Empire and Elites after the Muslim Conquest

The study of the early Islamic historical tradition has flourished in recent years with the emergence of new and innovative scholarship no longer dependent on more traditional narratival approaches. Chase Robinson's book, which takes full account of the latest research, interweaves history and historiography to interpret the political, social and economic transformations in northern Mesopotamia after the Islamic conquests. Using Arabic and Syriac sources to elaborate his argument, the author focuses on the Muslim and Christian élites, demonstrating that the immediate effects of the conquests were in fact modest ones. Significant social change took place only at the end of the seventh century with the imposition of Marwānid rule. Even then, the author argues, social power was diffused in the hands of local élites. This is a sophisticated study at the cutting-edge of a burgeoning field in Islamic studies.

CHASE F. ROBINSON is University Lecturer in Islamic History at the University of Oxford, and a fellow of Wolfson College.

CAMBRIDGE STUDIES IN ISLAMIC CIVILIZATION

Published titles in the series are listed at the back of the book

Empire and Elites after the Muslim Conquest

The Transformation of Northern Mesopotamia

CHASE F. ROBINSON
University of Oxford

CAMBRIDGE
UNIVERSITY PRESS

CAMBRIDGE UNIVERSITY PRESS
Cambridge, New York, Melbourne, Madrid, Cape Town, Singapore, São Paulo

Cambridge University Press
The Edinburgh Building, Cambridge CB2 2RU, UK

Published in the United States of America by Cambridge University Press, New York

www.cambridge.org
Information on this title: www.cambridge.org/9780521781152

First published 2000
This digitally printed first paperback version 2006

A catalogue record for this publication is available from the British Library

ISBN-13 978-0-521-78115-2 hardback
ISBN-10 0-521-78115-9 hardback

ISBN-13 978-0-521-02873-8 paperback
ISBN-10 0-521-02873-6 paperback

To Emiko

Contents

Preface

This study is intended to demonstrate that one can write Islamic provincial history in the post-conquest and Umayyad periods (c. 640–750 CE), a time for which the source material is patchy, late and frustratingly inconsistent. The book's method is to marry history and historiography; its concern is with Muslim and non-Muslim élites who lived in a peripheral area at a time of political and social change. The area – for the most part, present-day northern Syria and Iraq – was peripheral because the caliphs lived in the south, while the Muslim–Byzantine frontier lay to the north. It was a time of political and social change because, in defeating Byzantine and Sasanian armies, the Muslims would begin to transform a region heretofore divided between Byzantine east and Sasanian west into the northern tier of the Umayyad and Abbasid empires.

To write seventh- and eighth-century history we must come to terms with our sources; and as long as early Islamic archaeology, epigraphy, papyrology and numismatics remain as underdeveloped as they presently are, this means coming to terms with authors who wrote well after the events they describe. We are thus forced to rely in large measure on the learned élite's representation of its past, and, this being representation rather than record, we can no longer subordinate the study of early Islamic historiography to historical reconstruction. The reader may find frustrating the interweaving of history and historiography that follows; and he may frequently feel that he is taking two steps forward only to take a third back. But he can at least take consolation in being forewarned, and perhaps also in knowing that the approach reflects what is now twenty years of fierce debate – and measurable progress – in the study of the early Islamic historical tradition.

History and historiography are thus intertwined in several ways. We begin with northern Mesopotamia writ large, and then focus on the city of Mosul, then as now the principal city of northern Iraq. Although this plan certainly reflects the growing political significance of the city, it more closely corresponds to the quantity and quality of our sources. One can say something in detail about Mosul in the eighth century for the simple reason that a Mosuli native, Yazīd b. Muḥammad al-Azdī (d. c. 334/945) did, writing a history of Mosul that survives in part; one can say nothing comparable about Edessa or Nisibis – to take two of the most obvious examples from western northern Mesopotamia (the Jazira) – because they failed to produce an Azdī. For provincial traditions of historiography grew where the soil was most fertile. The great Islamic conquests of the early seventh century set in motion waves of settlement and urbanisation whose ripples travelled up the Tigris as far as northern Iraq, producing early medieval Mosul; the result was an Islamic city recognisable not only by its institutions (e.g. mosques, tribal quarters, governing palaces), but also by its politics and élite culture more generally. Mosul inherited Nineveh's enviable position astride the Tigris, became an administrative and military centre early on, and, by the end of the eighth century, had established itself as an entrepôt for riverine trade to the heart of the empire. An ambitious élite was the result; and it was this élite that generated the learning out of which al-Azdī's city record – and thus ours too – emerged. More precisely, al-Azdī's historiography was produced by a maturing local historiographic tradition that found itself, at the turn of the tenth century, in one of the two capitals of an ambitious provincial dynasty (the Ḥamdānids), one that actively patronised learning and had an interest in the past (Umayyad and Abbasid); al-Azdī's exceptional interest in local tribes of a century and half earlier – that is, the very material on which we must base our account of Umayyad (and Abbasid) politics – is not unrelated to the (tribal) Ḥamdānid milieu in which he wrote.

By contrast, cities of the early Islamic Jazira such as Edessa and Nisibis suffered multiple misfortune. The Euphrates, Balīkh and Khābūr rivers, and even more so the Syrian steppe, failed to conduct the same forces of settlement and urbanisation as did the Tigris; and such Muslim settlement as there was in the Jazira on the whole seems to have been conditioned by opportunism and desperation, rather than by the Qurashī élite's enthusiasm. Moreover, if a fortuitous combination of geography and Christology had endowed these cities with disproportionate political and cultural significance in Christian Late Antiquity, they were quickly marginalised in the pattern of regional politics ushered in by the conquests: too far south to serve as effective garrisons on the northern frontier on the one hand, and so well skilled in expressing local identity in Christian terms on the other, they had little appeal to, and apparently little interest in, the Muslim élite. Syriac learning, at least as measured by the barometer of (non-Edessan) historiography, more and more retreated to the monasteries; but Islamic learning did little to fill the consequent breach, most of it being concentrated in al-Raqqa. Writing a history of Mosul might fairly be called re-writing al-Azdī, whereas writing a history of the Jazira is writing almost *ex nihilo*. The present book's coverage illustrates precisely this. The experience of cities within the early Islamic north thus contrasts sharply, and it is precisely from the contrast that lessons can be learned; this is the principal reason why I treat together an area that was politically divided in the pre-Islamic period by the Byzantine–Sasanian frontier, and administratively divided in the early Islamic period.

Chapter 1 replaces the conventional survey of sources with a close examination of the conquest traditions of the Jazira and Mosul; the purpose of the chapter is not simply to distinguish what is valuable for reconstructing conquest history from what is not, but to draw some conclusions about the character of the conquest tradition and that of early Islamic rule itself. We shall see that the conquest tradition does provide invaluable evidence for understanding the conquests; but in greater amounts it records the controversies that arose as the post-conquest north was transformed into two imperial provinces, controversies conducted by the Christian and Muslim urban élites who shared the stewardship of what were now Abbasid cities. This transformation is the topic of chapters 2, 3, 4 and 5.

In the Jaziran west, a relatively loose, tribute-based rule in the post-conquest period yielded to a relatively formal, taxation-based provincial administration during the late seventh and eighth centuries (chapter 2); it was only with the imposition of direct Muslim rule under the Marwānids that the increasingly articulated state began to make consistent claims to sovereignty, these being expressed principally in the demand for provincial revenues. Here in the Jazira, where Syrian authority remained attenuated throughout the post-conquest and Sufyānid periods (c. 640–85), conquest had had but a minimal effect on local élites; the social power of some urban Christian notables, who seem to have enjoyed virtual autonomy, may have actually increased. It was also in the early Marwānid Jazira, when Muslims began to rule in earnest, that we begin to discern a form of Islamic belief (Khārijism) that took hold among some of those members of the Islamic élite who had failed to sedentarise in the wake of the conquests, particularly those who had material grievances of one kind or another (chapter 5). Stubbornly insisting on a conquest-era fusion of kinship, piety and undifferentiated *jihād*, Jaziran Khārijites illustrate how articulating primeval Islamic belief could channel what might otherwise have been mere banditry on the part of pastoralists and semi-pastoralists into a coherent (if ultimately futile) programme of rebellion. These Khārijites were an ascetic élite, one that acquired its status by exemplifying the community's passing virtues.

Meanwhile, in the Mosuli east, a garrison founded and ruled by Kufans was transformed by the Marwānids into what turned out to be an unruly city (chapter 3). Mosul, which lay on the western bank of the Tigris, now eclipsed the Sasanian settlement that had grown in the weeds of ancient Nineveh on its eastern bank, the shift from garrison to city being neither gradual nor natural, but rather resulting from a Marwānid commitment of resources and energies that established Syrian rule in Mosul for the first time. In practice this meant appointing kinsmen to rule as governors, and acquiring and developing land; the result was the partial eclipse of a conquest élite by a land-owning élite. The signs of Mosul's transformation appear not only in brick and mortar, but in the pattern of politics itself, since the urban forces that the Marwānids unleashed overtook them within two generations. In the Mosuli hinterland, where imperial pressure was considerably lighter and Arab settlement all but non-existent, change was predictably much slower (chapter 4). Here a landed gentry formed the élite of a number of towns and villages, retaining their (deviant) Christianity and their land until well into the Abbasid period.

In chapters 6 and 7 I turn to the first and greatest crisis of state–provincial relations in the early medieval history of Mosul: the dreadful massacre committed by the Abbasid army only months after its defeat of the last Umayyad caliph, Marwān II, on the nearby Zāb river in 132/750. Since al-Azdī's description of the events is exceptionally valuable, here too my method is to carry out historiographic and historical inquiries in tandem. That the Marwānid city could become unruly reflects a truism of pre-modern Islamic social history: limitations imposed by technology and geography meant that state power was almost always made effective by locals, rather than by its agents and armies. What makes the case of late Marwānid and early Abbasid Mosul noteworthy is our evidence, which allows us a glimpse of state–local relations a century before they can be discerned elsewhere. Here we can see that the so-called 'politics of notables', whereby locals acquired (or preserved) social power by acting as intermediaries between the state and provincial subjects, did not simply appear, perhaps in accordance with some kind of centre–periphery functionalism unmoored in history; rather, locals and imperialists (the categories overlap) only reluctantly made their way towards compromise. For a relatively brief historical moment, provincials seem to have experimented with autonomy.

In different ways then, these chapters are all generally concerned with how two provinces experienced projections of power from the south and west, which varied in intensity and character; they are particularly concerned with how provincial élites, indigenous and immigrant alike, responded to the opportunities and challenges posed by the conquests, the Marwānids, and finally the Abbasid Revolution. By 'élites' I mean those social groups whose assertions of high status were underpinned by economic and/or cultural resources, these being principally (but not exclusively) land, descent, history and piety – the economic, cultural and symbolic 'capital' of some contemporary sociology. Whether these groups had a clear sense of corporate identity – the 'collective consciousness' sometimes held necessary for the designation of class – is usually impossible to determine, but in my view less significant than the effectiveness with which they broadcast their claims; with one exception (the Khārijites), all of these élites did enjoy some real and enduring success. It almost goes without saying that the picture is incomplete, focused in spots and unfocused in others, sometimes still and sometimes moving; the evidence rarely allows us to describe the élites as the dynamic, self-reproducing things that they generally are. Still, it is clear enough that the driving force of social change for these élites – their creation, adaptation, transformation and disappearance – was power projected by the Qurashī clans that ruled successively from Medina, Syria and Iraq, and which, starting in the last decade of the seventh century, began to construct a framework for their own long-term reproduction: a dynastic state.

The speed and character of change among the élites of northern Mesopotamia were determined by the confluence of history, settlement and geography that distinguished the Jazira and Mosul from other regions – and indeed from each other. On its western flank a part of Syria, and on its eastern flank a part of Iraq, northern Mesopotamia can shed some light on early Islamic state building in both its Umayyad and Abbasid phases.

Acknowledgements

The publication of this book is the final instalment in a process of thinking, researching and writing that was longer than I care to admit, and this is something that I mention only in order to thank Roy Mottahedeh, who helped set it into motion, and William Graham, Wolfhart Heinrichs, Michael Cook and Fred Donner, who kindly read an early version; the last showed an exceptional kindness in sharing not only his knowledge of Mosul with a very green researcher, but indeed the topic itself. Since then I have also benefited from the expertise of Michael Morony, Sebastian Brock, Jeremy Johns, Donald Richards and Luke Treadwell, the last four members of the Faculty of Oriental Studies at Oxford University; no scholar could reasonably wish for a more pleasant place to work. Aloysious Mowe, Peter Starr and Mary Starkey improved the manuscript in several ways, Rachel Ward helped to choose and secured the cover illustration, and Marigold Acland and David Morgan deftly guided the book through the Press. To Lawrence Conrad, Patricia Crone and Emikam Elad, who read and criticised the penultimate draft of what follows, I have incurred still more costly debts. But it is two of the happier features of research and writing that readers' debts can occasionally be repaid, and that their investment in time and effort entails no real risks; these the author takes alone.

Abbreviations

BSOAS	*Bulletin of the School of Oriental and African Studies*
CSCO	*Corpus Scriptorum Christianorum Orientalium*
DI	*Der Islam*
EI	*Encyclopaedia of Islam*
EI^2	*Encyclopaedia of Islam* (second edition)
GAL	C. Brockelmann, *Geschichte der arabischen Literatur*
GAS	F. Sezgin, *Geschichte des arabischen Schrifttums*
IJMES	*International Journal of Middle Eastern Studies*
JA	*Journal Asiatique*
JAOS	*Journal of the American Oriental Society*
JESHO	*Journal of the Economic and Social History of the Orient*
JNES	*Journal of Near Eastern Studies*
JRAS	*Journal of the Royal Asiatic Society*
JSAI	*Jerusalem Studies in Arabic and Islam*
PO	*Patrologia Orientalis*
SI	*Studia Islamica*
ZDMG	*Zeitschrift der Deutschen Morgenländischen Gesellschaft*

Note on dates and citations

For the sake of simplicity, I use Christian dates throughout, but in order to remain faithful to the sources cited, I frequently add *hijrī* dates as well. It is in the nature of this period of history that all death dates should be preceded by an implicit *circa*; these generally come with both sets of dates, in the form of *hijrī*/Christian.

Whereas very few of the Islamic sources used in this study have been translated, nearly all of the Christian sources (mostly Syriac) do exist in translations, almost always in Latin, and quite frequently in modern European languages; these I have cited in the form of Syriac/translation.

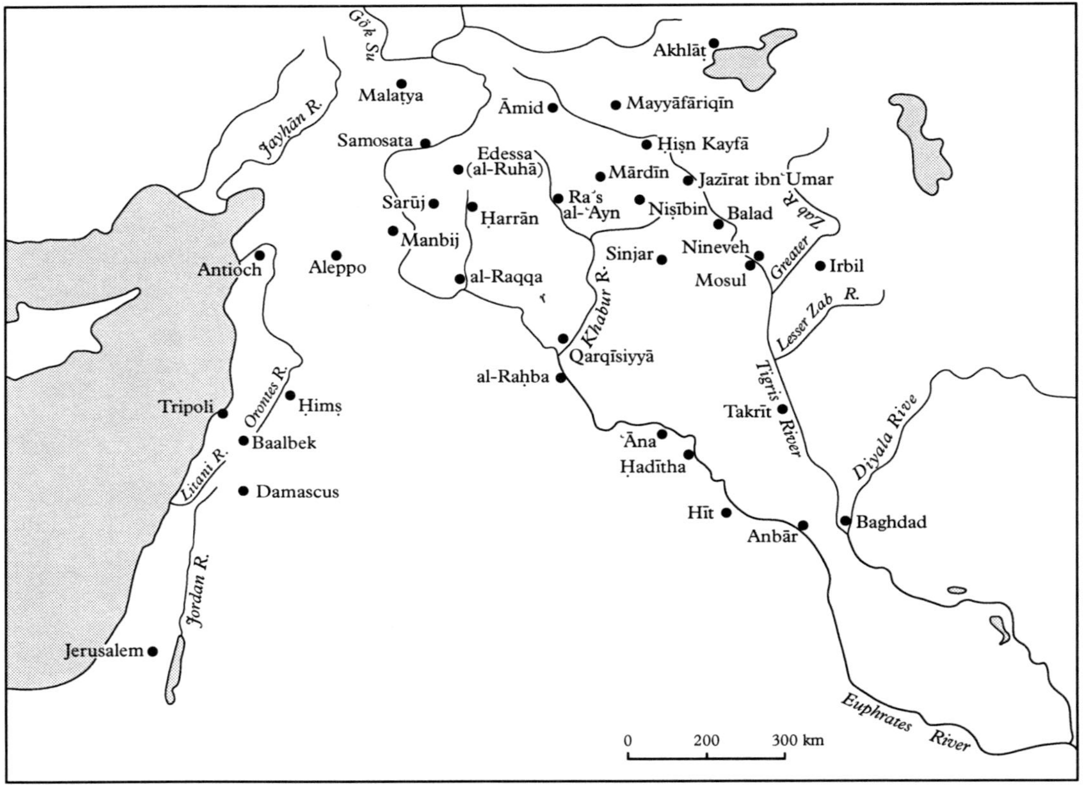

The Fertile Cresent in the early Abbasid period

ONE

Conquest history and its uses

The literary material upon which one must base a seventh- and eighth-century history of the Jazira and Mosul generally dates from the ninth and tenth; with the exception of al-Azdī's history, it was also written by non-Jazirans and non-Mosulis. To use this material, which is clustered in accounts concerned with the conquests of the 630s and 640s, the two civil wars of the 650s and 680s, and the Abbasid Revolution of 750, we need to know something of how it came together and how it was understood. In general terms, the approach taken here is thus source and form critical, and if varieties of source and form criticism are hardly new to the field,[1] the implications of much of this work continue to be wished away. In part this is because the criticism has more frequently served to undermine credulous reconstructions of the tradition than it has to erect sound reconstructions of its own. It is positive results that most historians want, however: Dennett's views on early Islamic taxation have staying power not so much because his criticisms of Becker were fatal, but rather because his reconstructions were put so boldly and concisely; Dennett was (and remains) extremely useful.[2] If it is uncharitable to say that source and form criticism has been its own worst enemy, it remains fair to say that its tools must now be handled differently.

This is what I propose to do. In the following I shall play the role of critic and architect: in criticising conquest accounts, one can begin to describe not only the emergence of the historiographic tradition, but something of the social and political milieu in which it emerged; as we shall see, this was a competitive and (sometimes) fractious milieu of local and imperial élites.

[1] For two recent – and quite different – examples, see N. Calder, *Studies in Early Muslim Jurisprudence* (Oxford, 1993); and Albrecht Noth, *The Early Arabic Historical Tradition: A Source-critical Study* (Princeton, 1994; second edn, in collaboration with Lawrence I. Conrad (originally published 1973)).

[2] See D. C. Dennett, *Conversion and the Poll Tax in Early Islam* (Cambridge, MA, 1950). Cf. A. Noth, 'Die literarisch überlieferten Verträge der Eroberungszeit als historische Quellen für die Behandlung der unterworfenen Nicht-Muslime durch ihre neuen muslimischen Oberherren', in T. Nagel *et al.*, eds., *Studien zum Minderheitenproblem im Islam I* (Bonn, 1973), pp. 282–314; and K. Morimoto, *The Fiscal Administration of Egypt in the Early Islamic Period* (Kyoto, 1981), Introduction.

We can begin with a chapter in the *Kitāb al-Kharāj* attributed to the jurist Abū Yūsuf (d. 182/798), a legal work concerned primarily with taxation issues and their origins in the conquest period.[3] The chapter in question, 'On the land of Syria and the Jazira', is in fact only about the latter, and it opens with the work's conventional response to the caliph ('O Commander of the Faithful, concerning what you asked about . . .'), and then unconventionally – and somewhat apologetically – turns to an invaluable description of how our author worked. To answer questions about conquest history, Abū Yūsuf typically relies on *fiqh* – here knowledge of the past transmitted more or less continuously by reputable authorities; but in this section he relies instead on an anonymous native of the Jazira, who himself disclaims any such transmitted knowledge:

I have written to a learned man from the Jazira (*shaykh min ahl al-Jazīra*)[4] who possesses knowledge (*ʿilm*) about the matter of the conquests of the Jazira and Syria, asking him about this. He wrote me [the following]: 'May God preserve you and your health! I have compiled for you what I happen to know about Syria and the Jazira (*mā ʿindī min ʿilm al-Shām wa'l-Jazīra*);[5] it is nothing that I learned orally (*ḥafiẓtuhu*) from any jurists (*fuqahāʾ*), nor from anybody who can provide it with a chain of authorities to any jurists (*wa-lā ʿamman yusniduhu ʿan al-fuqahāʾ*). It is merely one of many reports from one who can be described as possessing knowledge in this matter (*ḥadīth min ḥadīth man yūṣaf bi-ʿilm dhālika*), and I have not asked any of them [i.e. the jurists] to provide a chain of authorities for it.

Our *shaykh* is unsure of what he knows. Precisely how good is his knowledge? Two pages later he suggests part of an answer. The commander of the conquering armies of the Jazira, ʿIyāḍ b. Ghanm, is said to have imposed a universal capitation tax that consisted of one dīnār, two *mudd*s of wheat and two *qisṭ*s of oil and vinegar.[6] Our authority cannot vouch for the reliability of the report, in part for reasons already stated (he does not have access to formally transmitted accounts), but also because he 'was not told if this [arrangement] was based on a *ṣulḥ* text, on a practice that I can verify (*amr uthbituhu*), transmission from jurists, or an authoritative chain of authorities (*isnād thābit*)'.[7] What he means by this is clarified on the same page. Discussing a distinction between city and rural folk introduced by the early caliphs (*fa-ammā man*

[3] Abū Yūsuf, *Kitāb al-Kharāj* (Būlāq, 1302). As will become clear, I have learned a great deal from Calder's discussion of Abū Yūsuf (*Studies*, chapter 6; for Jaziran material, pp. 137ff.), but I remain unpersuaded by his redating and reattribution of the text. For some criticisms, see M. Q. Zaman, *Religion and Politics under the Early ʿAbbāsids: The Emergence of the Proto-Sunnī Elite* (Leiden, 1997), pp. 91ff.; and cf. H. Motzki, 'The prophet and the cat: on dating Mālik's *Muwaṭṭaʾ* and legal traditions', *JSAI* 22 (1998), pp. 18–83.

[4] Abū Yūsuf, *Kitāb al-Kharāj*, p. 39; I follow the reading in the Taymūriyya manuscript; see also the edition by I. ʿAbbās (Beirut and Cairo, 1985), p. 136.

[5] So the Salafiyya edition (Cairo, 1927); ʿAbbās's edition reads *min al-ʿilm bi-amr al-Jazīra wa'l-Shām*.

[6] In early Islamic Iraq, a *mudd* was approximately 1.05 litres (of dry measure), and a *qisṭ* between 1.07 and 2.14 kg. (W. Hinz, *Islamische Masse und Gewichte* (Leiden, 1955), s.vv.).

[7] Abū Yūsuf, *Kitāb al-Kharāj*, p. 41.

waliya min khulafāʾ al-muslimīn),[8] he writes that 'a learned man who claims expertise in this matter' (*baʿḍ ahl al-ʿilm mimman zaʿama anna la-hu ʿilm bi-dhālika*) argues that the rural folk must provide for armies (*arzāq al-jund*) because they are producers; this explains why city folk, who are not producers, are exempt from this obligation. The argument is then clinched with an appeal to shared ignorance:

By way of proof, learned people argue (*fa-ahl al-ʿilm biʾl-ḥujja yaqūlūna*): our right is in our possession, and those before you held us to it; it is [also] established in your records (*wa-huwa thābit fī dawāwīnikum*). You are now ignorant, as we are now ignorant, of how things were at the beginning (*wa-qad jahiltum wa-jahilnā kayfa kāna awwal al-amr*). How can you see fit to impose on us something for which you can provide no established precedent, and how can you break from this practice, which is verifiable in our records, and according to which we still operate?[9]

The local authorities upon which this *shaykh* draws – here almost certainly Edessan urban notables – thus resist attempts to change their fiscal status by appealing to shared ignorance of 'how things were at the beginning'. As Calder points out, the (presumably) Edessan appeal can only be a response to an earlier, positive assertion about 'the beginning', which he takes to be a government claim that the *ṣulḥ* reached at Edessa stipulated that taxes were to be yielded according to one's ability to pay.[10] The parties to the dispute may, or may not, be the government on the one hand and locals on the other. There can be no question, however, that this fiscal controversy generated conflicting claims about conquest history, and that a party to the dispute argued on the strength of a *ṣulḥ* treaty, one probably in text form.[11]

Here comparing Abū Yūsuf with Ibn Isḥāq (d. 144/761), Sayf b. ʿUmar (d. 180/796), Abū ʿUbayd (d. 223/837) and the sources quoted by al-Balādhurī (d. 279/892) is instructive. Abū Yūsuf's informant is confident that the battle of Edessa ended with a *ṣulḥ* agreement, but he suspends judgement on the crucial question of fixed versus flexible tribute, stressing instead that the determined resistance of the Edessans persuaded ʿIyāḍ to agree to their terms: 'He [ʿIyāḍ] entered into a *ṣulḥ* with them on the terms they requested. Only God knows more than that a *ṣulḥ* was concluded, according to which

[8] These would apparently include Muʿāwiya, who transformed a levy (*waẓīfa*) into *jizya* (see al-Balādhurī, *Futūḥ al-buldān* (Leiden, 1866), p. 173), as well as ʿAbd al-Malik b. Marwān (as I suggest below). The earliest instance of the term *waẓīfa* in the literature is probably found in Ibn al-Muqaffaʿ, *Risāla fī al-ṣaḥāba*, ed. and trans. C. Pellat as *Conseilleur du calife* (Paris, 1976), pp. 59/58, where it is a calculation levied upon districts (*kuwar*); see also F. Løkkegaard, *Islamic Taxation in the Classic Period* (Copenhagen, 1950), pp. 126f.; and C. E. Bosworth, 'Abū ʿAbdallāh al-Khwārazmī on the technical terms of the secretary's art', *JESHO* 12 (1969), p. 139.

[9] Abū Yūsuf, *Kitāb al-Kharāj*, p. 41. Cf. Calder, *Studies*, p. 139, who calls it a 'genuine echo of arguments produced at either Edessa or Harran expressing objections to reforms in taxation'.

[10] Calder, *Studies*, p. 139.

[11] Cf. an Egyptian case recorded in a papyrus (dated 90/709), where the appropriate 'documents' (*kutub*) cannot be adduced; see A. Grohmann, *Arabic Papyri in the Egyptian Library* (Cairo, 1934–), III, pp. 19ff.

the city was conquered; [about this latter point] there is no doubt.'[12] He cites no text; indeed, he implies that all claims based on treaty proofs are bogus: 'You are now ignorant, as we are now ignorant, of how things were at the beginning.' Meanwhile, Ibn Isḥāq and Sayf knew that Edessa's *ṣulḥ* was granted in exchange for payment of the *jizya*;[13] Abū ʿUbayd had access to an Edessan treaty text, which was then reproduced by Ibn Zanjawayh (d. 251/865),[14] and al-Balādhurī knew no fewer than three (and possibly four) treaty texts.[15] The first of these, which is attributed to the Jazarī scholar Sulaymān b. ʿAṭāʾ al-Qurashī (d. 195/810), is only summarised;[16] but the next two al-Balādhurī cites in full, the first on the authority of al-Wāqidī (d. 208/823),[17] and the other on the authority of a Raqqan *qāḍī*, Dāwūd b. ʿAbd al-Ḥamīd, here transmitting on the authority of his father and grandfather.[18] Both have ʿIyāḍ stipulate the terms, and both are directly germane to the controversy to which Abū Yūsuf's informant is speaking; while the first specifies a tribute (one *dīnār* and two *mudd*s of wheat), the second does not (*idhā addū al-ḥaqq alladhī ʿalayhim*) ('if they yield that owed by them').[19] This second one is almost certainly a fuller version of that cited by Abū ʿUbayd.[20]

Now Calder argues that the final redaction of Abū Yūsuf is a product of the 860s, hearing in it echoes of the fiscal crisis of the Sāmarrāʾ period;[21] Hill would presumably argue that all notice of fixed tribute belongs in ʿUmar's reign, and that Abū Yūsuf has faithfully recorded history;[22] I see nothing in this part of the text that cannot be reconciled with a late Umayyad milieu, and no reason to doubt a middle to late eighth-century *floruit* for our anonymous informant. Why then does he fail to adduce a treaty text – such as that known

[12] Abū Yūsuf, *Kitāb al-Kharāj*, p. 40.

[13] Al-Ṭabarī, *Taʾrīkh al-rusul waʾl-mulūk* (Leiden, 1879–1901), I, pp. 2505 and 2507; I leave aside exactly what *jizya* means here.

[14] Abū ʿUbayd, *Kitāb al-Amwāl* (Cairo, 1968), p. 298; Ibn Zanjawayh, *Kitāb al-Amwāl* (Riyadh, 1986), p. 474.

[15] See al-Balādhurī, *Futūḥ*, pp. 172ff.

[16] And so too in Qudāma b. Jaʿfar, *Kitāb al-Kharāj wa-ṣināʿat al-kitāba* (Baghdad, 1981), p. 312, which is heavily indebted to al-Balādhurī.

[17] The account begins at *Futūḥ*, p. 172:9 (I take the *qālū* of p. 174:2 to refer to al-Wāqidī). Ibn Aʿtham al-Kūfī (*Kitāb al-Futūḥ* (Hyderabad, 1968–1975), I, pp. 326ff.) seems to be drawing loosely on al-Wāqidī too; he reports a *ṣulḥ* with a four-*dīnār* tribute.

[18] The account begins at *Futūḥ*, p. 174:14. Little can be said about Dāwūd, a Kufan native and *qāḍī* who settled in al-Raqqa, except that he appears fairly frequently as a source for al-Balādhurī (thus *Futūḥ*, pp. 57, 167, 468; and al-Balādhurī, *Ansāb al-ashrāf*, V (Jerusalem, 1936), p. 313 where he reports on the authority of *mashāyikh min al-Qaysiyyīn*), and that in *ḥadīth* matters he was considered *ḍaʿīf* or *munkar al-ḥadīth*; see Ibn Abī Ḥātim al-Rāzī, *Kitāb al-Jarḥ waʾl-taʿdīl* (Beirut; reprint of Hyderabad, 1953), III, p. 418; and Ibn Ḥajar, *Lisān al-mīzān* (Hyderabad, 1331), II, pp. 420f.

[19] Al-Balādhurī, *Futūḥ*, p. 174.

[20] Abū ʿUbayd, *Kitāb al-Amwāl*, p. 298; Ibn Zanjawayh, *Kitāb al-Amwāl*, p. 474. It is addressed in Abū ʿUbayd's version 'to the people of Edessa', and in al-Balādhurī's to 'the bishop of Edessa'.

[21] Calder, *Studies*, pp. 147f., where he tentatively proposes that the work is to be credited to al-Khaṣṣāf (d. 261/874).

[22] D. R. Hill, *The Termination of Hostilities in the Early Arab Conquests AD 634–656* (London, 1971), pp. 95 and 98.

to both Dāwūd and Abū ʿUbayd – in support of his argument? It could be argued that our informant did know of existing *ṣulḥ* texts, but that he chose to suppress them, or, very differently, that although appropriate *ṣulḥ* texts did exist, he was simply ignorant of them. Both explanations are unpromising, however: one suppresses not all *ṣulḥ* texts, but rather only those that do damage to one's argument; and Abū Yūsuf – who was, after all, Hārūn al-Rashīd's chief *qāḍī* – chose his informant precisely because he *was* so learned in his province's history.

One is attracted to the conclusion that provincial authorities' knowledge of early Islamic history grew over time.[23] Much of this growth probably took place in early Abbasid al-Raqqa,[24] which dominated Jaziran learning in this period. This is the impression created not only by al-Balādhurī's frequently Raqqan sources (e.g. Sulaymān b. ʿAṭāʾ, Dāwūd b. ʿAbd al-Ḥamīd,[25] Abū Ayyūb *al-muʾaddib*, ʿAmr al-Nāqid, Abū ʿAffān and 'learned men from among the Raqqan scribes'), but also by Abū ʿUbayd's treaty text, which comes on the authority of another Raqqan native, Kathīr b. Hishām (d. 207/822),[26] who transmitted from his teacher and fellow Raqqan, Jaʿfar b. Burqān (d. 151/768).[27]

To judge by the *Kitāb al-Kharāj*, knowledge of an increasingly remote past was thus at once both obscure and deeply controversial. Abū Yūsuf lacks expertise in Jaziran traditions, so he writes to an anonymous local *shaykh*, who clearly does not; but his testimony suggests that the problem is systemic, for it turns out that he too suffers from a dearth of information. This is a pattern discernible

[23] The production of knowledge in this period is certainly not unique to the Jazira: for an argument that biographical details of the Prophet's life grew during the late eighth and early ninth centuries, see M. Cook, *Muhammad* (Oxford, 1983), pp. 62f.; and for a response, M. Lecker, 'The death of the Prophet Muḥammad's father: did Wāqidī invent some of the evidence?', *ZDMG* 145 (1995), pp. 9–27.

[24] Cf. M. Abiade, *Culture et education arabo-islamiques au Šām pendant les trois premiers siècles de l'Islam* (Damascus, 1981), p. 174 (which shows a clear Raqqan predominance in the Jaziran authorities cited by Ibn ʿAsākir). On some scholarship in al-Raqqa in this period, see now J. van Ess, *Theologie und Gesellschaft im 2. und 3. Jahrhundert Hidschra* (Berlin and New York, 1997), II, pp. 471ff. (which provides an overview of Sulaymān al-Raqqī and Raqqan Shīʿism).

[25] Since the famous *kātib* ʿAbd al-Ḥamīd is said to have left descendants in al-Raqqa (thus al-Ṣafadī, *al-Wāfī bi'l-wafayāt* (Leipzig, Istanbul and Beirut, 1931–), XVIII, p. 86), it is tempting to finesse the obvious chronological difficulties and identify Dāwūd as his (long-lived) son; W. al-Qāḍī ('Early Islamic state letters: the question of authenticity', in A. Cameron and L. I. Conrad, eds., *The Byzantine and Early Islamic Near East I: Problems in the Literary Source Material* (Princeton, 1992), p. 236) does precisely this.

[26] See Ibn Saʿd, *Kitāb al-Ṭabaqāt al-kubrā* (Leiden, 1905–40), VII², p. 76; al-Mizzī, *Tahdhīb al-kamāl fī asmāʾ al-rijāl* (Beirut, 1992), XXIV, pp. 163ff.; Ibn Ḥajar, *Tahdhīb al-tahdhīb* (Hyderabad, 1327), VIII, pp. 429f.

[27] See Ibn Saʿd, *Kitāb al-Ṭabaqāt*, VII², p. 181; al-Mizzī, *Tahdhīb al-kamāl*, V, pp. 11ff. (where he, along with the Syrians and Jazirans, is said to have transmitted from al-Zuhrī while the latter was resident at Hishām's court in Ruṣāfa); Ibn Ḥajar, *Tahdhīb*, II, pp. 84ff.; al-Dhahabī, *Tadhkirat al-ḥuffāẓ* (Hyderabad, 1958), pp. 171f.; al-Qushayrī, *Taʾrīkh al-Raqqa* (Damascus, 1998), pp. 86ff.; see also M. Lecker, 'Biographical notes on Ibn Shihāb al-Zuhrī', *Journal of Semitic Studies* 41 (1996), pp. 31f. It is hard to see how Jaʿfar, as some authorities would have it, was actually illiterate; thus al-Mizzī, and see also M. Cook, 'The opponents of the writing of Tradition in early Islam', *Arabica* 44 (1997), p. 495, note 516.

elsewhere in the north,[28] and should give us reason to pause when we read Iraqi versions of Jaziran history. The problem is not only that the historical tradition is in some measure discontinuous (which it clearly is);[29] it is that our informant seems to have belonged to the last generation in which historical *naïveté* of this kind was intellectually possible. Thus the length of ʿIyāḍ's siege at Edessa escapes him, which is perhaps not so surprising; in and of itself, the duration of a siege was of no lasting legal significance – in the long run, it simply did not matter. But so too do the specifics of the *ṣulḥ* treaty escape him, and this is surprising, since Edessa, as we shall see, frequently plays a paradigmatic role for the conquest of the Jazira. When pressed for precedents, our informant rejects all representations of this past as spurious, explaining fiscal arrangements with reference to contemporary practice. A generation or two later he almost certainly would have provided historical precedents of his own.

Treaties: forms and functions

That an Edessan treaty seems to have come into being well after the conquest of Edessa can hardly be taken to mean that no treaties existed in the aftermath of the conquest, that all treaty texts preserved in our historical sources are forgeries, or, of course, that the conquest of Edessa did not end with a treaty of some kind.[30] The élites of northern Mesopotamia were accustomed to bargaining and negotiating terms for their cities: treaties were a common feature of the great Persian–Byzantine wars of the late sixth and early seventh centuries;[31] and local Arabs, *foederati* and otherwise, appear in treaties frequently enough that one must infer that they understood their significance.[32] Indeed, there is every reason to think so, for there was a practice of Jāhilī treaty writing

[28] In the case of Mosul too it seems that local authorities knew less about conquest history than did those living (and learning) in the centres of scholarship in the south; for al-Azdī's reliance on second-century Iraqi authorities for the conquest history of his own town, see chapter 6.

[29] The argument for discontinuity in historical transmission is most vigorously put by P. Crone, *Slaves on Horses* (Cambridge, 1980), chapter 1; and more recently, Lawrence I. Conrad, 'The conquest of Arwād: a source-critical study in the historiography of the early medieval Near East', in Cameron and Conrad, eds., *The Byzantine and Early Islamic Near East*, esp. at p. 363.

[30] On treaties of the very early period, see M. Muranyi, 'Die Auslieferungsklausel des Vertrages von al-Ḥudaibiya und ihre Folgen', *Arabica* 23 (1976), pp. 275–95; Noth, 'Verträge'; Noth/Conrad, *Early Arabic Historical Tradition*, pp. 63ff.; and W. al-Qāḍī, 'Madkhal ilā dirāsat ʿuhūd al-ṣulḥ al-islāmiyya zaman al-futūḥ', in A. al-Bakhit and I. Abbas, eds., *Proceedings of the Second Symposium on the History of Bilād al-Shām during the Early Islamic Period up to 40 AH/640 AD* (Arabic articles) (Amman, 1987), pp. 193–269.

[31] See, *inter alia*, the 'document' that the bishop of Sergiopolis sets down at Khusraw's request (Procopius, *A History of the Wars*, ed. and trans. H. B. Dewing (London and New York, 1914–1940), II.v.30); and the events that followed Qawād's unsuccessful siege of Amida, when the city folk demanded compensation for the foodstuffs and wine that his Sasanian army had confiscated: see ps.-Zacharias Rhetor, *Historia ecclesiastica Zachariae Rhetori vulgo adscripta*, ed. and trans. E. W. Brooks (Paris, 1919, 1921, 1924; *CSCO* 83–4, 87–8), II, pp. 25f./16f. (Syr./translation). According to one early sixth-century chronicle, the signing of peace treaties is said to have triggered huge outpourings of joy among the people of the north; see ps.-Joshua, *The Chronicle of Joshua the Stylite*, ed. and trans. W. Wright (Cambridge, 1882), pp. 90f./75f.

[32] For examples, see J.-B. Chabot, ed. and trans., *Synodicon Orientale ou Recueil de synodes Nestoriens* (Paris, 1902), pp. 526f./532f. (from a synod of 484); I. Shahid (Kawar), 'The Arabs

among the Arabs of the Peninsula,[33] which was apparently sanctioned by the Qur'ān itself,[34] and put into practice by the so-called 'Constitution of Medina'. It may be credulous to think that the caliph ʿUmar possessed a trunk crammed full of treaty documents;[35] but this is not the same as saying that commanders would not have thought to give written form to conquest arrangements.

In formal terms, one can distinguish in Jaziran accounts between treaty conditions enumerated as part of continuous narrative and those reproduced as part of a treaty document. The first is signalled by the form 'and he [the commander] reached a *ṣulḥ*/*amān* agreement on the (following terms)' (*fa-ṣālaḥa(ū)-hu(hā) ʿalā . . .* /*wa-āmana(ū)-hu(hā) ʿalā*); the conditions (sometimes unilateral, sometimes bilateral) are then enumerated, after which the narrative moves directly on, usually in itinerary fashion, to the next battle. The second type purports to record the treaty *verbatim*, and its most distinctive feature is a striking concern with authenticity. It generally begins with a *praescriptio* consisting in a *basmala* and names of the addresser and addressee,[36] and marks its end with concluding formulae of various kinds (e.g. *wa-kafā bi'l-llāh shahīdan*). It is occasionally prefaced or followed by the compiler's attestation to authenticity (e.g. *wa-khatama ʿIyāḍ bi-khātimihi*; *wa-kataba la-hum kitāb nasakhtuhu*).[37] Despite

in the peace treaty of AD 561', *Arabica* 3 (1956), pp. 192ff.; I. Shahid, *Byzantium and the Arabs in the Sixth Century*, I, part 1 (Washington, D.C., 1995), pp. 266ff. Cf. ps.-Joshua, *Chronicle*, pp. 82/69f., where five Arab chiefs (*rīshānē*; Wright translates 'shaikhs') are executed for failing to follow orders; the *foederati* are clearly involved here too.

33 On Jāhilī treaty writing, see G. Schoeler, 'Schreiben und Veröffentlichen. Zu Verwendung und Funktion der Schrift in den ersten islamischen Jahrhunderten', *DI* 69 (1992), pp. 2ff.; J. Pedersen, *The Arabic Book*, trans. G. French (Princeton, 1984), p. 10; cf. G. Khan, 'The pre-Islamic background of Muslim legal formularies', *Aram* 6 (1994), pp. 193–224; and for literacy in Medina, see now M. Lecker, 'Zayd b. Thābit, "A Jew with two sidelocks": Judaism and literacy in pre-Islamic Medina (Yathrib)', *JNES* 56 (1997), pp. 259–73.

34 E.g. Qur'ān 5: 1 and 2:282, the latter calling explicitly for the writing down of contracted debts; on this, and some of the relevant *ḥadīth*, see J. A. Wakin, *The Function of Documents in Islamic Law* (Albany, 1972), pp. 5f.

35 See M. Ḥamīd Allāh, *Majmūʿat al-wathā'iq al-siyāsiyya li'l-ʿahd al-nabawī wa'l-khilāfa al-rāshida*, 4th edn (Beirut, 1983), p. 24. For a brief survey of conquest treaties, see W. Schmucker, *Untersuchungen zu einigen wichtigen bodenrechtlichen Konsequenzen der islamisichen Eroberungsbewegung* (Bonn, 1972), pp. 24ff.

36 A relatively full example appears in ps.-Wāqidī, (*Futūḥ al-Shām* (Calcutta, 1854), II, p. 94), and concerns Ḥimṣ: *min Abī ʿUbayda b. al-Jarrāḥ al-Fihrī ʿāmil amīr al-mu'minīn ʿUmar b. al-Khaṭṭāb ʿalā al-Shām wa-qā'id juyūshihi*.

37 Thus al-Balādhurī, *Futūḥ*, pp. 173f. Cf. the account preserved by Ibn Aʿtham (*Futūḥ*, I, p. 327), which has the bishop of al-Raqqa insist that ʿIyāḍ give written form to his spoken offer of safe passage; ʿIyāḍ does so, duly authenticating it as well (*fa-kataba la-hu ʿIyāḍ amān wa-baʿatha ilayhi manshūr qad khatamahu bi-khātimihi*). Abū ʿUbayda first folds, then seals, his letter to ʿUmar: ps.-Wāqidī, *Futūḥ al-Jazīra, Libri Wakedii de Mesopotamiae expugnatae historia* (Göttingen, 1827), p. 1; cf. Qur'ān 21: 104; and, for a discussion of the relevant techniques of folding and storing papyri and parchment, N. Abbott, *The Ḳurrah Papyri from Aphrodito in the Oriental Institute* (Chicago, 1938), pp. 14f. This ps.-Wāqidī is one of several Iraqi conquest texts ascribed to al-Wāqidī, none of which appears to be early. In addition to the Göttingen MS, there is a Copenhagen MS (no. 137; for a discussion and partial translation of the Göttingen MS, with notes to the Copenhagen, see B. G. Niebuhr and A. D. Mordtmann, *Geschichte der Eroberung von Mesopotamien und Armenien* (Hamburg, 1847)), and now an edition, based on photographic copies of an Istanbul MS (*Ta'rīkh futūḥ al-Jazīra wa'l-Khābūr wa-Diyār Bakr wa'l-ʿIrāq* (Damascus, 1996)). In general, see Brockelmann, *GAL*, I, p. 136; and Sezgin, *GAS*, I, p. 296.

the apparent artificiality of the second type, which in its essentials conforms to the *amān* letters prescribed by Ibn Qutayba (d. 276/889),[38] it is facile to assume that form can predict authenticity – that, in other words, the less concerned a text is with authenticity, the more authentic it is likely to be. In fact, sometimes the opposite might be argued: in al-Wāqidī's account of the conquest of Edessa it is the treaty representation of the first type that falls foul of Noth's criteria for authenticity,[39] while the accompanying treaty text is in some respects promising.[40]

Here it bears remembering that while inauthenticity can be demonstrated relatively easily, ascertaining that a treaty is both authentic and original is in practice extremely difficult, and generally requires a control of some kind.[41] An illustration comes in an account concerning the conquest of Edessa, which is attributed to Sulaymān b. ʿAṭāʾ, one of several Jaziran natives involved in building the tradition.[42] On the one hand, it arouses suspicion on at least three counts: it includes transparently legendary ingredients (ʿIyāḍ is mounted on a chestnut-brown horse),[43] apparently classical features of Muslim–non-Muslim relations ('if they fail to fulfil any of these conditions, they will forsake their protected status (*dhimma*)'), and it has the treaty for Edessa function paradigmatically for the entire Jazira.[44] On the other hand, none of these criticisms can clinch an argument for secondary forging, especially in the light of the report's reassuring imprecision (*fa-in tarakū shayʾ mimmā shuriṭa la-hum*); it contains no identifiable anachronisms.

Considering that independent control on the Islamic tradition appears so infrequently, we might subordinate questions about the authenticity of conquest treaties to questions about their social function; in other words, we should concern ourselves less with their truth value and more with two related questions of post-conquest history. First, how were treaties perceived to govern relations between local Muslims and Christians on the one hand, and imperial authorities and local Christians on the other? Second, what is the consequent literary effect of the treaty on the text in which it was finally deposited? Of the

38 Ibn Qutayba, *ʿUyūn al-akhbār* (Cairo, 1925), II, p. 225.

39 See his 'Verträge', esp. p. 312 (where the *ad hoc* character of the tax is taken to signal an early date), and Noth/Conrad, *Early Arabic Historical Tradition*, pp. 63ff.

40 The prohibition of 'committing offences' (*wa-lam yuḥdithū maghīla*), along with the Syriacism (*baʿūthā*; cf. Thomas of Marga, *The Book of Governors*, ed. and trans. E. A. Wallis Budge (London, 1893), pp. 237/447) must have been as obscure to ninth-century readers as it is to modern ones.

41 Cf. Conrad, 'The conquest of Arwād', p. 399, note 213. For one effort to control the Arabic conquest tradition with an early Syriac source, see C. F. Robinson, 'The conquest of Khūzistān: a historiographical reassessment', in L. I. Conrad, ed., *History and Historiography in Early Islamic Times: Studies and Perspectives* (Princeton, forthcoming).

42 Al-Balādhurī, *Futūḥ*, p. 172.

43 Given as *faras kumayt*, but reports naturally differed about the precise colour: cf. al-Qushayrī, *Taʾrīkh al-Raqqa*, pp. 24f. (*maḥdhūf aḥmar*).

44 The idea is ubiquitous in the literature; for jurists' examples, see Abū ʿUbayd, *Kitāb al-Amwāl*, p. 298; Ibn Zanjawayh, *Kitāb al-Amwāl*, p. 474; Qudāma b. Jaʿfar, *Kitāb al-Kharāj*, p. 313; Abū Yūsuf, *Kitāb al-Kharāj*, pp. 39ff. Cf. Calder, *Studies*, pp. 138f.

second issue I have relatively little to say, since my intentions here are stubbornly conservative; suffice it to say, the choice of one or the other treaty form was presumably conditioned by the availability of exemplars *and* desired narrative effect, treaty texts providing a documentary authority that *isnād*less *akhbār* so frequently lacked. It is on the first of the two questions that I should like to concentrate, for historical narrative seems to have had an archival function; and this, more than fire or the ravages of time, probably explains why virtually no treaties survive independently.[45] Whether copied *verbatim*, loosely paraphrased or excerpted,[46] the texts preserved in the historical tradition had played crucial roles in the hurly-burly of politics and social relations in early Islamic towns.

They might appear fixed and immutable, but treaties had first and foremost been living documents, their lives extended by recopying[47] and, of course, forging.[48] Copies seem to have been retained by Christian and Muslim authorities in the provinces, the former apparently storing theirs in church archives;[49] one infers from Abū Yūsuf's passage that imperial authorities kept theirs in

[45] Cf. M. Chamberlain, *Knowledge and Social Practice in Medieval Damascus, 1190–1350* (Cambridge, 1994), pp. 2f.

[46] Thus Abū ʿUbayd (*Kitāb al-Amwāl*, p. 297; Ibn Zanjawayh, *Kitāb al-Amwāl*, p. 473) preserves the operative section of Khālid b. al-Walīd's treaty with the Ḥimṣīs, along with its close; but the material between the two he did not bother to record.

[47] For a particularly good example, see Abū Yūsuf, *Kitāb al-Kharāj*, p. 54, where Mūsā b. Ṭalḥa volunteers his confusion (*ʿindanā kitāb katabahu al-nabī (ṣ) li-Muʿādh aw qāla nuskha aw wajadtu nuskha hākadhā*). The Prophet's letter concerning the Thaqīf is said to have been written on a *ṣaḥīfa*, the copying of which was witnessed by ʿAlī, Ḥasan and Ḥusayn, whereas his letter to the people of Dūmat al-Jandal, written on vellum, was simply copied word by word, without witnesses; see Ibn Zanjawayh, *Kitāb al-Amwāl*, pp. 456ff.

[48] The treaty of Khaybar was particularly notorious among medieval authorities: presented with a text purporting to come from the Prophet's hand, Ibn al-Furāt detected *tazwīr* on dating grounds – the city actually fell sixty-seven days after the date recorded in the letter; see Hilāl al-Ṣābiʾ, *Kitāb Tuḥfat al-umarāʾ fī taʾrīkh al-wuzarāʾ* (Leiden, 1904), pp. 67f.; cf. al-Ṣafadī, *al-Wāfī biʾl-wafayāt*, I, pp. 44f. On Khaybar (and its forgeries), see A. Noth, 'Minderheiten als Vertragspartner im Disput mit dem islamischen Gesetz: Die 'Nachkommen der Juden von Ḫaibar' und die Ǧizya', in H. R. Roemer and A. Noth, eds., *Studien zur Geschichte und Kultur des Vorderen Orients* (Festschrift for B. Spuler) (Leiden, 1981), pp. 289–309, esp. 294f.; M. Gil, *A History of Palestine, 634–1099*, trans. E. Broido, rev. edn (Cambridge, 1992), p. 152; and M. Schöller, *Exegetisches Denken und Prophetenbiographie* (Wiesbaden, 1998), pp. 334ff. and 433ff.

[49] Khalīfa b. Khayyāṭ (*Taʾrīkh* (Beirut, 1995), p. 77) tells us that the *ṣulḥ* contracted by ʿIyāḍ was retained by the inhabitants of the Jazira, but not precisely where; cf. the case of Mayyāfāriqīn (C. F. Robinson, 'Ibn al-Azraq, his *Taʾrīkh Mayyāfāriqīn*, and early Islam', *JRAS* 3, 6, 1 (1996), p. 22), where a church is specified. A yellowed copy of the Najrān treaty, bearing the Prophet's stamp, is said to have been found in 265/878 in a *daftar* in the possession of Ḥabīb the monk, who claimed that it came from the *Bayt al-Ḥikma*; see the *Histoire Nestorienne*, II (2) ed. and trans. F. Nau in *PO* 13 (1919), pp. 601ff. The Latin loan word used here (*sijill*) had already entered Arabic via Aramaic by the time of the Qur'ān, and it appears in Syriac conquest accounts too; thus Michael the Syrian, *Chronique de Michel, patriarche jacobite d'Antioche (1166–1199)*, ed. and trans. J.-B. Chabot (Paris, 1899–1924), xi.vii ('livre'.'chapitre') (the document ʿUmar writes for Sophronius, bishop of Jerusalem, forbidding a Jewish presence in the city). One can fairly assume the existence of state archives from the Marwānid period, but these remain difficult to describe; cf. M. M. Bravmann, 'The State archives in the early Islamic period', *Arabica* 15 (1968), pp. 87ff., which is reprinted in his *The Spiritual Background of Early Islam* (Leiden, 1972), pp. 311ff.

the capital. Abū ʿUbayd's Edessa treaty text is said to have come to light when the caliph ʿUmar II (r. 717–720) directed one of his subordinates to 'ask the people of al-Ruhā [Edessa] if they have a *ṣulḥ*', whereupon 'their bishop' (*usqufuhum*) promptly produced one, stored in a cylindrical container of some kind: 'This is the letter (*kitāb*) from ʿIyāḍ b. Ghanm and those Muslims with him to the people of Edessa: "I have granted them security (*amān*) for their lives, possessions, children and women, their city and their mills, provided they pay what they rightly owe."'[50] According to one of al-Balādhurī's Takritī *shaykh*s, a conquest treaty (*kitāb amān wa-shuraṭ la-hum*) had been in the possession of the people of Takrit until a certain al-Ḥ/J/Kh-r-sh-ī ripped it up;[51] the person in question is almost certainly Yaḥyā b. Saʿīd al-Ḥarashī,[52] who was appointed governor of Mosul in 796, and whose methods in levying taxes were as destructive as they were effective.[53] In shredding the Takritī treaty, Yaḥyā b. Saʿīd was not so much rejecting a specific treaty stipulation as he was announcing that the rules had changed: he was now going to exact what he liked, regardless of what this or any other treaty stipulated. In any case, the event was probably a bit of theatre: when al-Maʾmūn's tax agents later tried to modify *kharāj* practices in Mosul, they claimed ignorance of the written precedent upon which city notables had insisted; at this point, a copy of the document was kept in the *dīwān* in Baghdad.[54]

Treaty copies were retained (and produced) in part because they were held to govern the character and amount of tribute to be levied on Christian subjects. We have already seen that the informant quoted by Abū Yūsuf reflects a local controversy regarding the rate and method of taxation. He concedes that Edessa fell according to a *ṣulḥ* treaty, but disputes the existence of a surviving text, since it apparently prescribed a tax arrangement contrary to his interests. If the existence of a text was not in question, the issue then frequently turned on who was liable to pay, and, in the language of the classical jurists, whether the amount of tribute was specified (*ʿalā shayʾ musammā/sammawhu*),[55] or variable according

[50] Abū ʿUbayd, *Kitāb al-Amwāl*, p. 298; Ibn Zanjawayh, *Kitāb al-Amwāl*, p. 474; see also al-Qushayrī, *Taʾrīkh al-Raqqa*, p. 26. Cf. the case in Damascus, where fifteen churches are said to have been specified in the city's *ṣulḥ*; when one of these is confiscated, the Christians take their grievance to ʿUmar II, who rebukes Ḥassān b. Mālik al-Kalbī: 'If this is one of the fifteen churches which are in their treaty (*ʿahd*), then you have no claim on it' (*fa-lā sabīl la-ka ilayhā*); see Ibn Manẓūr, *Mukhtaṣar taʾrīkh madīnat Dimashq* (Damascus, 1988), I, p. 290.

[51] Al-Balādhurī, *Futūḥ*, p. 333; de Goeje reads 'al-Jurashī', but his name is frequently garbled: see p. 311, note c; al-Azdī, *Taʾrīkh al-Mawṣil* (Cairo, 1967), p. 286, note 3; and Crone, *Slaves*, p. 145.

[52] Cf. M. Morony, *Iraq after the Muslim Conquest* (Princeton, 1984), p. 200, note 123, and 'The effects of the Muslim conquest on the Persian population of Iraq', *Iran* 14 (1976), p. 52, note 133, where he is taken to be a Khārijite.

[53] Al-Azdī, *Taʾrīkh*, pp. 286f. and 32 (for Yaḥyā's father in the service of Hishām in 112/731). On al-Ḥarashī, see also P. G. Forand, 'The governors of Mosul according to al-Azdī's *Taʾrīkh al-Mawṣil*', *JAOS* 89 (1969), pp. 97f.

[54] Al-Azdī, *Taʾrīkh*, pp. 410f. (in this case, the document in question was not a conquest treaty, but an Abbasid-era tax document).

[55] One occasionally comes across variants, e.g. *kharāj maʿlūm* (Ibn Zanjawayh, *Kitāb al-Amwāl*, p. 187).

to the capacity of those paying (*ʿalā qadr al-ṭāqa*). Al-Balādhurī's authorities preferred the former; thus accounts of the conquest of al-Raqqa put the tribute at one and four *dīnārs*, sometimes including a portion in kind.[56] By the time the tradition reaches us, a consensus had emerged among Muslim authorities that all adult males were liable; but Christian accounts, which were by definition written by men of the church, frequently argue that priests and bishops were exempt, a point not infrequently disputed by Muslim sources.[57]

In addition to governing tribute obligations, treaty texts were also held to determine the legal status of the Christians' public worship and churches;[58] it is here, more than in matters of tax and tribute, that we can see how conquest history was adduced in local controversies. According to al-Azdī, al-Mahdī adjudicated between the Christians and Muslims of Mosul in 163/779 in a dispute over the status of the church of Mār Thomas; here the issue was plainly the legality of *iḥdāth* – post-conquest maintenance and repairs. It seems that the Christians of the city had enlarged the church at the expense of an adjacent mosque, with the result that city folk had it razed. Al-Mahdī summoned the two parties of the controversy (*al-farīqān*) to the nearby town of Balad, presumably to distance the proceedings from angry crowds; there he ultimately decided in favour of the Muslims.[59] The events are also preserved in the biographies of the city's *qāḍī*, al-Ḥasan b. Mūsā al-Ashyab (d. 824); the Christians offer him a generous sum to judge in their favour, but he declines.[60] Later, when Hārūn visited Edessa in 793, the Muslims (*ṭayyāyē*) of the city claimed that the Christians had been spying for the Byzantines, that the emperor himself had been praying in the city's church, and that the 'great church' (*ʿidtā*) should be razed, and its bell cease ringing.[61] The first allegation

56 Al-Balādhurī, *Futūḥ*, pp. 173f.

57 Thus ʿUmar II is said to have proposed a tax of 2 dīnārs on monks; see Ibn Zanjawayh, *Kitāb al-Amwāl*, p. 163; and, for Egyptian evidence, Morimoto, *Fiscal Administration of Egypt*, p. 82. For an overview on the *jizya*, see U. Rubin, 'Quran and *Tafsīr*: the case of "*ʿan yadin*"', *DI* 70 (1993), pp. 133–44.

58 See, for example, al-Wāqidī's text (*lā yuḥdithū kanīsa wa-lā bīʿa wa-lā yuẓhirū nāqūs wa-lā bāʿūth wa-lā ṣalīb*) in al-Balādhurī, *Futūḥ*, p. 173; cf. Ibn Zanjawayh, *Kitāb al-Amwāl*, p. 280; Abū ʿUbayd, *Kitāb al-Amwāl*, pp. 137ff.; and al-Shaybānī, *Sharḥ kitāb al-siyar al-kabīr* (Cairo, 1960), pp. 56ff.

59 Al-Azdī, *Taʾrīkh*, pp. 244 and 340.

60 See al-Khaṭīb al-Baghdādī, *Taʾrīkh Baghdād* (Cairo, 1931), VII, pp. 426ff.; J. M. Fiey, *Mossoul Chrétienne: Essai sur l'histoire, l'archéologie et l'état actuel des monuments chrétiens de la ville de Mossoul* (Beirut, 1959), p. 20. Al-Ḥasan, who also served as the *qāḍī* of Ḥimṣ, was a man of some learning, transmitting *ḥadīth*s to Aḥmad b. Manṣūr al-Ramādī among others; see the literature cited in G. H. A. Juynboll, *Muslim Tradition: Studies in Chronology, Provenance and Authorship of Early Ḥadīth* (Cambridge, 1983), p. 227; al-Azdī, *Taʾrīkh*, pp. 335ff. (first appointed in 199/814 and dismissed in 206/821). A collection of his *ḥadīth*s is apparently preserved in the Ẓāhiriyya Library; see M. N. al-Albānī, *Fihris makhṭūṭāt Dār al-Kutub al-Ẓāhiriyya* (Damascus, 1970), p. 178.

61 See the *Chronicle of 1234* (trans. J.-B. Chabot as *Chronicon anonymum ad annum Christi 1234 pertinens*), I (Paris, 1916 and 1937; *CSCO* 81 and 109) and II (Paris and Louvain, 1920 and 1974; *CSCO* 82 and 354), II, pp. 3/1; J. B. Segal, *Edessa, 'The Blessed City'* (Oxford, 1970), pp. 200f.; J. M. Fiey, *Chrétiens syriaques sous les Abbassides surtout à Bagdad (749–1258)* (Louvain, 1980; *CSCO* 420), p. 49.

echoes treaty clauses that call upon city folk to 'help Muslims against their enemies',[62] and perhaps northern Syrian anxieties about a Byzantine *reconquista* too.[63]

The fullest example is provided by the Monophysite patriarch Dionysius of Tell Maḥrē (d. 845) in his history, here cited by the late twelfth-century patriarch Michael the Syrian.[64] The point at issue was patriarchal authority, particularly vis-à-vis that of the *qāḍī* of Mosul; according to his first-person testimony, Dionysius argued the Christian case on their behalf as follows: 'The Mosulis [that is, the city's Christians] say that they willingly handed their city over to the Muslims (*ṭayyāyē*), [that is, that it was a *ṣulḥ*] and that he who conquered it entered into a treaty (*qyāmā*) with them, according to which their church would not be razed and that their laws would not be abolished; but this judge devastated their cathedral (lit: "great church") and put an end to their laws.'[65] In response to the patriarch's words, the caliph ordered the chief *qāḍī*, at this point Yaḥyā b. Aktham,[66] to adjudicate the case, telling him: 'If the Mosulis demonstrate to you that their city was taken peacefully, let them retain their laws, which he who conquered it granted to them.' Much like the anonymous Edessans quoted by Abū Yūsuf's informant, the Mosulis knew that conquest history was no settled thing: it was the stuff of controversy.

In prescribing conquest arrangements, conquest history thus describes post-conquest history; and in the absence of genuine documentary sources, it is hard to see how we can say a great deal more than that. Christians might claim that bishops were not to be held liable for tribute, and this in the form of history and law codes alike,[67] but we know that they frequently were;[68] in

[62] Thus al-Balādhurī, *Futūḥ*, p. 172. For views that would support a much earlier date for clauses such as this, see W. Kaegi, 'Heraklios and the Arabs', *The Greek Orthodox Theological Review* 27 (1982), p. 122.

[63] See S. Bashear, 'Apocalyptic and other materials on early Muslim–Byzantine wars: a review of Arabic sources', *JRAS* 3,1 (1991), pp. 173–207; and also M. Cook, 'The Heraclian dynasty in Muslim eschatology', *al-Qanṭara* 13 (1992), pp. 3–23, esp. 18, note 92.

[64] On Dionysius and his work, see R. Abramowski, *Dionysius von Tellmahre, jakobitischer Patriarch von 818–845* (Leipzig, 1940); R. Hoyland, *Seeing Islam as Others Saw it: A Survey and Evaluation of Christian, Jewish and Zoroastrian Writings on Early Islam* (Princeton, 1997), pp. 416ff.; and, for a translation of the work as it is preserved in Michael and the *Chronicle of 1234*, A. Palmer, *The Seventh Century in the West-Syrian Chronicles* (Liverpool, 1993), pp. 85ff. For a tentative argument that Tell Maḥrē is to be identified with Tell Sheikh Hassan, which lies c. 40 km north of al-Raqqa, see K. Bartl, 'Tell Sheikh Hasan: a settlement of the roman-parthian to the Islamic period in the Balikh valley/northern Syria', *Archéologie Islamique* 4 (1994), pp. 14f.

[65] Michael the Syrian, *Chronique*, xii.xiv, which is also cited in Fiey, *Mossoul*, pp. 26f.

[66] On Yaḥyā (d. 243/857), author of a *shurūṭ* work and prominent in the *miḥna*, see al-Azdī, *Ta'rīkh*, pp. 369, 373, 395, and 405; al-Khaṭīb al-Baghdādī, *Ta'rīkh Baghdād*, XIV, 191ff.; Ibn Ḥajar, *Tahdhīb*, XI, pp. 179ff.; Ibn Khallikān, *Wafayāt al-aʿyān* (Beirut, 1977), VI, pp. 147ff.; Wakin, *The Function of Documents*, p. 18, note 7.

[67] In addition to the *Life* of Gabriel cited below, see the Christian account preserved in the (Islamic) *Ta'rīkh Mayyāfāriqīn wa-Āmid* of Ibn al-Azraq (MS BM OR 5803, fol. 5a); Robinson, 'Ibn al-Azraq', p. 21, note 140 (history).

[68] Thus Chabot, ed. and trans., *Synodicon Orientale*, pp. 225/489f.; see also A. Palmer, *Monk and Mason on the Tigris Frontier* (Cambridge, 1990), p. 187; and R. J. Bidawid, *Les Lettres du patri-*

the Jazira, the practice seems to have begun in the early Abbasid period.[69] Similarly, the Islamic conquest tradition frequently prohibits the striking of sounding-boards, but we know that monks and priests kept on striking.[70] Since the question of church building is relatively well documented, it can suggest some of the ways we can turn the (relatively late) tradition to our advantage; it can also reinforce a point made already: as far as confessional relations are concerned, it is in the early Abbasid period that conquest history clearly began to matter.

Conquest treaties frequently limit or prohibit church construction in cities such as Edessa and al-Raqqa.[71] Jurists, being jurists, disagreed about the particulars, some prohibiting maintenance and construction alike, some only construction *de novo*,[72] while others apparently restricted these prohibitions to the *amṣār*.[73] But regardless of what jurists of the ninth and tenth centuries may have said, in the north (particularly Edessa and Ṭūr ʿAbdīn) we have epigraphic evidence of continued church building,[74] along with a range of documentary and literary material.[75] The city of Mosul, which was a *miṣr* by any reasonable definition, witnessed the birth of a vibrant church and monastic

arche nestorien Timothée I (Vatican, 1956), p. 2 (Mūsā b. Muṣʿab exceptionally exempts Timothy, Nestorian patriarch; on Mūsā, see chapter 7).

69 If we follow the *Zuqnin Chronicle*, ed. J.-B. Chabot as *Incerti auctoris chronicon anonymum pseudo-Dionysianum vulgo dictum II* (Paris and Louvain, 1933 and 1989; *CSCO* 104 and 507), pp. 259f./204f.

70 Thus Thomas of Marga, *Governors*, pp. 30/54. For the practice more generally, see L. I. Conrad, 'A Nestorian diploma of investiture from the *Taḏkira* of Ibn Ḥamdūn: the text and its significance', in W. al-Qāḍī, ed., *Studia Arabica et Islamica* (Festschrift for Iḥsān ʿAbbās) (Beirut, 1981), pp. 99f.

71 The prohibition of new church building is well attested in the Arabic literature, and it is included in the 'covenant of ʿUmar'; see A. S. Tritton, *The Caliphs and their Non-Muslim Subjects* (London, 1930), pp. 37ff. and for a more recent – and in many respects, more optimistic – reading, see A. Noth, 'Abgrenzungsprobleme zwischen Muslimen und nicht-Muslimen: Die 'Bedingungen ʿUmars (*aš-šurūṭ al-ʿumariyya*)' unter einem anderen Aspekt gelesen', *JSAI* 9 (1987), pp. 290–315.

72 Whereas the clause in Sulaymān b. ʿAṭāʾ's treaty (*lā yuḥdithū kanīsa illā mā kāna la-hum*) assumes that *iḥdāth* means maintenance and repair, elsewhere it is taken to mean building as well as rebuilding; thus al-Balādhurī, *Futūḥ*, p. 172; cf. also Abū Yūsuf, *Kitāb al-Kharāj*, p. 138.

73 Thus Ibn Abī Shayba, *al-Muṣannaf* (Beirut, 1989), VII, pp. 635f.; al-Shaybānī, *Sharḥ kitāb al-siyar*, p. 58 (where a distinction is drawn between *al-qurā* and *al-amṣār*); Ibn Ḥanbal, *Masāʾil* (Beirut, 1981), p. 260 (I owe this last reference to Michael Cook).

74 See M. M. Mango, 'The continuity of the classical tradition in the art and architecture of Northern Mesopotamia', in N. G. Garsoian, *et al.*, eds., *East of Byzantium: Syria and Armenia in the Formative Period* (Washington DC, 1982), pp. 115–34 (several eighth-century examples from Ṭūr ʿAbdīn). This appears to be in line with Syria and Palestine in the same period; thus I. Shahid (Kawar), *Byzantium and the Arabs in the Fourth Century* (Washington DC, 1984), pp. 425f.; and R. Schick, *The Christian Communities of Palestine from Byzantine to Islamic rule* (Princeton, 1995), esp. pp. 112ff.

75 For Ṭūr ʿAbdīn, see Palmer, *Monk and Mason*, chapter 5 (drawing on, *inter alia*, the *Life* of Simeon, which documents the holy man's enthusiasm for building), and table 2, on pp. 194f.; for Athanasius' building projects in Edessa, see the *Chronicle of 1234*, I, pp. 294f./229; and, in general, W. Hage, *Die syrisch-jakobitische Kirche in frühislamischer Zeit* (Wiesbaden, 1966). pp. 59ff. ('Das 7. und 8. Jahrhundert sah die syrisch-jakobitische Kirche in einer regen Bautätigkeit, die auch unter der Herrschaft des Islams keine Einschränkung erkennen ließ').

culture during the seventh and eighth centuries.[76] As far as the Christians were concerned, the evidence suggests that the controversy lay not in the legality of church building under Islam, but rather in who had authority over the churches once built. According to a Nestorian synod of 676, churches and monasteries were to be built under the supervision of the bishop; there is no mention here of Muslim restrictions.[77] Writing as the Nestorian bishop of Nineveh soon after the conquest of Mosul, Īshōʿyab III complained of the construction of a Monophysite church;[78] had the legal distinction between building and rebuilding then existed, one might have expected him to invoke it – particularly since the Nestorians could claim pre-Islamic foundations in Mosul, while the Monophysites could not. What seems to have upset Īshōʿyab was his adversaries' ability to curry favour with the authorities, and the meddling of Takritī Monophysites in Nineveh affairs. Simeon of the Olives is singled out for having used funds from Ṭūr ʿAbdīn to rebuild a church in Nisibis that had been destroyed by Jews and Nestorians, and which was completed in 706/7;[79] once again, the issue turns on Nestorian and Monophysite competition for Muslim favour, rather than the legality of church construction *per se*.[80]

Spotty as it is, the evidence also suggests that it was only in the middle of the eighth century that some restrictions began to appear; in other words, they relate to the imposition of Abbasid rule from Iraq.[81] As we have seen, it is Abbasid caliphs and judges who adjudicate these disputes, and it may even be that the Abbasid caliphs' episodic visits to towns in the north served to hone polemical skills;[82] certainly this dating would explain an awkward account of the construction of a church near Ṣalaḥ around 755.[83] It follows that conquest

[76] For an overview, see Fiey, *Mossoul*.

[77] See Chabot, ed. and trans., *Synodicon Orientale*, pp. 217f./483; cf. E. Sachau, *Syrische Rechtsbücher* (Berlin, 1907–14), II, pp. 36f.

[78] This in the collection of his letters edited and translated by R. Duval as *Išōʿyahb patriarchae III Liber epistularum* (Paris, 1904 and 1905; *CSCO* 11–12), pp. 82/63f.; see also Fiey, *Mossoul*, p. 19, note 1. The Nestorian *History of Rabban Hôrmîzd* is filled with similar stories, many of which are certainly legendary; see Rabban Hormizd, *The Histories of Rabban Hôrmîzd the Persian and Rabban Bar ʿIdtâ*, ed. and trans. E. A. W. Budge (London, 1902).

[79] See the discussion in Palmer, *Monk and Mason*, p. 160.

[80] Cf. the case of Takrit, discussed by J. M. Fiey, 'Tagrît. Esquisse d'histoire chrétienne', *L'Orient Syrien* 8 (1963), pp. 312f.; reprinted in his *Communautés syriaques en Iran et Irak des origines à 1552* (London, 1979).

[81] The dislocation in the countryside so vividly portrayed in the *Zuqnin Chronicle* thus seems to have had an urban echo as well; see C. Cahen, 'Fiscalité, propriété, antagonismes sociaux en Haute-Mésopotamie au temps des premiers ʿAbbāsides d'après Denys de Tell Mahré', *Arabica* 1 (1954), pp. 136–152; cf. Fiey, *Chrétiens syriaques*, pp. 24f.

[82] In addition to the accounts already cited, see the *Chronicle of 1234*, II, pp. 22f./16, where al-Maʾmūn goes to Ḥarrān, and enters into controversy with Theodore Abū Qurra; the debate is recorded in writing. On the historicity of the debate, see S. Griffith, 'Reflections on the biography of Theodore Abū Qurrah', in S. K. Samir, ed., *Actes du 4e Congrès International d'Etudes Arabes Chrétiennes* (Cambridge, 1992), *Parole de l'Orient* 18 (1993), pp. 156ff.

[83] Where, in Palmer's words, 'the builders of the church . . . apparently called it a "renovation", whereas it was clearly no less than a total reconstruction'; see Palmer, *Monk and Mason*, pp. 187 and 206 (for the inscription).

traditions that feature restrictions of the variety discussed here are unlikely to have stabilised before the early eighth century, when they were required by Muslim and Christian élites in intraconfessional controversies.

Christian conquest accounts

Treaty texts thus played a crucial role in a living tradition of conquest history, and we have seen that something of their *Sitz im Leben* can be inferred from accounts of Umayyad and early Abbasid administration. It is out of this controversial milieu that our finished treaties emerged.

The eventual resting-place of the confessional claims they expressed need not be the tradition that produced them. The conquest account attributed to Sulaymān b. ʿAṭāʾ (preserved by al-Balādhurī) may or may not be authentic, but that the treaty was put in circulation by local Christians, only to be recorded by a Muslim native of Ḥarrān, and finally pass into the imperial tradition, is suggested by a number of features: the distinction between the single (and definite) 'cathedral church and precinct' (*haykalahum wa-mā ḥawlahu*) and the indefinite 'any church' (*kanīsa*); the permission given to repairing pre-existing churches (*lā yuḥdithū kanīsa illā mā kāna la-hum*); and, finally, the complete omission of any tribute requirement.[84] Similarly, al-Wāqidī's long account of the conquest of al-Raqqa, Ḥarrān and Edessa seems to preserve the (pagan) Ḥarrānians' special pleading.[85] This said, Christian perspectives are naturally most abundant in the surviving Syriac tradition, and there one finds that the function of many Christian accounts is not so much to record history as it is to prescribe harmonious coexistence, an accommodating *modus operandi* that was rooted in, and exemplified by, lines of patronage. Within this retrojected framework of coexistence and patronage is then made a set of claims: claims about Church institutions (e.g. churches and monasteries), the poll tax and public rituals (e.g. the striking of sounding-boards and processions on holy days).

There are many examples, including one in the *Life* of Simeon of the Olives (d. 734): wishing to build churches and monasteries in Nisibis, Simeon secures a document (*ktābā*) from the governor (*shallīṭā*) of city, which he takes to the 'great king of the Arabs', along with a variety of precious gifts; he duly returns with another document, this one written by the 'king', which stipulates that the 'laws of the Christians' be respected in the Arabs' territory.[86] Another example appears in the Syriac *Life* of Gabriel of Qarṭmīn, the metropolitan bishop of Dārā from 634 to 648.

84 Al-Balādhurī, *Futūḥ*, p. 172. 85 Al-Balādhurī, *Futūḥ*, p. 174.

86 See the *Life* of Simeon, ed. P. Dolabani, *Maktabzabnē d-ʿumrā qaddīshā d-Qarṭmīn* (Mardin, 1959), p. 134. For a summary of the contents, see S. P. Brock, 'The Fenqitho of the monastery of Mar Gabriel in Tur 'Abdin', *Ostkirchliche Studien* 28 (1979), pp. 168–82; see also Palmer, *Monk and Mason*, pp. 159ff. (where Dolabani's text is called 'drastically edited'); and Hoyland, *Seeing Islam*, pp. 168ff.

Now this Mor Gabriel went to the court of the sovereign (*shulṭānā*) of the Arabs [lit. 'sons of Hagar'], who was ʿUmar the son of Khaṭṭāb, in the city of Jazirē. He was received with great gladness and after a few days the Blessed One [i.e. Gabriel] petitioned the commander (*amīrā*) and received his written authority concerning the statutes (*qnōnē*) and laws (*nmūsē*) and orders and warnings and judgements and observances pertaining to the Christians; to churches and monasteries; and to priests and deacons, that they should not pay the head tax [lit.: vertebrae], and to monks that they should be exempt from tribute (*mdattā*), and that the (use of the) wooden gong would not be banned; and that they might practise the chanting of anthems at the bier of a dead man when he leaves his house to be taken for burial, together with many (other) customs. The sovereign (*shallīṭā*) was pleased that the Blessed One had come to him; and the holy man returned to the abbey with great joy.[87]

Palmer argues that the text is legendary, partly on the grounds that the caliph ʿUmar would have had nothing to do with securing a conquest treaty in the backwoods of Ṭur ʿAbdīn; he must be correct, even if the ʿUmar in question may be a local figure.[88] Considering the wide range of evidence, we have no choice but to regard Gabriel's account, and equally those treaties that stipulate the precise contrary to the arrangements set down by Gabriel, as polemical assertions and counter-assertions, which freeze, and then embellish upon, episodes in an ongoing process whereby Christian communities and Muslim authorities negotiated and adjusted their way towards coexistence. The affected reference to the caliph's 'written authority' merely underlines the view, held equally by Christians and Muslims alike, that negotiations were to be carried out with reference to what Abū Yūsuf's 'learned people' called 'how things were at the beginning'; they were also to be written down.[89]

It was not enough that relations between Christians and Muslims simply be given contractual form. In a political culture conditioned by emerging norms rather than fixed rules and institutions, Christian claims that churches could be rebuilt or that sounding-boards could be struck were most effectively made by those who enjoyed the favour of Muslim authorities. Harmonious relations prescribed by dry treaty stipulations were thus vividly exemplified by individuals – principally bishops and holy men; Gabriel, his hagiographer writes, 'was received with great gladness'. Christians, for their part, reciprocated, and are often given to receive the conquerors warmly, frequently offering provisions and food. The conquest story that appears in the Syriac *Ecclesiastical History* of Bar Hebraeus (d. 1286) is a case in point. The protagonist is Mārūtā, the Monophysite maphrian of Takrit, and the section in question begins with his reforms of 629, which resulted in the establishment of Takrit as the see of the Monophysite metropolitan; it then turns to the events of the conquest itself:

[87] See microfilm 1 enclosed in Palmer, *Monk and Mason*, LXXII; I follow Palmer's translation closely. [88] Robinson, 'Ibn al-Azraq', p. 20.

[89] Cf. accounts concerning the conquest of Tustar, where instructions are emphatically written; see Ibn Aʿtham, *Futūḥ*, II, p. 11 (*wa-aʿṭāhum ʿahd wa-kitāb maktūb*).

When these [matters] were settled, Mārūtā went to Tagrīt, and he decorated and adorned it with monasteries and churches, which he built there. In his days, the kingdom of the Arabs (*malkūtā d-ṭayyāyē*) took control of Persia (*bēt parsāyē*), and in his wise administration he opened the fortress (*ḥesnā*) of Tagrīt to them; [as a result], not a soul was injured.[90]

There is little hope of reconciling this account with those preserved by the Islamic tradition, which is itself inconsistent on the fate of the city, and Posner sensibly discarded it in favour of the Islamic material.[91] Although the provenance of this report is difficult to pin down, it is unlikely to be early. Unlike much in Bar Hebraeus, it does not derive from Michael the Syrian, whose sources are not only better known to us, but are often quite early. More important, it is not included in the biography of Mārūtā, which was penned by his successor, Denha.[92] In fact, the account is too lean and confused to inspire any confidence at all: it lacks any temporal precision ('When these [matters] were settled . . .'), and fails to mention any figures by name. It rather shows all the signs of being legendary, and is absent in Denha's biography for the simple reason that the legend had not yet emerged.

For later authorities, it did have two things to offer, however. The first, particular to Mārūtā, was praise for his firm stewardship of the church in a time of crisis, when bishops not infrequently fled their sees. A western synod of 636, for example, expressly prohibits bishops from moving around, despite 'the many disturbances and discords'.[93] The second, common to a large number of accounts, was to project a harmonious and orderly set of confessional relations, which were to be anchored by lines of patronage and authority; the conquest past could serve to underpin Christian and Muslim authority alike. In this particular narrative Mārūtā's acknowledgment of Muslim authority is

90 Bar Hebraeus, *Chronicon ecclesiasticum*, ed. and trans. J. B. Abbeloos and T. J. Lamy (Paris and Louvain, 1872–77), III, cols. 123–6 (Syriac and Latin). For criticisms of Fiey's account in his 'Tagrît', see N. Posner, 'The Muslim Conquest of Northern Mesopotamia: An Introductory Essay into its Historical Background and Historiography', Ph.D. thesis (New York University, 1985), pp. 320ff. On Bar Hebraeus and his sources, see Y. M. Isḥāq, 'Maṣādir Abī al-Faraj al-Malaṭī al-ta'rīkhiyya wa-atharuhā fī manāhijihi', *Aram* 1 (1989), pp. 149–72; on the events of 629, see Morony, *Iraq*, pp. 377f.

91 See Posner, 'Muslim Conquest', pp. 314ff.; Fiey, 'Tagrît', p. 311. Cf. W. Kaegi, *Byzantium and the Early Islamic Conquests* (Cambridge, 1992), p. 154; and Morony, *Iraq*, p. 378.

92 See Denha, *Histoire des divins actions de saint Mar Marouta l'ancien* in the *Histoires d'Aḥoudemmeh et de Marouta*, ed. and tr. by F. Nau in *PO* 3 (1909), pp. 79ff.; Posner, 'Muslim Conquest', pp. 320f.

93 See A. Vööbus, ed. and trans., *The Synodicon in the West Syrian Tradition I* (Louvain, 1975; *CSCO* 367–8), pp. 91/99 and 113/117. Cf. Mārūtā of Maipherqaṭ, *The Canons Ascribed to Mārūtā of Maipherqaṭ*, ed. and trans. A. Vööbus (Louvain, 1982; *CSCO* 439–40), pp. 52/42; S. P. Brock, 'Christians in the Sasanid empire: A case of divided loyalties', in S. Mews, ed., *Religion and National Identity: Papers Read at the Nineteenth Summer Meeting and the Twentieth Winter Meeting of the Ecclesiastical History Society* (Oxford, 1982; Studies in Church History 18), p. 15, where he notes not only the synod of 554, but also the bridal imagery that lies behind it: 'In the synod of 554 the transfer of bishops from one see to another is forbidden on the grounds that this is a form of adultery; each bishop's see being "a pure spiritual wife who has been given to him".'

expressed with some economy ('he opened the fortress of Tagrīt to them, and not a soul was injured'); others are considerably less economical. Mār Emmeh, the (Nestorian) bishop of Nineveh at the time of the conquests, is said to have provided provisions for the conquering Muslim armies, and to have yielded the land to them as well; for his co-operation with the Muslim commander in the conquests he was duly rewarded with the patriarchate in 646/7.[94] He would later receive a letter of investiture from ʿAlī, conferring upon him authority over (Nestorian) Christians, which he would display to Muslim military officials as proof of his status.[95] To Landron, accounts such as these suggest that the Nestorians reacted to the conquests with a certain 'passivity' that was born of their experiences as a persecuted minority in the Sasanian empire;[96] Hill, who revives the old bogey that the conquest of the north was facilitated by Melkite persecution of the Monophysites, would probably agree.[97] But the eirenic tone cannot be explained by earlier oppression, be it Sasanian or Byzantine; it rather functions as a generic model for Muslim–Christian relations, and this, no doubt more than simple historiographic exchange, explains why similar accounts appear in the Islamic tradition as well.

Thus, according to Ibn Aʿtham's account of conquest events at Edessa, the bishop of the city, having prepared a great feast in the cathedral, invites ʿIyāḍ to dine with him; ʿIyāḍ's attendance, we read, will impress the bishop's fellow Christians. But ʿIyāḍ, citing ʿUmar's humble entrance into Jerusalem and his refusal to dine with its bishop, refuses. The bishop then suggests that the commander have his men accept the invitation, but again he declines.

The bishop stood before ʿIyāḍ not knowing what to say. So ʿIyāḍ said to him: O bishop! You are only doing this for us out of fear for your land; you should rather do it for those who come after us (*bi-man ya'tīka min baʿdinā*). We have granted you a *ṣulḥ*, so do not fear any oppression on our part; nor shall we impose upon you something beyond your means. So the bishop returned to his men saying, 'This is the finest man there could ever be!' (*hādhā afḍal rajul yakūn*).[98]

[94] See the *Histoire Nestorienne*, II (2), pp. 629f.; Mārī b. Sulaymān (attrib.), *Kitāb al-Majdal* (*Maris Amri et Slibae, De patriarchis Nestorianorum commentaria*, ed. and trans. H. Gismondi (Rome, 1899), p. 62) (this, presumably, drawing on the preceding: on the authorship and sources of the work, see B. Holmberg, 'A reconsideration of the *Kitāb al-Mağdal*', in S. K. Samir, ed., *Actes du 4e Congrès International d'études Arabes chrétiennes* (Cambridge, 1992), *Parole de l'Orient* 18 (1993), pp. 255–73); and Fiey, *Mossoul*, p. 16.

[95] *Wa-kataba la-hu ʿAlī b. Abī Ṭālib ʿalayhi al-salām kitāb bi'l-waṣāh ʿalayhi bi'l-naṣārā wa-riʿāyat dhimmatihim*); thus Mārī b. Sulaymān, *Kitāb al-Majdal*, p. 62. The 'commanders' (*amīrē*) of Nisibis, Ḥarrān, Edessa and Amida were impressed not only by the holiness of Simeon of the Olives but also by his possession of the caliph's written orders; see his *Life* in Dolabani, *Maktabzabnē*, p. 134. For diplomas, see Conrad, 'Nestorian diploma', pp. 99ff.; and P. Kawerau, *Die jakobitische Kirche im Zeitalter der syrischen Renaissance* (Berlin, 1960), pp. 86ff.

[96] M. B. Landron, 'Les Relations originelles entre Chrétiens de l'est (Nestoriens) et Musulmans', *Parole de l'Orient* 10 (1981–2), p. 192.

[97] Hill, *Termination*, p. 84; cf. G. Wiet, 'L'Empire néo-byzantin des omeyyades et l'empire néo-sassanide des Abbasides', *Cahiers d'Histoire Mondiale* 9 (1953), p. 64.

[98] Ibn Aʿtham, *Futūḥ*, I, p. 331. Conquest accounts in demonstrably late compilations (e.g., ps.-Wāqidī) frequently take the form of intra-confessional dialogues.

The point here, as elsewhere,[99] is to contrast the pious modesty of the (victorious) early Muslims with the arrogant wealth of the (ignominiously defeated) Christians; it is also to anchor ideals of co-operation and co-existence in a formative beginning.

In the examples adduced so far, bishops and holy men have played starring roles; this is because the narratives served not only communal interests, but also factional interests in intra-Christian competition for Muslim favour.[100] Their prominence should not be taken to mean that conquest accounts featuring civil authorities do not appear in the tradition, however. A fairly complex example comes in the treaty account recorded in a number of Christian sources (i.e. the Syriac history of Michael the Syrian and the *Chronicle of 1234*), the Christian Arabic chronicle of Agapius (Maḥbūb) of Manbij (d. c. 950), and the Greek history usually attributed to Theophanes (d. 818);[101] it is particularly noteworthy because it figures prominently in a number of modern reconstructions of the conquest of the north.[102] Aside from relatively minor chronological inconsistencies, the accounts are at one in describing a treaty concluded between a Byzantine figure (usually John) on the one hand and (almost invariably) ʿIyāḍ b. Ghanm on the other. According to the treaty, the Byzantines were to pay an annual tribute of 100,000 gold coins, in return for which the Muslims, having already conquered Syria, would refrain from crossing the Euphrates into the Jazira proper. It is only in the second (or third) year, when the Byzantines fail to make good on the tribute, that ʿIyāḍ crosses the river, moving first to Edessa; this campaign results in the conquest of Byzantine Mesopotamia. Now below I will argue that the conquering Muslims did march into the Jazira from Syria, and indeed that Edessa was the first major city to fall. But what meaning did the account bear in the early period, and what is its exact provenance?

The authority responsible for the accounts, whom we can assume to be Theophilus of Edessa (d. 785),[103] is anything but naïve about Islamic rule, knowing what can only be described as a fairly arcane point of imperial history, namely that in the post-conquest period Qinnasrīn and Ḥimṣ were

[99] For an example from the south (Hurmuzān), see Robinson, 'The conquest of Khūzistān'.

[100] A particularly good example involves the Nestorian patriarch Ḥnānīshōʿ (d. 699 or 700); see Mārī b. Sulaymān, *Kitāb al-Majdal*, p. 63; and further Hoyland, *Seeing Islam*, pp. 200ff.

[101] Michael the Syrian, *Chronique*, xi.vii; *Chronicle of 1234*, I, pp. 256f./200f.; *The Chronicle of Theophanes Confessor*, trans. C. Mango and R. Scott (Oxford, 1997), AM 6128 and 6130; Agapius of Manbij, *Kitāb al-ʿUnvān, histoire universelle* 2(II), ed. and trans. A. A. Vasiliev in *PO* 8 (1912), p. 476 (hereafter *Kitāb al-ʿUnwān*).

[102] Thus Kaegi, *Byzantium and the Early Islamic Conquests*, pp. 159ff.; Posner, 'Muslim Conquest', pp. 274ff. and 356; Palmer, *Monk and Mason*, pp. 158f.

[103] For the argument in favour of Theophilus as the common 'Eastern' source behind Dionysius (as preserved in Michael the Syrian and the *Chronicle of 1234*), Agapius and Theophanes, see L. I. Conrad, 'Theophanes and the Arabic historical tradition: some indications of intercultural transmission', *Byzantinische Forschungen* 15 (1988), pp. 4ff.; Conrad, 'The conquest of Arwād', pp. 330ff.; the editors of Theophanes (*Chronicle*, pp. lxxxii ff.) accept it as a 'working hypothesis'; and so too Hoyland, *Seeing Islam*, pp. 631ff., where his work is reconstructed.

administratively connected until the reign of Yazīd b. Muʿāwiya;[104] as Kaegi has noted, a passage in Theophanes' version ('that he would not cross the Euphrates either peacefully or by force of arms') may also echo the *ṣulḥ*/*ʿanwa* distinction of the Muslim lawyers.[105] It is thus imprecise to call the account merely Christian, particularly since Theophilus, a Maronite by confession, is unmistakably hostile to the emperor Heraclius and his Monothelitism; it is out of his arrogance that he refuses to pay the tribute.[106] In fact, the account betrays an unmistakably Edessan pedigree: in opening the gates of their city to the conquerors, the Edessans are given to enter into an agreement that generously preserves not only their own possessions but (inexplicably) the lives of the Byzantine garrison; and in coming to peaceful terms with the Muslims, the townsfolk possess a foresight unknown to Heraclius, and also to the people of Tella and Dārā, who capitulated only after a Muslim attack.

In a political milieu where the legacy of the past conditioned the law of the present, the stakes in history writing were high. There is no room in Theophilus' account for a violent attack, much less any heroic resistance on the part of the city folk, for the Edessan élite stood to gain nothing by generating or transmitting such a conquest memory: familiar as he was with the Islamic tradition, Theophilus would have known of the legal consequences of *ʿanwa* conquests, just now starting to crystallise; and (apparently) comfortable as he was as part of the caliph's court, he knew equally well the gains to be had from coexistence. This, rather than the events' facticity, is sure: for other accounts have Edessa falling not peaceably, but rather under military attack, or reneging on their first agreement, just as other accounts have Dārā and Tella entering into the same *ṣulḥ* as had Edessa.[107]

Administration and apologia

Conquest traditions were thus shaped by confessional relations in the early Islamic north. Christian and Muslim élites came to share the view that conquest events set precedents and were to be adduced to adjudicate disputes between their communities; they naturally disagreed about what exactly these precedents were. It is in the light of these disagreements, as well as those of Muslim jurists, that we must read conquest accounts that narrate sieges, capit-

[104] See al-Balādhurī, *Futūḥ*, pp. 131f.

[105] Kaegi, *Byzantium and the Early Islamic Conquests*, p. 159; whether it was 'original' is another matter. On Theophanes' reliance on the Arabic tradition more generally, see Conrad, 'Theophanes'.

[106] Thus the *Chronicle of 1234*, I, pp. 256/200: 'God had removed His Hand from the kingdom of the Romans' (so Palmer, *Seventh Century*, p. 163). On Theophilus, see Hoyland, *Seeing Islam*, pp. 400ff.; on Heraclius' Monothelitism, see F. Winkelmann, *Die östlichen Kirchen in der Epoche der christologischen Auseinandersetzungen* (Berlin, 1980); and J. F. Haldon, *Byzantium in the Seventh Century* (Cambridge, 1990), chapter 8. Cf. Eutychius' account in *Das Annalenwerk des Eutychios von Alexandrien*, ed. and trans. M. Breydy (Louvain, 1985; *CSCO* 471–2), pp. 141f., where it is the Muslims who provoke the conquest.

[107] Thus al-Balādhurī, *Futūḥ*, pp. 174ff.

ulations, treaty conditions and the like. Of course tribute sums and authority to build churches were not the only controversies that arose as a result of the conquests; nor were questions of Islamic rule limited to urban relations between Christians and Muslims. Administration posed problems too; and two of the most salient narrative patterns – chains of command and conquest itineraries – are inexplicable without reference to the administrative history of the north.

The conquest tradition was conditioned by administrative history in two ways. Although the administrative history of the north was discontinuous, it was only infrequently recognised as such; in general, Abbasid historians, as historians before and after them, wrote knowingly and prescriptively about a past that was now as remote to them as it was confusing. In practical terms, this means that they assumed conquest origins for the Marwānid-era administrative geography that they inherited; the conquest tradition brims with anachronisms as a result. Second – and again due to these discontinuities – controversies arose about administrative geography, principally about the inclusion or exclusion of tax districts; and while scholars occasionally discussed administrative issues in the light of their understanding of pre-Islamic administrative geography,[108] much more frequently they turned to conquest history to settle issues.[109]

We can begin with the Jaziran conquest account attributed to Sayf b. ʿUmar, and transmitted by al-Ṭabarī. Sayf begins by having ʿUmar dispatch ʿIyāḍ b. Ghanm and Suhayl b. ʿAdī from Iraq to relieve Abū ʿUbayda, now under attack by the Byzantines in Ḥimṣ.[110] The latter, following the Jaziran *firāḍ*,[111] arrives at al-Raqqa, to where the *ahl al-Jazīra* – here apparently natives of the Jazira enrolled in the Byzantine army – have moved, having heard of the approaching Kufan army (*ahl al-Kūfa*); after a siege, Suhayl concludes a *ṣulḥ* treaty with the Raqqans, doing so under the command of ʿIyāḍ. Another of ʿIyāḍ's commanders, ʿAbd Allāh b. ʿAbd Allāh b. ʿItbān, who has followed a different route along the Tigris, reaches Mosul, crosses over to Balad and finally arrives at Nisibis. There he reaches a *ṣulḥ*, now on the model of the Raqqan *ṣulḥ*; once again ʿIyāḍ's authority over the campaign is acknowledged, and the same *dhimmī* status granted. Here we come to a disturbance in

108 The notable exception is Abū Yūsuf, *Kitāb al-Kharāj*, p. 39, where the Byzantine–Sasanian border is located.

109 See, for example, al-Balādhurī, *Futūḥ*, p. 332 and Ibn ʿAbd al-Munʿim al-Ḥimyarī, *al-Rawḍ al-miʿṭār fī khabar al-aqṭār* (Beirut, 1975), p. 26 (based on al-Balādhurī), where the *kharāj* history of Urmiya is anchored in conquest events (the town belonged to the province of Mosul, but later its *kharāj* was transferred away). The campaigns of ʿUtba b. Farqad, according to one authority, extended over 'all the [tax] districts of [the region of] Mosul'; see al-Nuwayrī, *Nihāyat al-arab fī funūn al-adab* (Cairo, 1975), XIX, p. 237.

110 The account begins at al-Ṭabarī, *Taʾrīkh*, I, p. 2506:8.

111 Usually described as the (fortified) Sasanian side of the Sasanian–Byzantine frontier; see Ibn Ḥubaysh, *Kitāb al-Ghazawāt* (Cairo, 1987), II, p. 70; see also R. N. Frye, 'The Sasanian system of walls for defense', in M. Rosen-Ayalon, ed., *Studies in Memory of Gaston Wiet* (Jerusalem, 1977), pp. 8ff.

al-Ṭabarī's text;[112] the author has apparently broken up and rearranged Sayf's narrative, interpolating material concerning al-Walīd b. ʿUqba and the Taghlib that properly belongs on the next page. Having secured the capitulation of al-Raqqa and Nisibis, ʿIyāḍ now summons his two sub-commanders, and the unified force takes Ḥarrān; Suhayl and ʿAbd Allāh then take Edessa. The two cities agree to what appears to be identical terms, which include the imposition of the *jizya*. The section ends with a brief retrospective and accompanying poetry; what immediately follows is again misplaced and should be restored to the beginning of the section.[113] Sayf then turns to the vexing problem of the Taghlib, and a new section now begins.

What are some of the concerns behind Sayf's narrative? The first is to make absolutely clear what is being conquered and on whose authority. When Sayf describes the three routes taken by ʿIyāḍ and his two sub-commanders from Kufa to the north – Suhayl along the Euphrates, ʿAbd Allāh up the Tigris, and ʿIyāḍ himself neatly poised between the two[114] – he has done nothing less than to describe the geographical borders of the province of al-Jazīra. The choreography may function as a geographical introduction to the scenes that follow; it certainly expresses the view that a single front, under a single commander, established Islamic rule over a unitary province. Al-Wāqidī is at pains to insist on the same point.[115] Since the early Syriac tradition identifies ʿIyāḍ as the principal commander leading forces east of the Euphrates, one infers that at issue was not so much ʿIyāḍ's identity as the composition of his forces and the character of this authority. In having ʿIyāḍ unify and co-ordinate all the battles on the front, Sayf reflects a widespread concern to anchor a unified and uniform provincial administration in conquest events, and to counter claims made on behalf of other commanders;[116] this is why he distinguishes ʿIyāḍ from his sub-commanders at the start, and repeatedly underlines his authority in all of the treaty accounts.

Representations of unified command had two virtues: not only did they illustrate the proper delegation of caliphal authority,[117] they provided precedents for administrative arrangements of a later period. Such is the case for the refrain of identical treaty arrangements (*wa-ajraw . . . majrā*; *wa-ṣanaʿū kamā ṣanaʿa*), which are said to have followed those of al-Raqqa. In fact, the prominence of al-Raqqa (Syr.: Qalliniqos) in the Islamic tradition is striking when compared with its failure to appear in any local, Christian history of the

112 Al-Ṭabarī, *Taʾrīkh*, I, p. 2507: 8–11 are to be restored to p. 2508: 12.

113 Al-Ṭabarī, *Taʾrīkh*, I, p. 2508: 6–12.

114 Note that ʿIyāḍ is curiously positioned *fī manzil wāsiṭ min al-Jazīra* (al-Ṭabarī, *Taʾrīkh*, I, p. 2506, with note p), a position that asserts his leadership of the Jaziran army, while it accommodates accounts that credit treaty negotiations to others (in this connection, note the ambiguity of *qabila*).

115 Thus the account preserved by al-Balādhurī (*Futūḥ*, p. 175): 'Not a foot of the Jazira was left unconquered by ʿIyāḍ b. Ghanm during the reign of ʿUmar b. al-Khaṭṭāb.'

116 Such as ʿUmayr (or ʿUmar) b. Saʿd: see al-Balādhurī, *Futūḥ*, p. 177; al-Ṭabarī, *Taʾrīkh*, I, pp. 2505f.; Ibn al-Azraq, *Taʾrīkh*, fol. 6b.

117 See Noth/Conrad, *Early Arabic Historical Tradition*, pp. 111ff.

conquest, be it early or late.[118] This, combined with the anachronistic appearance of a uniform tax regime, might be taken to suggest a *terminus post quem* of 796–7, when Hārūn made the city his capital; certainly the city also had its champions: we have already seen that the Raqqans are responsible for much of the Jaziran historical tradition. Be this as it may, the treatment of al-Raqqa contrasts with that of Edessa, for while Edessa is also given to provide a treaty that functions as a paradigm for the entire (and now unified) Jazira, its appearance as the first major city to fall east of the Euphrates can at least be corroborated by independent sources, which give it a crucial role in the fall of the Byzantine north to the Persians;[119] the Syriac tradition (Edessan and non-Edessan alike) also makes it clear that Edessa served Heraclius as his base for his defence.[120] The presumption of a uniform tax administration, one understood to have been inspired by a model constructed at the first, great conquest, thus appears to have overwhelmed the tradition in general; but concerning the question of sequence, which clearly preoccupied several of al-Balādhurī's sources, sound material seems to survive.

A reconstruction that places Edessa before al-Raqqa forces us to reject al-Wāqidī's account, the striking feature of which is ʿIyāḍ's march from al-Raqqa, to Ḥarrān and then Edessa.[121] Both al-Balādhurī and al-Wāqidī seem to have sensed the awkwardness: the former cites it only after Sulaymān b. ʿAṭāʾ, who has ʿIyāḍ in Edessa first, and before al-Zuhrī (as transmitted by al-Wāqidī!), who has Ḥarrān, Edessa, al-Raqqa; al-Wāqidī himself begins the report by equivocating. The account should probably be explained as a cumbersome attempt to accommodate two conflicting reconstructions, one which had al-Raqqa falling first, and another that had the Edessa treaty functioning paradigmatically for the entire Jazira; this is presumably why the report ends with the feeble 'And ʿIyāḍ would make raids from Edessa, and return there.'[122] Confusion about the orthographically similar al-Ruhā and al-Raqqa, which is betrayed by ʿIyāḍ's manoeuvres around the 'Edessa Gate (*bāb al-Ruhā*), which is one of its [al-Raqqa's] gates',[123] may have compounded the problem.

118 An exception is Elias of Nisibis, *Opus chronologicum*, ed. and trans. E. W. Brooks (Paris, 1910; *CSCO* 62), p. 133; but here as elsewhere he is drawing directly on the Islamic tradition.

119 Thus, the late seventh-century Armenian history attributed to Bishop Sebeos, *Histoire d'Héraclius par l'évêque Sebéos*, trans. F. Macler (Paris, 1904), pp. 61f. The text remains controversial; see, for instance, M. Krikorian, 'Sebēos, historian of the seventh century', in T. J. Samuelian, ed., *Classical Armenian Culture: Influences and Creativity* (Chico, CA, 1982), pp. 52–67; Z. Arzoumanian, 'A critique of Sebēos and his *History of Heraclius*, a seventh-century Armenian document', in *ibid.*, pp. 68–78; and, more recently, R. Hoyland, 'Sebeos, the Jews and the rise of Islam', in R. L. Nettler, ed., *Medieval and Modern Perspectives on Muslim–Jewish Relations* (Luxembourg, 1995), pp. 89–102; Hoyland, *Seeing Islam*, pp. 124ff.

120 Thus the *Zuqnin Chronicle*, pp. 150/112; cf. Abū Yūsuf, *Kitāb al-Kharāj*, p. 40 (where Edessa is *madīnat malik al-Rūm*).

121 Al-Balādhurī, *Futūḥ*, pp. 172ff.

122 Al-Balādhurī, *Futūḥ*, p. 175.

123 Al-Balādhurī, *Futūḥ*, p. 173; cf. Qudāma b. Jaʿfar, *Kitāb al-Kharāj*, p. 312:10 (*ḥattā nazala min al-Raqqa ʿalā al-bāb al-musammā biʾl-Ruhā*). The account may have originally formed part of an Edessan scene, such as that described by Sulaymān b. ʿAṭāʾ (al-Balādhurī, *Futūḥ*, p. 172:10–11).

If the report is so problematic, why did al-Balādhurī see fit to include it? For one thing, it enjoyed some verisimilitude.[124] For another, it was very appealing. Not only is it equipped with all the precision for which al-Wāqidī is (in)famous – three dates, a list of sub-commanders and their positions in the army, detailed treaty arrangements[125] – but its section on the capitulation of al-Raqqa is a particularly striking example of conquest narrative. The repeated emphasis on the speed and manoeuvres of ʿIyāḍ and his conquering horsemen (*fa'ntahat ṭalīʿat ʿIyāḍ fa-aghārū ʿalā ḥāḍir; fa-aqbala ʿIyāḍ fī ʿaskarihi . . . thumma ta'akhkhara; wa-rakiba wa-ṭāfa ḥawla al-madīna wa-waḍaʿa ʿalā abwābihā rawābiṭ thumma rajaʿa ilā ʿaskarihi wa-baththa al-sarāyā*) contrasts with a city paralysed by the siege, watching impotently as hostages are taken and crops ripen in the surrounding fields. The passage then culminates in ʿIyāḍ's victory cry ('The land is ours! We have trodden on it and made it a safe refuge!'), which has Qur'ānic and poetic echoes.[126] Taken as a whole, the passage thus expresses a conquest truth as compelling to medieval as it is to modern historians: the Arabs were faster than their adversaries – simply put, they moved better.

Al-Balādhurī's treatment of the conquest of Mosul is amenable to the same analysis, for the simple reason that the administration of the north was fluid for much of the Marwānid and early Abbasid period; despite jurists' attempts to systematise, this may have been true of Iraq in general.[127] Of course an administrative context of the *Futūḥ al-buldān* is discernible in the very organisation of the work itself; and in distinguishing between the campaigns that resulted in the conquest of Mosul from those in the southeastern districts of Shahrazūr,[128] al-Ṣāmaghān,[129] and Darābādh,[130] al-Balādhurī does nothing less than provide a

[124] Thus two more Jazirans (al-Ḥajjāj b. Abī Manīʿ al-Ruṣāfī and Abū Ayyūb al-Raqqī) report a Raqqa–Edessa–Ḥarrān sequence (al-Balādhurī, *Futūḥ*, p. 175), and a very different reconstruction has Suhayl b. ʿAdī, one of ʿIyāḍ's sub-commanders, move up into the Jazira via al-Raqqa (al-Ṭabarī, *Ta'rīkh*, I, p. 2506).

[125] On al-Wāqidī's chronology (some of which can be vindicated), see J. M. B. Jones, 'The chronology of the *maghāzī*', *BSOAS* 19 (1957), pp. 245–80 (called 'characteristically precise' at p. 261); and for his attractive precision, P. Crone, *Meccan Trade and the Rise of Islam* (Princeton, 1987), p. 224.

[126] Thus Q 33: 27 (*wa-awrathakum arḍahum wa-diyārahum wa-amwālahum wa-arḍan lam taṭa'ūhā*) (trans. A. J. Arberry, *The Koran Interpreted* (New York, 1955) as 'And he bequeathed upon you their lands, their habitations, and their possessions, and a land you never trod'). See also Ibn Hishām, *al-Sīra al-nabawiyya* (ed. M. al-Saqqā *et al.*, Beirut, n.d.), III, p. 333 (trans. A. Guillaume as *The Life of Muhammad* (Oxford, 1955), p. 513: 'We will tread you down'); cf. al-Ṭabarī, *Ta'rīkh*, II, p. 1781; and Ibn al-Athīr, *al-Kāmil fī al-ta'rīkh* (Beirut, 1965), II, p. 534.

[127] Thus Ibn al-Muqaffaʿ, *Conseilleur*, pp. 59/58: 'There is not a single tax district (*kūra*) whose tax charge (*waẓīfa*) has not changed several times, disappearing here and remaining there.'

[128] Thus al-Balādhurī, *Futūḥ*, pp. 333f. The first of three toponyms is in Iranian Kurdistān and the area north of Hamadān; see W. Barthold, *An Historical Geography of Iran*, trans. S. Soucek (Princeton, 1984), pp. 207ff.

[129] This district lay to the south of the Lesser Zāb, to the east of Shahrazūr; see G. Hoffmann, *Auszüge aus syrischen Akten persischer Märtyrer* (Leipzig, 1880); Abhandlungen für die Kunde des Morgenlandes, 7, number 3), pp. 257 and 260; and J. M. Fiey, *Assyrie chrétienne* (Beirut, 1965–8), II, p. 500, note 1.

[130] This district lay to the south of the Greater Zāb, east of Irbil; see Fiey, *Assyrie chrétienne*, II, p. 644. If, following Brock's suggestion, we identify the 'Arbad' mentioned in the Life of John

precedent for the administrative articulation of regions that had formerly fallen under a loose Kufan penumbra. For according to al-Balādhurī's own sources,[131] Shahrazūr and its tax districts had formed part of the province of Mosul until the end of Hārūn's reign, when it was combined with Darābādh and al-Ṣāmaghān; this reconstruction is corroborated in part by al-Azdī, who counts Shahrazūr among the districts of Mosul in 113,[132] and by revenue lists attributed to the time of Hārūn himself, where Shahrazūr and its dependencies are listed separately from Mosul.[133] According to al-Bakrī, it was al-Mahdī who removed Darābādh and al-Ṣāmaghān from the province.[134] A similar pattern can be detected in the south. Whatever truth there is to the view that Ṭīrhān and Takrit were granted an *amān* by ʿUtba b. Farqad, one independent of the Mosul/Nineveh settlements, by the middle of the Abbasid period administrative history would have put a premium on appropriate conquest narrative. Al-Azdī counts the districts of Ṭīrhān and Takrit within Mosul in the year 113/731–2,[135] and as late as Hārūn's time Takrit continued to be counted as part of the province.[136] Soon thereafter, al-Muʿtaṣim is said to have removed the two districts, shifting them both into the emerging (Iraqi) district of Sāmarrā'.[137]

Of course in none of these cases is it at all clear that the tradition has misrepresented conquest events; it may actually be that the capitulation of Takrit was distinct from that of Mosul. But how, in the absence of any independent corroboration, are we to decide? How do we distinguish conquest material actually preserved by the tradition – 'the neutral data of history'[138] – from conquest history coined in the course of administrative controversy? One writes history because there is a story to tell and a point to the story; and whatever the state of conquest knowledge among second-century authorities, the conquest history of a *miṣr* such as Mosul had to be told; an unknowable past had neither meaning nor use.[139] That the two protagonists – ʿArfaja b. Harthama

of Daylam with this Darābādh, we have late seventh or early eighth-century corroboration of the inclusion of this site in the province of Mosul; see S. P. Brock, 'A Syriac Life of John of Dailam', *Parole de l'Orient* 10 (1981–2), pp. 187/164.

131 Al-Balādhurī, *Futūḥ*, p. 334; Ibn ʿAbd al-Munʿim al-Ḥimyarī, *al-Rawḍ al-miʿṭār*, p. 350. For an overview of the conquest of Mosul and al-Balādhurī's accounts, see L. Caetani, *Annali dell'Islām* (Milan, 1905–26), IV, pp. 215ff.

132 Al-Azdī, *Ta'rīkh*, pp. 32f.

133 See al-Jahshiyārī, *Kitāb al-Wuzarā' wa'l-kuttāb* (Cairo, 1938), p. 285; A. von Kremer, 'Ueber das Budget der Einnahmen unter der Regierung des Hârûn alrasîd nach einer neu aufgefundenen Urkunde', *Verhandlungen des VII. internationalen Orientalisten-Congresses* (Vienna, 1888), pp. 6 and 11; S. A. El-ʿAli, 'A new version of Ibn al-Muṭarrif's list of revenues in the early times of Hārūn al-Rashīd', *JESHO* 14 (1971), pp. 305ff.; and B. Spuler, *Iran in früh-islamischer Zeit* (Wiesbaden, 1952), p. 474.

134 See al-Bakrī, *Muʿjam mā istaʿjama min asmā' al-bilād wa'l-mawāḍiʿ* (Cairo, 1951), p. 1278; cf. Qudāma b. Jaʿfar, *Kitāb al-Kharāj*, p. 175.

135 Al-Azdī, *Ta'rīkh*, pp. 32f.

136 Al-Jahshiyārī, *Wuzarā'*, p. 285.

137 Al-Bakrī, *Muʿjam*, p. 1278. Little wonder then that authorities continued to debate how Mosul related administratively to the Jazira (see al-Azdī, *Ta'rīkh*, p. 226).

138 The phrase is J. Wansbrough's: *The Sectarian Milieu: Content and Composition of Islamic Salvation History* (Oxford, 1978), p. 31.

139 The point, needless to say, applies elsewhere; cf. P. Magdalino, ed., *The Perception of the Past in Twelfth-century Europe* (London and Rio Grande, OH, 1992), for a variety of essays.

and ʿUtba b. Farqad – both fathered notable families,[140] does not necessarily speak against the reliability of the material; but it certainly does speak in favour of familial contributions to oral history in early Islam;[141] and combined with the view that restricted conquest command to fully fledged *ṣaḥāba*,[142] hardly makes for disinterested history.

What is clearer is that these and other conquest accounts expressed tribal apologetics; and we can see this if we examine the Takrit/Mosul events in more detail. According to Sayf's account of the conquest of Takrit, in 16/637–8 a Byzantine commander called al-Anṭāq led a force that consisted of Byzantine troops, quasi-heretical Christian notables (*shahārija*) and Arab tribesmen from the Iyād, Taghlib and al-Namir. After a forty-day siege, the Arab tribesmen had a change of heart, and they chose to co-operate with the besieging Muslims and to convert to Islam; their co-operation led to the collapse of the Byzantine defence and the violent capitulation of the city. A force under the leadership of Ribʿī b. al-Afkal was then sent to al-Ḥiṣnayn (=Mosul), which it quickly conquered;[143] there too the tribesmen play a crucial role. We have already seen that this account is at odds with a Syriac account of events at Takrit; here it it more important to note that it also contradicts Arabic/Islamic reports that have the city falling by treaty,[144] proposes the aberrant date of 16 AH for its capitulation,[145] and, finally, leaves loose ends that later historians felt compelled to tie. Al-Anṭāq's movements before the battle, for example, are altogether vague, and Sayf's suggestion that he came from Mosul,[146] was resolved by Ibn al-Athīr into certainty,[147] while the Persian translation of al-Ṭabarī's history claims that he was usually stationed in Takrit.[148] Little wonder then that the report failed to command a consensus.

140 On the Harāthima, see al-Azdī, *Taʾrīkh*, p. 24; on the Farāqid, al-Balādhurī, *Ansāb al-ashrāf* MS Reisülkuttap 598, fol. 595b (hereafter *Ansāb*, Reis. 598).

141 Cf. R. S. Thomas, *Oral Tradition and Written Record in Classical Athens* (Cambridge, 1992).

142 See Ibn Ḥajar, *al-Iṣāba fī tamyīz al-ṣaḥāba* (Cairo, 1977), VI, p. 412 (concerning ʿArfaja b. Harthama). It is presumably this view that explains why one candidate for conquest leadership, ʿUmayr b. Saʿd (al-Balādhurī, *Futūḥ*, pp. 176f.), is described as 'young in age'; cf. al-Ṭabarī, *Taʾrīkh*, I, p. 2505 (*ghulām ḥadath al-sinn*). Early teenage years (fourteen or fifteen) appear to have been the minimum age for battle: see Jones, 'Chronology', p. 273; and Lecker, 'Zayd b. Thābit', pp. 262f.

143 Al-Ṭabarī, *Taʾrīkh*, I, pp. 2474ff. The account was transmitted by al-Azdī as well; thus Ibn al-Athīr, *Usd al-ghāba* (Būlāq, 1871), III, p. 401.

144 Thus al-Balādhurī, *Futūḥ*, p. 249 (where an *amān* is granted to the city folk); and al-Balādhurī, *Ansāb*, Reis. 598, fol. 596a.

145 The years 18, 19 and 20 AH seem to have prevailed. See Khalīfa b. Khayyāṭ, *Taʾrīkh*, p. 77; and, for a detailed discussion, Posner, 'Muslim Conquest', pp. 314ff.

146 *Kataba Saʿd fī ijtimāʿ ahl al-Mawṣil ilā al-Anṭāq wa-iqbālihi ḥattā nazala bi-Takrīt* (al-Ṭabarī, *Taʾrīkh*, I, p. 2474).

147 *Wa-sabab dhālika anna al-Anṭāq sāra min al-Mawṣil ilā Takrīt* (Ibn al-Athīr, *al-Kāmil*, II, p. 523).

148 *Chronique de Abou Djafar-Mohammed-ben-Yezid Tabari*, trans. H. Zotenberg (Paris, 1958, reprint of 1867–1874), III, pp. 420f. Although Kaegi (*Byzantium and the Early Islamic Conquests*, pp. 154f.) has identified a plausible rationale for a continued Byzantine presence in northern Iraq, he has also noted the poverty of our evidence in its favour.

One can still wonder why it was put into circulation. Aside from the legendary attraction of 'al-Anṭāq',[149] the answer must be that it reconstructed conquest events in line with the interests of Rabīʿa tribesmen. More precisely, the account was circulated apparently to rehabilitate those local Rabīʿa who had resisted the kerygma of Arab Islam; it is a variant on what Donner has called the 'Euphrates Arab' tradition, in which the conquest experience of stubborn Shaybānīs was revised in a more positive light.[150] Conversion *en masse* is the principal marker; it is at once fittingly drawn from the stock formulary of *akhbār* scholarship, the *takbīr*,[151] and at the same time contradicted by the Syriac ecclesiastical literature, which counts the Taghlib as part of the fold well into the Islamic period,[152] and equally the Islamic tradition, which concedes the Taghlibīs' stubborn refusal to convert.[153] It may also be that Sayf manifests his notorious Kufan sympathies in pushing the conquest date back from 20 (or 18) to 16 AH; this, in any case, eliminates an embarrassing period during which the Kufans sat on their hands.[154] What is beyond question is that these sympathies lie behind his view on the Jazira: for if virtually all authorities could agree that Mosul was a Kufan conquest, in asserting Kufan origins for the armies that conquered al-Jazīra, Sayf clearly – if not uniquely[155] – expressed Kufan claims much further west.

The problem for Sayf went beyond the issue of claims, however; the very course of the conquest had been unsatisfactory in the eyes of his informants. Thus we read that 'the Jazira was the easiest province to conquer and rule (*fa-kānat al-Jazīra ashal al-buldān amran wa-aysarahu fatḥan*); but this ease was ignominious for them [i.e. for the defeated Jazirans] and also for those Muslims who settled amongst them [i.e. for the conquerors]'. Compensatory poetry ascribed to ʿIyāḍ b. Ghanm then follows, relating – albeit awkwardly – the glorious battle.[156] If Sayf's prose account functions in at least two ways (to rehabilitate Rabīʿa tribesmen and eliminate Kufan indifference to the north), the poem seems to respond apologetically to a dearth of conquest drama; and it is tempting to see it as a fossil, one produced fairly early on, perhaps in the course of *fakhr* debates among conquest veterans or their offspring.[157]

149 The figure also appears in the ps.-Wāqidī texts.
150 F. M. Donner, *The Early Islamic Conquests* (Princeton, 1981), p. 199.
151 See Noth/Conrad, *Early Arabic Historical Tradition*, pp. 143ff.
152 On the Taghlib, see chapter 2.
153 The ongoing controversy regarding the fiscal status of Christian Arab tribes reflects precisely this; see, for examples, Ibn Zanjawayh, *Kitāb al-Amwāl*, pp. 125ff. See also below, chapter 2.
154 Hill, *Termination*, p. 97.
155 Thus Ibn Isḥāq (al-Ṭabarī, *Taʾrīkh* I, p. 2505) has 'Umar direct the governor of Kufa, Saʿd b. Abī Waqqāṣ, to 'dispatch an army from where you are'.
156 Al-Ṭabarī, *Taʾrīkh*, I, pp. 2507f.
157 On the social production of tribal poetry, see S. Caton, *'Peaks of Yemen I Summon': Poetry as Cultural Practice in a North Yemen Tribe* (Berkeley and Los Angeles, 1990), esp. pp. 50ff.; on the social production of embarrassing family history, see M. Lecker, *Muslims, Jews and Pagans: Studies on Early Islamic Medina* (Leiden, 1995), pp. 150ff.

Conclusions

The point in the preceding is not to argue that the tradition is incoherent, and thus useless for the purposes of historical reconstruction. Far from it: medieval Muslim historians were not bad historians; it is rather we who are bad historians if we read legal and administrative discourse as though it were Thucydides. In this sense, Brett is correct: *ta'rīkh* is not history (in this conventional sense), but information 'arranged with a passion for chronology',[158] and, as we have already seen, with sequence too: 'Not a foot of the Jazira was left unconquered by ʿIyāḍ b. Ghanm during the reign of ʿUmar b. al-Khaṭṭāb, may God be pleased with him; ʿIyāḍ conquered Ḥarrān, Edessa, al-Raqqa, Qarqīsiyā, Nisibis, and Sinjār.'[159] When *akhbārī*s as respected as Ibn Saʿd, al-Wāqidī and al-Zuhrī are associated with a report such as this, we can reasonably conclude that the stuff of 'real' history (e.g. chronology, topography, character and motive) was irrelevant: for all that ʿIyāḍ b. Ghanm is ubiquitous in the tradition, we can say virtually nothing about what he was like, or why he conquered.[160] Of the geography and topography of the north we learn nothing; ʿIyāḍ's men simply push across empty space, their numbers – indeed the logistics of the campaigns more generally – appearing in the narratives only incidentally. To write conventional military history from evidence such as this is to misunderstand the character of the tradition: two pages of Theophylact Simocatta can probably teach us more about late antique warfare than 200 pages of al-Ṭabarī; to conjure up what happened in the siege of Edessa we are well advised to read 'Joshua the Stylite' and pseudo-Zacharias on Amida at the turn of the sixth century.

The surviving tradition betrays its interests elsewhere; it may have been set down by individual compilers, but the reports themselves reflect corporate ideals more clearly than they do these compilers' individual interests:[161] Christian and Muslim élites alike were concerned to prescribe communal norms by describing conquest events and documents; *akhbārī*s anchored administrative precedents in conquest itineraries and hierarchies of command, and asserted tribal claims in battle narratives. Now the problem is not simply that in expressing these interests the *akhbārī*s failed to provide an objective account of what happened in the early seventh century; it almost goes without saying that all claims about the past reflect socially conditioned ideas of what is important. What modern historians of medieval Islam do is

158 M. Brett, 'The way of the nomad', *BSOAS* 58 (1995), p. 252.

159 Al-Balādhurī, *Futūḥ*, p. 175.

160 For the lean biographical details (early conversion; fought at al-Ḥudaybiyya; became sub-commander for Abū ʿUbayda; took command of the Jazira; died in Syria or the Jazira), see Ibn Saʿd, *Kitāb al-Ṭabaqāt*, VII^2, p. 122; al-Balādhurī, *Ansāb al-ashrāf*, V (Beirut, 1996), pp. 595f.; al-Khaṭīb al-Baghdādī, *Ta'rīkh Baghdād*, I, pp. 183f.; al-Dhahabī, *Siyar aʿlām al-nubalā'* (Beirut, 1982), II, pp. 354f.; Ibn ʿAsākir, *Ta'rīkh madīnat Dimashq* (Beirut, 1998), XLVII, pp. 264ff. (I am indebted to A. Elad for reminding me of Ibn ʿAsākir).

161 On the homogeneity of the conquest tradition, see Noth/Conrad, *Early Arabic Historical Tradition*, introduction.

essentially comparable to what al-Ṭabarī did: we select, rearrange and synthesise (to greater or lesser degrees) accounts of the past, producing narratives that are coherent, meaningful and which teach lessons; the lessons may be more explicit from one historian to the next, but they are all in a broad sense political.[162] The problem for us more precisely lies in describing how history was endowed with political meaning. As far as northern Mesopotamia is concerned, a consensus that conquest history conditioned social conduct seems to have appeared several generations after the events in question; out of reach of authentic memory, it was now plastic enough to be impressed upon a wide variety of contemporary issues.

We have already seen that inasmuch as the fate of northern churches reflects broader patterns, it was only with the Abbasids that confessional relations began to be governed by laws imputed by the tradition to the conquest period. More of a sense of the emerging role of conquest history can be gathered from John of Fenek, who was writing very soon after the end of the Second *fitna*:

> Before calling them [the Muslims], [God] had prepared them beforehand to hold Christians in honour; thus they also had a certain commandment (*pūqdanā maram*) from God concerning our monastic station, that they should hold it in honour. Now when these people came, at God's command, and took over as it were both kingdoms, not with any war or battle, but in a menial fashion, such as when a brand is rescued out of the fire; not using weapons of war or human means, God put victory into their hands in such a way that the words written concerning them might be fulfilled, namely, 'One man chased a thousand and two men routed ten thousand'. How, otherwise, could naked men, riding without armour or shield, have been able to win, apart from divine aid, God having called them from the ends of the earth so as to destroy, by them, 'a sinful kingdom' and to bring low, through them, the proud spirit of the Persians.[163]

Five pages later he returns to the honourable position enjoyed by Christians, and this in a passage of some interest to historians of Islamic law:[164]

> For they held, as I have said above, a certain commandment, stemming from the man who was their guide, concerning the people of the Christians and the monastic station. Also as a result of this man's guidance they held to the worship of the One God, in accordance with the customs of ancient law. At their beginnings they kept to the tradition (*mashlmānūtā*) of Muḥammad, who was their instructor (*tār'ā*), to such an extent that they inflicted the death penalty on anyone who was seen to act brazenly against his laws (*namūseh*).[165]

[162] Something which is no more true of orientalists' historiography than it is of others'; see P. Novick, *That Noble Dream: The 'Objectivity Question' and the American Historical Profession* (Cambridge, 1988).

[163] See John's *Ktābā d-rīsh mellē* in A. Mingana, *Sources Syriaques* (Mosul, 1907), pp. *141f., which is translated by S. P. Brock, 'North Mesopotamia in the late seventh century: Book XV of John Bar Penkāyē's *Rīš Mellē*', *JSAI* 9 (1987), p. 57 (whose translation I otherwise follow), who renders it as 'a special commandment'; for the *terminus post quem* of 693, see p. 52.

[164] See John of Fenek, *Rīsh mellē* in Mingana, *Sources*, p. *146f.; Brock, 'North Mesopotamia in the late seventh century', p. 61 (who translates 'an ordinance').

[165] Cf. the *sīra* accounts that have the Christian Waraqa b. Nawfal proclaim that Muḥammad has received *al-nāmūs al-akbar*; thus Ibn Hishām, *al-Sīra al-nabawiyya*, I, pp. 233ff.

The passage may be significant for the light it sheds on pre-classical *sunna*; what is notable here is that John, writing just as the Marwānids began to make sovereign claims in the north, is naïve of conquest arrangements, and thus anchors his claim for Christian status not in conquest negotiations, but in a 'certain commandment' given by God to Muḥammad. Unfamiliar as he was with the requirements imposed upon historical writing by (later) Marwānid and Abbasid history, he was concerned to teach that in forsaking God, the Christians had brought His wrath upon them; the Muslims were nothing more (or less) than instruments for this wrath. Of specific battles and their settlements he had no interest, for they had not yet begun to teach lessons of their own.

It might be suggested then that John of Fenek is as valuable a witness of historiographic trends as he is of conquest events;[166] in fact, he highlights a perspective that is shared by others. It is not just that Sayf b. ʿUmar was short on heroism, or that Abū Yūsuf's informant was also ignorant of conquest details. A very early (and very laconic) account knows only of some fighting at Mardīn and Raʾs al-ʿAyn;[167] the *Zuqnin Chronicle*, which is neither very early nor very laconic, has ʿIyāḍ take Edessa and alludes to some fighting and a treaty at Dārā, but knows no details;[168] and even Theophilus of Edessa knew more about conquest events in Syria and Palestine than he did about those of his native Jazira and Edessa. Indeed, when the ninth-century tradition finally does turn its attention to the conquest, it fails to produce a single example of detailed battle narrative; instead, it manifests an interest in the personalities concerned, many of which imply Islamic inspiration, and in examples of negotiated settlement. The spread of the evidence thus suggests a provisional conclusion: detailed knowledge of the conquests emerged only during the late eighth and early ninth centuries, particularly – indeed, to some degree because – early Muslim and Christian élites were working out a long-term *modus vivendi*.

So much for historiographic conclusions. What can we say about seventh- and eighth-century history? Can the conquest traditions tell us something about the capital on which northern Mesopotamian élites drew to claim or maintain their status?

As far as reconstructing conquest history is concerned, we must set our sights relatively low; the general contours of the conquest can be made out, but of the precise course of ʿIyāḍ's campaigns or of the individual experience

166 Of course John's thoroughly topological account hardly amounts to disinterested history; for the Biblical parallels, see the notes to Brock's translation, 'North Mesopotamia in the late seventh century'.

167 Thus the *Chronicle of 724*, ed. and trans. E. W. Brooks as *Chronicon miscellaneum ad annum domini 724 pertinens* (Louvain, 1904; *Chronica Minora* II of *CSCO* 3–4), pp. 148/114; for an early dating of the text, see Palmer, *Seventh Century*, pp. 5ff.; and now Hoyland, *Seeing Islam*, pp. 118f. The fortress of Mardīn seems to have been a particularly important Byzantine stronghold on the eve of the conquests; see, for example, Michael the Syrian, *Chronique*, x.xxv.

168 *Zuqnin Chronicle*, pp. 150f./112f.

of northern Mesopotamian settlements, little can be said with much confidence. Although it has recently been argued that accounts identifying Iraq as the base for Jaziran conquest forces can be reconciled with those that posit Syrian origins,[169] there can be no doubt that the principal assault was launched from Syria and led by ʿIyāḍ b. Ghanm. Wellhausen argued the Syrian case on the grounds that al-Balādhurī's material, corroborated by the Byzantine history attributed to Theophanes, was more reliable than Sayf *apud* the recently published al-Ṭabarī, who remains the principal advocate of the Iraqi line.[170] If the jury is still out on Sayf in general,[171] a wide variety of sources strengthens Wellhausen's hand considerably. Theophanes, it turns out, here reflects a mid-eighth-century view (that of Theophilus of Edessa), which, in its essential component – that the Muslim conquerors of Syria crossed the Euphrates, moving into the Jazira from the west – is corroborated by the *Zuqnin Chronicle*, which was written around 775, and which is independent of the so-called 'common source' and the Islamic tradition alike.[172] To the objection that north-western Jaziran sources would naturally privilege Syria over Iraq, it can be countered that the seventh-century administrative history tells the same story: just as accounts subordinating Mosul's administration to Kufa can corroborate Kufa's (uncontroversial) claims to have conquered the city, so too does the Syrian–Jaziran administrative continuum corroborate a Syrian conquest of the Jazira.[173] Manifestly late accounts outfitting Edessa with a paradigmatic treaty appear to have been grafted onto authentic history.

As far as reconstructing post-conquest history is concerned, one can infer some generalities, for as a discourse generated by élites and for élites, conquest narrative both describes and prescribes an economic and social model.

Assuming that élite wealth was disproportionately weighted in favour of land,[174] one might expect land ownership to figure prominently in conquest narrative. Indeed it does so appear, while mercantile interests, such as they were, remain unexpressed. It should also be noted that Muslim claims on the land, which are expressed in *ʿanwa* traditions, are generally restricted to rural properties (*al-arḍ*), while cities and towns are given *ṣulḥ* arrangements; and the resulting impression of urban continuity in land tenure is reinforced by

[169] See N. Posner, 'Whence the Muslim conquest of northern Mesopotamia?', in F. Kazemi and R. D. McChesney (eds.), *A Way Prepared: Essays on Islamic Culture in Honor of Richard Bayly Winder* (New York, 1988), pp. 27–52; and Posner, 'Muslim Conquest,' esp. pp. 5ff.

[170] J. Wellhausen, *Skizzen und Vorarbeiten* (Berlin, 1884–9), VI, pp. 5ff. For more criticisms of Sayf, see Hill, *Termination*, pp. 92ff.

[171] See E. Landau-Tasseron, 'Sayf Ibn ʿUmar in medieval and modern scholarship', *DI* 67 (1990), pp. 1–26.

[172] At least for conquest material; see the *Zuqnin Chronicle*, pp. 150/112.

[173] On this, see chapter 2.

[174] Even if one is now ill-disposed towards Jones's oft-cited estimate that revenue from agriculture was roughly twenty times that from trade and industry; see A. H. M. Jones, *The Later Roman Empire, 284–602: A Social, Economic and Administrative Survey* (Norman, 1964), I, p. 465 (which draws on Edessa and Egypt); also see A. H. M. Jones, *The Greek City from Alexander to Justinian* (Oxford, 1940), p. 265.

al-Balādhurī's (admittedly incomplete) survey of Jaziran landholding, in addition to the *Zuqnin Chronicle*, which documents all manner of rural dislocation in the first decades of the Abbasid period.[175] How much reshuffling of land ownership took place within the towns, cities and their hinterlands is another matter; one might expect the church to have expanded its already substantial holdings. Lay and Church authorities alike possessed wealth in movable forms, and no doubt some of this was lost, being buried, confiscated or taken away by civil and military figures who withdrew;[176] but insofar as Byzantine-era élites in Jaziran towns and cities anchored their privilege in the land, we should assume that they continued to do so in the Islamic period too. It was presumably military pragmatism that led the conquering Muslims to extend to the city élites of the Jazira a series of very generous offers, according to which land and *de facto* autonomy were granted in return for *de jure* recognition of Islamic sovereignty; the pattern may not be unique to the north, but here, where the Muslim presence was so thin, autonomy was real. It is the subject of chapter 2.

Of course economic capital was one of several resources upon which the Church could draw; it also gave public and symbolic form to its privileged status. It is in this context that one should read accounts insisting that Christians (that is, the Church) retain the right to build and renovate churches, to sound wooden boards and to process. Indeed, conquest history itself, written on the Christian side as it invariably was by monks and bishops, itself underpins the post-Byzantine authority of the Church by exemplifying its leadership in leading figures, be they bishops (e.g. Mārūtā) or holy men (Simeon of the Olives, Gabriel of Qarṭmīn – the two categories overlap), who are given to represent Christian communities in conquest negotiations. When Dionysius of Tell Maḥrē recorded conquest negotiations between conquerers and conquered, he established a paradigm of Muslim–Christian élite relations that he himself re-enacted whenever he (or any other bishop) met Abbasid caliphs and governors. Writing history, like writing theology, was one way of transforming Byzantine defeat into the Church's victory.[177]

175 I leave open the question of how the predominantly rural location of the Marwānid *quṣūr* relates to this.

176 For one discussion of silver, which was probably the mainstay of the church's movable wealth, see M. M. Mango, 'The uses of liturgical silver, 4th–7th centuries', in R. Morris, ed., *Church and People in Byzantium* (Birmingham, 1990), pp. 245–61.

177 On the patriarch Sophronius, see D. M. Olster, *Roman Defeat, Christian Response, and the Literary Construction of the Jew* (Philadelphia, 1994), p. 111.

TWO

The seventh-century Jazira

In describing the conquests, Muslim historians and jurists are arguing that the kerygma of the Arabic-speaking one God was to take political expression beyond the Arabian Peninsula. The world, not just the Meccans, Ḥijāzīs, or Arabs, was to acknowledge the dominion of God, duly delegated first to His Messenger and then his deputies. The universal currency of this acknowledgement was to be tribute: an alms tax (usually called the *ṣadaqa*) for those who professed Islam, and for those who did not, a head tax (usually called the *jizya*).[1] This is a fairly sophisticated view of political power, and one that legitimises not only the Syrian post-prophetic state, but also its claims on revenue, in part by rationalising in theocratic terms the community's conquests: whatever their truth, accounts that have Muḥammad campaign at Tabūk shortly before his death press the Prophetic *imprimatur* on military engagements outside the Peninsula.[2] Sophisticated ideas usually take some time to become sophisticated, however; and as far as the Umayyad al-Jazīra is concerned, there is no good evidence that this classical view of sovereignty and power applied. The constituent elements ingredient to later, classical views can be identified relatively early on, but the system emerged only secondarily.[3]

To understand seventh-century history in the north we must disabuse ourselves of the anachronistic conceptions of territory and power that underlie our ninth-century sources. Our mental map of al-Jazīra – a unitary province circumscribed by borders, taxed, and administered by Muslim civil and military officials (*wulāt*, *ʿummāl*) from a capital city – is the achievement

[1] The *dhimma* contract is expressed particularly well in a dialogue between ʿIyāḍ b. Ghanm and the bishop of al-Raqqa in Ibn Aʿtham, *Futūḥ*, I, p. 327.

[2] Occasionally the connection is made explicit; thus a *ṣaḥābī* participant at Tabūk is dispatched to al-Raqqa to call its *ṣāḥib* to convert; see ps.-Wāqidī, *Futūḥ al-Jazīra*, p. 6. In general, see Donner, *Conquests*, pp. 101ff. On the reliability of the coverage of these raids, see T. Nöldeke, 'Die Tradition über das Leben Muhammeds', *DI* 5 (1914), pp. 166ff.

[3] There is no question that a head tax of some variety was imposed by early Muslims on non-Muslims in Iraq (for inferences from the Arabic terminology, see Dennett, *Conversion*, pp. 26ff.; Løkkegaard, *Islamic Taxation*, p. 130f.; and for two late first-century Syriac examples, see Crone, *Slaves*, pp. 16 and 215; and also Hoyland, *Seeing Islam*, p. 194); that it was applied universally and uniformly is another thing entirely.

of eighth- and early ninth-century administrators and historians; both were engaged in an imperialist project. While Abbasid officials built an administrative system upon the shaky Marwānid foundations they had inherited, Abbasid historians transmitted and transformed Umayyad-era stories, in the process rationalising their administrators' work in conquest narrative. This narrative is complemented by the historical material relating to the Muslim presence in the post-conquest Jazira, which generally appears only coincidentally to political dramas (e.g. *fitnas*) that arose in the south and west; and although this material was preserved as much to express factional, family and tribal credit as it did imperial ideals, it certainly came to be understood by later Muslims as the natural follow-up to the kerygma of the conquests – the unfolding of *dār al-Islām* – and continues to be read by modern historians as evidence for Islamic 'rule' and 'administration'. But what is true for al-Balādhurī is not necessarily true for us; and in what follows I shall argue that it is not until the 680s – at the earliest – that one can meaningfully speak of Islamic rule in the north. It was the decade from 685 to 695, rather than that of 635 to 645, that signals a break in Jaziran history.

To varying degrees, the same thing could be said about other regions, for inasmuch as the events of the Second Fitna demonstrated the obsolescence of the Sufyānid system as such,[4] changes in the administration of al-Jazīra might be explained simply with reference to the evolution of the polity itself. Yet this would explain little. The ruling élite evolved not in a vacuum, but in the Peninsula and in Syria, and it is with the diversity of the Late Antique Near East that it had to cope; the pace of change differs from region to region for precisely this reason.[5] The lands east of the Euphrates were different; and for all that the Jazira might appear culturally homogeneous,[6] only ambitious administrators and imperial historians would conceive of it in unitary terms. Like the Alpine ranges of Italy, the region's topography obscures local diversity; the Jazira is rather like the Mediterranean, an ocean of steppe, punctuated by archipelagos of river valleys and hills, and settled only unevenly on its shores. Communication and travel, except towards the south, were difficult; news (often bad) did travel, and the élite of one city only occasionally

[4] Thus Cameron: 'major cultural change came only with the arabisation policies of Abd al-Malik and Walid II in the late seventh century onwards' (A. Cameron, 'The eastern provinces in the seventh century AD: Hellenism and the emergence of Islam,' in S. Said, ed., *Hellenismos: Quelques jalons pour une histoire de l'identité grecque* (Leiden, 1991), p. 298). For the eclipse of Sufyānid arrangements, see Crone, *Slaves*, chapters 4 and 5.

[5] For an account of the 'collision' of Islam and the Late Antique provinces of the Near East, see M. Cook and P. Crone, *Hagarism: The Making of the Islamic World* (Cambridge, 1977), pp. 83ff.; on the province of Mosul, the standard is now Morony, *Iraq*, pp. 131ff.

[6] Compare J. B. Segal, 'Mesopotamian communities from Julian to the rise of Islam', *Proceedings of the British Academy* (1955), pp. 109–39; and F. Millar, *The Roman Near East, 31 BC–AD 337* (Cambridge, MA, 1993), p. 495 (Northern Mesopotamia has 'no very clearly defined cultural identity in the eyes of outsiders'). See also A. D. Lee, *Information and Frontiers: Roman Foreign Relations in Late Antiquity* (Cambridge, 1993), pp. 49ff.

responded to problems suffered by another.[7] In political terms, the region had been unequally halved by the partition of 363;[8] and the split was deepened by confessional divisions, as Chalcedonians, Monophysites and Nestorians competed both for imperial favour and new converts.[9] In a political culture as fragmented as this, horizons were low: loyalties were either local or locally expressed; and in one so familiar with the *Sturm und Drang* of imperial warfare and the accompanying changes to local politics, the city folk placed their trust in their walls, in local saints and their relics.[10]

If geography militates against any rapid imposition of imperial control on the part of early Muslims, so does the early evidence for administration. This is something noted already in 1913 by Lammens who, struck by the curious absence of Jaziran governors in the pre-Marwānid period, argued that

> la Mésopotamie continuait à jouir d'une véritable autonomie administrative. Si elle se trouvait rattachée au reste du califat, c'est par les liens assez relâchés d'une sorte de protectorat, par le paiement d'un tribut. Cette situation spéciale devait échapper à la perspicacité des ces auteurs, unanimes à attribuer toutes les conquêtes dans l'Asie sémitique au règne de ʿOmar. Incapables d'autre part de rétablir la liste des gouverneurs de la Mésopotamie antérieurement à la période marwânide, ils s'en sont tirés en rattachant ce pays au *ǧond* de Qinnasrîn. C'était peut-être la façon la moins inexacte de préciser une situation mal définie.[11]

In the idea of a protectorate Lammens went well astray; but in questioning the extent to which al-Jazīra was at all integrated into the still-nascent *dār al-Islām*, his view marks real progress from Wellhausen's, and anticipates many of mine here.[12] Eighty years on, it remains to make some more progress. We can begin by comparing Jaziran lands with the province of Mosul.

[7] In times of localised famine, grain could be transported from an area of plenty, but this was remarkable; for two examples, see ps.-Joshua, *Chronicle*, pp. 77f./66; and Īshōʿyab III, *Liber epistularum*, p. 90/69f. (Īshōʿyab III, at this point bishop of Nineveh, sends grain to Nisibis to relieve famine there). On communications in general, see Lee, *Information and Frontiers*.

[8] For an overview, see L. Dillemann, *Haute mésopotamie orientale et pays adjacents: contribution à la géographie historique de la région, du Ve s. avant l'ère chrétienne au VIe s. de cette ère* (Paris, 1962), esp. pp. 218ff.

[9] For examples of the anxiety, see John of Fenek, *Rīsh mellē* in Mingana, ed., *Sources*, p. *147; Brock, 'North Mesopotamia in the late seventh century', p. 62; and, in general, Morony, *Iraq*, pp. 372ff.

[10] Of these, the *mandylion* of Edessa is the most famous example; see Segal, *Edessa*, pp. 215f.; and also A. Cameron, 'The history of the image of Edessa: the telling of a story', in C. Mango and O. Pritsak, eds., *Okeanos: Essays Presented to Ihor Ševčenko on his Sixtieth Birthday by his Colleagues and Students* (Cambridge, MA, 1983; Harvard Ukranian Studies 7), pp. 80–94. For others, see M. Whitby, 'Procopius and the development of Roman defences in Upper Mesopotamia', in P. Freeman and D. Kennedy, eds., *The Defence of the Roman and Byzantine East* (Oxford, 1986), pp. 722f. In general, see A. Cameron, 'Images of authority: elites and icons in late sixth-century Byzantium', *Past and Present* 84 (1979), pp. 3–35.

[11] H. Lammens, 'Le Califat de Yazîd Ier (suite et fin) xxv', *Mélanges de la Faculté Orientale* (Université Saint-Joseph) 6 (1913), p. 441; reprinted in his *Le Califat de Yazid Ier* (Beirut, 1921), p. 446.

[12] Cf. J. Wellhausen, *The Arab Kingdom and its Fall*, trans. M. G. Weir (Beirut reprint, 1963), p. 59.

Mosul and the Jazira

Prima facie, Mosul conforms to a pattern first systematically described by Wellhausen and Becker, according to which each province was ruled by a small Arab/Muslim élite of conquering tribesmen that consisted in a governor (or sub-governor), who enjoyed civil and military authority, along with a garrison of tribesmen settled in, or near, a pre-existing town or city; this small élite of conquerors sat atop a rump Byzantine or Sasanian administrative system, which, left largely undisturbed at its lower levels, was held responsible for levying taxes and tribute. In Mosul, the élite was based in the city itself, which soon eclipsed the Sasanian settlement at Nineveh; and at least some of the taxing that took place in the rural hinterland was left largely in the hands of an indigenous landed gentry called the *shahārija*, who levied a collective tribute on village headmen. These issues will occupy us in chapters 3 and 4; here it is enough to say that at this very general level, the emergence of Mosul can be reconciled with every Islamic historian's model for the early period. Once we look more closely at our evidence, however, the model begins to strain.

Conquest-era appointments for Mosul are confusing, in part because authorities disagreed about the date of the city's capitulation, some (e.g. Sayf b. ʿUmar) arguing for 16/637–8, and others for 20/641–2. Al-Ṭabarī, forced to wrestle with Sayf's chronology, concedes that his sources are contradictory when it comes to the governors of 16/637–8, some putting ʿUtba b. Farqad in charge,[13] some ʿAbd Allāh b. al-Muʿtamm,[14] and finally others Ribʿī b. al-Afkal and ʿArfaja b. Harthama jointly.[15] Al-Balādhurī, who holds to a conquest date of 20/641–2, simply has ʿArfaja succeed ʿUtba;[16] late Syriac sources may know only of the latter.[17] The confusion is utterly unexceptional in conquest historiography, and says as much about the high standards of ninth-century historians as it does the shortcomings of the eighth-century tradition with which they were forced to work. It is more important to note that traditions generally identify Mosul as a Kufan conquest; in this case they

[13] A Kufan *sharīf* of the Sulaym, on whom see Ibn al-Athīr, *Usd al-ghāba*, III, pp. 365f.; Ibn Ḥajar, *al-Iṣāba*, VI, pp. 379f.; and M. Lecker, *The Banū Sulaym: A Contribution to the Study of Early Islam* (Jerusalem, 1989), pp. 125ff. (with more literature).

[14] Of whom very little is known, and whose name is sometimes recorded as al-Muʿtamar. Al-Azdī, citing Sayf b. ʿUmar (Ibn al-Athīr, *Usd al-ghāba*, III, pp. 263f.; Ibn Ḥajar, *al-Iṣāba*, VI, p. 221) calls him an ʿAbsī (Ghaṭafān).

[15] Al-Ṭabarī, *Taʾrīkh*, I, p. 2481; see also pp. 2394 and 2474ff. Of ʿArfaja b. Harthama once again little is known, and indeed authorities even disagreed about the sequence of his names. I follow Ibn al-Kalbī (*Ǧamharat al-nasab* (Leiden, 1966), II, p. 192) in reading ʿArfaja b. Harthama, but the family name (al-Harāthima, al-Azdī, *Taʾrīkh*, p. 24) may speak in favour of Harthama b. ʿArfaja, which appears often enough in a variety of sources.

[16] Al-Balādhurī, *Futūḥ*, pp. 332, which is apparently followed by Ibn al-Faqīh, *Kitab al-Buldān* (Leiden, 1885; Bibliotheca Geographorum Arabicorum V), pp. 128f.; see also al-Balādhurī, *Ansāb*, Reis. 598, fol. 595b, where ʿUtba goes to Azarbayjān from either Mosul or Shahrazūr.

[17] Bar Hebraeus, *Chronicon syriacum*, trans. E. A. W. Budge as *The Chronography of Gregory Abuʾl-Faraj . . . Known as Bar Hebraeus* (Oxford, 1932), p. lv; Thomas of Marga, *Governors*, I, p. clxiii.

are correct,[18] the effective limit of Kufan claims being signalled by an account that lists Qarqīsiyā, along with Mosul, Ḥulwān and Māsabadhān, as Kufa's four *thughūr*.[19] One of the earliest reports has the reputed builder of Kufa, Saʿd b. Abī Waqqāṣ, instruct ʿAbd Allāh b. al-Muʿtamm to appoint Muslim b. ʿAbd Allāh as his successor in 17/638–9; the latter is said to have been among the captured *asāwira* who had converted and enrolled in Islamic armies, and in this appointment we have another sign that Mosul was counted among the *thughūr*.[20]

While appointments made by ʿAlī and Muʿāwiya might be taken to signal the integration of the city and province into a centralising caliphate, all that the evidence allows us to conclude is that Mosul continued to be a Kufan outpost, garrisoned by and for Kufans. In the appointment of Ḥukaym/Ḥakīm b. Salāma al-Ḥizāmī in 34/654–5, one can see the beginning of the administrative detachment of Mosul from Kufa; the province, according to this view, was now coming under the direct control of the caliph.[21] But the account also preserves the earlier pattern: for while the appointment may or may not have been made by the caliph (the text itself is ambiguous), it is clear that the appointee was, like ʿUtba b. Farqad almost a generation earlier, a Kufan *raʾīs*.[22] One might expect ʿAlī to have appointed a Kufan sympathetic to his cause, and that is exactly what happened: thus ʿAmr b. al-Ḥamiq, one of ʿAlī's most enthusiastic partisans, governed the city on his behalf.[23] Indeed, as late as the Second Civil War, Mosul remained under a Kufan aegis: al-Dīnawarī subsumes Mosul under Kufa in his enumeration of al-Mukhtār's provinces,[24] and when ʿAbd Allāh b. al-Zubayr appointed the Kufan Muḥammad b. al-Ashʿath over Mosul, he pointedly made him subordinate to Ibn Muṭīʿ, his governor of Kufa.[25] Although the appointment of Muḥammad

[18] For one example where traditions are incorrect, see M. Hinds, 'The first Arab conquests of Fārs', *Iran* 22 (1984), pp. 39–53, which is reprinted in J. Bacharach, L. I. Conrad, and P. Crone, eds., *Studies in Early Islamic History* (Princeton, 1996), pp. 197–229.

[19] Al-Ṭabarī, *Taʾrīkh*, I, pp. 2497f.; cf. I, pp. 2673f. Cf. al-Yaʿqūbī, *Taʾrīkh* (Leiden, 1883), II, p. 277 (where *kharāj* figures for Mosul follow upon Ḥulwān's).

[20] Al-Ṭabarī, *Taʾrīkh*, I, pp. 2485 and 2497. On the withdrawal of Arab tribesmen from the *thughūr* and their replacement by *asāwira*, see Donner, *Conquests*, p. 239.

[21] Thus Morony, *Iraq*, p. 135. [22] Al-Ṭabarī, *Taʾrīkh*, I, p. 2928.

[23] On ʿAmr b. al-Ḥamiq, see al-Maqdisī, *Kitāb al-Badʾ waʾl-taʾrīkh* (Paris, 1918), V, p. 113; al-Balādhurī, *Ansāb al-ashrāf* IVa (Jerusalem, 1971), pp. 236f.; Ibn Saʿd, *Kitāb al-Ṭabaqāt*, VI, p. 15; al-Yaʿqūbī, *Taʾrīkh*, II, p. 274; Ibn ʿAsākir, *Taʾrīkh madīnat Dimashq*, XLV, pp. 490ff.; al-Shābushtī, *al-Diyārāt* (Beirut, 1986 reprint of ʿAwwād edn, Baghdad, 1951), p. 179 (ʿAmr's tomb lay near the Dayr al-Aʿlā). According to Ibn al-Athīr, *al-Kāmil*, III, p. 380 (here almost certainly drawing on the first section of al-Azdī's *Taʾrīkh*), a Khathʿamī appointee of ʿAlī was killed by Taghlibīs while en route to the city.

[24] When al-Dīnawarī (*al-Akhbār al-ṭiwāl* (Leiden, 1888), p. 300) states that al-Mukhtār's control extended over Kufa, all of (central) Iraq, and the rest of the empire's provinces (read: the East) 'except the Jazira, Syria, and Egypt, which were under ʿAbd al-Malik's control', we are clearly to understand Mosul as part of Kufa, an inference which is confirmed by ʿAbd al-Raḥmān b. Saʿīd's appointment over Mosul that immediately followed. See also al-Yaʿqūbī, *Taʾrīkh*, II, p. 308.

[25] But Ibn al-Zubayr retained the right to dismiss Muḥammad b. al-Ashʿath; see al-Ṭabarī, *Taʾrīkh*, II, p. 635. On the Kufan family of Muḥammad b. al-Ashʿath, see R. Sayed, *Die Revolte des Ibn al-Ašʿaṯ und die Koranleser* (Freiburg, 1977), pp. 74ff.; Crone, *Slaves*, pp. 110f.

b. al-Ashʿath suggests that the Kufan pattern started to strain during the Second Fitna, it is only under the earliest Marwānids that things clearly changed for good; as we shall see, at this point the Syrians clearly did stake and enforce claims in Mosul.

As far as one can tell – and lacking the coinage, one cannot claim to control the administrative history of the town in this period – the Mosuli pattern is thus overwelmingly Yamani and Kufan through the early 60s AH.[26] A Kufan conquest, it was settled primarily by Kufan tribesmen (principally the Azd, in addition to the Hamdān, ʿAbd al-Qays, Ṭayyiʾ and Kinda), from among whom were drawn the city's governors. All this may be enough to question how Sufyānid the city actually ever was: it may be that most Mosulis of this period no more acknowledged Muʿāwiya's authority than the Syrians acknowledged ʿAlī's.[27] There is some confusion regarding the name of ʿUthmān's governor, Ḥakīm/Ḥukaym b. Salāma/Salām al-Ḥizāmī/Khizāmī, and Muʿāwiya seems to have appointed an otherwise undistinguished nephew over the city, ʿAbd al-Raḥmān b. ʿAbd Allāh b. ʿUthmān b. ʿAbd Allāh;[28] in neither case is there any good evidence that Sufyānid authority was actually made effective. As we shall see, the earliest evidence attesting to Muʿāwiya's rule extends as far east as Sinjār, but no further,[29] and although being Kufan is not the same thing as being Shīʿite, it is intriguing that one of Thomas of Marga's sources synchronises the reign of George the Catholicos with that of the king (*malkā*) Ḥasan bar ʿAlī (Ḥasan b. ʿAlī).[30] Certainly die-hard Kufan Shīʿite opponents of Muʿāwiya, such as Karīm b. ʿAfīf al-Khathʿamī, chose to live out their lives in Mosul,[31] apparently leaving behind a Jazira that was considered ʿUthmānī by persuasion.[32] Be this as it may, there is no reason to think that Syrians ever enjoyed Mosuli spoils or tribute throughout the Sufyānid period; if the city did pass some of its revenues on, it was to Kufa rather than Damascus. From the perspective of Mosul then, the end of the Second Civil War marks a radical break; far from reconstituting Syrian rule, the Marwānids seem to have imposed it for the first time, replacing, as we shall see, a conquest with a landholding élite.

26 The one exception being the obscure ʿAbsī, ʿAbd Allāh b. al-Muʿtamm. Note as well that another Hamdānī, ʿUbayd Allāh b. Abī Baltaʿa, is also occasionally mentioned in this period; see Abū al-Faraj al-Iṣfahānī, *Kitāb al-Aghānī* (Cairo, 1984), XVII, pp. 143f.

27 On the evidence from early eighth-century Syriac king lists, which omit the reign of ʿAlī, see Crone, *Slaves*, p. 214, note 102.

28 On Ḥakīm/Ḥukaym b. Salāma/Salām al-Ḥizāmī/Khizāmī, see al-Ṭabarī, *Taʾrīkh*, I, p. 2928; Ibn al-Athīr, *al-Kāmil*, III, p. 147. On ʿAbd al-Raḥmān b. ʿAbd Allāh b. ʿUthmān al-Thaqafī (otherwise known as ʿAbd al-Raḥmān b. Umm al-Ḥakam), see al-Yaʿqūbī, *Taʾrīkh*, II, p. 275; al-Ṭabarī, *Taʾrīkh*, II, pp. 128 and 181; Ibn ʿAsākir, *Taʾrīkh madīnat Dimashq*, XXXV, pp. 43ff.; and Crone, *Slaves*, pp. 124f.

29 On John of Fenek's testimony, see below.

30 See Thomas of Marga, *Governors*, pp. 88/207f.

31 See W. Madelung, *The Succession to Muḥammad: A Study of the Early Caliphate* (Cambridge, 1997), pp. 337f.

32 Thus Ibn Aʿtham al-Kūfī, *Futūḥ*, II, p. 350; Abū Isḥāq al-Thaqafī, *Kitāb al-Ghārāt* (Beirut, 1987), p. 213.

In the Jazira, Marwānid change was no less radical. Although it fell under a very broad Syrian penumbra, Qurashī authority was even more attenuated there; for unlike in Mosul, where a Kufan élite was garrisoned, and where one can chart continuity in both administrative geography and personnel, the land to the west had neither garrison nor capital. Mosul was Kufan, and operated more or less autonomously from the Syrian capital; it is hard to see how the Jazira operated at all.

The province of al-Jazīra was in fact a Marwānid invention. Strictly (that is, administratively) speaking, it only came into being well after the conquests had ended, and this in a two-step process.[33] The first of these steps was the detachment of the *jund* of Qinnasrīn from that of Ḥimṣ, this being effected no earlier than the reign of Yazīd b. Muʿāwiya (680–3).[34] It was followed by ʿAbd al-Malik's detachment of al-Jazīra from Qinnasrīn, an event recorded in some detail by al-Balādhurī, an administrator's historian if there ever was one. There we read that the caliph, at the request of his brother Muḥammad b. Marwān, established a *jund* that was independent of that of Qinnasrīn, and which began to draw its provisions from the region's tax base (*fa-ṣāra junduhā ya'khudhūna aṭmāʿahā bi-hā min kharājihā*):[35] the marriage of provincial administration and taxation could not be clearer. Before this step was taken the Islamic tradition construes these lands, which are consistently and anachronistically identified as al-Jazīra, as an administrative dependency of Syria. This view is articulated explicitly;[36] it also underlies the stray account, such as when an unidentified *ʿāmil* of Nisibis writes directly to Muʿāwiya (now ʿUthmān's governor of Syria and the Jazira) complaining of scorpions,[37] or when another unidentified *ʿāmil*, now given authority over al-Jazīra, rules from Ḥarrān and al-Raqqa, apparently under the authority of the governor of Ḥimṣ.[38]

What do we make of these accounts, and, more generally, of the paucity of Sufyānid-era administrative evidence east of the the Euphrates? The anonymity of these figures contrasts sharply with the *horror anonymitatis* that characterises Iraqi and Syrian administration in general,[39] and with that of Mosul in particular. And it is clear enough that just as the Islamic historical tradition had difficulty accommodating the political autonomy of

33 Anomalous accounts that describe al-Jazīra as a *miṣr* in the wake of the conquests (see, for example, al-Yaʿqūbī, *Ta'rīkh*, II, p. 176; al-Balādhurī, *Ansāb*, V (Beirut), p. 382) are manifestly topological and mistaken; here, as elsewhere (see Noth/Conrad, *Early Arabic Historical Tradition*, index, s.v. ʿUmar I), ʿUmar functions as a magnet for all manner of administrative reforms, and Qinnasrīn even appears as a *jund*.

34 Thus al-Balādhurī, *Futūḥ*, p. 132. Sayf in al-Ṭabarī, *Ta'rīkh* I, p. 2673, credits the step to his father, while an Andalusian source, the *Akhbār majmūʿa* (Beirut, 1981), p. 57, first cited by P. Crone, 'Were the Qays and Yemen of the Umayyad period political parties?', *DI* 71 (1994), p. 45, note 239, puts it after the revolt of al-Mukhtār, a dating that has much to recommend it. On the tribal migrations that probably underlay the new *jund*, see Crone, *Slaves*, p. 34.

35 Al-Balādhurī, *Futūḥ*, p. 132.

36 Al-Balādhurī, *Futūḥ*, pp. 131f.

37 Al-Balādhurī, *Futūḥ*, p. 178.

38 Al-Ṭabarī, *Ta'rīkh*, I, p. 2914.

39 Crone, *Slaves*, p. 16.

pre-Marwānid Armenia,[40] so too did it misrepresent the Jazira's liminal character. One might thus be attracted to the solution proposed by Lammens, who considered the Qinnasrīn connection little more than an ingenious fiction, one devised by early Muslim historians who failed to find officials to staff a Jaziran administration that they presumed to have existed. But if a Qinnasrīn connection is anachronistic, there clearly was something to the Syrian connection, if only because eighth-century *akhbārīs* would have retrojected not a Syrian–Jaziran union, but rather the one of their day, i.e. a 'super province' consisting of Mosul and al-Jazīra.[41] Even if accounts subordinating al-Jazīra to Syria schematise and oversimplify, particularly since the status of a city as important as Nisibis remained unclear, they still retain echoes of the post-conquest period, when what might be called a 'Sufyānid sphere of influence' operated east of the Euphrates. This explains, on the one hand, the episodic appearance of Muslim commanders and the élite's *dirigiste* policies vis-à-vis the tribesmen, and, on the other, the continuity of settled Christian authority in the cities. This, however, is to anticipate things; before we turn to a positive reconstruction of seventh-century history, we must criticise the received wisdom.

Exercising some influence over the region's tribesmen apparently did interest the Sufyānids – but nothing more. Had they been determined to rule the Jazira – that is, with the view to extracting revenues and making at least modest claims to sovereignty – we might expect to find some evidence for administrative continuity from the Byzantine and Sasanian period; in other words, we might expect a role to be played by Edessa and Nisibis, the two great cities of Late Antique northern Mesopotamia. We might also expect some compelling evidence that the region was systematically taxed, if not by Muslims then at least by indigenous élites as their proxies; for in taxing the élite could begin not only to profit from the region's revenues, but to develop some of the networks of clients and notables through which claims to legitimate rule could be broadcast. But if evidence survives for a good measure of social continuity within Edessa, along with some *ad hoc* tribute taking, one searches in vain to see the two cities' function in administrative terms, or to discern any provincial system of taxation. The absence of a fixed capital militates against any administrative continuity in the north, be it Byzantine or Sasanian;[42] similarly, the absence of a provincial taxation system should dis-

[40] See A. Ter-Ghévondian, 'L'Arménie et la conquête arabe', in D. Kouymjian, ed., *Armenian Studies/Etudes arméniennes in memoriam Haïg Berbérian* (Lisbon, 1986), pp. 773–92; A. Ter-Ghévondian, *The Arab Emirates in Bagratid Armenia*, trans. N. Garsoïan (Lisbon, 1976), pp. 19ff.

[41] On the evidence for this, see below.

[42] This is not to rule out links between Sasanian or Byzantine administrative patterns and those that eventually emerged in the eighth century; it is to insist that the north was distinctive, and to argue that this distinctiveness lay in its discontinuous character: insofar as they existed, such links must have been recovered by the Marwānids and Abbasids, rather than intentionally preserved or modified by the Sufyānids.

suade us from thinking in imperial terms. We shall take these two problems – administrative continuity and taxation – in turn.

Edessa and Nisibis

Edessa was the cultural and political centre of the Byzantine east during the fifth and sixth centuries. For early geographers (both Armenian and Pahlavi), Edessa enjoys pride of place in surveys of the north,[43] and its importance in the first decades of the seventh century is also signalled by the local Edessan historical tradition.[44] For these and other reasons it is clear that Islamic conquest reports accurately reflect Edessa's central role in Heraclius' administration of the north, and to some degree too its experience in the conquest itself; as we have seen, Edessa was the first major city east of the Euphrates to fall to the Muslims under the command of ʿIyāḍ b. Ghanm. Equally for these reasons, we might assume that it would retain some significance in an early Islamic administration in the north; it was the natural place to concentrate imperial rule.

But Edessa, to put it bluntly, more or less falls off the political map of early Islam. Accounts that have the city provide paradigmatic treaty terms for the entire region are manifestly anachronistic, and in any case can be counterbalanced by those that have Ḥarrān – its closest neighbour – entering into a treaty of its own.[45] No doubt some Muslims settled there,[46] and there is no reason to doubt a range of reports that have Muʿāwiya rebuild the dome of the city's cathedral, which had been brought down by the earthquake of 678/9.[47] Still, one comes away from the sources with the impression that this intervention was exceptional, and indeed the contrast between Byzantine and Sasanian policies on the one hand, and Sufyānid indifference on the other, could hardly be sharper: for whereas Byzantine emperors waded into the city politics of Edessa – appointing governors, exiling notables, dismissing and appointing bishops – Muslim caliphs ignored the city almost entirely.[48] Meanwhile, neither the Arabic nor the Syriac tradition documents any systematic Muslim

[43] See J. Markwart, *A Catalogue of the Provincial Capitals of Ērānshahr* (Rome, 1931), pp. 13 and 63ff. (first cited by Morony, *Iraq*, p. 128); and R. H. Hewsen, trans., *The Geography of Ananias of Širak* (Wiesbaden, 1992), p. 71a (and index, s.v.). [44] See below, notes 139 to 142.

[45] Thus al-Ṭabarī, *Taʾrīkh*, I, pp. 2505f. (Sayf b. ʿUmar). As we have already seen, al-Balādhurī's sources are keen to reconcile Edessa's paradigmatic role with a conquest sequence at odds with it; cf. D. S. Rice, 'Medieval Ḥarrān: studies on its topography and monuments, I', *Anatolian Studies* 2 (1952), pp. 36ff. (where Ibn Shaddād's account is translated and discussed).

[46] One of the few notable examples is Ḥanẓala b. al-Rabīʿ, who is said to have been one of the Prophet's scribes; he died in Edessa during the lifetime of Muʿāwiya (al-Jahshiyārī, *Wuzarāʾ* p. 13); Ibn al-Athīr (*Usd al-ghāba*, II, p. 58), puts his death in Qarqīsiyā. For the conspicuous absence of any Muslims in seventh-century Ṭūr ʿAbdīn, see Palmer, *Monk and Mason*, pp. 165ff.

[47] See *Chronicle of 1234*, I, pp. 288/224; Michael the Syrian, *Chronique*, xi.xiii; Theophanes, *Chronicle*, AM 6170.

[48] On Edessa on the eve of Islam, see Posner, 'Muslim Conquest', pp. 182ff.; and Segal, *Edessa*, chap. 4.

settlement or administration in the city; and when Edessa and Ḥarrān do appear, the accounts merely illustrate how the north, once the battleground and frontier of the Byzantine and Sasanian empires, had become the battleground of intra-Muslim politics. And in this, there was no important role to be played by the city as such.[49]

The evidence concerning Nisibis, which Morony identifies as the early Islamic 'capital' of Diyār Rabīʿa, tells very much the same story. Adducing several administrators connected either to the city or the region, which in his view fairly closely reconstitutes Sasanian ʿArbāyestān, he argues that it 'survived as the major administrative center in this part of the Jazira after the Islamic conquest'.[50] While it is entirely possible – indeed, probable – that the eighth-century emergence of city and district owes something to Sasanian precedents, we cannot adequately chart the passage of the north from Sasanian imperial administration to Islamic imperial administration. For one thing, an argument for continuity must now come to grips with the seal evidence; and unless one dismisses as accidental the striking absence of Sasanian seals from ʿArbāyestān,[51] it is hard to discern exactly what the precedent was. That the area, like that of Nōd Ardashīragān, had been intensely militarised by the late sixth and early seventh centuries, is fairly clear;[52] but the burden of proof now lies with those who would describe it as an integral part of the Sasanian state, at least in terms similar to those of the Iraqi heartland, which is documented by a concentration of material evidence.[53] Moreover, even if we assume that Nisibis presented itself to the Muslim conquerors as a promising administrative centre, the evidence from the early Islamic period is too mixed to argue for continuity. While it is true that a geographer such as Ibn Ḥawqal gives pride of place to Nisibis in Diyār Rabīʿa, it is just as true that others do not; al-Muqaddasī, for one, identifies Mosul as none other than the capital (*qaṣaba*) of Diyār Rabīʿa.[54] Whatever the case, the geographers of the late ninth and tenth centuries – interested as they were in providing synchronic surveys of *dār al-Islām* – are hardly the most promising sources from which to chart the changes of the seventh and eighth centuries.

[49] 'Avec la conquête arabe, Édesse perdit l'importance politique qui lui avait créée la rivalité des empires qui se disputaient la possession de la Mésopotamie.' See R. Duval, *Histoire d'Edesse, politique, religieuse et littéraire* (Amsterdam, 1975 reprint of *JA* 18–19 (1891–1992)), p. 236.

[50] Morony, *Iraq*, p. 129ff.

[51] See R. Gyselen, *La Géographie administrative de l'empire sassanide: les témoignages sigillographiques* (Paris, 1989), p. 79 (she does not).

[52] See J. Howard-Johnston, 'The two great powers in late antiquity: a comparison', in A. Cameron, ed., *The Byzantine and Early Islamic Near East III: States, Resources and Armies* (Princeton, 1995), pp. 189f.; M. Morony, 'Syria under the Persians 610–629', in M. A. al-Bakhit and I. ʿAbbas, eds., *Proceedings of the Second Symposium on the History of Bilād al-Shām during the Early Islamic Period up to 40 AH/640 A.D* (English and French articles) (Amman, 1987), p. 91.

[53] Gyselen, *La Géographie administrative*, chap. 4.

[54] Al-Muqaddasī, *Aḥsan al-taqāsīm fī maʿrifat al-aqālīm* (Leiden, 1877; Bibliotheca Geographorum Arabicorum 3), p. 137.

In the absence of any early coinage from Nisibis, it is on the back of the historical record that we must ride, and here the impression created is hardly that of administrative continuity: the city appears now as part of al-Jazīra and now part of Mosul.[55] That it served as occasional base of Kufan and Syrian garrisons can hardly be doubted;[56] but far from being concentrations of 'imperial' power, these garrisons appear significant again only in the context of intra-Qurashī civil war. Thus ʿAlī's 'governor' (*ʿāmil*) of al-Jazīra, Mālik b. al-Ḥārith al-Ashtar, was appointed over Nisibis,[57] and he is said to have been appointed to take on the ʿUthmānids of the (apparently western) al-Jazīra;[58] his successor Shabīb b. ʿĀmir raided Syrian territories as far as Baʿlabakk.[59] According to his *Life*, Theodotus of Amida (d. 698) travelled widely in the north; only in Amida did he come across a garrison (and mosque) worthy of note.[60]

Indeed, when one turns to evidence that is both local and early, one is immediately delivered from the classicising perspectives of the Abbasid tradition. That the Nestorian Patriarch Īshōʿyab III, writing in Ctesiphon probably a decade after the conquest of the north, has the heretical bishop Sahdōna returning from 'the land of the Romans' (by which he means Edessa) to 'the land of the Persians' (by which he means Iraq),[61] should hardly surprise: one could hardly expect the effects of Islamic rule to be felt immediately. That John of Fenek, writing a full two generations later, should have been just as unfamiliar with the great Islamic conquests, is striking, particularly since he recycles pre-Islamic categories in his discussion of the Second Civil War. Here the conflict over Nisibis between ʿUbayd Allāh b. Ziyād and al-Mukhtār is said to turn on its status under Byzantine and Sasanian rule: the 'westerners' (i.e. the Muslim Arabs settled in Syria) argued that since the city had belonged to the Byzantines, it should now belong to them; meanwhile, the 'easterners' (i.e. Muslims settled in Iraq) held that since it had belonged to the Persians, it should now belong to them. One has the

[55] Contrast al-Balādhurī (*Futūḥ*, p. 178), who subordinates Nisibis to Syria, with a Nestorian source (Mārī b. Sulaymān, *Kitāb al-Majdal*, p. 64), according to which Nisibis is clearly anchored in an Iraqi ecclesiastical pattern.

[56] By far the earliest evidence for any Muslim administration is the unidentified *amīrā d-mdittā* ('*amīr* of the city [of Nisibis]') mentioned in the *Khuzistan Chronicle* (written c. 670–80), ed. and trans. I. Guidi as *Chronicon anonymum* (Paris, 1903; *Chronica Minora* I of *CSCO* 1–2), pp. 31/26; see also T. Nöldeke, 'Die von Guidi herausgegebene syrische Chronik uebersetzt und commentiert', *Sitzungsberichte der kaiserlichen Akademie der Wissenschaften*, Phil.-Hist. Klasse 128 (1893), p. 34.

[57] Thus al-Ṭabarī, *Ta'rīkh*, I, p. 3392; Ibn al-Athīr, *al-Kāmil*, III, 352; Wellhausen, *Arab Kingdom*, p. 95. [58] Ibn Aʿtham, *Futūḥ*, II, pp. 350ff. [59] Ibn al-Athīr, *al-Kāmil*, III, p. 379.

[60] See Palmer, *Monk and Mason*, pp. 166f. On the Islamic side, Ibn Aʿtham (*Futūḥ*, II, pp. 350f.) mentions the *ahl al-Raqqa* during the First Civil War.

[61] See Īshōʿyab III, *Liber epistularum*, pp. 203ff./148ff., and also the discussion in J. M. Fiey, 'Īšōʿyaw le Grand: Vie du catholicos nestorien Īšōʿyaw III d'Adiabène (580–659)', *Orientalia Christiana Periodica* 36 (1970), pp. 20ff. where (p. 25, note 6) the expression is called 'purement géographique', and more an archaism than anachronism, 'car, depuis 637, les Arabes règnent partout'.

impression that the controversy is a new one, and that the region was experiencing direct Islamic rule for the first time.[62]

Taxation

The lands east of the Euphrates had no formal administrative status in the Sufyānid period because they were not subject to systematic taxation; in other words, the Jazira was invented when the Marwānids determined that lands in the north should be taxed. During the Sufyānid period it appears that only occasional tribute was taken, and it took the Marwānids to impose an increasingly formal regime of taxation, one that was apparently perceived by Jaziran Christians as a sign of Islamic sovereignty.

Dennett's view may be taken as conventional wisdom.[63] He posits a three-stage development of Jaziran taxation: first, a conquest-era regime that consisted of a land tax (*kharāj*) levied in kind, along with a poll tax (*jizya*) levied in cash; second, a 'later' rationalisation, whereby the city folk bore the responsibility for taxes in cash and the country folk for taxes in kind; and third, a 'sweeping reform' by ʿAbd al-Malik, according to which each adult male was to pay a 4-dīnār *jizya*, and the land tax was levied proportionally and in cash. The reconstruction is typically Dennett in its simplicity and clarity; it also exemplifies the principal thesis of his book: 'This picture of historical development is a nice criticism of the Wellhausen–Caetani thesis that the jurists, including Abū Yūsuf, described only the rigid practices of their time, but attributed these practices to an earlier origin.'[64]

Pace Dennett, none of the early evidence suggests that during the Sufyānid period al-Jazīra was integrated into a uniform system of taxation; the evidence can suggest only that occasional tribute was taken. Aside from his misunderstanding of a crucial passage in Abū Yūsuf,[65] Dennett's discussion of the north presumes not only that the administrative geography of al-Jazīra was born in its classical form, but that the taxation regime in Mesopotamia was in line with the rest of the empire.[66] Here, as elsewhere (at least outside Egypt),

[62] John of Fenek, *Rīsh mellē* in Mingana, ed., *Sources*, pp. *156f.; Brock, 'North Mesopotamia in the late seventh century', pp. 64f.

[63] Dennett, *Conversion*, pp. 43ff., which is followed not only by scholars in cognate fields (thus W. Witakowski, *The Syriac Chronicle of Pseudo-Dionysius of Tel-Maḥrē: A Study in the History of Historiography* (Uppsala, 1987), p. 45), but by a scholar as learned in Islamic taxation and administration as Cahen ('Fiscalité', p. 137). Some objections, it is true, have been raised: A. Fattal (*Le Statut légal des non-musulmans en pays d'Islam* (Beirut, 1958), pp. 328f.), was struck by Dennett's seductive simplicity ('Ainsi l'organisation foncière des premiers temps de l'Islam était loin d'être aussi simple et lumineuse que le voudrait Dennett'), but he still followed al-Balādhurī and Abū Yūsuf otherwise; see also Calder, *Studies*, p. 140, note 20.

[64] Dennett, *Conversion*, p. 47.

[65] See M. J. Kister, 'The social and political implications of three traditions in the *Kitāb al-Kharādj* of Yahya b. Adam', *JESHO* 3 (1960), pp. 328f.

[66] See also A. N. Poliak, 'Classification of lands in the Islamic law and its technical terms', *American Journal of Semitic Languages and Literatures* 57 (1940), p. 60.

Dennett's views are essentially Abbasid, for the simple reason that his sources are Abbasid; his method is to adduce one Abbasid jurist's views to corroborate another's,[67] and to reject those early and local sources that contradict Abbasid administrative conceptions.

One might rather privilege these other sources. According to the *Zuqnin Chronicle*,[68] which was written around 775 near Āmid:

> In the year 1003 (691–2) ʿAbd al-Malik carried out a *taʿdīl* on the Syrians [i.e. the Christian inhabitants of the north]. He issued a harsh order that everyone go to his region, village, and father's house, so that everyone would register his name, his lineage [literally: 'whom he was the son of'], his crops and olive trees, his possessions, his children, and everything he owned. From this time, the *gizya* began to be levied *per capita* [lit: 'on the skulls of men']; from this time, all the evils were visited upon the Christians.[69] [For] until this time, kings had taken tribute from land (*mdattā d-arʿā*), rather than from men. From this time the sons of Hagar began to inflict on the sons of Aram servitude like the servitude of Egypt. Woe is us! Because we sinned, slaves now rule us. This was the first *taʿdīl* that the Muslims (*ṭayyāyē*) carried out.

Dennett was aware of this text, but he rejected it in favour of Michael the Syrian; for in describing a *taʿdīl* under ʿUmar, Michael did him the service of corroborating the Islamic tradition.[70]

To Michael's account we can raise at least two objections. First, had ʿUmar's reputed *taʿdīl* taken place as Michael describes it, one might fairly expect to read in the Christian sources something of its effect; after all, the Christian tradition refers to draconian tax measures during the brief Sasanian occupation of the north that preceded it,[71] as it recounts, *ad nauseam*, examples of Marwānid overtaxation that followed ʿAbd al-Malik's reform (some of which we will survey below). We might fairly conclude that the litany of woes breaks off for the simple reason that systematic taxation was broken off; the truth of universal taxation having its origins in Syria is probably a biblical, rather than historical, truth.[72] Second, not only did Michael write some 500 years after our anonymous chronicler, but his source here (presumably Dionysius of Tell Maḥrē) drew on an Iraqi-centred strain of the Islamic tradition. Here the chronicle is therefore less useful in reconstructing Jaziran history than it is in charting how Islamic historiographic concerns – in this case, the crediting of all manner of administrative precedents to the caliph ʿUmar – entered the

67 Thus al-Balādhurī is adduced to 'confirm' Abū Yūsuf (Dennett, *Conversion*, pp. 44f.).

68 *Zuqnin Chronicle*, pp. 154/116.

69 Hespel (*Zuqnin Chronicle*, p. 116) has followed J.-B. Chabot's translation here (*Chronique de Denys de Tell-Maḥré* (Paris, 1895), p. 10), with the result that some of the Syriac has been lost.

70 Michael the Syrian, *Chronique*, xi.vii; see also xi.xii.

71 Michael the Syrian, *Chronique*, xi.iii; *Chronicle of 1234*, I, pp. 220f./173f.; Theophanes, *Chronicle*, AM 6112.

72 Thus Luke 2: 1–2. See also J. Barton, *Oracles of God: Perceptions of Ancient Prophecy in Israel after the Exile* (London, 1986), p. 134 (David is rebuked by 'the prophets' for taking a census).

Syriac tradition. By contrast, our chronicler from Zuqnin was parochial to a fault,[73] and hence all the more useful for writing local history. He is ignorant not of history more faithfully preserved by other Christian sources, but rather of an imperial historiography that homogenises distinct provincial histories.

The *Zuqnin Chronicle* is thus to be preferred to Michael the Syrian; but what does it mean, and can its reconstruction be corroborated by other sources? The account describes the introduction of an entirely unprecedented tax regime – the levy of the *gizya* – rather than simply an increase in the rate of a pre-existing tax; it was because the region was being systematically taxed for the first time that it now had (and could support) a *jund*. The procedure that effected the change was the *taʿdīl*, a technical term given to describe a fiscal survey frequently accompanied by the forced repatriation of tax payers; although it might be carried out as part of the *kharāj* reforms of the classical period,[74] there is no necessary connection between the two, and other accounts explicitly associate it with the *gizya*. Here, in this pre-classical period, it signals a tax regime that figures proportional levies on collectivities, and one that can summon real forces of coercion. Of course in the Syriac *gizya*, we have a loan word from the Arabic *jizya* – that is, the proportional tax levied on individual non-Muslims, which, in one form or another, is traceable back to Qurʾān 9:29.[75] Whether the proportions were now specified (at 12, 24 and 36 dirhams), as they seem to have been in Mosul a generation later,[76] is impossible to know. It is more important to remember that usage of *jizya* in this early period was not restricted to the head tax;[77] nor does it imply a particular method of collection.[78] What it does seem to signify, however, is the lower status of those

[73] See Witakowski, *Pseudo-Dionysius of Tel-Maḥrē*, pp. 91ff. and 105 ('Practically no events are related except those which took place in Mesopotamia and – more rarely – in Syria'). I leave aside the important question of the composite nature of the work. For a general introduction, see S. Brock, 'Syriac historical writing: a survey of the main sources', *Journal of the Iraqi Academy* 5 (1979–80), pp. 10ff.; and for a more detailed discussion, L. I. Conrad, 'Syriac perspectives on Bilād al-Shām during the Abbasid period', in M. A. al-Bakhit and R. Schick, eds., *Bilād al-Shām during the Abbasid Period (132 AH/750 AD–451 AH/1059 AD): Proceedings of the Fifth International Conference on the History of Bilād al-Shām* (Amman, 1992), pp. 24ff.

[74] The fullest description is provided by Ibn ʿAbd al-Ḥakam, *Futūḥ Miṣr wa'l-Maghrib* (Cairo, 1995), p. 183; see also Dennett, *Conversion*, pp. 45f.; M. Shimizu, 'Les Finances publiques de l'état ʿabbāsside', *DI* 42 (1966), p. 20 (citing al-Jahshiyārī); Fattal, *Statut légal*, p. 329; Morimoto, *Fiscal Administration of Egypt*, pp. 43 and 246; and P. G. Forand, 'The status of the land and inhabitants of the Sawād during the first two centuries of Islām', *JESHO* 14 (1971), p. 29.

[75] See Rubin, 'Quran and *Tafsīr*', and Schmucker, *Untersuchungen*, pp. 74ff.; earlier work is usefully summarised in P. Crone, 'Two legal problems bearing on the early history of the Qurʾān', *JSAI* 18 (1994), p. 1, note 3. Nestorian sources of Iraq begin to make mention of the *gizya* in the wake of the Second Fitna; see above, note 3.

[76] Al-Azdī, *Taʾrīkh*, p. 3, where the governor of the city, Yaḥyā b. Yaḥyā al-Ghassānī, is ordered by ʿUmar II to 'adjust the head tax of Mosul (*diyat al-Mawṣil*) to 48 dirhams for the wealthy, 24 for [those in] the middle, and 12 for the poor, annually'. Cf. also Morimoto, *Fiscal Administration of Egypt*, pp. 48f. (for the complex evolution of *jizya* in Egypt, including criticisms of Dennett).

[77] As pointed out by Dennett, *Conversion*, and Løkkegaard, *Islamic Taxation*.

[78] As pointed out by Cahen for the early Abbasid north, 'Fiscalité', pp. 143ff.

paying it,[79] be they Arab, or non-Arab,[80] and this is why it sometimes designates the tribute imposed by the Islamic state on Byzantium.[81] This also explains why its (belated) introduction in late seventh-century Jazira was felt so keenly by the Christians.

Once we follow the *Zuqnin Chronicle*, several pieces of evidence begin to fall into place. The first is the unsystematic and politically inert character of pre-Marwānid tribute. Writing in or around Sinjār no later than 693, when the civil war, plague and Marwānid tax measures were just starting to take hold, John of Fenek waxed nostalgic about the bygone days of Muʿāwiya's reign, when 'justice flourished . . . and there was great peace in the regions under his control'; and when

> their robber bands went annually to distant parts and to the islands [?], bringing back captives from all the peoples under the heavens. Of each person they required only tribute (*madattā*), allowing him to remain in whatever faith he wished. Among them were also Christians in no small numbers: some belonged to the heretics [i.e. Monophysites], while others to us. Once Mʿawyā had come to the throne, the peace throughout the world was such that we have never heard, either from our fathers or from our grandparents, or seen that there had ever been any like it.[82]

The passage does not necessarily describe what the chronicler from Zuqnin called the *mdattā d-arʿā* ('land tax'), nor should it. In fact, John of Fenek's account resembles that of John of Daylam, who describes how tribute was extracted in the eastern Mosuli hinterland; there, headmen were taken hostage, only to be ransomed by a Nestorian holy man.[83] What it reflects, then, is the diversity of early tribute taking in the north.

79 For examples, see Abū Yūsuf, *Kitāb al-Kharāj*, p. 40; al-Ṭabarī, *Kitāb Ikhtilāf al-fuqahā'* (Leiden, 1933), p. 231; and Rubin, 'Quran and *Tafsīr*', pp. 137f. and 141f.; M. J. Kister, 'Land property and *jihād*', *JESHO* 34 (1991), p. 274.

80 Thus the Arab Taghlib insist on paying a double *ṣadaqa*, rather than the humiliating *jizya* (see below); and the Ghassānid Jabala b. al-Ayham also refuses to pay a *jizya* of the *ʿulūj* (al-Yaʿqūbī, *Taʾrīkh*, II, p. 161; see also Landau-Tasseron's comment in her review of Donner, *Conquests*, in *JSAI* 6 (1985), p. 505). When, following the Second Fitna, al-Ḥajjāj is said to have 'sealed the necks' of companions of the Prophet, he did it 'in order to humiliate them' (*li-yadhillahum bi-dhālika*); they had become symbolic *jizya* payers (al-Yaʿqūbī, *Taʾrīkh*, II, p. 325); and when Turkish commanders make a show of their obedience to al-Mustaʿīn in 251/865, 'they put their belts on their necks, humiliating and submitting themselves thereby' (*tadhallulan wa-khuḍūʿan*) (al-Ṭabarī, *Taʾrīkh*, III, p. 1544). On sealing, see A. Mez, *The Renaissance of Islam*, trans. S. K. Bakhsh and D. S. Margoliouth (Patna, 1937), pp. 47ff.; I return to the issue of sealing in an article currently in preparation.

81 Thus, one late seventh- or early eighth-century Syriac historian has Muʿāwiya imposing a *gizya* on the Byzantines: 'If the Romans want peace, let them hand over their arms and pay *gizya*'; see the *Maronite Chronicle* (ed. E. W. Brooks and trans. J. B. Chabot as *Chronicon maroniticum* in the same volumes as the *Chronicle of 724*), pp. 71f./56 (Chabot translates 'dent arma sua et tributam solvant' and Palmer, *Seventh Century*, p. 32, 'let them surrender their weapons, and pay the tax'). It is in the same sense that one Abbasid poet uses *jizya* in a panegyric for Hārūn; thus Ibn Abī Ḥafṣa (*wa-kullu mulūki Rūm aʿṭāhu jizya*) in al-Ṭabarī, *Taʾrīkh*, III, p. 741.

82 John of Fenek, *Rīsh mellē* in Mingana, *Sources*, p. *147; Brock, 'North Mesopotamia in the late seventh century', p. 61 (whose translation I cite). The impression was not only John's; see the evidence collected by Hoyland, *Seeing Islam*, p. 263, note 14.

83 See Brock, 'John of Dailam', pp. 187/163f. For a discussion of this text, see chapter 4.

The *Zuqnin Chronicle* thus puts John of Fenek's nostalgia for the Sufyānid past into clearer focus; it also gives us a firmer hold on the account provided by Abū Yūsuf's anonymous informant, and allows a securer – and considerably earlier – dating of the passage than that proposed by Calder.[84] Here we read that for the purposes of taxing lands in the formerly Sasanian lands of al-Jazīra, 'later caliphs' (*man waliya min khulafā' al-muslimīn*) treated the country folk as the city folk, except that they were also to provide sustenance (in kind) for the *jund* (*qad ja'alū ahl al-rasātīq iswat ahl al-madā'in illā fī arzāq al-jund fa-innahum ḥamilūhā 'alayhim dūn ahl al-madā'in*).[85] The temptation to translate passages such as these loosely should be resisted: by 'later caliphs' we are to understand the early Marwānids, and by *jund* we are to understand the newly garrisoned force which, according to al-Balādhurī, 'began to draw its provisions there from its *kharāj*'.[86] Only now, in the early Marwānid period, can we begin to speak of a revenue system that tried to extract surplus with some regularity, one which necessarily required maintenance costs.

It is also in the light of Marwānid measures that one is to read three apocalyptic texts written in the north in the decade following the Second Fitna: the *Apocalypse* of pseudo-Methodius (written in the region of Sinjār in the early 690s);[87] the *Apocalypse* of pseudo-John the Less (written in or near Edessa, most probably in the very late seventh or very early eighth century);[88] and a fragment of another Edessan apocalypse.[89]

Writing *ex eventu*, pseudo-Methodius details the appearance of the 'Devastator', 'Abd al-Malik b. Marwān, when

[84] Calder, *Studies*, pp. 139ff., esp. p. 140, note 20: 'Dennet (*sic.*) believes that 'Abd al-Malik reformed what 'Iyāḍ had imposed. I believe that the stories of 'Iyāḍ and 'Abd al-Malik in the form they have in Abū Yūsuf emerged in the middle of the third cent. in order to bolster rival arguments about the tax rates to be imposed on the people of Edessa.'

[85] Abū Yūsuf, *Kitāb al-Kharāj*, p. 40. For a detailed discussion of how city folk enjoyed systematic advantages over rural folk in the Ḥanafite school, see B. Johansen, '*Amwāl ẓāhira* and *amwāl bāṭina*: town and countryside as reflected in the tax system of the Ḥanafite school', in al-Qāḍī, ed., *Studia Arabica et Islamica*, pp. 247–63.

[86] See above, note 35.

[87] For a detailed discussion of the provenance and dating of the text, see now *Die syrische Apokalypse des Pseudo-Methodius*, ed. and trans. G. J. Reinink (Louvain, 1993; *CSCO* 540–1), Einleitung; see also G. J. Reinink, 'Ps.-Methodius: a concept of history in response to the rise of Islam', in Cameron and Conrad, eds., *The Byzantine and Early Islamic Near East*, pp. 149–87; Brock's comments in Palmer, *Seventh Century*, pp. 222ff. (discussion and partial translation); H. Suermann, *Die geschichtstheologische Reaktion auf die einfallenden Muslime in der edessenischen Apokalyptik des 7. Jarhrhunderts* (Frankfurt, Bern, New York, 1985); and Hoyland, *Seeing Islam*, pp. 263ff.

[88] *The Gospel of the Twelve Apostles*, ed. and trans. J. R. Harris (Cambridge, 1900), pp. 15ff./34ff.; for discussions, see H. J. W. Drijvers, 'The Gospel of the Twelve Apostles: a Syriac apocalypse from the early Islamic period', in Cameron and Conrad, eds., *The Byzantine and early Islamic Near East*, pp. 189–213; H. J. W. Drijvers, 'Christians, Jews and Muslims in northern Mesopotamia in early Islamic times: the Gospel of the Twelve Apostles and related texts', in P. Canivet and J. P. Rey-Coquais, eds., *La Syrie de Byzance à l'Islam* (Damascus, 1992), pp. 67ff.; and Hoyland, *Seeing Islam*, pp. 267ff.

[89] See Brock's discussion and translation in Palmer, *Seventh Century*, pp. 243ff.

Egypt and Syria and the places of the east will be subjugated to the yoke of tribute (*mdattā*) and tax (*shaqlā*), [and the inhabitants of Egypt and those who live in Syria will be in great tribulation,] seven times worse than the tribulation of those in captivity . . . Deserted lands, left uncultivated, will belong to them. The tyrants will inscribe [them] for themselves . . . They will be so joyful in wrath and pride that they will impose tribute (*mdattā*)[90] on the dead who lie in the dust, and take the capitation tax (*ksef rīshā*) from orphans, from widows, and from holy men.[91]

Similar things are 'predicted' by pseudo-John the Less:

He [i.e. Ishmael] shall lead captive a great captivity among all the people of the earth, and they shall spoil a great spoiling, and all the ends of the earth shall do service and there shall be made subject to him many lordships; and his hand shall be over all, and also those that are under his hand he shall oppress with much tribute (*mdattā*); and he shall oppress and kill and destroy the rulers of the ends [of the earth]. And he shall impose tribute on [the earth], such as was never heard of; until a man shall come out from his house and shall find four collectors who collect tribute (*tbōʿē*) and men shall sell their sons and daughters because of their need.[92]

Of course apocalypticists are generally bad historians, and these are guilty of exaggerating state power, here represented by the ubiquitous tax collector;[93] by Abbasid standards, the Marwānids were probably neither terribly rapacious nor terribly efficient. For evidence of the deep social dislocation that taxation can put into motion, we need to wait until the second half of the eighth century, when the Abbasids could combine unprecedented powers of coercion with real bureaucratic expertise.[94] What is significant is therefore not state power, but Marwānid resolve: there were at least three, and possibly four, *taʿdīl*s, over a period of twenty years. The chronicler from Zuqnin records *taʿdīl*s in AG 1003 (691–2) and again in 1020 (708–9); the second of these is said to have been a follow-up to the first.[95] This first *taʿdīl* is also known to the Edessan and Islamic traditions. In Abū Yūsuf it is credited to al-Ḍaḥḥāk b. ʿAbd al-Raḥmān,[96] a point apparently corroborated by the *Chronicle of 846*, which, along with the *Chronicle of 819*, mentions *taʿdīl*s in 1008 (696–7) and 1022 (710–11); the account dated to 1020 (708–9) by the *Chronicle of 846*, which may mark the beginning of the *taʿdīl* of 1022,[97] was undertaken by Maslama b. ʿAbd al-Malik

90 Following Reinink's suggestion (*Apokalypse*, p. 27, note 26).
91 See ps.-Methodius, *Apokalypse*, pp. 27ff./47ff.
92 The translation follows Drijvers's closely ('The Gospel', p. 204).
93 See P. J. Alexander, *The Oracle of Baalbek: The Tiburtine Sibyl in Greek Dress* (Washington, DC, 1967), p. 113; in general, see P. J. Alexander, 'Medieval apocalypses as historical sources', *American Historical Review* 73.4 (1968), pp. 997–1018 (reprinted in his *Religious and Political Thought in the Byzantine Period* (London, 1987)).
94 For an overview, see Cahen, 'Fiscalité'.
95 *Zuqnin Chronicle*, pp. 154f./116f.
96 Abū Yūsuf, *Kitāb al-Kharāj*, p. 41; Dennett, *Conversion*, pp. 45f.
97 See the *Chronicle of 819* (*Chronicon anonymum ad annum domini 819 pertinens*, which is edited by A. Barsaum and translated by J.-B. Chabot in the first two volumes of the *Chronicle 1234*), I, pp. 13/9 (a certain ʿAṭiyya carries out the *taʿdīl*) and 14f./10; the *Chronicle of 846* (*Chronicon ad annum domini 846 pertinens*, which is edited by E. W. Brooks and translated by J.-B. Chabot in the same volumes as the *Chronicle of 724*), pp. 232/176; Michael the Syrian, *Chronique*, xi.xvi (ʿAṭiyya's *taʿdīl*, here dated to 1009).

(here called the governor of the whole of the Jazira – *amīrā d-kullāh gāzartā*): 'Maslama sent officers throughout northern Mesopotamia in order to measure lands, make a census of vineyards, plantations, livestock and people, and to hang lead seals on everyone's neck.' The pace of these measures suggests that the Marwānids were making up for lost time.

The Second Fitna and its consequences

Inasmuch as tribute lies at the heart of any meaningful definition of empire,[98] the Sufyānid Jazira was on its edge, in this respect more fruitfully compared with first-century Ṭabaristān than it is with Syria or Mosul.[99] The apocalypticists' anxiety at the end of the seventh century is to be interpreted primarily in the light of the appearance of an unprecedented taxation regime; for Christians, it was taxation that signalled Islamic rule.[100] Here it should be emphasised that what I have called 'Islamic rule' is little more than a trope, and although it corresponds to any number of Syriac (or Arabic) terms, local Christians responded to the social practices and emerging institutions through which it was actualised: the introduction of taxation and, as we shall see, the political disenfranchisement of city élites. That Arabs one generation out of Arabia now ruled the civilised Near East in the name of a deviant monotheism obviously took some getting used to; but the main problem for the Church, at least as it is reflected in the apocalypses of this period, was the threat to its authority posed by conversion, now apparently made attractive because of the new tax regime. Thus the monk and bishop Jacob of Edessa responded to Marwānid changes by writing an apocalypse of his own, the principal themes of which are observing Church canons and Church leadership;[101] pseudo-Methodius called for a last world emperor to protect Christianity.[102]

On the Islamic side of things, the family of Ibrāhīm b. al-Ashtar most clearly signals the region's changing fortunes in the 60s and 70s. Al-Ashtar himself had served as ʿAlī's commander in Kufan territories extending up through ʿĀnāt, Hīt, and Sinjār, to Mosul, Dārā, Nisibis and Āmid; meanwhile, al-Ḍaḥḥāk b. Qays served Muʿāwiya, ruling over Syrian territories that reached as far as Edessa and Ḥarrān.[103] The two agents exemplify the contested politics of the day; and if Muʿāwiya's could claim victory over ʿAlī's,

[98] Put crisply by G. Woolf, 'World-systems analysis and the Roman empire', *Journal of Roman Archaeology* 3 (1990), p. 47 ('The logic of the world-empire . . . is the tributary mode of production').

[99] See P. Gignoux, 'Le *spāhbed* des Sassanides à l'Islam', *JSAI* 13 (1990), pp. 1–14 (in particular 13f., on the 'gouverneurs du Ṭabaristān').

[100] Cf. Reinink, 'Ps.-Methodius', pp. 178f.; Hoyland, *Seeing Islam*, p. 267. Cf. G. J. Reinink, 'The Romance of Julian the Apostate as a source for seventh-century Syriac apocalypses', in Canivet and Rey-Coquais, eds., *La Syrie de Byzance à l'Islam*, p. 85.

[101] H. J. W. Drijvers, 'The Testament of our Lord: Jacob of Edessa's response to Islam', *Aram* 6 (1994), pp. 112f. [102] Reinink, 'Ps.-Methodius'.

[103] Naṣr b. Muzāḥim al-Minqarī, *Waqʿat Ṣiffīn* (Cairo, 1981), p. 12; Khalīfa b. Khayyāṭ, *Taʾrīkh*, p. 121 (the latter calling him the *ʿāmil* of the Jazira).

the tradition puts no flesh on the administrative skeleton erected in the north-east. By contrast, al-Ashtar's son Ibrāhīm not only defeated ʿUbayd Allāh b. Ziyād on the Khāzir in 67/686,[104] but he followed up his victory by appointing governors over every Jaziran town worthy of note: taking Mosul for himself, Ibrāhīm appointed his brother ʿAbd al-Raḥmān over Nisibis (including Dārā and Sinjār), and Ḥātim b. al-Nuʿmān al-Bāhilī over Edessa, Ḥarrān and (apparently) Shimshāṭ.[105] We are pointedly told that al-Mukhtār collected taxes for eighteen months in the Sawād, al-Jabal, Iṣfahān, Rayy, Azarbayjān, and al-Jazīra.[106] In the administrative union of Mosul and Jazira we have a clear departure from Sufyānid precedent, and one so compelling that it was followed by the Zubayrids under Muhallab b. Abī Ṣufra,[107] and the Marwānids under Muḥammad b. Marwān.[108]

The literary sources thus record the decoupling of the Jazira and Qinnasrīn in the early 680s, and in the appointment of Muḥammad b. Marwān as governor of al-Jazīra and Mosul they also record the Marwānids' adoption of Mukhtārid administrative geography. Both changes can be discerned in the coinage. It seems that in the decades following the conquests, such local copper coinage as there was in the north consisted of residual Byzantine issues, the continuing circulation of Byzantine issues across the frontier, and finally, coins minted 'privately' on Byzantine models;[109] the most recent study has the influx of Byzantine coppers come to an end between 655 and 658, the imitations being struck to address the resulting shortage.[110] For centrally

[104] Al-Ṭabarī, *Taʾrīkh*, II, pp. 707ff.; al-Balādhurī, *Ansāb*, V (Jerusalem), pp. 247ff. For John of Fenek's testimony, see his *Rīsh mellē*, in Mingana, ed., *Sources*, pp. *157f.; Brock, 'North Mesopotamia in the late seventh century', pp. 65ff.; and for the events of the Second Civil War in the north, G. Rotter, *Die Umayyaden und der zweite Bürgerkrieg (680–692)* (Wiesbaden 1982), pp. 214ff.

[105] See al-Ṭabarī, *Taʾrīkh*, II, 716; al-Balādhurī, *Ansāb al-ashrāf*, XI (Greifswald, 1883), p. 114; Crone, *Slaves*, p. 105.

[106] Al-Dīnawarī, *Akhbār*, p. 306; al-Balādhurī, *Ansāb*, V (Jerusalem), p. 251; Morony, *Iraq*, pp. 135f.

[107] Al-Balādhurī, *Ansāb*, V (Jerusalem), pp. 274 and 332ff.; al-Balādhurī, *Ansāb*, XI, p. 111; al-Ṭabarī, *Taʾrīkh*, II, pp. 750, 753, 765 and 807.

[108] An appointment that is almost universally mentioned in the Arabic tradition, even if some of the details conflict; thus al-Azdī, *Taʾrīkh*, p. 25 (Mosul); al-Balādhurī, *Futūḥ*, p. 332 (Jazira and Armenia); al-Ṭabarī, *Taʾrīkh*, II, p. 1873 (Jazira, Armenia, Mosul, Azarbayjān). See also Michael the Syrian, *Chronique*, xi.xvi (Edessa); *Chronicle of 1234*, I, pp. 293/228 (Mesopotamia, Mosul and Armenia).

[109] C. Morrison, 'La monnaie en Syrie byzantine', in J.-M. Dentzer and W. Orthmann, eds., *Archéologie et histoire de la Syrie II: La Syrie de l'époque achéménide à l'avènement de l'Islam* (Saarbrücken, 1989), pp. 191–204; C. Morrison, 'Le trésor byzantin de Nikertai', *Revue Belge de Numismatique* 118 (1972), pp. 29–91; J.-P. Sodini and G. Tate, 'Déhès (Syrie du Nord) campagnes I–III (1976–1978), recherches sur l'habitat rural', *Syria* 57 (1980), pp. 267ff.; W. E. Metcalf, 'Three seventh-century Byzantine gold hoards', *Museum Notes* (American Numismatic Society) 25 (1980), pp. 87–108. For coins struck by Constans II found in Assur, see S. Heidemann's comments in P. A. Miglus, *Das Wohngebiet von Assur: Stratigraphie und Architektur* (Berlin, 1996), pp. 356 and 367.

[110] See S. Heidemann, 'The merger of two currency zones in early Islam: the Byzantine and Sasanian impact on the circulation in former Byzantine Syria and Northern Mesopotamia', *Iran* 36 (1998), pp. 98f.

organised copper minting we must wait until the appearance of the so-called 'standing caliph' issues, which were struck in a large number of north Syrian towns, in addition to Edessa and Ḥarrān; the consensus is that these issues were minted from about 74 to 77 (692–5).[111] These 'standing caliph' coppers postdate the 'imperial image' coppers minted in Syria proper; when these were first struck remains very controversial, Bates holding to 72–74, others pushing the date back to considerably earlier in the century.[112] There is no question regarding the sequence, however: no one would argue that the 'standing caliph' coppers preceded the 'imperial image' coins.

Two conclusions suggest themselves. First, if we leave aside one difficult report,[113] we might infer from the presence and variety of Byzantine issues and Byzantine imitations that Muslim claims to sovereignty – such as they were – did not include the exclusive right to strike coins; pre-conquest Byzantine issues were not withdrawn from circulation, and the ill-defined frontier slowed, but did not stop, the flow of coinage from Byzantium. Second, the secondary appearance of copper coins east of the Euphrates may be taken to signal the belated political integration of the area, an argument that grows in strength if caliphal minting in Syria began during Muʿāwiya's reign. A common design connects Edessa to the north Syrian mints, and this too points to the region's lingering ties to Syria; 'official' coinage thus spread from the west to the east, mirroring the eastward extension of administrative geography.[114] In short, there is no question that the 70s/690s mark something of a watershed: we are now in a different world, one in which coinage was centrally managed, its value (both economic and symbolic) recognised. The issue of a single type from as many as twenty mints shows that provincial minting was now subject to some manner of central supervision; the absence of Byzantine gold coins in early eighth-century hoards suggests that they were systematically withdrawn in favour of the new, epigraphic, standard.[115] Moreover, the intense (and short-lived) period of experimentation in design, which began with the 'standing caliph' issues and ended with the purely epigraphic coins of the reform, shows that the Marwānids were now pressing coinage into service for ideological purposes.

111 Morrison, 'La monnaie en Syrie byzantine', p. 199; M. Bates, 'History, geography and numismatics in the first century of Islamic coinage', *Revue Suisse de Numismatique* 65 (1986), pp. 254f.; M. Bates, 'Byzantine coinage and its imitations, Arab coinage and its imitations: Arab-Byzantine coinage', *Aram* 6 (1994), pp. 381–403.

112 When Muslims began to strike coppers continues to be debated by numismatists. The closest one comes to a consensus is Bates's chronology, which I follow here; although this has attracted a fair share of criticism (see, for example, S. Qedar, 'Copper coinage of Syria in the seventh and eighth century AD', *Israel Numismatic Journal* 10 (1988–1989), pp. 27–39), it has not yet been disproved, and Heidemann ('Merger', p. 99) appears to accept it with reservations.

113 Namely, the *Maronite Chronicle*, pp. 71/55f. (which has Muʿāwiya mint gold and silver coins, but these are said to have been rejected because they lacked crosses).

114 Cf. Ibn Zanjawayh, *Kitāb al-Amwāl*, pp. 157f., who has Syria and Jazira share the same tax rates.

115 Heidemann, 'Merger', p. 96.

If the copper coinage reflects the *laissez-faire* character of Sufyānid rule and the detachment of al-Jazīra from Syria, the silver coins shed more light on Marwānid rule in the north. Bates has demonstrated that starting in 73/692–3, a single, peripatetic mint struck dirhams in al-Jazīra, Mosul, Armenia, Azarbayjān, and Arrān; synchronising the movement of this mint (as reflected in mint names) and the movement of the caliphs (as recorded in the literary sources), he also argues that the mint mirrors a single governorship first occupied by Muḥammad b. Marwān.[116]

Given the movement of the silver mint, it is tempting to suggest that the silver coins were minted to pay soldiers in this and other *junds*. The coinage record is compelling, and so too is the familial symmetry that it suggests: ʿAbd al-Malik as caliph, flanked by his two brothers, Muḥammad in the north and Bishr in the south; in combination with Arabic and Syriac literary evidence, it clearly shifts the burden of evidence to those who argue that Mosul and al-Jazīra were administratively distinct in this period.[117] It is hard to see how this administration actually worked, however. One has the impression that the joint governorship remained controversial well into the eighth century;[118] and the coinage cannot be taken so far to suggest a single, administrative unit: by Abbasid standards, administration still remained inchoate.[119] There is no doubt, however, that the Jazira had come to be ruled directly: it now had a governor with broad responsibilities, and, alongside him, a *jund*. We can now begin to speak of the balance between the resources necessary to maintain the *jund* (along with what one presumes to have been an increasingly ambitious tax administration), and the resources extracted by its real or threatened use.

[116] See M. Bates, 'The dirham mint of the northern provinces of the Umayyad caliphate', *Armenian Numismatic Journal* 15 (1989), pp. 89–111; Bates, 'History, geography and numismatics', p. 237. As Bates notes ('Dirham mint', p. 90 note 5), it is only with Ibn al-Athīr (d. 630/1232) that we have a date for Muḥammad's governorship (*al-Kāmil*, IV, p. 361), and this no doubt because he, unlike al-Ṭabarī, used the now-lost first volume of al-Azdī's *Taʾrīkh al-Mawṣil*. Whether Ibn al-ʿAdīm (d. 660/1261) had the same information from the same source is another matter; see his *Zubdat al-ḥalab min taʾrīkh Ḥalab*, I (Damascus, 1951), p. 44.

[117] It was on the strength of al-Azdī's evidence that Forand argued that Mosul was administratively distinct from al-Jazīra (Forand, 'Governors', pp. 101f.). Evincing no knowledge of Forand's article, G. Rotter agreed five years later, but did so by arguing against al-Azdī, who 'took it for granted that Mosul had always been the capital or at least a part of the province of al-Jazīra', and by adducing the copper coinage; see his 'The Umayyad Fulūs of Mosul', *Museum Notes* 19 (1974), pp. 167 and 189.

[118] Concerning Marwān II's responsibilities, see al-Azdī, *Taʾrīkh*, p. 18 ('the governor of Mosul, its tax districts (*aʿmālihā*) and the entire Jazira'), and the *Zuqnin Chronicle*, pp. 188f./144 (where he appoints governors – typically expressed with an Arabism, *ʿamlē* – over all the cities, 'even Mosul'). For mixed evidence from the 160s, see M. Bonner, *Aristocratic Violence and Holy War: Studies in the Jihad and the Arab–Byzantine Frontier* (New Haven, 1996), p. 76, note 36.

[119] Thus Maymūn b. Mihrān (d. 116/734), who is sometimes anachronistically identified as the *qāḍī* of the Jazira and sometimes as its *wālī*, was apparently invested with authority over the fisc, in addition to the administration of justice (including its execution); see Ibn Saʿd, *Kitāb al-Ṭabaqāt*, VII^2, pp. 177f.; al-Balādhurī, *Ansāb al-ashrāf*, III (Wiesbaden/Beirut, 1978), pp. 100f.; al-Jahshiyārī, *Wuzarāʾ*, pp. 53f.; al-Qushayrī, *Taʾrīkh al-Raqqa*, pp. 42ff. Cf. the case of Yaḥyā b. Yaḥyā al-Ghassānī (see below, chapter 3, note 113).

Christian authority in the Sufyānid Jazira

Of the local consequences of Sufyānid *laissez-faire* policies little can generally be said; a partial exception concerns city life. Immediately following its account of the Second Fitna, the *Chronicle of 1234* begins a section entitled 'The evils committed by Ḥajjāj and Muḥammad bar Marwān in their lands'.[120] According to the account, upon taking authority of 'the lands of Persia' (i.e. the East), al-Ḥajjāj 'destroyed without mercy, killing Arab leaders (*rīshānē d-ṭayyāyē*) and looting their houses'. The account then continues:

Muḥammad bar Marwān did the same in his dominion, killing the élite (*rīshānē*) without mercy, even plotting against the Christian leaders (*rīshānē d-krestyānē*). These [too] he killed, and looted their houses. He killed Mardānshāh bar Zarnūsh and his son, who were the administrators (*mdabbrānē*) of Nisibis, and Shamʿūn bar Nōnā [the administrator of] Ḥalūgā, crucifying them.[121] The leaders of Armenia he gathered together in a church, and he set this alight, burning them alive. He then killed Anastās bar Andrā, the administrator of Edessa, and looted his house. Still, the Christians continued to be the scribes (*kutūbē*), élite, and administrators in Arab lands (*atrawwatā d-ṭayyāyē*).[122]

The account is manifestly Christian,[123] and one can safely assume that it was part of the ninth-century history of Dionysius of Tell Maḥrē. Michael the Syrian had access to it also,[124] but left us a briefer version, dropping the sentence concerning Mardānshāh and his son in Nisibis; Bar Hebraeus seems to know most of the details, but here the narrative is garbled.[125]

Textual questions aside, it is the social and political role of the *mdabbrānē* – the term I have translated as 'administrators' – that demands our interest here. The term itself is often used generically in Syriac to describe someone who possesses authority of one kind or other,[126] thus, 'leader', 'administrator', and 'governor'.[127] Its meaning being so plastic, the term was used in a variety of contexts. Nestorian synodical records frequently use the term and derivatives to describe church authorities;[128] it appears in hagiographic and monas-

120 *Chronicle of 1234*, I, pp. 293f./228f.

121 That Simeon held the same position in Ḥalūgā as Mardānshāh and his son in Nisibis is expressed implicitly in the parallelism of the Syriac, and this is how Chabot translated the passage ('et Simeonem filium Nonni, *gubernatorem* Ḥalugae').

122 *Chronicle of 1234*, I, pp. 293/228f.

123 But note that al-Yaʿqūbī, who seems to have spent his youth in Armenia, frequently has good access to Armenian history, and he does preserve an account of Muḥammad b. Marwān's massacre of Armenian notables, putting it in Khilāṭ (*Taʾrīkh*, II, pp. 324f.); see also al-Balādhurī, *Futūḥ*, p. 205.

124 Michael the Syrian, *Chronique*, xi.xvi.

125 Bar Hebraeus, *Chronicon syriacum*, ed. P. Bedjan (Paris, 1890), p. 112 (=Budge, *Chronography*, p. 104); Dionysius is expressly credited with the report.

126 This is well attested in the Syriac New Testament; see G. A. Kiraz, *A Computer-generated Concordance to the Syriac New Testament* (Leiden, 1993), p. 661: 'guide', 'leader'.

127 K. Brockelmann, *Lexicon syriacum* (Hildesheim, 1966 reprint of 1928 edn), p. 140; R. Duval, ed., *Lexicon syriacum auctore Hassano Bar-Bahlule* (Amsterdam, 1970), col. 1010; G. Hoffmann, *Syrische–Arabische Glossen*, I (Kiel, 1874), p. 210 (*mudabbir*, *sāʾis*); J. Payne Smith, *A Compendious Syriac Dictionary* (Oxford, 1903), p. 252.

128 See Chabot, ed., *Synodicon Orientale*, pp. 74/326 (synod of 544); pp. 155/415 (585); and pp. 218/483 (676).

tic contexts among Nestorians and Monophysites alike ('leader'; 'abbot');[129] the so-called *Khuzistan Chronicle* (written c. 680) calls Muḥammad the 'leader of the Arabs' (*mdabbrānā d-ṭayyāyē*);[130] in a Christian–Muslim dialogue of the middle of the seventh century, God and Jesus are said to 'govern' the heaven and earth;[131] and when a (West Syrian) translator read *al-rawāsī* of Qur'ān 41:9 as *ru'asā'*, he quite sensibly translated it as *mdabbrānē*.[132]

Can we assign a more precise meaning to our text? In pairing *mdabbrānē* and *rīshānē*, our account is far from unique: 'headmen and city governors' (*rīshānē w-mdabbrānē d-mdinātā*) are also said to have been present at the Christian–Muslim dialogue in Syria.[133] Similarly, in describing events in Āmid after the Sasanians' successful siege of the city in 502/3, pseudo-Zacharias of Metylene has Qawād summon several notables, among whom are counted 'the chiefs (*rishānē*) and *mdabbrānē* of the city'. Here it is again impossible to discern any distinction between *rishānē* ('chiefs'; 'heads') and *mdabbrānē*, but pseudo-Zacharias then quickly uses *mdabbrānā* (in the singular), and now the sense is considerably narrower: Qawād is said to have left behind in the city 'Glōn, the commander (*rab ḥaylā*) as *mdabbrānā*, two *marzban*s, and something like three thousand soldiers, to rule the city'.[134] Here then *mdabbrānā* designates an imperially appointed governor, an idea more commonly expressed by *hegmōnā* and *shallīṭā*.[135] The crucial difference seems to be that the *mdabbrānā* enjoyed only

[129] A. Vööbus, ed. and trans., *Syriac and Arabic Documents Regarding Legislation Relative to Syrian Asceticism* (Stockholm, 1960), index; Rabban Hormizd, *Rabban Hôrmîzd and Rabban Bar-'Idtâ*, pp. 197/298 (he translates 'governor'). For the semantic overlap of *rīshā* and *amīrā*, see S. P. Brock, 'Syriac views on emergent Islam', in G. H. A. Juynboll, ed., *Studies on the First Century of Islamic Society* (Carbondale and Edwardsville, 1982), p. 14.

[130] *Khuzistan Chronicle*, pp. 30/26 (noted by Brock, 'Syriac views', p. 202, note 34). Cf. John of Fenek's use of *mhaddyānā*, 'guide' (*Rīsh mellē* in Mingana, *Sources*, pp. *146f.; Brock, 'North Mesopotamia in the late seventh century', p. 61); and *rīshā* (in this case, 'caliph'); see the *Zuqnin Chronicle*, pp. 152ff./114f.

[131] See F. Nau, 'Un colloque du patriarch Jean avec l'émir des Agaréens et faits divers des années 712 à 716', *JA* 11.5 (1915), pp. 249/258f. The text is dated by Cook and Crone to 644 (*Hagarism*, p. 162, note 11), but this part may not be integral to the original (*ibid*, p. 168, note 20); see also S. H. Griffith, 'Disputes with Muslims in Syriac Christian texts: from Patriarch John (d. 648) to Bar Hebraeus (d. 1286),' in B. Lewis and R. Niewöhner eds., *Religionsgespräche im Mittelalter* (Wiesbaden, 1992), pp. 257ff.

[132] 'And he placed in it [the earth] stable mountains (*rawāsī*) above it, and he blessed it and measured in it its sustenance in four days, alike for [all] who ask'; see A. Mingana, 'An ancient Syriac translation of the Ḳur'ān exhibiting new verses and variants', *Bulletin of the John Rylands Library* 9 (1925), pp. 208 and 218. The term is legible in the reproduction of the Syriac MS, which is appended onto the article, fol. 77b, right column, line 13. The text is not as old as Mingana would have it; see T. Nöldeke and F. Schwally, *Geschichte des Qorans* (Leipzig, 1909–38), III, pp. 100ff. [133] Nau, 'Colloque', pp. 251/261.

[134] Ps.-Zacharias, *Historia ecclesiastica*, II, pp. 30/20. For a parallel passage in Procopius, see his *Wars*, I.vii. 33. According to *Wars* I.ix 18, Glōn occupied the sanctuary of a local holy man named Simeon.

[135] The last of these (along with *amīrā*, borrowed from Arabic) seems to appear more in Syriac of the early Islamic period: it can describe the Byzantine governor of a settlement such as Fallūja on the Euphrates (*Khuzistan Chronicle*, pp. 33/28; Nöldeke, 'Die von Guidi herausgegebene syrische Chronik', p. 36 translates 'Oberbeamte') or the Muslim governor of Mosul in the early Islamic period; see Rabban Hormizd, *Rabban Hôrmîzd and Rabban Bar 'Idtâ*, pp. 65/97.

temporary and delegated – indeed perhaps even improperly delegated – authority. According to 'Joshua the Stylite', when one governor of Edessa left the city for Constantinople, a certain Eusebius was deputised over 'his administration of the city' (*l-madbareh mdittā*).[136] Similarly, 'Joshua' identifies the rebel Constantine as the *mdabbrānā* of Arzan al-Rūm (Theodosiopolis).[137] Later Syriac historical prose also uses the term in the sense of 'deputy'.[138]

So much for terminology; what can the history of Edessa on the eve of the Islamic conquest tell us? After a century of warfare, the city had grown a thick skin. The city's landed élite occasionally worked alongside imperial authorities,[139] but they were stubbornly independent-minded; and it is this aspect of Edessan notable politics that the Edessan historical tradition naturally highlights. Perhaps only some were implicated in Narsē's (Narses') rebellion against Phocas,[140] but clearly most opposed Khusraw's appointment of a city notable named Qūrā (Cyrus) as governor after the Persian conquest. Despite (or perhaps because of) this, Qūrā did Khusraw's bidding, sending off huge sums of money to Iraq, and soon afterward, Khusraw ordered that the Edessans be deported.[141] It was presumably also the notables' opposition that had led Khusraw to abandon his appointment of the Nestorian Aḥīshmā as bishop; the uneasy compromise was to appoint Monophysite bishops from the east, one occupying the Edessan office. Heraclius, in his turn, would later exile the Monophysite Isaiah, who had also been brought from the east, turning the city's cathedral over to the Chalcedonians of the city. This is said to have aroused the ire of the city's four leading families; 'this time,' Dionysius of Tell Maḥrē reports, 'they could not oppose the emperor's command,' and some were apparently exiled.[142] Earlier, the Jews of the city are said to have allied with the Persian garrison in resisting Heraclius' brother Theodoric, when he came to re-impose Byzantine rule after Heraclius' victories.

In sum, we seem to have a fairly robust culture of élites operating in Edessa on the eve of the conquest; and in the light of terminology and history one might

[136] Or, 'to administer the city'; see ps.-Joshua, *Chronicle*, pp. 35/30. The practice was perfectly ordinary; for a later example, see Nikephoros, *Brevarium historicum*, ed. and trans. C. Mango as *Nikephoros Patriarch of Constantinople Short History* (Washington, DC, 1990), pp. 55 and 180f. (commentary); and also Segal, *Edessa*, pp. 123ff.

[137] Ps.-Joshua, *Chronicle*, pp. 45/37; cf. trans. by A. Luther, *Die syrische Chronik des Josua Stylites* (Berlin and New York, 1997), p. 64 ('Der Befehlshaber').

[138] See, for example, the *Chronicle of 1234*, II, pp. 191/143 (year 1178, where the eunuch Mujāhid is identified as the *mdabbrānā* for ʿIzz al-Dīn, the brother of Sayf al-Dawla).

[139] Thus, it was John, of the celebrated Ruṣāfa family, who received and housed Khusraw II when he allied with Maurice; see Michael the Syrian, *Chronique*, x.xxiii; *Chronicle of 1234*, I, pp. 216/170.

[140] *Chronicle of 1234*, I, pp. 220/173; Michael the Syrian, *Chronique*, x.xxv; Theophanes, *Chronicle*, AM 6095.

[141] It is unclear how many of the city folk were actually moved, and in any case many returned, apparently after the fall of Shahrbarāz; see Michael the Syrian, *Chronique*, xi.i and xi.iii; the *Chronicle of 1234*, I, pp. 230/180f.

[142] *Chronicle of 1234*, I, pp. 236/185. For these Edessan events, see also Michael the Syrian, *Chronique*, xi.iv. On Edessa in this period, see Segal, *Edessa*, chap. 4; and much remains useful in Duval, *Édesse*.

suggest that the *mdabbrānē* can be identified as local figures charged with what Heraclius quite naturally thought to be temporary authority in the city; only locals could have managed the city in the absence of a Byzantine garrison. The appointments were presumably made in an atmosphere of some crisis; one imagines that they were *ad hoc*, the figures in question to be relieved as soon as Byzantine control was restored. Unfortunately, we cannot say from which families these *mdabbrānē* came, nor even if they were curial and/or clerical. Of course relief never came – at least not until the Crusades – and far from experiencing a Christian reconquest along with all the Byzantine *dirigisme* that it would bring,[143] the cities entered an Indian summer of *de facto* autonomy that ended only with Marwānid annexation and the imposition of direct Islamic rule.

Here it is worth noting that the participation of local élites in city affairs fits a broader, sixth-century pattern: Byzantinists may argue about how clearly bishops' local authority was recognised by Constantinople,[144] but that bishops and land owners were now wielding wide-ranging powers in the cities is anything but controversial.[145] More important, Edessa fits a regional pattern, for local (and early) hagiographies have Christians in charge of civil affairs in several towns of the north. According to the *Life* of Simeon, which reflects a late seventh- and early eighth-century world, George the son of Lazarus of Anḥel was 'in charge of the whole region of Ṭūr ʿAbdīn' (*shalīṭ hwā ʿal kulleh atrā d-Ṭūr ʿAbdīn*); it is to George that Simeon went for a corvée of 300 men to build a church.[146] Similarly, the *Life* of Theodotus of Amida describes Christian authorities (here called *arkhān*, in addition to *mdabbrānē*) in charge of Samosata, Ṭūr ʿAbdīn, Mayferqaṭ and Dārā.[147] Appointed bishop of Amida

143 For an overview of Heraclius' efforts, see Haldon, *Byzantium in the Seventh Century*, pp. 297ff.

144 See A. Hohlweg, 'Bischof und Stadtherr im frühen Byzanz', *Jahrbuch der österreichischen Byzantinistik* 20 (1971), pp. 51–62, *contra* D. Claude, *Die byzantinische Stadt im 6. Jahrhundert* (Munich, 1969).

145 It almost goes without saying that the two categories not infrequently overlapped. The relevant literature is very large here; some examples are G. Downey, 'Ephraemius, Patriarch of Antioch,' *Church History* 7 (1938), pp. 364–70; J. H. W. G. Liebeschuetz and H. Kennedy, 'Antioch and the villages of northern Syria in the fifth and sixth centuries AD: trends and problems', *Nottingham Medieval Studies* 32 (1988), pp. 65–90 (p. 78 note 81 for how little we know of sixth-century municipal institutions); J. H. W. G. Liebeschuetz, *Barbarians and Bishops: Army, Church, and State in the Age of Arcadius and Chrysostom* (Oxford, 1990), esp. 228ff.; W. Bayless, 'Synesius of Cyrene: a study of the role of the bishop in temporal affairs', *Byzantine Studies/Études Byzantines* 4 (1977), pp. 147–56; G. Dagron, 'Le christianisme dans la ville byzantine', *Dumbarton Oaks Papers* 31 (1977), pp. 1–25.

146 See Simeon's *Life* in Dolabani, *Maktabzabnē*, pp. 135f. The text also has Simeon build a magnificent mosque nearby, this to keep on the right side of Muslim authorities; since it also has him build a *madrasa*, there is good reason to suspect the hand of the text's later (twelfth-century?) redactor. Elsewhere (p. 148) one reads of 'chief (*rīshā*) Gabriel of Anḥel'; and Palmer (*Monk and Mason*, p. 162) speaks of Anḥel as the seat of a 'ruling Melkite ʿdynasty' of local governors'.

147 For Theodotus' material I draw on A. Palmer, 'Saints' lives with a difference: Elijah on John of Tella (d. 538) and Joseph on Theodotus of Amida (d. 698)', in H. Drijvers *et al.*, eds., *IV Symposium Syriacum 1984* (Rome, 1987=Orientalia Christiana Analecta 229), pp. 203–16; Palmer, *Monk and Mason*, pp. 162ff.; and Hoyland, *Seeing Islam*, pp. 156ff. On Mayferqaṭ a half century later, see the *Zuqnin Chronicle*, pp. 196ff./151ff.

shortly before his death in 698, Theodotus himself was invested by an unidentified 'authority over all the east'; here we probably have the first sign of Muḥammad b. Marwān's new regime.[148] Needless to say, change in a region as liminal as the north came relatively slowly: Dionysius reassures his readers that despite Muḥammad b. Marwān's measures, Christians continued to serve as 'administrators', and we read elsewhere of a certain Rūmī (a Chalcedonian?) 'head (*rīshā*) of Ṭūr ʿAbdin' in 751.[149] Indeed, Christians would reappear as civil authorities in the Islamic north, both in what remained the overwelmingly Christian cities of the west, as well as in Muslim foundations: Mosul, for example, had one thirteenth-century Christian governor.[150]

Late examples such as these reflect the continuing vitality and resilience of local Christian élites, as they do the pragmatism of local Muslim dynasties; they do not mean that little had changed, however. For already at the start of the eighth century one can see how Marwānid innovations presented attractive opportunities. Thus the Jacobite Athanasius, whom Palmer not unreasonably calls a 'seventh-century tycoon',[151] exemplifies – albeit spectacularly – the Edessans' ability to adapt to late seventh-century change. His *floruit* puts him squarely in the midst of the imposition of Marwānid rule, and from this he profited enormously, emerging as a wealthy land owner (of three hundred shops (*ḥnūtē*) and nine hostels (*pūtqē*) by one reckoning), a patron of church restorations and building in Edessa and Egypt, and finally a city worthy; it is Athanasius who produced 5,000 dīnārs demanded of the Edessan by a tax collector named Muḥammad,[152] thus saving the city's most famous icon. Some of his wealth may have been old, but much came from the Marwānids themselves. For ʿAbd al-Malik is said to have been so impressed by Athanasius' sagacity and secretarial skills that he had him manage the affairs of his son ʿAbd al-ʿAzīz, now governor of Egypt;[153] according to Dionysius, here drawing on his grandfather, Daniel bar Moses, Athanasius 'was the administrator, and assigned the tax (*maflāg gizyātā*) of Egypt'.[154] Athanasius' dexterity in handling the Marwānids, perhaps combined with confessional rivalries, explains why he engendered the hostility of the Melkite Sarjūn b. Manṣūr, who belonged to that

[148] See Hoyland, *Seeing Islam*, p. 159, note 157; Palmer, *Monk and Mason*, p. 167.
[149] See Dolabani, *Maktabzabnē*, p. 160; noted already by Palmer, *Monk and Mason*, pp. 6f.
[150] See F. de Blois, 'The Iftikhāriyān of Qazvīn', in K. Eslami, ed., *Iran and Iranian Studies: Essays in Honor of Iraj Afshar* (Princeton, 1998), pp. 16f.
[151] Palmer, *Seventh Century*, p. 93. On Athanasius, see the *Chronicle of 1234*, I, pp. 294f./229; Michael the Syrian, *Chronique*, xi.xvi (passages translated by Palmer, *Seventh Century*, pp. 202ff.). See also Hage, *Kirche*, pp. 59, 72, 75 and 84; Segal, *Edessa*, pp. 202f., 213f. and 240; Palmer, *Monk and Mason*, p. 169.
[152] Perhaps, following Chabot (Michael the Syrian, *Chronique*, II, p. 474, note 2), to be identified as Muḥammad b. Marwān himself. Cf. Bar Hebraeus, *Chronicon syriacum*, p. 112 (=Budge, *Chronography*, p. 103), which calls Muḥammad the *amīrā* of Gazirtā d-Qardō.
[153] The operative term is, once again, *mdabbrānā*; literally, 'He ordered that Athanasius become his scribe and administrator.'
[154] *Chronicle of 1234*, I, pp. 294/229; on Athanasius in the history of Egyptian taxation, see Morimoto, *Fiscal Administration of Egypt*, p. 114.

category of non-Muslim bureaucrat-scribes upon whom early Muslims depended so heavily in administering the conquered provinces; the latter naturally seems to have thought Athanasius an opportunist and *parvenu*, and conspired to have his wealth confiscated. In the event, he had only mixed success.

Conclusion: Sufyānid concerns

Conquest can create new élites (through the distribution of offices, land and titles), as it can destroy (through violence and confiscation) or incorporate (through conversion or assimilation more generally) pre-existing élites; to do so requires some kind of imperial programme, along with sufficient power. In the city and province of Mosul, we shall see how a conquest-era, Kufan-based programme yielded to a very different Marwānid programme, which turned on élite foundations and investment in the land; throughout, power was concentrated in the city. In the Jazira, conquest momentum dissipated entirely, and so far as it existed, the Ḥijāzīs' programme had nothing to do with building an empire on the backs of the region's settled, and something to do with exercising influence over its pastoral populations.

As far as one can judge, earliest Muslim conceptions of the north appear to have been as much ethnic as confessional or geographic. The Christian tradition preserves a striking account, according to which Abū Bakr sent out four conquest generals: one to Palestine, one to Egypt, one to Persia, and one against the Christian Arabs.[155] The account is imprecise at best, but it apparently captures the early élite's concern for the pastoralists of Syria and northern Mesopotamia, and perhaps too some ignorance of (and indifference towards) the territory of the north as such.[156] What is more, according to the Islamic tradition, the earliest post-conquest administrative appointment was not of a governor with responsibilities over a given territory, but rather of two officials charged with overseeing what was perceived as two separate populations: al-Walīd b. ʿUqba, appointed over the Arabs of al-Jazīra (*ʿarab al-jazīra*), and Ḥabīb b. Maslama, appointed over its non-Arab (and presumably settled) people (*ʿajam*).[157] Of Ḥabīb's responsibilities we revealingly hear nothing, but of al-Walīd's the sources do preserve some material. At least once he is called the *ʿāmil li-ʿUmar ʿalā Rabīʿa bi'l-Jazīra*,[158] a title that would be

[155] Michael the Syrian, *Chronique*, xi.iv; *Chronicle of 1234*, I, pp. 241/189; cf. Theophanes, *Chronicle*, AM 6123 and 6124.

[156] Thus the Byzantine defeat in *sūrat al-Rūm* is described in Qur'ān 30:1 as *fī adnā al-arḍ*, a phrase that exegetes took to mean *arḍ al-ʿarab* (e.g., al-Bayḍāwī, *Tafsīr* (Cairo, n.d.), p. 338), as well as the Jazira (ʿAbd al-Razzāq al-Ṣanʿānī, *Tafsīr* (Riyadh, 1989), II, p. 101). In Muʿāwiya's time Mosul is counted as one of the 'Arab lands' (*bilād al-ʿarab*); see al-Ṭabarī, *Taʾrīkh*, II, p. 142.

[157] Al-Ṭabarī, *Taʾrīkh*, I, p. 2508 and cf. p. 2843; Ibn Ḥubaysh, *Kitāb al-Ghazawāt*, III, p. 91; see also Donner, *Conquests*, p. 252. Ḥabīb had earlier participated in the conquest of the north, serving as a sub-commander of ʿIyāḍ b. Ghanm, and distinguishing himself in Armenia; see al-Balādhurī, *Futūḥ*, pp. 193ff.; *Zuqnin Chronicle*, pp. 152/114; and, more generally, al-Qushayrī, *Taʾrīkh al-Raqqa*, pp. 32ff.

[158] Ṭabarī, *Taʾrīkh* I, p. 2812.

eclipsed by the (classical) formulation of *ʿāmil Diyār Rabīʿa*. Meanwhile, none other than the caliph himself is said to have addressed the problem of the non-Rabīʿa Iyād, who reportedly scattered towards the north during the conquests; ʿUmar is given to write to the (unidentified) emperor, threatening the Christian populations within *dār al-Islām* if the Iyād were not returned. The account seems to contain a number of anachronisms – particularly the presence of borders across which the pastoralists are said to have crossed – as well as what may be an early dichotomy between *arḍ al-ʿarab* (land of the bedouins) and *arḍ al-Rūm* (Byzantium).[159]

The pastoralists of the Jazira naturally posed a threat to order, and we read that ʿUthmān directed Muʿāwiya to settle tribesmen in regions well distant from towns and villages, apparently because of the difficulty of maintaining security;[160] but this report appears to be unique, and in any case, the conquerors' concern would only have grown alongside their investment in the land.[161] In the earliest period, the threat appears to have been principally ideological, for in Taghlibī Christianity the pastoralists challenged the revolutionary fusion of (Arab) pastoral power and monotheism that Muḥammad had effected.[162] Thus Christian sources also have conversion being demanded of Taghlibī chiefs,[163] and the one clear instance of élite incorporation in the post-conquest Jazira also concerns the Taghlib. The account quite strikingly preserves the words of a Taghlibī disputant of al-Walīd b. ʿUqba, who is said to have demanded the universal conversion of his tribe. To this the disputant responded:

As for those who were appointed chiefs of their clans according to the treaty made with Saʿd [b. Abī Waqqāṣ], as well as those who have accepted him [the chief], for them you have the right to demand it [conversion]. But as for those over whom no chief was

159 Al-Ṭabarī, *Ta'rīkh*, I, pp. 2508f.; cf. al-Balādhurī, *Futūḥ*, p. 164; al-Masʿūdī, *Kitāb al-Tanbīh wa'l-ishrāf* (Leiden, 1894; Bibliotheca Geographorum Arabicorum 8), p. 206. On borders, see W. Kaegi, 'Reconceptualizing Byzantium's eastern frontiers in the seventh century', in R. W. Mathisen and H. S. Sivan, eds., *Shifting Frontiers in Late Antiquity* (Aldershot, 1996), p. 86 ('The term blurring, instead of fluidity, best describes what happened to the notion of frontiers in the east during the seventh century').

160 See al-Balādhurī, *Futūḥ*, p. 178; I follow Landau-Tasseron's reading in her review of Donner (cited above, note 80), p. 504; cf. Donner, *Conquests*, p. 248. This and related passages are also discussed in C. F. Robinson, 'Tribes and nomads in early Islamic northern Mesopotamia', in K. Bartl and S. R. Hauser, eds., *Continuity and Change in Northern Mesopotamia from the Hellenistic to the Early Islamic Period* (Berlin, 1996), pp. 431ff. That we hear so little of rural banditry probably says more about the concerns of the historians than it does the experience of those living in the north; cf. B. Isaac, *The Limits of Empire: The Roman Army in the East* (Oxford, 1990), p. 98.

161 We shall see precisely this in the Marwānid period.

162 The Taghlib are said to have been the 'fiercest people in the Jāhiliyya' and 'had Islam delayed even slightly, the Taghlib would have eaten everybody up'; see al-Khaṭīb al-Tibrīzī's commentary on the *muʿallaqa* of ʿAmr b. Kulthūm, *Sharḥ al-qaṣā'id al-ʿashr* (Aleppo, 1969), pp. 317f. There is still much to learn from H. Lammens, 'Le Chantre des Omiades', *JA* 9/4 (1894), pp. 94–176, 193–241 and 381–459.

163 Thus the caliph al-Walīd lectures a Taghlibī chief: 'As chief of the Arabs (*ṭayyāyē*), you disgrace all of them in worshipping the cross. Do what I want and convert'; see Michael the Syrian, *Chronique*, xi.xvii; Bar Hebraeus, *Chronicon syriacum*, p. 115 (=Budge, *Chronography*, p. 106).

appointed, and who did not follow those appointed, what is your claim on them [that is, how can you demand their conversion]?[164]

The argument was seen to be persuasive, the caliph ʿUmar instructing his governor that the right to demand conversion was limited to the Arabs of the Arabian Peninsula; the Taghlib could retain their Christianity, provided that they refrained from christening their children and paid a double *ṣadaqa* (rather than the ignominious *jizya*). Now we know that Taghlibī Christianity survived the first century of Islam,[165] and the northern Syrian Tanūkh also remained Christian, at least until the early Abbasid period;[166] on the other hand, we also know that some Taghlibī chiefs did convert, emigrating to Iraq, and that these had been given authority over non-Taghlibīs, i.e. Namir and Iyādī tribesmen.[167] In the short and long term, the caliphs' success vis-à-vis the pastoralists remained mixed, and this because the projection of power on the steppe always remained problematic. Although the sources adduce ʿUmar's concession of double *ṣadaqa* as evidence for his far-sighted and benign rule, it more clearly reflects the élite's understanding of the pastoralists' power on the steppe, and the good wisdom of bargaining and co-opting.[168]

What is particularly significant for this early period is thus the caliphs' attention to the region's Arab pastoralists, particularly when compared to their indifference to settled affairs. Indeed, it is apparently in this period that the tripartite administrative geography of the north emerged, each of the three regions (Diyār Rabīʿa, Diyār Bakr and Diyār Muḍar) taking its name from the settlement of Arab tribes. The geography of the north had earlier echoed its pastoral populations,[169] but the division is altogether striking, and reflects the tribal character of social power. One can plausibly argue that the *ajnād* of early Islamic Syria were modelled directly upon Heraclius' (or in any event Byzantine) military districts,[170] and that the Islamic province of Mosul was

[164] Al-Ṭabarī, *Taʾrīkh*, I, p. 2509.

[165] The perseverance of Taghlibī Christianity is signalled on the one hand by the Islamic tradition (for an overview, see Noth, 'Verträge', pp. 306ff.), and on the other by the Syriac ecclesiatical literature, which lists bishops over the Taghlib as late as the tenth century; see Michael the Syrian, *Chronique* III, pp. 450–82 (appendix iii); see also E. Honigmann, *Le Couvent de Barṣaumā et le patriarcat jacobite d'Antioche et de Syrie* (Louvain, 1954; *CSCO* 146), pp. 148f.

[166] Who are said to have converted during the reign of al-Mahdī; see Michael the Syrian, *Chronique*, xii.i (which is probably based on the near contemporaneous testimony of Dionysius of Tell Maḥrē). This report is corroborated by an inscription in Eshnesh on the Upper Euphrates (Palmer, *Seventh Century*, p. 71).

[167] Al-Ṭabarī, *Taʾrīkh*, I, p. 2482.

[168] See al-Ṭabarī, *Taʾrīkh*, I, pp. 2508f.; Abū ʿUbayd, *Kitāb al-Amwāl*, pp. 37ff.; Ibn Zanjawayh, *Kitāb al-Amwāl*, pp. 125ff. On ʿUmar and the Taghlib, see also S. Bashear, *Arabs and Others in Early Islam* (Princeton, 1997), pp. 28f.

[169] Namely ʿArab, Bēt ʿArabāyē, ʿArbāyestān; for a discussion and bibliography, see Posner, 'Muslim Conquest', pp. 96ff.

[170] For the most recent installments in what has become a protracted debate, see now J.F. Haldon, 'Seventh-century continuities: the *Ajnād* and the "Thematic Myth"', in Cameron, ed., *The Byzantine and Early Islamic Near East III: States, Resources and Armies*, pp. 379–423; and R.-J. Lilie, 'Araber und Themen. Zum Einfluß der arabischen Expansion auf die byzantinische Militärorganisation,' in *ibid.*, pp. 425–60.

modelled on the late Sasanian Nōdh Ardashīragān;[171] but it would be nonsense to explain the two *diyār*s of Bakr and Muḍar with reference to the Byzantine provinces of Osrhoene and Euphratensis. In this and other respects, the Muslims were building a tradition of rule from scratch. Heidemann has shown that when centrally organised minting finally did come to the north, it owed nothing to Byzantine precedents.[172]

Such as it was, Jaziran politics was thus thoroughly and exclusively tribal throughout the Sufyānid period; two generations would pass before the caliphs decided that the Syro-Mesopotamian steppe could be transformed from a theatre of tribal drama into a revenue-producing province of an empire. It is for this reason that early Muslims paid scant attention to the imperial legacy on offer in cities such as Edessa and Nisibis, for which the *mdabbrānē* could have functioned as the principal conduit; it is also for this reason that the latent potential for self-government by city élites in the Byzantine east was temporarily actualised in the form of the *mdabbrānē*.

[171] See Gyselen, *La géographie administrative*, pp. 78f.

[172] Heidemann, 'Merger', p. 99.

THREE

From garrison to city: the birth of Mosul

If the province of al-Jazīra was invented by the Marwānids, the city of Mosul emerged during the second half of the seventh century, its shallow roots lying in the late Sasanian period. And if the story of al-Jazīra is one of local autonomy within a Sufyānid sphere of influence, that of Mosul is the Marwānid appropriation of a Kufan preserve, the transformation of garrison to city, and the emergence of a city élite. Building, investment, patronage and politics became intertwined in the first decades of the eighth century, as the Marwānid family – outsiders here as much as the Turks were in Ayyubid and Mamluk Cairo – imposed a new social order on the city, building it, quite literally, from the ground up. Unlike the contested Jaziran steppe, early Marwānid Mosul seems to illustrate the maxim that 'over the long run and at a distance, cities and states have proved indispensable to each other';[1] but later Marwānid Mosul suggests that already in the eighth century rulers needed the city more than the city needed rulers.[2] Politics and building being so intimately linked, we can begin by describing the birth of the city.[3]

The origins of Mosul were initially described in Syriac for hagiographic purposes. The fullest account concerns a holy man named Īshōʿyab (Bar Qūsrā); it survives in a mid-eleventh-century anonymous history written by a Nestorian in Christian Arabic, which is sometimes known as the *Chronicle of Siʿirt*, after the northern town of Siʿirt. The chronicler was indebted to a number of earlier sources, and the provenance of this particular account is unfortunately impossible to pin down.[4] It is all but certain, however, that

[1] C. Tilly, *Coercion, Capital, and European States: AD 990–1992* (Cambridge, MA and Oxford, 1990), p. 2; see also pp. 51ff.

[2] I borrow the phrase from R. Bulliet, *The Patricians of Nishapur* (Cambridge, MA, 1972), p. 61.

[3] The following is not intended as a detailed reconstruction of the seventh- and early eighth-century city, a project that demands much more space, in addition to an intimate knowledge of local topography, neither of which I enjoy; for one recent attempt, see A. M. A. al-Salmān, *al-Mawṣil fī al-ʿahdayn al-rāshidī wa'l-umawī* (Mosul, 1985), pp. 55ff. Here I intend primarily to outline the social context in which local power was rooted, and in which local politics was conducted.

[4] A strong candidate is the four-part ecclesiastical history written by Daniel Bar Maryam, whose mid-seventh century *floruit* would put him within oral transmission of the events (so A. Baumstark, *Geschichte der syrischen Literatur* (Bonn, 1922), p. 207); but cf. E. Degen, 'Die Kirchengeschichte des Daniel Bar Maryam – eine Quelle der Chronik von Seʿert?', *ZDMG*

another version, preserved in the Christian Arabic history conventionally attributed to Mārī b. Sulaymān, is drawn directly from our Nestorian source.[5] Meanwhile, the only surviving Syriac account, which was set down by Īshōʿdnaḥ of Basra (writing after 849–50), is so frustratingly telescoped that identifying its provenance is even more difficult;[6] but since its source (or sources) does not appear to lie behind the version preserved by our Nestorian chronicler, it can shed some more dim light on the legend.

The Nestorian chronicle reads as follows:

It is said that he [Mār Īshōʿyab] once came upon shepherds eating meat. They invited him to eat with them, and despite the vow [of vegetarianism],[7] he agreed, eating three mouthfuls. So the monks who were with him repudiated (*ankara*) him,[8] and he shrank in their estimation (*ṣaghara fī ʿaynihim*) because of what he had done. Desiring to cross from Nineveh to the small garden (*al-junayna*), he drew a cross on the water, spread his cloak and sat down [on it]. He took the monks who had repudiated him because of [his] eating of the meat, sat them down on the cloak, and they crossed the water as if on land. The guards (*al-ḥurrās*), who were on the city's gate, saw him and thought him some kind of divine apparition (*fa-taṣawwarūhu ilāhan*). He then built near the [present-day?] city (*madīna*) a great church (*haykal ʿaẓīm*) to which two pious monks came to live with him.[9] At this time there was no [other] building facing (*bi-izāʾ*) the small garden. When Khusraw II came to rule, he built around the small garden a great structure (*bināʾ kathīr*) and people inhabited it.

We subsequently learn that buildings adjacent to this complex served as a refuge for neighbouring villagers during Arab raids, and that when the Muslims settled the area they expanded on the building done by Khusraw II, naming the site 'al-Mawṣil'. Only then, according to our source, did the settlement become a true city.[10]

The account enjoys a fair measure of verisimilitude. Monasticism was flourishing in the Sasanian north-west during the sixth and seventh centuries;

Footnote 4 (*cont.*)
Supplementa I (1969), 2, pp. 511–16 (which questions how important Daniel actually was to the anonymous chronicler). See, in general, L. Sako, 'Les Sources de la chronique de Séert', *Parole de l'Orient* 14 (1987), pp. 155–66.

5 Mārī b. Sulaymān, *Kitāb al-Majdal*, p. 55; see also Thomas of Marga, *Governors*, pp. 67/120, esp. note 2.

6 Īshōʿdnaḥ, *Le Livre de la Chasteté*, ed. and trans. J.-B. Chabot (Rome, 1896; Mélanges d'Archéologie et d'Histoire 16 (1896)), pp. 32/28. On Īshōʿdnaḥ, see Baumstark, *Geschichte*, p. 234; and J. M. Fiey, 'Îšôʿdnaḥ métropolite de Basra, et son oeuvre', *L'Orient Syrien* 11 (1966), pp. 435ff.

7 (*Bi-sabab al-yamīn*). The ninth-century Nestorian Īshōʿ Bar Nūn is said to have remarked that 'if a monk eats meat he is in a sin near to [that of] fornication'; see Vööbus, ed., *Documents*, p. 203. Mārī b. Sulaymān does not include the passage.

8 According to Mārī b. Sulaymān's version, the two monks were eating with the shepherds.

9 (*Rāhibān fāḍilān*); on plurals and duals in (south Palestinian) Christian Arabic (in this case, *ruhbān*), see J. Blau, *A Grammar of Christian Arabic* (Louvain, 1966; *CSCO* 267), p. 209. Cf. a slightly different account in the *Livre de la chasteté*, pp. 32/28.

10 See the *Histoire nestorienne* ii (1), ed. and trans. A. Scher in PO 7 (1911), pp. 199f. Local tradition in the nineteenth century also attributed the name 'al-Mawṣil' to the conquering Arabs; see G. P. Badger, *The Nestorians and their Rituals* (London, 1852) I, p. 77.

source after hagiographic source recounts monastic foundations in the north in this period. Among the most celebrated was that of Bēt ʿAbē, which was founded around 595 in the region of Margā; home at one point to as many as 300 men, it too was surrounded by a number of smaller buildings.[11] Mār Elīyā is said to have built a monastery to the south of Īshōʿyab's site.[12] Qaṣr Serīj was founded around 565 by the Monophysite bishop Aḥūdemmeh, approximately 60 kilometres north-west of Mosul; and there Khusraw II is said to have had a hand in its development as well, restoring the monastery after it had been torched by Nestorians.[14] Enclosing a monastery with defensive walls was hardly unique to Mār Īshōʿyab; John of Ephesus, for example, speaks of a monastery enclosure (*ṭīrā d-dayrā*), behind which one fled from attacking Arabs.[14] In other respects too the passage is a perfectly ordinary example of Syriac monastic hagiography. Thus it possesses many of the standard *topoi*, those '*coups de théâtre*',[15] that illustrated the power of the holy man:[16] breaking the ascetic vow of vegetarianism,[17] walking on water[18] and, shortly afterwards, the miraculous paralysis that strikes the arm of an attacking Arab.[19]

What poses the thorniest problem for reconstructing Mosul's origins is the hagiographical imperative that the holy man abandon the civilised world for the uncivilised,[20] perhaps reinforced by a lingering taboo against the construction

[11] See Thomas of Marga, *Governors*, I, p. xlvii; Rabban Hormizd, *Rabban Hôrmîzd and Rabban Bar 'Idtâ*, II, p. 64, note 1; Hoffmann, *Auszüge*, pp. 226f.; Fiey, *Assyrie Chrétienne*, I, pp. 236ff. This appears to have been a large monastery, but not exceptionally so (cf. Witakowski, *Pseudo-Dionysius of Tel-Maḥrē*, p. 52).

[12] *Khuzistan Chronicle*, pp. 23f./21 (Nöldeke, 'Die von Guidi herausgegebene syrische Chronik', p. 22); Thomas of Marga, *Governors*, pp. 28/50f.; Fiey, *Assyrie chrétienne*, II, pp. 639ff.

[13] For the archaeology and identification of the site, see D. Oates, *Studies in the Ancient History of Northern Iraq* (London, 1968), pp. 106ff.; St J. Simpson, 'Aspects of the Archaeology of the Sasanian Period in Mesopotamia', D.Phil. thesis (Oxford, 1992), pp. 113 and 495.

[14] John of Ephesus, *Lives of the Eastern Saints*, I, ed. and trans. E. W. Brooks in *PO* 17 (1923), pp. 40 and 81; see also the *Life* of Simeon in Dolabani, *Maktabzabnē*, p. 130.

[15] The term is P. Brown's, 'The rise and function of the holy man in Late Antiquity', *Journal of Roman Studies* 61 (1971), p. 81; the article is republished in his *Society and the Holy in Late Antiquity* (Berkeley, 1982).

[16] This is not to say that the hagiographic literature does not occasionally betray historiographic sophistication; see, in particular, Thomas of Marga's care in dating an event in his *Governors*, pp. 46f/80.

[17] See the extract from the *Life* of Abraham in S. P. Brock and S. A. Harvey, *Holy Women of the Syrian Orient* (Los Angeles and London, 1987), p. 33.

[18] For more crossings of the Tigris, see the *Life* of Sabrīshōʿ in Mingana, *Sources Syriaques* (Mosul, 1907), pp. 197/246; the *Life* of Samuel in Palmer, *Monk and Mason*, microfilm 1, fol. XXII; Rabban Hormizd, *Rabban Hôrmîzd and Rabban Bar 'Idtâ*, pp. 100/149 and 104/154; Thomas of Marga, *Governors*, pp. 250/465 and 315ff./515ff.; and the summary of the *Life* of John the Arab in S. P. Brock, 'Notes on some monasteries on Mount Izla', *Abr-Nahrain* 19 (1980/1), p. 9, with note 35 (where even more examples are cited).

[19] See John Moschus, *Le Pré Spirituel*, trans. M.-J. R. de Journel (Paris, 1946), p. 112; John of Ephesus, *Lives of the Eastern Saints* I, p. 20; Procopius, *Wars* I.vii.5–8; and the *Life* of Gregory Dekapolites in D. J. Sahas, 'What an infidel saw that a faithful did not: Gregory Dekapolites (d. 842) and Islam', *Greek Orthodox Theological Review* 31 (1986), p. 50.

[20] Thus Thomas of Marga turns Plato into a holy man, who builds a cell 'in the heart of the wilderness, beyond the habitation of man'; see Thomas of Marga, *Governors*, pp. 298/531 (Budge's translation).

of monasteries within cities.[21] Mār Īshōʿyab, according to the *Chronicle of Siʿirt*, constructs his cell at a time in which 'there was no [other] building facing (*bi-izāʾ*) the small garden'. Little wonder then that the holy man had to cross the river so miraculously: why bother building a bridge without a settlement worth visiting on the western bank? Īshōʿdnaḥ's account expresses the same hagiographic conceit: Mār Īshōʿyab 'came to Ḥesnā ʿEbrāyē, which is Mosul, because at this time the city (*mdittā*) was not [yet] built.' But the text then reads that '[There was nothing there] except a small fort (*ḥesnānā zʿūrā*),' which forces us to emend the *Chronicle of Siʿirt*'s *al-junayna* (small garden) to *al-ḥuṣayna* (small fort),[22] and relieves us of the awkward reading, 'he then built near the [present-day?] city . . .'

Of course this adjustment merely restores an earlier reading of the text: as it happens, there was no garden on the western side of the river; Īshōʿyab's monastery was built close by a pre-existing fort of some kind. What remains unchallenged is the authors' insistence that the western bank of the Tigris was unoccupied until Mār Īshōʿyab's miraculous crossing, a point that was accepted by authorities as critical as Sarre and Herzfeld.[23] Now it is true that ruins and abandoned forts often served as sites for erecting monasteries,[24] in part because they offered building materials for recycling;[25] but it is equally true that monks did not always insist on total solitude: the walls of Nineveh came to be home to Muslim holy men and Christian monks in the early Islamic period, when we know at least part of the site was occupied.[26] The presumption must rather be that the construction of Īshōʿyab's monastery forms merely one episode in a continuous history of occupation on the western bank. Put differently, positing an unoccupied western bank may satisfy a hagiographer, but it runs counter to most historical and geographical sense.

Late Antique Nineveh, it appears, was a settlement of some note. Leaving aside the question of Nineveh's immediate fortunes after the disaster of 612

[21] It is hard to know if legislation intended to reverse the prohibition, an example of which dates to 554, was at all effective; see Chabot, ed., *Synodicon Orientale*, pp. 106f./364.

[22] Cf. Mārī b. Sulaymān, *Kitāb al-Majdal*, p. 55 (*wa-banā haykal ḥasan bi'l-ḥuṣayna*).

[23] F. Sarre and E. Herzfeld, *Archäologische Reise im Euphrat- und Tigris-gebiet* (Berlin, 1920), II, p. 208.

[24] For some examples, see A. Vööbus, *History of Asceticism in the Syrian Orient* (Louvain, 1958–88; *CSCO* 184, 197 and 500), II, pp. 164f.; the *Life* of Simeon in Dolabani, *Maktabzabnē*, p. 133; Michael the Syrian, *Chronique*, xii.vi. *Ḥadīth* not infrequently locate Christian holy men in ruins (*khirab*); see J. D. McAuliffe, *Qurʾānic Christians: an Analysis of Classical and Modern Exegesis* (Cambridge, 1991), p. 225.

[25] Cf. F. R. Trombley, 'Monastic foundations in sixth-century Anatolia and their role in the social and economic life of the countryside', *Greek Orthodox Theological Review* 30 (1985), p. 54.

[26] Thus Ḥnānīshōʿ is said to have resided in the monastery of Jonah (*dayr Yūnān*) on the western walls of Nineveh; see ʿAmr b. Mattā (attrib.), *Kitāb al-Majdal*, ed. and trans. H. Gismondi in *Maris Amri et Slibae De patriarchis nestorianorum* (Rome, 1896–9), p. 59; see also M. Canard, *Histoire de la dynastie des H'amdanides de Jazîra et de Syrie* (Algiers, 1951), p. 116. Where on the walls one Muslim ascetic (*zāhid*) built his cell is not said by al-Azdī, *Taʾrīkh*, p. 216f.; cf. Ibn Ḥawqal, *Ṣūrat al-arḍ* (Leiden, 1939; Bibliotheca Geographorum Arabicorum 2), p. 217. On the continued occupation of Nineveh, see below.

BCE,[27] one can still note that a range of material evidence betrays Parthian and Sasanian occupation on the eastern bank of the river, and this through the late sixth century; in fact, the archaeological record suggests that it was the main centre of Sasanian settlement.[28] Although the town apparently played no clear administrative role in the late Sasanian period,[29] it was home to Christian and Jewish communities.[30] The Islamic tradition handles the terms Nineveh and Mosul roughly, but in the legendary Ṣuhayb b. Sinān, the historical record puts an Arab (and presumably pastoral) presence in the area as well.[31] On the opposite side of the river the material evidence is even thinner, the Islamic town of Mosul having sealed evidence from earlier phases, with the possible exception of a pair of sherds and a lamp.[32]

But certainly no *cordon sanitaire* insulated the site from Nineveh. In fact, the historical record preserves a number of toponyms that signal middle to late Sasanian occupation on the western bank. It is in the nature of our evidence that the Persian toponyms are only preserved in texts dating from the Islamic period.[33] Most of these credit Ardashīr with a foundation of some

[27] Older scholarship occasionally asserted the complete end of occupation in 612, which is said to have forced survivors to cross over to the western bank (thus M. Streck, *Assurbanipal und die letzten assyrischen Könige bis zum Untergange Nineveh's* (Leipzig, 1916)); but the site was not entirely depopulated and there appears to have been some cultural continuity (thus S. Dalley, 'Nineveh after 612 BCE', *Altorientalische Forschungen* 20 (1993), pp. 134–47).

[28] A. Pauly with G. Wissova, *Real-Encyclopädie der classischen Altertumswissenchaft*, Neue Bearbeitung (Stuttgart, 1894–1972), s.v. 'Ninos' cols. 641 and 642; Simpson, 'Aspects', p. 136 where the material evidence is surveyed and Nineveh called the region's 'main Sasanian settlement'; see also pp. 488 and 556; and St J. Simpson, 'From Tekrit to the Jaghjagh: Sasanian sites, settlement patterns and material culture in northern Mesopotamia', in Bartl and Hauser, eds., *Continuity and Change*, pp. 95ff.

[29] Gyselen (*La Géographie administrative*, p. 78) notes tentatively that 'Le Nōd-Ardaxšīragān du VIe siècle serait concentré alors autour de la ville moderne de Mossoul'; cf. Morony, *Iraq*, p. 136.

[30] Bishops from Nineveh are mentioned in the synods of 554, 576, and 585, and are attested through the seventh century; see Chabot, ed., *Synodicon Orientale*, p. 678; and for an overview with further bibliography, J. M. Fiey, *Pour un Oriens Christianus Novus: Répertoire des diocèses syriaques orientaux et occidentaux* (Beirut, 1993), pp. 115f. Evidence for Jews in Nineveh is sparse, but still adequate; see A. Oppenheimer, *Babylonia Judaica in the Talmudic Period* (Wiesbaden, 1983), pp. 313f.; and J. B. Segal, 'The Jews of North Mesopotamia before the rise of Islam', in G. M. Grintez and J. Liver, eds., *Sefer Segal: Studies in the Bible Presented to Professor M. H. Segal by his Colleagues and Friends* (Jerusalem, 1964), p. 37.

[31] Information on Ṣuhayb survived because of his piety and his status as the first 'Byzantine' (Rūmī) to convert. See al-Balādhurī, *Ansab al-ashrāf*, I (Cairo, 1959), pp. 180ff.; Ibn Saʿd, *Kitāb al-Ṭabaqāt*, III[1], pp. 161ff.; Ibn Qutayba, *al-Maʿārif* (Cairo, 1981), pp. 264f.; Abū Nuʿaym al-Iṣfahānī, *Ḥilyat al-awliyā'* (Cairo, 1938), I, pp. 151ff. For other sources, see I. Goldziher, *Muslim Studies*. trans. C. R. Barber and S. M. Stern (London, 1967), I, p. 128 note 7.

[32] Simpson, 'From Tekrit', p. 95, note 22 (sherds purportedly found at Bāsh Ṭābiya, which is located at the northernmost part of the medieval walls, near the river, and which was the site for al-Dayr al-Aʿlā; see A. Rücker, 'Das "Obere Kloster" bei Mossul und seine Bedeutung für die Geschichte der ostsyrischen Liturgie', *Oriens Christianus* 3rd ser., 7 (1932), pp. 186f.; Sarre and Herzfeld, *Reise*, II, p. 291; Canard, *Dynastie*, p. 119; and Fiey, *Mossoul*, p. 12 (lamp of unknown provenance).

[33] The best summary of this issue is J. M. Fiey, 'Mossoul d'avant 1915', *Sumer* 2 (1946), pp. 38f. See also Fiey, *Mossoul*, pp. 12f.; Sarre and Herzfeld, *Reise*, II, p. 208; E. Reitemeyer, *Die Städtegründungen der Araber im Islām nach den arabischen Historikern und Geographen* (Munich, 1912), p. 81.

kind,[34] while one suggests Qawād, who is said to have been an active builder in the north.[35] Although one might take some of these toponyms to refer to the region of Mosul,[36] at least one (Nōdh Ardashīr) appears to have been the name given to part of the nineteenth-century town itself.[37] In addition to these Persian toponyms, the Syriac term Ḥesnā ʿEbrāyē ('citadel of the Jews') is mentioned in a number of sources, and although none is securely datable to the pre-conquest period, there is no sign that the term was newly coined.[38] When it is occasionally located in Nineveh, we are to understand the region of Nineveh in its broadest sense,[39] for Ḥesnā ʿEbrāyē was clearly on the western side of the river,[40] and almost certainly refers to the *madīna* mentioned in Īshōʿdnaḥ's account, as well as the *ḥuṣayna* and *madīna* of our Nestorian chronicle.[41] One must therefore reject Honigmann's view that it designated Īshōʿyab's new building(s).[42] Daywahchjī and Fiey call this an abandoned Assyrian fort,[43] which the former locates in the easternmost

34 E.g. 'Būdh [read: Nōdh] Ardashīr'; see Ibn Khurdādhbih, *Kitāb al-Masālik wa'l-mamālik* (Leiden, 1889; Bibliotheca Geographorum Arabicorum 6), p. 17; Yāqūt, *Muʿjam al-buldān* (Leipzig, 1866–73), IV, p. 683; cf. Ḥamza al-Iṣfahānī, *Kitāb Ta'rīkh sinī mulūk al-arḍ wa'l-anbiyā'* (Petropoli, 1844), pp. 46f. G. Le Strange's suggestion that the 'Būdh' is 'undoubtedly a clerical error' (*The Lands of the Eastern Caliphate* (Cambridge, 1905), p. 87), is confirmed by Gyselen, *La Géographie administrative*, p. 56, note 134. For 'Khurrazād Ardashīr', see al-Dīnawarī, *Akhbār*, p. 47; and Yāqūt, *Muʿjam*, II, p. 422. According to al-Muqaddasī (*Aḥsan al-taqāsīm*, pp. 138f.), the pre-Islamic site was called 'Khawlān'.

35 Namely, 'Bih Hormuz Qawādh' (Hoffmann, *Auszüge*, p. 178, citing Bar Bahlūl, in Duval, ed., *Lexicon*, II, c. 943). This is one of the earliest attestations of the city's nickname *al-ḥadbā'*, and, if Hoffmann is correct that the passage derives from Dionysius of Tell Maḥrē, the earliest. According to the *Histoire nestorienne* II (1), p. 125, Qawād built extensively in Mosul and Iraq, transferred populations there, and had them work the land.

36 See, for example, al-Ṭabarī, *Ta'rīkh*, I, p. 820.

37 See the map drawn by Felix Jones in 1852, which is reproduced in, *inter alia*, J. M. Russell, *Sennacherib's Palace without Rival at Nineveh* (Chicago, 1991), p. 2.

38 See the dialogue included in Narsai, *Homiliae et carmina*, ed. A. Mingana (Mosul, 1905), II, p. 410 (glossed by Mingana in note b as an early name for Mosul); the history dubiously attributed to Mshīḥāzkā (*fl.* mid sixth century) and also edited by Mingana, *Sources*, pp. 11/87 (where it appears as a well-known landmark); and finally the *Khuzistan Chronicle* (written c. 660–80), pp. 23f./21.

39 Thus Thomas of Marga, *Governors*, pp. 198/386 (where one should translate 'by', rather than Budge's 'in').

40 Budge's speculation that it lay in Nineveh (Thomas of Marga, *Governors*, II, p. 337, note 2) cannot survive the explicit testimony of the text he himself edited (*Governors*, pp. 248/461, with note 2).

41 Here, as so frequently elsewhere, *madīna* says much less about size and population than it does about the presence of fortifications of some kind; it simply means 'fort'. As Sourdel-Thomine has noted, al-Harawī calls the ruined fort of Dārā a *madīna*; see his *Kitāb al-Ishārāt ilā maʿrifat al-ziyārāt*, trans. J. Sourdel-Thomine as *Guide des lieux de pèlerinage* (Damascus, 1957), p. 143. Cf. C. Foss's comments in his 'Archaeology and the "Twenty Cities" in Byzantine Asia', *American Journal of Archaeology* 81 (1977), p. 470; and the confusion of the ninth-century monk Cogitosus, who called a 'typical, near-circular, Irish monastery' nothing less than a city (thus R. Hodges and D. Whitehouse, *Mohammed, Charlemagne and the Origins of Europe* (Ithaca, 1989), pp. 84f.).

42 See *EI*, p. 609 (Honigmann); and *EI*², p. 899 (Honigmann, updated by Bosworth).

43 Fiey, *Mossoul*, p. 11. *Pace* S. Ṣā'igh (*Ta'rīkh al-Mawṣil* [Cairo, 1923], I, p. 40), the ruins described by Xenophon are those of Nineveh; the account sheds no light on the western side of the river.

quarter of the medieval city, called *al-qulayʿāt*;[44] the location is entirely plausible, but in the absence of corroborating archaeology, there is no way of knowing.

The conquest tradition also refers to a fort. That this was the most salient feature on the western bank in the early seventh century is suggested by the Arabic toponym used in the conquest account attributed to Sayf b. ʿUmar, al-Ḥiṣnān ('the Two Forts'),[45] and also by one of the accounts preserved by al-Balādhurī, according to which ʿUtba b. Farqad crossed over to 'the eastern fort'.[46] Echoes of early history seem to have survived; and thanks to another invaluable account preserved by al-Balādhurī, we can relate one of these forts to the newly built complex: al-Balādhurī's informant reports that when ʿArfaja b. Harthama succeeded ʿUtba b. Farqad as governor of Mosul, it consisted of 'the fort (*al-ḥiṣn*), chapels (*biyaʿ*) for the Christians [read: monks] – their cells were few in number in those chapels – and a Jewish area'.[47] One presumes that this *ḥiṣn* refers to Ḥesnā ʿEbrāyē. One can only speculate about the second fort, candidates being one of the two great mounds of Nineveh, Kuyunjik (the 'core mound' of the ancient city's remains) and Nebi Yunus, where Assyrian structures are also concentrated,[48] or, much less probably, one of Nineveh's gates along the Tigris or Khawṣar.[49] Of 'al-Ḥiṣnān' nothing more is heard after the conquests; it may not have been a local toponym at all, but rather a term used by the conquering tribesmen from the south.

The term 'al-Mawṣil' seems to have entered general currency only during the seventh century; it fails to appear in any text securely datable to the pre-conquest period.[50] This said, attempts made by medieval authorities to rationalise it in Arabic terms are dubious,[51] and an argument that early Muslims

44 S. al-Daywahchjī, 'Qalʿat al-Mawṣil fī mukhtalif al-ʿuṣūr', *Sumer* 10 (1954), p. 96; Ṣā'igh, *Ta'rīkh al-Mawṣil*, I, p. 40.

45 Al-Ṭabarī, *Ta'rīkh*, I, pp. 2474f. Ibn al-Athīr, *al-Kāmil*, II, p. 524 (where *al-ḥiṣn al-sharqī* is glossed as Nineveh, and *al-ḥiṣn al-gharbī* as Mosul); cf. al-Bakrī, *Muʿjam*, pp. 71 and 341.

46 Al-Balādhurī, *Futūḥ*, p. 331; cf. Khalīfa b. Khayyāṭ, *Ta'rīkh*, p. 77 (where ʿIyāḍ b. Ghanm, having conquered Mosul, puts ʿUtba in charge of one of its two *ḥiṣns*).

47 Al-Balādhurī, *Futūḥ*, p. 332; cf. the account in Īshōʿdnaḥ, *Le Livre de la Chasteté*, pp. 32/28.

48 The case for the first would be based on the site's well-attested post-Assyrian occupation (see D. Stronach and S. Lumsden, 'UC Berkeley's excavations at Nineveh', *Biblical Archaeologist* 55 (1992), p. 229; and S. Lumsden, 'Urban Nineveh', *Mār Šipri* 4 (1991), p. 3), in addition to the much later evidence that a *ḥesnā d-Nīnawā* sat atop it (see the references cited by Budge in Thomas of Marga, *Governors* II, p. 337, note 2; and the map executed by Jones). The case for the second would be based on al-Muqaddasī's note of a fort atop *madīnat Yūnus b. Mattā* (*Aḥsan al-taqāsīm*, p. 139); see also Oppenheimer, *Babylonia Judaica*, p. 313. It is presumably these two fortifications that one poet had in mind; see Yāqūt, *Muʿjam*, IV, p. 870. Cf. the *Chronicle of 1234*, I, pp. 321/251.

49 For a recent survey of the archaeology, and also a clear map, see M. L. Scott and J. MacGinnis, 'Notes on Nineveh', *Iraq* 52 (1990), pp. 63–73.

50 The toponym does appear in the Nestorian synod of 410 (Chabot, ed., *Synodicon Orientale*, pp. 616ff.), but this in a late thirteenth- or early fourteenth-century redaction, whose author, according to Chabot, 'a notablement modifié le texte pour l'accommoder à la discipline de son époque'.

51 Yāqūt (*Muʿjam*, IV, p. 683) provides no fewer than four aetiologies; see also Ibn al-Faqīh, *Kitāb al-Buldān*, p. 128; and al-Azdī, *Ta'rīkh*, p. 226. The caliph al-Rāḍī derided Mosul by glossing its name as *muwāṣilat al-ḥuzn*; see al-Ṣūlī, *Akhbâr ar-Râdî billâh*, trans. M. Canard (Algiers, 1946), I, p. 237.

Arabised (and thus Islamicised) a pre-existing Aramaic term is attractive,[52] particularly since they were not building *de novo*. Such an argument would rest precariously on the term's appearance in three seventh-century texts that may reflect pre-Islamic usage: the Armenian geography of Ananias of Shirak, which Hewsen argues was written before 636;[53] the Syriac *Khuzistan Chronicle*, whose author elsewhere draws attention to the Muslims' practice of founding – and naming – new cities;[54] and finally, the early Abbasid recension of the Pahlavi text published by Markwart,[55] which includes at least one section that apparently dates from the period of the Sasanian occupation of the west.[56] What is clearer is that Ḥesnā ʿEbrāyē – the one toponym we can be sure was used locally – remained in usage well into the Islamic period. Although Īshōʿdnaḥ simply glossed the term as 'al-Mawṣil', several passages in Thomas of Marga's *Governors* suggest that by his time (the middle of the ninth century) the term had come to identify only a part of the city, perhaps something akin to an 'old Mosul' around which the Islamic city grew, and in which the Christian population remained concentrated.[57] The term may have remained in use as late as the thirteenth century.[58]

A tentative reconstruction of the late sixth- and early seventh-century site is thus as follows. According to the material and historical record, Nineveh was the local focus of settlement during much – if not all – of the Sasanian period;[59] there was some settlement on the western side of the river, but it was thinner, and located on or near fortifications of unknown provenance. Although Sasanian interest in the site may have developed as early as the third century, it only becomes clear during the reign of Khusraw II; and the erection of walls around the nascent monastery complex credited to Īshōʿyab fits a late Sasanian pattern discerned by Wilkinson and Tucker, who see the appearance of walled enclosures and fortlets as a 'conspicuous feature' of the period.[60] Here, where the walls are explicitly said to have been erected as

[52] See Pauly/Wissova, *Real-Encyclopädie der classischen Altertumswissenschaft* L (1932), p. 1164 (which corrects Sarre and Herzfeld, *Reise*, II, p. 207); and Streck, *Assurbanipal und die letzten assyrischen Könige*, I, p. cdxxvi.

[53] See Hewsen, *The Geography of Ananias of Širak*, p. 74a ('the thirty-sixth [country of Asia], *Aruastan*, which is called Assyria, i.e. *Muçl*, is east of Mesopotamia and borders Armenia. It has mountains, rivers and the city of Nineveh'). See also J. Marquart (Markwart), *Ērānšahr nach der Geographie des ps.-Moses Xorenaci* (Berlin, 1901), p. 142.

[54] See the *Khuzistan Chronicle*, pp. 36/30; and Nöldeke, 'Die von Guidi herausgegebene syrische Chronik', p. 20.

[55] Markwart, *Catalogue*, p. 16.

[56] Markwart, *Catalogue*, pp. 82f.; Morony, *Iraq*, p. 128.

[57] Īshōʿdnaḥ, *Le Livre de la Chasteté*, pp. 32/28; Thomas of Marga, *Governors*, index, esp. pp. 248/461 with note 2.

[58] For a manuscript copied in Mār Mīkhāʾīl in Ḥesnā ʿEbrāyē in 1206–7, see R. Gottheil's note 'On a Syriac manuscript of the New Testament belonging to the Rev. Mr Neesan', *JAOS* 13 (1889), pp. clxxxi–clxxxiii (my gratitude to S. P. Brock for this reference).

[59] It is Nineveh, rather than a proto-Mosul, that figures in Heraclius' campaign against the Sasanians in 625; see, for example, Theophanes, *Chronicle*, AM 6118.

[60] T. J. Wilkinson and D. J. Tucker, *Settlement Development in the North Jazira, Iraq* (Warminster, 1995), pp. 70f.; for a map of the area surveyed – west of Balad (Eski Mosul) – see p. 147.

shelter against local Arab raiders, one is given to believe that the fort served primarily as a refuge from, and perhaps too as a base for military action against, pastoralist raiders;[61] for those looking for Sasanian *limes*,[62] the fort might be construed as a terminus on the Tigris. In either case, the site's military potential would have been plain to the Muslims who came to conquer it, and so too its geographical advantages: what the Muslims found was not only a modest fort, but one that commanded both the Tigris *and* the desert corridor between the river and Jabal Sinjār.

How this modest clustering of settlement on the western side of the river fits into a broader, regional pattern of settlement is hard to discern. Ripples of the Late Antique expansion of settlement so well attested in the eastern Mediterranean may have crossed the Euphrates into the western and central Jazira;[63] while the late Sasanian expansion of settlement in Iraq may have reached from the Gulf as far north as the Diyālā.[64] Against this tentative pattern of settlement expansion contrast the results of Wilkinson and Tucker's north Jazira survey, which suggest a steady decline in the number of settlements in the Roman/Parthian and Sasanian/early Islamic periods.[65] Other survey work in the north shows a similar decline in the Roman/Parthian period, with some very modest recovery in the Sasanian;[66] between the two Zābs, in al-ʿAqr/Assur, it was only in the early Islamic period that the site

[61] On 'waste' material associated with an expansion of pastoralism in this period, see Wilkinson and Tucker, *Settlement Development*, p. 70; on the various functions of forts, see Isaac, *The Limits of Empire*, p. 254f. Of course the foundation story of Mosul itself mentions Arab raids.

[62] On the fraught question of Sasanian *limes* in the north, see Wilkinson and Tucker, *Settlement development*, p. 71; A. Northedge, A. Bamber, and M. Roaf, *Excavations at ʿAna* (Warminster, 1988), p. 8; Howard-Johnston, 'Two great powers', pp. 189f.; Isaac, *The Limits of Empire*, pp. 255ff.; and for the Roman lines that might have served as a foundation from Sinjār to Balad, S. Gregory and D. Kennedy, eds., *Sir Aurel Stein's Limes Report* (Oxford, 1985), I, chapters 1–3 (on Sinjār to Balad *limes*).

[63] The evidence being as sparse as it is mixed, it is premature to reach conclusions about the area as a whole. The case is fairly strong for the region of Edessa (thus T. J. Wilkinson, *Town and Country in Southeastern Anatolia* (Chicago, 1990), pp. 117ff., which also guardedly argues for a dramatic contraction of settlement in the early Islamic period), but much less so for the Khābūr: cf. W. Röllig and H. Kühne, 'The lower Habur: second preliminary report on a survey in 1977', *Les Annales Archéologiques Arabes Syriennes* 33 (1983), pp. 187–99, with B. Lyonnet, 'Settlement pattern in the Upper Khabur (N.E. Syria) from the Achaemenids to the Abbasid period: methods and preliminary results from a survey', in Bartl and Hauser, eds., *Continuity and Change*, pp. 351ff. For continued settlement in Tell Tuneinir, see M. Fuller and N. Fuller, 'Continuity and change in the Syriac population at Tell Tuneinir, Syria', *Aram* 6 (1994), pp. 259–77 (with further bibliography for the Khābūr).

[64] On the Diyālā region, see R. M. Adams, *Land behind Baghdad: A History of Settlement on the Diyala Plains* (Chicago, 1965); and on Susiana, R. J. Wenke, 'Western Iran in the Partho-Sasanian period: the imperial transformation', in F. Hole, ed., *The Archaeology of Western Iran: Settlement and Society from Prehistory to the Islamic Conquest* (Washington, DC, 1987), pp. 257f. (I am indebted to J. Johns for the latter).

[65] Wilkinson and Tucker, *Settlement Development*, p. 71; see also Simpson, 'From Tekrit', esp. pp. 91 and 99 (perhaps some late Sasanian recovery).

[66] W. Ball, 'The Upper Tigris area: new evidence from the Eski Mosul and North Jazira projects', in Bartl and Hauser, eds., *Continuity and Change*, pp. 417ff. Cf. J. K. Ibrahim, *Pre-Islamic Settlement in Jazirah* (Baghdad, 1986), pp. 87f.

recovered from early Sasanian destruction.[67] Of course these results are very tentative, and the picture may change as more work is undertaken. At this point, however, it can still be said that insofar as large-scale development was driven by the Sasanian state,[68] or vulnerable to environmental and political crises (especially plague and imperial warfare),[69] the eastern Jazira held little promise for urbanisation.[70] What little momentum there was towards urban growth in the late Sasanian period cannot explain the growth of the eighth-century Islamic city; Marwānid politics explains it.

The post-conquest site

In the absence of good archaeological evidence, describing early Muslim settlement is almost as perilous as describing the Sasanian site. The reconstruction that follows is drawn together from stray accounts from Abbasid historians – chiefly al-Azdī – and geographers; it is also guided by the assumption that since Mosul was built by Kufans soon after they had built Kufa, its morphology may in some measure be indebted to the Kufan prototype. Such as it is, the literary evidence suggests that earliest Muslim settlement and growth were concentrated in the nascent Mosul, while Nineveh's devolution into suburb and pilgrimage centre was protracted. Jews and Christians were present on both sides of the river; mention is occasionally made of a Persian quarter in Mosul,[71] but the evidence is late and dubious.[72] It seems that Nestorians and Monophysites alike continued to build in Nineveh, a toponym that continued in use well after the foundation of Mosul;[73] it was there, according to an eleventh-century redaction of a seventh-century source, that a Jewish tailor lived.[74]

It is ʿArfaja b. Harthama, ʿUtba b. Farqad's successor, who is conventionally given credit for transforming the conquest settlement into a *miṣr*, and this apparently during the reign of ʿUthmān. According to al-Balādhurī, the

67 S. Heidemann, 'Al-ʿAqr, das islamisiche Assur: Ein Beitrag zur historischen Topographie in Nordmesopotamien', in Bartl and Hauser, eds., *Continuity and Change*, pp. 260f.; see also Miglus, *Das Wohngebiet von Assur*.
68 As argued by Howard-Johnston, 'Two great powers', pp. 198ff.
69 The classic example comes from much further west; see C. Foss, 'The Persians in Asia Minor and the end of Late Antiquity', *English Historical Review* 90 (1975), pp. 721–47. For the western Jazira, see now C. Gerber, 'Die Umgebung des Lidar Höyük von hellenistischer bis frühislamischer Zeit: Interpretation der Erbegnisse einer Geländebegehung', in Bartl and Hauser, eds., *Continuity and Change*, p. 310; and for the north-eastern Jazira, Simpson, 'From Tekrit', p. 101.
70 Cf. M. van de Mieroop, *The Ancient Mesopotamian City* (Oxford, 1997), pp. 233f.
71 S. al-Daywahchī, 'Khiṭaṭ al-Mawṣil fī al-ʿahd al-umawī', *Sumer* 7 (1951), p. 223.
72 Thus ps.-Wāqidī, *Taʾrīkh futūḥ al-Jazīra*, p. 236; al-ʿUmarī, *Munyat al-udabāʾ fī taʾrīkh al-Mawṣil al-ḥadbāʾ* (Mosul, 1955), p. 31.
73 Fiey, 'Īšōʿyaw le Grand', p. 5; Thomas of Marga, *Governors*, pp. 53/95f.
74 Rabban Hormizd, *Rabban Hôrmîzd and Rabban Bar ʿIdtâ*, pp. 172/261; Thomas of Marga, *Governors*, II, p. 337 note 2; see also Morony, *Iraq*, pp. 307f. Tenth-century Mosul was apparently home to Jewish scholars and study groups; see D. E. Sklare, *Samuel Ben Ḥofni Gaon and his Cultural World* (Leiden and New York, 1986), pp. 118ff.

tamṣīr involved settling Arabs, setting out tribal quarters, and building a congregational mosque; according to al-Azdī (as cited by Ibn al-Athīr and Ibn Ḥajar), it meant transferring and settling 4,000 tribesmen of the Azd, Ṭayyiʾ, Kinda and ʿAbd al-Qays.[75] Whatever it implies about urbanism or administration, here the term *tamṣīr* quite clearly involves establishing a permanent garrison,[76] and this is why reports also associate ʿArfaja with the site's *tajnīd*,[77] and also why it is occasionally called a *jund* rather than a *miṣr*.[78] As a garrison site, the site thus seems to have retained in some measure its pre-Islamic function; and it is tempting to speculate that such building as was undertaken in the first decades of Islamic rule was located within or near the enclosure walls built by Khusraw II. To establish pre-Marwānid walls of some kind we must rely on two relatively late sources, however. The hagiography of Rabban Hormizd mentions the 'gate of the city of Mosul' during the rule of a governor (*shallīṭā* and *amīrā*) named ʿUqba, who might be identified as ʿUtba b. Farqad, or perhaps ʿUqba b. al-Walīd.[79] The historian of Mayyāfāriqīn, Ibn al-Azraq, also remarks that al-Anṭāq's authority stretched from 'the gate of Constantinople to the gate of Mosul'.[80] Neither of these accounts is incompatible with the tradition's broad consensus that the Marwānids were the first to build Mosul's walls – that is, true circuit walls – the early tradition being interested not in urbanism as such, but rather in Islamic city building.[81]

How space was organised is also very difficult to say, particularly since the existing settlement and topography would have made it nearly impossible to import – at least wholesale – a Kufan model originally imposed on a virgin site.[82] The arrangement of the city's tribal quarters occupied al-Azdī in what appears to have been a monograph devoted to the topic,[83] some echoes of

[75] Al-Balādhurī, *Futūḥ*, p. 332; Ibn al-Athīr, *Usd al-ghāba*, III, p. 401; Ibn Ḥajar, *al-Iṣāba*, VI, p. 412 (citing al-Azdī). See also Reitemeyer, *Die Städtegründungen*, p. 81; al-Daywahchī, 'Khiṭaṭ', p. 224; Donner, *Conquests*, pp. 196f.; and K. Athamina, 'Arab settlement during the Umayyad caliphate', *JSAI* 8 (1986), pp. 191f.

[76] When Sayf b. ʿUmar describes plots laid out in Kufa for 'tribesmen manning the frontier areas and Mosul' (*ahl al-thughūr wa'l-Mawṣil*) (al-Ṭabarī, *Taʾrīkh*, I, p. 2490; see also Ibn al-Athīr, *al-Kāmil*, II, p. 530), he is describing Kufa before these changes in Mosul had taken place.

[77] Cf. the description of Muʿāwiya's transformation of Qinnasrīn from a mere *rustāq* of Ḥimṣ to a *miṣr*, effected by the garrisoning of troops (*ḥattā maṣṣarahā Muʿāwiya wa-jannadahā bi-man taraka al-Kūfa wa'l-Baṣra*) (al-Ṭabarī, *Taʾrīkh*, I, p. 2673).

[78] Thus Ibn Ḥazm, *Jamharat ansāb al-ʿarab* (Cairo, 1977), p. 367; Ibn Durayd, *Kitāb al-Ishtiqāq* (Göttingen, 1854), p. 282. See also al-Yaʿqūbī, *Taʾrīkh*, II, p. 176 (a very schematic account that identifies Mosul as a *jund*, along with Filasṭīn, al-Jazīra (!) and Qinnasrīn).

[79] Rabban Hormizd, *Rabban Hôrmîzd and Rabban Bar ʿIdtâ*, pp. 75/110.

[80] See the *Taʾrīkh Mayyāfāriqīn wa-Āmid*, MS BM OR 5803, fol. 7a.

[81] In the city of Marv, the earliest Muslim settlement was apparently intramural; there, earliest Muslim settlement within the Sasanian walls moved west into the *rabaḍ* during the Marwānid period (*EI*[2] s.v. 'Marw al-Shāhidjān').

[82] For an overview, see H. Djaït, *al-Kūfa, naissance de la ville islamique* (Paris, 1986), pp. 73ff. For a discussion of Muslim settlement in and around Syrian towns, see D. Whitcomb, 'Amṣār in Syria?: Syrian cities after the conquest', *Aram* 6 (1994), pp. 16ff.

[83] In al-Azdī's words, 'in a book [I] entitled the tribes and quarters [of Mosul]' (*fī kitābin tarjamtuhu* [or: *tarjamatuhu*] *al-qabāʾil wa'l-khiṭaṭ*); see the *Taʾrīkh*, pp. 96 and 101. Traces of the city's (presumably original) *khiṭaṭ* were discernible as late as Ibn Ḥawqal's time; see his *Ṣūrat al-arḍ*, p. 215.

which can be heard in the surviving chronicle.[84] Of the city's first congregational mosque nothing seems to remain;[85] we must wrestle with literary evidence. Al-Balādhurī's account, which features ʿArfaja b. Harthama, actually masks something of a controversy, since no less an authority than al-Azdī himself transmitted accounts that credited ʿUtba b. Farqad with building a *dār* and *masjid*.[86] This, however, is unlikely; and we should probably follow al-Balādhurī's judgement here. It is apparently this first mosque that, renovated by Marwān II and enlarged by al-Mahdī in 783–4,[87] survived well into the medieval period, coming to be called the 'old mosque' (*al-masjid al-ʿatīq*) after the construction of Nūr al-Dīn's larger mosque.[88] We also read that it lay on elevated ground, an 'arrow's shot' from the bank of the river,[89] which presumably would put it within about 500 metres of the Tigris.[90]

Thanks to one of al-Azdī's massacre reports, we also know that one of the mosque's portals 'was adjacent to the church' (*bāb al-masjid mimmā yalī al-bīʿa*).[91] This church is not given a name, but if we assume that it survived,[92] and further that Christians would not have been permitted to build immediately

[84] See, for example, the long discussion of the Azdī clan of Jābir b. Jabala in year 129 (al-Azdī, *Taʾrīkh*, pp. 77ff., in particular 101).

[85] Al-Daywahchī, ('al-Jāmiʿ al-umawī fī al-Mawṣil', *Sumer* 6 (1950), pp. 211–19; and cf. ʿUmarī, *Munyat al-udabāʾ*, p. 209) argues that the modern *jāmiʿ* al-Muṣaffī is a renovation of a mosque originally built by ʿUtba b. Farqad and expanded by ʿArfaja b. Harthama and Marwān II. No archaeological or epigraphic evidence is adduced, however; and the attribution appears more traditional than historical (see, for example, the *Guide Book to the Mosul Museum* (Baghdad, 1966), p. 8). The earliest connection between the mosque and the so-called 'broken minaret' that lies nearby appears to have been made only in the eighteenth century (see al-ʿUmarī, *Munyat al-udabāʾ*, p. 36); although Sarre and Herzfeld note some circumstantial evidence (location and scale) in favour of the antiquity of this minaret, the case collapses on stylistic grounds (*Reise*, II, p. 232). The most one can therefore say is that local tradition held this mosque to be old. Cf. G. Bell, *Amurath to Amurath* (London, 1911), p. 259.

[86] See Ibn al-Athīr, *Usd al-ghāba*, III, p. 366.

[87] See Yāqūt, *Muʿjam*, IV, p. 684 (renovation); al-Azdī, *Taʾrīkh*, p. 248 (enlargement; the author transcribes an inscription from al-Mahdī's construction).

[88] Abū Shāma, *Kitāb al-Rawḍatayn fī akhbār al-dawlatayn* (Cairo, 1287), I, pp. 29f.; al-Harawī, *Guide*, pp. 71/158 with note 3; Ibn al-Athīr, *al-Taʾrīkh al-bāhir fī al-dawla al-atābakiyya* (Cairo, 1963), pp. 31 and 77 (where the mosque now stands in abandoned land); Ibn Jubayr, *Riḥla* (Leiden and London, 1907), p. 235; cf. ʿAbd al-Munʿim al-Ḥimyarī, *al-Rawḍ al-miʿṭār*, p. 563.

[89] Al-Muqaddasī, *Aḥsan al-taqāsīm*, p. 138.

[90] Of course distance is determined by the composition of the bow and arrow, along with the skill of the archer. This distance is about the limit of the classical *ramyat sahm*; see Djaït, *al-Kūfa*, p. 92 with note 6 thereto; and J. D. Latham and W. F. Patterson, *Saracen Archery: An English Version and Exposition of a Mameluke Work on Archery (ca AD 1368)* (London, 1970), pp. 109f. (good archers putting down a barrage at 400 yards, and a world record of 972!); some seventh-century evidence suggests a shorter distance (thus A. D. H. Bivar, 'Cavalry equipment and tactics on the Euphrates frontier', *Dumbarton Oaks Papers* 26 (1972), p. 283). In any case, the layout of the Kufan mosque is probably the *locus classicus* (see al-Ṭabarī, *Taʾrīkh*, I, pp. 2488ff.)

[91] Al-Azdī, *Taʾrīkh*, p. 147 (the editor reads *bayʿa*, which makes little sense here). Early mosques were not infrequently built adjacent to – or even onto – pre-existing churches; for the Damascus example, see the third part of the (anonymous) *Kitāb al-ʿUyūn wa'l-ḥadāʾiq fī akhbār al-ḥaqāʾiq*, III, ed. M. de Goeje and P. de Jong as *Fragmenta historicorum arabicorum* (Leiden, 1869), p. 5; and, for Ḥimṣ, Ibn Ḥawqal, *Ṣūrat al-arḍ*, p. 176.

[92] The leading candidate among those churches that did not survive would be Mār Zena; see Fiey, *Mossoul*, pp. 19f.

next to the congregational mosque, only three churches fulfil the dual requirement of a seventh-century foundation (or earlier) and proximity to the river: the church of Mār Īshōʿyab, which, rebuilt and renamed, survives as that of Mār Īshaʿyā,[93] the ancient church of the Syrian Catholics,[94] and, finally and even less likely, the church of Ṭāhira/Dayr al-Aʿlā.[95] All three of these lie in the north-eastern part of the nineteenth-century old city, a location that makes reasonable the apparent western expansion of the city that began in the early eighth century.[96] In any case, by the time of the Abbasid Revolution the mosque had a minaret of some height.[97]

The presumptive *dār/qaṣr al-imāra* goes unmentioned by al-Balādhurī in his description of ʿArfaja's building, but the Kufan pattern, which we might expect to have been followed by the Kufan immigrants to Mosul, called for a *qaṣr* in the immediate vicinity of, and almost certainly attached to, the congregational mosque; one also expects that this *qaṣr* lay on the *qibla* side of the mosque.[98] Fortunately, Mosul's first *qaṣr* figures prominently in al-Azdī's entry on the year 133/750–1, and the text shows the Kufan model was indeed followed. There we read that Yaḥyā b. Muḥammad was present in the *qaṣr al-imāra*, which is described as 'attached' (*mulāṣiq*) to the congregational mosque; a page later Yaḥyā is located in the *maqṣūra*, which presumably reveals where the *qaṣr al-imāra* joined the mosque.[99] By the end of the seventh or early eighth century this *qaṣr* had a rival in al-Ḥurr b. Yūsuf's very elaborate palace, which he had erected by 725–6.[100]

In addition to the city's congregational mosque, there were other *masjids*, and many (if not all) might fairly be called tribal mosques, erected to serve the needs of a tribe and its adjacent area; here, as elsewhere, each *qawm* was to have its own place to pray.[101] A tribal quarter and mosque (*khiṭṭa* and *masjid*) located in the northern part of the town – the 'upper *rabaḍ*' of al-Azdī's day – were named after al-Qaṭirān b. Akma al-Shaybānī, who was appointed governor in 745–6. Since he came onto the scene with Shaybānīs in tow, the mosque may have have been built to serve their needs.[102] The Sulayma branch

93 Sarre and Herzfeld, *Reise*, II, p. 291; Fiey, *Mossoul*, pp. 13 and 104ff., in which this church, as well as the two that follow, are marked on the city plan.

94 Fiey, *Mossoul*, pp. 136ff.; Sarre and Herzfeld, *Reise*, II, pp. 295ff. (here mistakenly called Mār Yaʿqūb). Fiey suggests (*Mossoul*, p. 19) that this is the church to which Īshōʿyab III alludes (see Īshōʿyab III, *Liber epistularum*, pp. 82/63f.)

95 Fiey, *Mossoul*, pp. 126ff.; al-Shābushtī, *al-Diyārāt*, pp. 176ff.; al-ʿUmarī, *Masālik al-abṣār* (Cairo, 1924), I, pp. 293ff.

96 Cf. Simpson, 'From Tekrit', p. 95.

97 Al-Azdī, *Taʾrīkh*, pp. 147f., where a town crier is ordered to ascend the minaret; the account would presumably be dismissed as topological by J. Bloom, *Minaret: Symbol of Islam* (Oxford, 1989), who argues that mosques were towerless throughout the Umayyad period.

98 For a discussion and plans, see Djaït, *al-Kūfa*, pp. 91ff. Cf. the case of Marv, where Naṣr b. Sayyār is first removed from his rooms (*bayt*) to his *maqṣūra*, and then from his *maqṣūra* to the courtyard of his house (*sāḥat dārī*); see the anonymous *Akhbār al-dawla al-ʿAbbāsiyya* (Beirut, 1971), p. 310.

99 Al-Azdī, *Taʾrīkh*, pp. 145f.

100 The anecdote explaining the construction of the 'Open Canal' (see below) puts al-Ḥurr in the palace.

101 See the *ḥadīth* transmitted by Ibn ʿAbbās in al-Azdī, *Taʾrīkh*, p. 320.

102 Al-Azdī, *Taʾrīkh*, p. 68. The text reads *fī rabaḍ al-aʿlā*, which presumably alludes to the Dayr al-Aʿlā, founded sometime in the early period (Fiey, *Mossoul*, pp. 127f.).

of the Azd had their settlement in the city's west, along the Sikka Kabīra in the area of Bāb Sinjār of al-Azdī's day; its mosque originally took the name of the first Sulamī settler of the city, Jābir b. Jabala, and later adopted the name of al-Muʿāfā b. ʿImrān, the most famous figure of second-century Mosuli learning.[103] An area of the city took the name of another branch of the Azd, the Ṭamthāniyyūn.[104] The only tribal mosque we can describe in any detail is identified as the *masjid Banī Asbāṭ/Ṣābāṭ al-Ṣayrafī*.[105] It was located next to the church of Mār Tūmā, near or along the Sikkat Sirrī of al-Azdī's day, which must have run on an east–west axis, from Bāb Sirrī on the Tigris, and the Darb Banī Īliyā, which would have run from Dayr Saʿīd/Mār Īliyā in the south. We know something about this mosque only because the Christians of Mār Īliyā are said to have annexed a large part of it, and the church was razed as result. This, as we have seen, led the Christians to take their grievances to al-Mahdī, who was passing through Mosul in year 163/779–80; the caliph eventually ruled in favour of the Muslim claimants. Since the annexation was only discovered at a fairly late stage, one infers that the mosque had been abandoned by this time.[106] An echo of Kufa's tribal cemeteries/gathering areas (*jabbānāt*) can be heard in the early Abbasid period.[107]

Beyond these meagre passages, any record of urban growth during the Sufyānid period has perished along with the first part of al-Azdī's history. It is unlikely, however, that we are missing much at all: the sources consistently credit building projects to Marwānids rather than Sufyānids;[108] al-Balādhurī had access to some of the same sources that underlie al-Azdī in this period;[109] and whereas Marwānid-era investments along the Euphrates echo those of Marwānid Mosul, Sufyānid Bilād al-Shām apparently saw relatively little urban growth in general. Seventh-century building was thus modest enough in Mosul, consisting of a mosque–palace complex, along with some residential building that goes entirely unrecorded. The considerable – and costly – building activity that would finally come in the early eighth century required the retention of provincial revenues and the commitment of imperial and local figures alike, and as long as the settlement remained a Kufan depen-

[103] See al-Azdī, *Ta'rīkh*, pp. 91f., and 113; and C. F. Robinson, 'al-Muʿāfā b. ʿImrān and the beginnings of the *ṭabaqāt* literature', *JAOS* 116 (1996), pp. 114–120. Is the Bāb Jābir to be identified as Bāb Sinjār? The Sikka Kabīra presumably ran from east to west, and may have been, along with the north–south-running street that Ibn Ḥawqal knew as the *darb dayr al-aʿlā*, one of the principal thoroughfares of the medieval city. Cf. Ibn Jubayr, *Riḥla*, p. 235; Sarre and Herzfeld, *Reise*, II, p. 210; and Fiey, *Mossoul*, p. 126.

[104] Al-Azdī, *Ta'rīkh*, pp. 77f. and 312.

[105] See al-Azdī, *Ta'rīkh*, pp. 244 (where the text may be awry); the toponym is apparently to be reconstructed in the light of p. 364 (Asbāṭ b. Ayyūb al-Bajalī), p. 341 (Asbāṭ b. Muḥammad), or the Azdī lineage of Mālik b. Fahm (F. Wüstenfeld, *Register zu den genealogischen Tabellen der arabischen Stämme und Familien* (Göttingen, 1853), p. 283; al-Azdī, *Ta'rīkh*, pp. 94 and 335. See also Oppenheimer, *Babylonia Judaica*, pp. 391f.

[106] For the account, see chapter 1, note 59. Al-Mahdī was infamous for his destruction of churches, but there is no reason to doubt the authenticity of this report.

[107] Al-Azdī, *Ta'rīkh*, p. 248; see also below.

[108] For several examples, see below.

[109] On these sources, see chapter 6 below.

dency, both were apparently lacking. Of course the site's history in this period can be construed in more positive terms: the site's defensive potential was recognised by the conquering Muslims; and since stationing a Kufan garrison in the north required little building, little took place. It is under the Marwānids that the Kufan pattern was broken, and the garrison transformed into a city.

That Islamic cities in Iraq grew out of garrison sites is clear,[110] but how this happened much less so. In what follows I should like to argue that in the case of Mosul, the transformation was radical and precipitous, and that alone among Iraqi settlements, it passed through a distinctly Marwānid – and one heretofore held to be exclusively Syrian – phase of élite patronage.

The birth of the city

In the decades following the conquest, Mosul grew into a garrison of a few thousand Arab settler/soldiers and their dependants. With no clear Sasanian administrative antecedent, its site is to be explained in military terms: it occupied a strategic and fortified position on the northern Tigris. In terms of administration, it was considered Kufan, and its governing élite was drawn from among Kufan chiefs.

The shift from Kufan garrison to Marwānid city is in part signalled by Muḥammad b. Marwān's transfer of Basrans to Mosul,[111] but more clearly in administrative terms. As we have already seen, the most one can say about the post-conquest and Sufyānid periods is that authority appears to have been delegated principally to immigrant Kufan tribes of the Azd and Hamdān; if they had a policy at all, the Sufyānids took a hands-off approach. In the absence of clear numismatic evidence and the first third of al-Azdī's history, the initial sequence of Marwānid governors remains incomplete and confused until the reign of al-Ḥurr b. Yūsuf, who was appointed in 108 or early 109/726–7; but problems of sequence aside, we can still be sure that the pattern is now altogether different: unlike the Sufyānids, the Marwānid house did lay their hands on Mosul, appointing kinsmen as governors. Thus Saʿīd b. ʿAbd al-Malik, Yūsuf b. Yaḥyā b. al-Ḥakam (Marwān I's nephew), and Muḥammad b. Marwān are all counted as governors during the reign of ʿAbd al-Malik (685–705), and some reports put Muḥammad in the north well into the reign of Sulaymān (715–17).[112] The Damascene Yaḥyā b. Yaḥyā al-Ghassānī, already serving as governor when the extant section of al-Azdī's *Ta'rīkh* begins in 101/719–20, may represent a brief interregnum during which the Umayyads delegated authority

[110] For some archaeologists' views, see A. Northedge, 'Archaeology and new urban settlement in early Islamic Syria and Iraq', in G. R. D. King and A. Cameron, eds., *The Byzantine and Early Islamic Near East II: Land Use and Settlement Patterns* (Princeton, 1994), pp. 231–65; and Whitcomb, 'Amṣār in Syria?', pp. 13–33.

[111] Al-Yaʿqūbī, *Ta'rīkh*, II, p. 324 (the tribesmen in question were Azdīs and Rabīʿa).

[112] For an overview, see Forand, 'Governors', pp. 88ff., and Rotter, 'Fulūs', 166ff.

to trusted protegés;[113] but the pattern reasserts itself quickly, first with Marwān b. Muḥammad b. Marwān (governor from 102/720 to 105/724), al-Ḥurr b. Yūsuf b. Yaḥyā (governor from c. 108/727 to 113/731–2) and his son Yaḥyā b. al-Ḥurr (governor for a few months thereafter).[114] Al-Azdī has the latter immediately follow his father, but the overstrike evidence puts al-Walīd b. Talīd (governor from 114–21/732–9) between the two.[115]

As far as Mosul is concerned, the Marwānids were about building; perhaps as much as direct Marwānid family administration, building must be seen as an integral part of their programme of rule. It is Muḥammad b. Marwān who is conventionally credited with constructing the medieval city, and this by local, Islamic, and Syriac sources;[116] when his son Marwān entered the city in 745–6 to eject Shaybān the Khārijite, he announced that he would do no harm to the people of the city built by his father.[117] The most impressive building project undertaken in the early Marwānid period was the digging of the so-called Open Canal (*al-nahr al-makshūf*).[118] According to the anecdote recorded by al-Azdī in 107/725–6,[119] the governor of the city, al-Ḥurr b. Yūsuf, distressed by the sight of a woman struggling to carry water from the Tigris into the city, promptly wrote to Hishām about the inaccessibility of drinking water, and the caliph responded by directing him to cut the canal.[120] Workers and engineers were brought into the city; in year 729–30 5,000 men were engaged in the project. Work continued into the governorship of al-Walīd b. Talīd, and was finally completed in 738–9, reportedly with an outlay of 8,000,000 dirhams.[121] Al-Azdī repeatedly emphasises how the costs consumed

[113] On Yaḥyā, whose father is said to have commanded the *shurṭa* of Marwān b. al-Ḥakam, see al-Azdī, *Ta'rīkh*, pp. 3 and 10; Ibn Sa'd, *Kitāb al-Ṭabaqāt*, VII², p. 169; Abū Zur'a al-Dimashqī, *Ta'rīkh* (Damascus, 1980), pp. 203, 254, 339, and 711; Ibn Ḥajar, *Tahdhīb*, XI, pp. 299f. (citing al-Azdī); and Forand, 'Governors', pp. 89 and 103. In part based on overstrike evidence, Rotter ('Fulūs', pp. 173ff.) puts the beginning of Yaḥyā's reign in 99.

[114] The sequence of these governors is certain (with one exception), but the chronology less so, not only because the coins are undated, but also because the governorships of Mosul and the Jazira frequently overlap (cf. the confusion surrounding 'Umar b. Hubayra in al-Azdī, *Ta'rīkh*, p. 16; cf. al-Ṭabarī, *Ta'rīkh*, II, p. 1349). For al-Azdī's evidence, see Forand, 'Governors', pp. 89f.; for the numismatic, Rotter, 'Fulūs', pp. 175ff.

[115] I am indebted to L. Ilisch for making available to me the results of his unpublished study of Mosuli overstrikes.

[116] Naṣr b. Muzāḥim, *Waq'at Ṣiffīn*, p. 149; Isḥāq b. al-Ḥasan al-Zayyāt, *Dhikr al-aqālīm* (Barcelona, 1989), p. 165; and Bar Bahlūl, in Duval, ed., *Lexicon*, c. 943.

[117] Al-Azdī, *Ta'rīkh*, p. 75.

[118] On the construction of the canal, see al-Azdī, *Ta'rīkh*, pp. 26ff.; and Ibn al-Athīr, *al-Kāmil*, V, pp. 132f. (here, as throughout this period, drawing on al-Azdī).

[119] Following al-Kindī, Rotter ('Fulūs', pp. 178f.) and Forand ('Governors', p. 90) push the date of al-Ḥurr's appointment in Mosul to late 108 or early 109/726–7; if this is correct, the date of the canal must be so pushed as well.

[120] The anecdote has a Syrian parallel in Ibn Shaddād, *al-A'lāq al-khaṭīra fī dhikr umarā' al-Shām wa'l-Jazīra (ta'rīkh Lubnān wa'l-Urdunn wa-Filasṭīn)* (Damascus, 1962), pp. 15f. But water did remain a chronic problem in Mosul: see, for examples, al-Muqaddasī, *Aḥsan al-taqāsīm*, p. 138; Yāqūt, *Mu'jam*, IV, p. 684.

[121] Preferring Ibn al-Athīr's (*al-Kāmil*, V, p. 241) reading of al-Azdī (*Ta'rīkh*, p. 43), which now reads 80,000,000.

Mosul's revenues, to the point that none was passed on to Hishām, who is said to have asked al-Ḥurr to slow construction in 731–2. He also related Hishām's order that twenty mills be set into the canal in 115/733–4, a full eight years after construction began, and eighteen millstones are said to have been installed; revenues from the mills went into a *waqf* that defrayed their cost. The canal seems to have survived in Ibn Ḥawqal's day, and, apparently under the name of *Nahr Zubayda*, in al-Muqaddasī's too; according to the former, its water lay about 60 *dhirā*ʿ below ground level.[122] Ṣāʾigh proposes a location, and claims that traces of the canal were visible in his day, but the argument is problematic.[123]

Shaban might have been tempted to argue that the canal was dug because of overpopulation in the city.[124] The city had certainly grown, and al-Azdī is at pains to note that the province's revenues were especially high in this period, and its tax districts at their most expansive.[125] In fact, the completion of the Open Canal represents the end of a golden age for building in the city, which had begun with the first Marwānids. As we have already seen, relatively late sources put walls in conquest-era Mosul, but other sources are explicit that walls appeared only after the conquest,[126] and relatively early accounts attribute these to the Marwānids. The attribution, however, was controversial. Al-Wāqidī credits Saʿīd b. ʿAbd al-Malik,[127] Yāqūt proposes Marwān II,[128] and al-Azdī remarks with some frustration that 'Muḥammad [b. Marwān] built the walls of Mosul in AH 80[/699–700], without any disagreement among those Mosulis knowledgeable in history' (*bayna man yaʿlam al-sīra min ahl al-Mawṣil*).[129] Marwān II is a candidate only if we accept reports of a first tenure as governor in the city in 102–5/720–4, unless one can somehow explain why he would later erect walls that ran between the congregational mosque and the city's most lavish palace, which was built shortly before 725–6.[130] One rather imagines that twenty to twenty-five years of growth pushed the city beyond walls designed to enclose a fairly modest settlement; in other words,

[122] Al-Azdī, *Taʾrīkh*, p. 197; Ibn Ḥawqal, *Ṣūrat al-arḍ*, pp. 214f.; al-Idrīsī, *Opus geographicum* (Rome, 1984), p. 659; al-Muqaddasī, *Aḥsan al-taqāsīm*, p. 138.

[123] See Ṣāʾigh, *Taʾrīkh al-Mawṣil*, I, pp. 64f., followed in part by Salman, *al-Mawṣil*, pp. 89f. The location is probably too far north, and in any case the purported traces appear to be Fiey's 'plaine d'alluvions . . . qui représente l'ancien lit du fleuve il y a quelques décades' (*Mossoul*, pp. 124f. and note 4); Canard, *Dynastie*, pp. 118f. It seems that the canal had disappeared by Ibn al-Athīr's time (*al-Kāmil*, V, p. 133).

[124] M. A. Shaban, *Islamic History: A New Interpretation I* (Cambridge, 1971), pp. 143f. (where he sees population growth in the Jazira in this period).

[125] Al-Azdī, *Taʾrīkh*, pp. 32f. The wealth of the town in this period may account for the relatively large issues of coins struck in the name of al-Ḥurr b. Yūsuf and al-Walīd b. Talīd, both of which are frequently overstruck.

[126] Thus ps.-Wāqidī, *Taʾrīkh futūḥ al-Jazīra*, p. 236, explains the success of the conquest by the absence of walls; see also al-ʿUmarī, *Munyat al-udabāʾ*, p. 33.

[127] Al-Balādhurī, *Futūḥ*, p. 332, which is accepted by S. al-Daywahchī, 'Sūr al-Mawṣil,' *Sumer* 3 (1947), pp. 117f. [128] Yāqūt, *Muʿjam*, IV, p. 683. [129] Al-Azdī, *Taʾrīkh*, p. 25.

[130] On this *qaṣr* see below, and al-Azdī, *Taʾrīkh*, pp. 26f. and 146 (the latter makes it clear that it was built outside the city walls).

the city grew very rapidly during the first quarter of the eighth century. These Marwānid walls were razed by Hārūn in 796–7.[131]

In addition to these walls, the Marwānids oversaw a range of other building projects. The streets were paved by (some combination of) Muḥammad b. Marwān, Saʿīd b. ʿAbd al-Malik, and al-Walīd b. Talīd.[132] Saʿīd is also credited with building a canal that bore his name, as well as a mosque;[133] and later Marwān II is said to have erected a bridge and renovated the congregational mosque.[134] In year 128/745–6 a bath is mentioned.[135] Hishām built a palace complex (*qaṣr*) of mud and unbaked brick that eventually passed on to Wāʾil b. al-Shaḥḥāj.[136] It was the governor al-Ḥurr b. Yūsuf who, by 725–6, had built the most impressive Marwānid palace, this to serve as his *qaṣr al-imāra*. It was called *al-manqūsha* ('the one with carved ornament') because it was ornamented with 'teak and glass [or stone] mosaics (*fasāfis*) and the like'; 'the like' included marble.[137] Al-Ḥurr eventually passed this *qaṣr*, along with his other properties, to his son Yaḥyā, who also governed the city, and one of its *dār*s took Yaḥyā's name. Al-Azdī's massacre narrative puts this *qaṣr* outside the Marwānid walls built a generation earlier; other accounts locate the palace near the canal and several markets, and one imagines that it was this part of the settlement that Yāqūt knows as *al-Ḥurr*.[138] It survived in al-Muqaddasī's day, but by Ibn al-Athīr's it was in ruins.[139]

The Marwānids thus built and invested in Mosul on a large scale, radically altering the urban landscape; by the Abbasid Revolution the city shows all the signs of having enjoyed something of a boom, and it is tempting to think that taxation may have had a hand in triggering it.[140] Newly built walls had been overrun, perhaps in part as the canal allowed settlement further west;[141]

[131] Al-Azdī, *Taʾrīkh*, p. 289; al-Balādhurī, *Futūḥ*, p. 332.

[132] Al-Balādhurī, *Futūḥ*, p. 332 (on the authority of the Mosuli al-Muʿāfā b. Ṭāwūs); al-Balādhurī, *Ansāb al-ashrāf*, vii/i (Beirut, 1997), p. 452 (al-Walīd b. Balīd); Yāqūt, *Muʿjam*, IV, p. 683.

[133] Al-Balādhurī, *Futūḥ*, p. 332; Ibn ʿAbd al-Munʿim al-Ḥimyarī, *al-Rawḍ al-miʿṭār*, p. 564 (reproducing al-Balādhurī).

[134] Yāqūt, *Muʿjam*, IV, p. 683. The bridge was apparently built by the year 128/745; see al-Azdī, *Taʾrīkh*, pp. 70 and 75.

[135] Al-Azdī, *Taʾrīkh*, p. 75.

[136] Al-Azdī, *Taʾrīkh*, pp. 24 and 158. On *qaṣr* as fortified enclosure, see L. I. Conrad, 'The *quṣūr* of medieval Islam: some implications for the social history of the Near East', *al-Abḥāth* 29 (1981), pp. 7–23; Rotter ('Fulūs', p. 178) 'castle'.

[137] Al-Azdī, *Taʾrīkh*, pp 24f. and 27; Ibn al-Athīr (*al-Kāmil*, V, pp. 132f.) replaces and glosses *al-fasāfis* (following the editor's emendation) with *al-fuṣūṣ al-mulawwana*; see also F. Gabrieli (*Il califfato di Hishâm* (Alexandria, 1935)), p. 131. Cf. G. Bisheh, 'From castellum to palatium: Umayyad mosaic pavements from Qasr al-Hallabat in Jordan', *Muqarnas* 10 (1993), pp. 49–56.

[138] Yāqūt, *Muʿjam*, II, p. 239.

[139] Al-Muqaddasī, *Aḥsan al-taqāsīm*, p. 138; Ibn al-Athīr, *al-Kāmil*, V, pp. 132f.; Ibn Baṭṭūṭa, *Riḥla* (Beirut, 1975), p. 254 (the wide and long avenue mentioned here must be the Darb Dayr al-Aʿlā).

[140] Cf. K. Hopkins, 'Taxes and trade in the Roman Empire (200 BCE–AD 400)', *Journal of Roman Studies* 70 (1980), pp. 101–25.

[141] That the city was built up considerably is clear not only from al-Azdī, but also the flood account preserved by a contemporary source (*Zuqnin Chronicle*, pp. 228/178). For an example of the damage caused by floods in a much later period, see Bell, *Amurath to Amurath*, p. 261.

the congregational mosque had been renovated by Marwān II; residential housing and markets had been erected; ostentatious and monumental architecture had appeared. A conservative guess would count the settled population of the city well into the tens of thousands,[142] perhaps even as high as 50,000; it is based on two sets of mortality figures. Accounts cited by al-Azdī for the massacre of 133 put the death toll at either 11,000 or 30,000 'ring wearers', a term which al-Azdī apparently took to designate adult males, since elsewhere the number of those killed 'aside from women and children' is also put at 30,000; meanwhile, al-Yaʿqūbī, working independently of al-Azdī and his sources, put the death toll at 18,000 men 'of pure Arab stock' (*min ṣalīb al-ʿarab*), here in addition to slaves and *mawālī*.[143] A generation later, when the population would have recovered somewhat from the massacre, the contemporaneous *Zuqnin Chronicle* tells us that 1,000 corpses were taken out of Mosul in a single day during the plague of 774–5.[144] Now the figure may be round, but it is not necessarily far-fetched,[145] and it certainly compares favourably to the more hyperbolic number of 30,000 deaths in a hailstorm in Mosul in 846–7;[146] even allowing for continued growth, this does seem excessive. A mid-eighth-century population of about 50,000 would make Mosul a relatively large city, but not unreasonably so, contemporaneous Basra and Kufa being considerably larger, and tenth-century Nishapur three or four times as populous.[147]

It was al-Azdī's view that revenues flowing from the province's especially expansive tax districts fuelled the building boom, at least insofar as it was symbolised by the Open Canal.[148] His view is echoed a generation later by an early Abbasid monk from the monastery of Zuqnin, who remarked in about 770 that the 'Mosulis, who lived in the land of Mesopotamia, were extremely rich in this period [i.e. year 769–70]', precisely because, it appears, they were such rapacious taxers.[149] Re-stated in somewhat broader terms – the city's wealth was based on the extraction of rural surplus – this view must be true in the main. But it is also banal, and leaves unanswered how this surplus was produced and extracted, and exactly who benefited from it; the *Zuqnin Chronicle* only gives us to believe that they were Muslim Arabs.

142 Ṣā'igh suggested a population of over 100,000 for the early Abbasid period (*Ta'rīkh al-Mawṣil*, I, p. 91); the reasons he adduces are unconvincing, and the number seems too high, even for the eve of the Abbasid Revolution.

143 See al-Azdī, *Ta'rīkh*, pp. 148, 151 and 153; al-Yaʿqūbī, *Ta'rīkh*, II, pp. 428f. On the sources of the massacre, see chapter 6.

144 *Zuqnin Chronicle*, pp. 368/300.

145 See L. I. Conrad, 'Epidemic disease in central Syria in the late sixth century: Some new insights from the verse of Ḥassān ibn Thābit', *Byzantine and Modern Greek Studies* 18 (1994), p. 57; and L. I. Conrad, 'Die Pest und ihr soziales Umfeld im Nahen Osten des frühen Mittelalters', *DI* 73 (1996), pp. 85ff.

146 See the *Chronicle of 1234*, II, pp. 39/28.

147 As early as 64/683 Basra is said to have had 150,000 *mawālī* alone (Wellhausen, *Arab Kingdom*, p. 402); Kufa is usually held to have been somewhat smaller. On Nishapur, see now R. Bulliet, *Islam: The View from the Edge* (New York, 1994), p. 135, note 9; and in general, D. Ayalon, 'Regarding population estimates in the countries of medieval Islam', *JESHO* 28 (1985), pp. 1–19.

148 Al-Azdī, *Ta'rīkh*, p. 24.

149 See the *Zuqnin Chronicle*, pp. 254/199.

The scale and cost of building leave no doubt that the city was a large-scale consumer of this rural surplus, which was extracted in variable combinations of cash and kind. Raising revenue in the form of taxation was even difficult for taxers as efficient as the Abbasids,[150] however, and we should be alert to the sources' exaggerated estimates of the sums collected. Even if we allow that the province expanded and contracted over time, it is hard to see how *kharāj* figures attributed to the time of Muʿāwiya (45,000,000 dirhams) and Hārūn (24,000,000 dirhams) can be correct.[151] For the city's canal seems to have cost 8,000,000 dirhams, and it is said to have exhausted at least two years' revenues in the process. Later, when some years' worth of tax arrears were collected in year 180/796–7, they amounted to no more than 6,000,000 dirhams.[152] It is thus only when we arrive at the figures recorded by Qudāma b. Jaʿfar (6,300,000) and Ibn Khurdādhbih (4,000,000) that the figures start to make some sense, even if the province at this point was considerably smaller than that of the late Umayyad period.[153] In the case of Mosul then, the early tax figures are too unreliable to demonstrate a precipitous drop in revenues from the Umayyad to the middle Abbasid period;[154] and if revenues did reach a modest peak in the later Umayyad period, they reflect intensive Marwānid investments during times of relative peace, rather than the *Fortleben* of Sasanian agriculture, which seems to have been the case in the south.

Of course tax collection throughout the eighth century was difficult and inefficient. For one thing, it was predicated on a loose network of intermediaries and imperial agents, and these cost the state dearly: we shall see that *shahārija* middlemen pocketed large sums, and that imperial accountants embezzled too.[155] For another, collection also depended on a measure of rural security, and this was hard to guarantee.[156] Evidence for the coercive force

150 For a parallel, see P. A. Brunt, 'The Revenues of Rome', *Journal of Roman Studies* 71 (1981), pp. 161–172.

151 See al-Yaʿqūbī, *Taʾrīkh*, II, p. 277 (*kharāj al-Mawṣil wa-mā yuḍāf ilayhā wa-yattaṣil bi-hā*) (Muʿāwiya); al-Jahshiyārī, *Wuzarāʾ*, p. 285 (Hārūn); see also von Kremer, 'Ueber das Budget der Einnahmen', pp. 6 and 11, and El-ʿAli, 'A new version of Ibn al-Muṭarrif's list of revenues', p. 309.

152 See al-Azdī, *Taʾrīkh*, pp. 29ff. and 287.

153 Qudāma b. Jaʿfar, *Kitāb al-Kharāj*, p. 175; Ibn Khurdādhbih, *Masālik*, p. 94; Isḥāq b. al-Ḥasan al-Zayyāt, *Aqālīm*, p. 165 (6,000,000 dirhams or dīnārs); cf. the fourth part of the anonymous *Kitāb al-ʿUyūn wa'l-ḥadāʾiq fī akhbār al-ḥaqāʾiq*, IV (Damascus, 1973), p. 387 (3,600,000 dirhams in 331/942). Restoring the districts that had formerly belonged to Mosul (e.g. Takrit, al-Sinn, Shahrazūr and al-Ṣāmaghān) would push the sum to c. 10,000,000 dirhams p.a.

154 See, for example, E. Ashtor, *A Social and Economic History of the Near East in the Middle Ages* (London 1976), pp. 66ff.; cf. also Morony's warning (*Iraq*, pp. 119f.).

155 On the Islamic side of things, perhaps the best example is the letter written by al-Manṣūr to his uncle (and governor of the city) Ismāʿīl b. ʿAlī in Shawwāl of 152/Oct.–Nov. 769 and reproduced by al-Azdī (*Taʾrīkh*, pp. 214f.); according to the text, the caliph had sent a *daftar* to Ismāʿīl providing the names and addresses of local tax officials involved in embezzlement. On the Christian side, an example is the apparent allusion to the *muṣādara* undertaken when Mūsā b. Muṣʿab was appointed governor of Mosul in 770 (*Zuqnin Chronicle*, pp. 289f./231).

156 For one example of how rural gangs could resist the tax man during the Abbasid period, see Thomas of Marga, *Governors*, pp. 293f./523ff.

required to collect may first appear as early as the reign of ʿAbd al-Malik, in the person of al-Walīd b. Talīd, who is identified as the *ṣāḥib al-shurṭa* of Muḥammad b. Marwān;[157] what is certain is that al-Walīd was later appointed governor, and in 115 and 120 (733–4 and 737–8) his responsibilities are said to have included the city's *aḥdāth*, in addition to the conventional *ṣalāt* and *ḥarb*.[158] The term *aḥdāth* seems to have disappeared from usage in Mosul fairly quickly, replaced by the *rawābiṭ*, a mounted militia that had taken firm institutional hold by 762–3.[159] This is because bandits and Khārijites did reappear – and in the Marwānid and Abbasid periods with some frequency – costing the state in a variety of ways: banditry in the countryside could force the closure of the *dār al-kharāj* within the city;[160] having 'cut off' peripheral areas from the tax collectors, Khārijites could levy tributes of their own,[161] or force local governors to deliver huge sums as ransom;[162] bandits and Khārijites alike – and the distinction between the two is often hard to discern – required the state to hire posses.[163] Imperial force had only a shallow reach onto the steppe to the west and into the valleys and mountains of the east;[164] later, the Abbasids had to rely on local tribesmen for the dirty work of levying taxes.[165]

Given the difficulty experienced by the Abbasids in levying taxes, it might be suggested that what had earlier fuelled Mosul's boom was a variety of economic activities, of which taxing the rural hinterland was merely one. In fact, it is the site's great economic potential that takes the mystery out of the Marwānids' attachment to Mosul.[166] Mosul, like Nineveh, benefited enormously from geography. Not only did it lie on the edge of the fertile areas of al-Marj and Adiabene, but it occupied the terminus of riverine and land routes

157 Al-Balādhurī, *Futūḥ*, p. 332.
158 Al-Azdī, *Taʾrīkh*, pp. 35 and 40; Forand, 'Governors', pp. 90f.; Rotter, 'Fulūs', pp. 180ff.
159 See al-Azdī, *Taʾrīkh*, p. 195; and chapter 7 below.
160 See al-Azdī, *Taʾrīkh*, p. 293, where banditry is presented as a response to al-Ḥarashī's rapacious taxation, which sent the peasantry fleeing to Azarbayjān (see p. 287). Cf. also pp. 364 (tribesmen 'cut' the Khurāsān road) and 367 (Christians of Kuḥayl attacked by local tribesmen).
161 For two examples, see al-Azdī, *Taʾrīkh*, pp. 275f.; and Michael the Syrian, *Chronique*, xii.iii (Walīd b. Ṭarīf). Note that when al-ʿAṭṭāf b. Sufyān rebelled, 'he levied taxes and imprisoned the tax officials' (*al-ʿummāl*); al-Azdī, *Taʾrīkh*, p. 279.
162 Thus Ḥumayd b. Qaḥṭaba, the governor of the Jazira, is said to have paid al-Mulabbad 100,000 dirhams; see al-Ṭabarī, *Taʾrīkh*, III, pp. 120f.; al-Azdī, *Taʾrīkh*, pp. 166f.; al-Balādhurī, *Ansāb*, III, p. 248f.
163 For examples, see al-Azdī, *Taʾrīkh*, p. 379.
164 Thus Thomas of Marga, writing a full century after the Abbasid Revolution, is unable to distinguish between Abbasid generals, their armies, and their proxies, reducing them all to colourless *ṭayyāyē*. As Brock remarks ('Syriac sources for seventh-century history', *Byzantine and Modern Greek Studies* 2 (1976), p. 27), 'Were it not for one or two passing references, the reader would be left totally unaware that Thomas was writing under Islamic rule.'
165 For an overview, see H. Kennedy, 'Central government and provincial élites in the early ʿAbbāsid caliphate', *BSOAS* 44 (1981), pp. 26–38. The state's reliance on local tribesmen is one of the enduring features of northern Mesopotamian politics; see, for example, F. E. Peters, 'Byzantium and the Arabs of Syria', *Les Annales Archéologiques Arabes Syriennes* 27–8 (1977–8), pp. 100f.; and Isaac, *The Limits of Empire*, pp. 235ff.
166 See Athamina, 'Arab settlement', p. 191 ('For unknown reasons, al-Mawṣil attracted the attention of some Umayyad Caliphs').

from the west and north,[167] and although it was not the northernmost point from which goods could be quickly and cheaply shipped downstream on rafts,[168] it was certainly the most 'practicable' one;[169] this explains why it so frequently enjoys pride of place among the northern *débouchés.*[170] The site could thus be made to command a productive hinterland, to produce in its own right, and finally to tax the goods it distributed.

That the early eighth-century city came to produce as well as consume wealth is clear: a shift from conquest-era underdevelopment to Marwānid-era investment is signalled by changes in landholding and land use. Thus Hishām purchased a large piece of land (fifty-nine *jarībs* by one reckoning) from the Buraydạ clan of the Azd for the sum of 70,000 dirhams,[171] putting it under cultivation, and thereby producing what al-Azdī's informant considered exceptional land, 'the best ever seen'.[172] The property was so valuable that it was later targeted by an anti-Umayyad mob, and then granted to one of the city's notables. The family of al-Ḥurr b. Yūsuf also owned a variety of properties, including agricultural estates (*ḍiyāʿ*);[173] they had held these properties already during the reign of Sulaymān b. ʿAbd al-Malik.[174]

It is in the context of Marwānid family landholding that we are to understand the digging of the Open Canal, the installation of the river mills – indeed, early eighth-century building in general. The high cost of the canal, in

167 On the (almost proverbial) fertility of the Nineveh plain, see Fiey, *Assyrie chrétienne*, I, p. 225; Thomas of Marga, *Governors*, II, 43, note 2. The 200 mm isohyet cuts across the Jaziran plain just north of the ancient Assur; and the geographers describe Mosul's agriculture as rain-fed: see al-Iṣṭakhrī, *Kitāb Masālik al-mamālik* (Leiden, 1870; Bibliotheca Geographorum Arabicorum 1), p. 73; Ibn Ḥawqal, *Ṣūrat al-arḍ*, p. 215; al-Muqaddasī, *Aḥsan al-taqāsīm*, p. 138.

168 Jazīrat b. ʿUmar may have had the honour; see Ibn Ḥawqal, *Ṣūrat al-arḍ*, pp. 224f. (epitomised by al-Idrīsī, *Opus geographicum*, p. 664).

169 The word is G. Algaze's, 'Habuba on the Tigris: archaic Nineveh reconsidered', *JNES* 45 (1986), p. 130. In the early modern period, only passenger boats and rafts with shallow drafts (e.g. *zawraqs* or small *keleks*) could navigate north of Mosul, and these only with difficulty because of rapids and whirlpools; meanwhile, deep draft, goods-carrying ships often had difficulty navigating north of Sāmarrā'; see *A Handbook of Mesopotamia* I (London, 1916–17), pp. 252f. and 287ff.

170 The provenance of Tigris-borne trade from the north is frequently identified as Azarbayjān, Armenia, Diyār Rabīʿa and Mosul (see, for examples, al-Yaqūbī, *Kitāb al-Buldān* (Leiden, 1892; Bibliotheca Geographorum Arabicorum 7), pp. 237f. and 263), but Mosul alone (the only city mentioned) is occasionally used as shorthand for the north in general; see al-Yaqūbī, *Buldān*, p. 265; Ibn al-ʿIbrī (Bar Hebraeus), *Ta'rīkh mukhtaṣar al-duwal* (Beirut, 1983), p. 211; and Ibn al-Ṭiqṭaqā, *al-Fakhrī* (Paris, 1895), p. 219. Cf. also Ibn ʿAbd al-Munʿim al-Ḥimyarī, *al-Rawḍ al-miʿṭār*, p. 301.

171 This presumably took place while he lived in the city either during the governorships of Muḥammad b. Marwān or Saʿīd b. ʿAbd al-Malik; see al-Azdī, *Ta'rīkh*, p. 24.

172 At least some of these estates were vandalised by what must have been a Mosuli mob shortly after the Abbasid Revolution (al-Azdī, *Ta'rīkh*, pp. 171f.), but this may reflect long-suppressed resentment towards Hishām, rather than towards the dynasty itself; thus Marwān II is said to have ordered that Hishām's estates on the Euphrates be destroyed (Agapius, *Kitāb al-ʿUnwān*, p. 517). Elsewhere we read that Hishām's plans to rebuild the bridge at Āmid were foiled only by his death; see the *Zuqnin Chronicle*, pp. 176/133.

173 For details, see chapter 7.

174 See Ibn ʿAsākir, *Ta'rīkh madīnat Dimashq*, XX, p. 142; Ibn al-ʿAdīm, *Bughyat al-ṭalab fī ta'rīkh Ḥalab* (Damascus, 1988), p. 4187.

addition to that of all the millstones,[175] can only have been recouped by monopolising (or at least radically centralising) the grinding of wheat in a mill owned or operated by those who had invested in it. In fact, a document recorded in 139/756 mentions *en passant* 'the caliphal mill' (*raḥā amīr al-mu'minīn*),[176] and an early Abbasid account suggests that milling was restricted to what would be called banal mills in the medieval west.[177] What we seem to have, therefore, is Marwānid origins for the large-scale Tigris milling that was such a prominent feature of the ninth- and tenth-century Iraqi economy, from Āmid down to Baghdad.[178] One can only wonder how much wealth these activities produced,[179] but sources occasionally report that Hishām earned more revenue from his Euphrates and Tigris estates than he did from the *kharāj* of all the provinces.[180]

We do know something about Mosul mills of a later period; these were called *'urūb*.[181] According to Ibn Ḥawqal, an *'arba* consisted of four millstones, each

175 According to Ibn Ḥawqal (*Ṣūrat al-arḍ*, p. 222), an Iraqi millstone comparable in quality to that found in the Jazira could fetch more than 50 dīnārs in the ninth century. Baghdad's famous Mills of the Patrikios had 100 millstones, and are said to have required an initial investment of 1,000,000 dirhams (see J. Lassner, *The Topography of Baghdad in the Early Middle Ages* (Detroit, 1970), pp. 75f. and generally; and J. Lassner, *The Shaping of 'Abbāsid Rule* (Princeton, 1980), pp. 231ff.).

176 See al-Azdī, *Ta'rīkh*, pp. 171f.; for the *darb raḥā amīr al-mu'minīn*, see al-Muqaddasī, *Aḥsan al-taqāsīm*, p. 138.

177 According to al-Azdī (*Ta'rīkh*, p. 362) in 206/821–2 wheat prices had dropped precipitously, and when a peasant took his wheat to a Nineveh miller, the latter refused to grind it, leaving him hungry; the account only has verisimilitude in the absence of (or severe restrictions upon) hand-milling. Cf. Thomas of Marga, *Governors*, pp. 153f./313. Talmudic evidence puts hand mills in Late Antique Iraq (thus J. Newman, *The Agricultural Life of the Jews in Babylonia between the Years 200 CE and 500 CE* (London, 1932), pp. 91 and 144ff.); although they are said to have been eclipsed by water mills during the late second and third centuries (L. A. Moritz, *Grain-mills and Flour in Classical Antiquity* (Oxford, 1958), p. 137), they are common enough finds in archaeological sites of the Islamic period in Bilād al-Shām (J. Johns, personal communication).

178 Already by c. 775 we have evidence that Tigris mills were a prominent feature of the landscape (thus the *Zuqnin Chronicle*, pp. 228/178). There is good evidence for private water mills in a later period (G. Makdisi, 'The topography of eleventh-century Baghdad: materials and notes, I', *Arabica* 6 (1959), pp. 189f.); and as we might expect, these were taxed; see Ibn Ḥawqal, *Ṣūrat al-arḍ*, p. 214; and Q. al-Sāmarrā'ī, *al-Mu'assasāt al-idāriyya fī al-dawla al-'Abbāsiyya fī khilāl al-fatra 274–334/861–945* (Damascus, 1971), pp. 227f. The problem is knowing how often and how much: to judge from the stray account in Ibn Miskawayh (*Tajārib al-umam* (London, 1922), III, pp. 71 and 78), taxing was exceptional.

179 According to al-Ya'qūbī (*Buldān*, p. 243), the Mills of the Patrikios in Baghdad are said to have produced 100,000,000 dirhams annually, a figure that is accepted by Mez (*Renaissance of Islam*, p. 467), but apparently not by G. Wiet, *Le Pays* (Cairo, 1937), p. 20 ('d'un million de dirhems').

180 See Agapius, *Kitāb al-'Unwān*, p. 505; cf. Michael the Syrian, *Chronique*, xi.xix; and Bar Hebraeus, *Chronicon syriacum*, p. 118 (=Budge, *Chronography*, p. 109).

181 On the *'urūb*, see also al-Shābushtī, *al-Diyārāt*, pp. 69 (with note 3 for further bibliography), and 176 (Dayr al-A'lā overlooks the Tigris and the *'urūb*; this would put them in the northern part of the town); al-Qazwīnī, *Kitāb 'Ajā'ib al-makhlūqāt*, ed. F. Wüstenfeld as *Kosmographie* (Göttingen, 1848), I, p. 309 (and p. 320 for mills in Nineveh); Bosworth, 'Abū 'Abdallāh al-Khwārazmī', p. 156. These mills were probably variations on the 'ship mills' of the Roman period; for a sixth-century example, see Procopius, *Wars* V.xix.19–23; and Moritz, *Grain-mills*, p. 139, note 1.

pair of which was capable of grinding fifty camel-loads of wheat in a twenty-four-hour period; twenty of these were strung across the river.[182] There is also abundant evidence that southern Iraq came to bake with Mosuli flour transported down the Tigris on *zawraqs*,[183] and in the year of al-Azdī's death (945) we can see why: on the eastern side of Baghdad, where Mosuli flour was available, one dirham bought five *raṭls* of bread, while on the western side, where it was not, one and a quarter dirhams bought a single *raṭl*.[184] No doubt the demand for Mosuli wheat and flour increased after the Abbasid Revolution, with the growth of Kufa and Basra, not to mention the foundation of Baghdad and Sāmarrāʾ. Even so the Mosulis are said to have acquired their reputation as merchants by the Revolutionary period,[185] and the city's function as entrepôt for goods from the north is said to have been apparent to al-Manṣūr.[186] Among the measures taken by the Abbasids to mend fences with the city's élite was Ismāʿīl b. ʿAlī's transfer of the city's markets to the former burial ground, along with the construction of a new *masjid*.[187]

The character and consequences of Marwānid building

To say that Mosul on the eve of the Abbasid Revolution anticipated Mosul of Miskawayh's time is to judge the Marwānid city by its future role within a more intensively urbanised Iraqi economy. What, to conclude, can we say about Mosul within its Marwānid context? What did the Marwānids actually intend? The answer must be that they intended in Mosul whatever they intended in a number of Syrian élite foundations and settlements (and this need not be a single thing); in other words, this Marwānid building programme, which unfolded on the easternmost flank of the Syro-Mesopotamian steppe, should be interpreted primarily in the light of those still ill-defined Marwānid building projects that took place in Greater Syria to the west.[188]

[182] Ibn Ḥawqal, *Ṣūrat al-arḍ*, p. 219. A conservative estimate (see R. Bulliet, *The Camel and the Wheel* (Cambridge, MA, 1975), pp. 20, 168, and 281f.) puts a camel load at 500 pounds. If Ibn Ḥawqal's figures are correct, these would be very productive mills, indeed far more productive than the Vitruvian water-wheel; see K. D. White, *Farm Equipment of the Roman World* (Cambridge, 1975), p. 15.

[183] See, for examples, Ibn Miskawayh, *Tajārib al-umam*, I, p. 405 (*daqīq* and *shaʿīr*); the anonymous *Kitāb al-ʿUyūn wa'l-ḥadāʾiq*, IV, p. 323; al-Ṣūlī, *Akhbâr ar-Râḍî billâh*, I, p. 177; Mez, *Renaissance of Islam*, pp. 486ff. *Keleks* (large rafts with huge carrying capacities) could make the journey from Mosul to Baghdad in as few as two or three days, depending on the flood; see *A Handbook of Mesopotamia*, pp. 287ff.; Thomas of Marga, *Governors*, pp. 383/651.

[184] See Ibn Miskawayh, *Tajārib al-umam*, II, p. 91.

[185] Al-Balādhurī, *Ansāb*, iii, p. 281.

[186] See al-Yaʿqūbī, *Buldān*, pp. 237f. In this passage al-Manṣūr probably had wheat in mind, but Mosulis would also trade in textiles (see al-Jāḥiẓ, *Kitāb al-Tabaṣṣur bi'l-tijāra* (Cairo, 1966), p. 42, which is one of the sources cited by R. B. Serjeant, *Islamic Textiles: Material for a History up to the Mongol Conquest* (Beirut, 1972), pp. 38f.).

[187] This apparently paved the way for al-Mahdī's expansion of the mosque; see al-Azdī, *Taʾrīkh*, p. 248. Was construction around Mosul's congregational mosque initially restricted, as Sayf says it was in Kufa (al-Ṭabarī, *Taʾrīkh*, I, p. 2489)?

[188] For Marwānid building and the question of the *quṣūr*, see now J. Bacharach, 'Marwanid

The evidence is twofold. First, there is the striking combination of Marwānid patronage (here in the persons of Hishām and al-Ḥurr b. Yūsuf), élite residential compounds (usually *qaṣr*s) and hydraulic works related to agricultural development. Although the combination is generally associated with the heartland of Syria and Palestine, examples can be found as far east as the Euphrates and (perhaps) the Balīkh;[189] this may be why historians coupled together Hishām's Euphrates and Tigris estates.[190] Second, even if continued occupation has put Marwānid settlement beyond detailed reconstruction, several ingredients of nascent Mosuli urbanism are as strikingly Syro-Byzantine as they are anomalous within the early Islamic building tradition of Iraq: these include paving stones, urban walls, mosaics, and at least one bath. Syrian tastes on the Tigris need not surprise, for insofar as Marwānid building was élite driven, we might expect a consistency of forms and styles, particularly since labour could move between Iraq and Syria.[191] In short, history would make Mosul an Iraqi city, but Marwānid rule in the city was in large part about making it Syrian.

The Marwānid programme thus worked in a number of discrete but overlapping ways. As we have seen, administration was put in the hands of family members and their kinsmen; the concentration of Kufan settlers was diluted by settling Basrans; land was purchased and confiscated by family members, undercutting older (Kufan) landholding patterns; lands were put under cultivation, resulting in a shift from military garrison to Marwānid demesne. Finally – and perhaps most important – the Kufan pattern of settlement, consisting of mosque and *dār al-imāra*, was overshadowed by a Marwānid foundation, which featured a new and more ambitious language of élite legitimisation: building on a large scale made Marwānid rule public (and impressively so) not simply because the Marwānids outbuilt the Kufans, but because their building was so expensive and ostentatious: the Manqūsha palace replaced the *dār al-imāra* in administrative terms, but it also reflected a new rhetoric of rule. The Marwānids, lacking both conquest experience and local roots, came to rule *more regio*, to consume and patronise, to acquire and display wealth.

Umayyad building activities: speculation on patronage', *Muqarnas* 13 (1996), pp. 27–44; and Northedge, 'Archaeology and new urban settlement'.

189 See C.-P. Haase, 'Is Madinat al-Far, in the Balikh region of northern Syria, an Umayyad foundation?', *Aram* 6 (1994), pp. 245–57. Hishām's Euphrates canals are mentioned in the poetry (thus R. Nadler, *Die Umayyadenkalifen im Spiegel ihrer zeitgenössischen Dichter* (Erlangen-Nuremberg, 1990), p. 261), and his investments are described in some detail by the local Christian sources. According to the *Chronicle of 846*, pp. 235/178, he built 'houses' (*bātē*), 'irrigated lands' (*zar'ātā*) and 'workshops' (*ḥānwātā*), and cut a canal from the Euphrates to irrigate the surrounding land; see also the *Zuqnin Chronicle*, pp. 175/133; *Chronicle of 1234*, I, pp. 309/241; and Michael the Syrian, *Chronique*, xi.xix.

190 See above, note 180.

191 By the time of al-Walīd b. 'Abd al-Malik, masons from Qardā had travelled to Syria to quarry the stones for the caliph; see P. Mouterde, 'Inscriptions en syriaque dialectal à Kāmed (Beq'a)', *Mélanges de l'Université Saint-Joseph* 22 (1939), pp. 71ff.; noted by K. A. C. Creswell, *A Short Account of Early Muslim Architecture*, rev. and supp. J. W. Allan (Adershot, 1989), p. 124; and Northedge, 'Archaeology and new urban settlement', p. 234, note 13.

The consequences of these changes for the social history of Mosul were far-reaching. Put very schematically, an élite of tribesmen/soldiers yielded to an élite of landholders and office holders as the Kufan garrison was eclipsed by the Marwānid and Abbasid city, the two principal factors being the growing value of the land and the city's increased administrative differentiation as it was integrated into an imperial system.[192] In other words, Marwānid designs on the city fundamentally altered its long-term character, in the short term even setting into motion forces for Mosuli particularism amongst a newly ambitious and restive élite, a topic that will occupy us in chapter 7.

This is not to say that landholding had no hand in determining the social make-up of the Sufyānid-era city; lands must have been granted outright in Mosul (as elsewhere), and at least some of the army's salaried soldiers must have converted their wealth into land. Nor is it to say that history ceased to matter: the Kufans may have been indifferent to the economic potential of the land, but they had conquered it after all, and early settlers would continue to benefit from the prestige accorded to conquest participants and their progeny: this would explain why second-century families such as the Harāthima and Farāqid retained names that anchored them in conquest history. Indeed, we can sometimes see how some families with deep Mosuli roots adapted themselves to Marwānid changes, the best example being the family of the ascetic and *muḥaddith* al-Muʿāfā b. ʿImrān (d. 801). Al-Muʿāfā's great-grandfather had been among the first of the Banū Sulayma branch of the Azd to settle in the city. At least part of his wealth was in the form of land, and so too al-Muʿāfā's; but the family extended its influence beyond landholding, into politics and scholarship too.[193]

So there was a measure of continuity. On the other hand, Hishām's rule clearly opened the way for new families to emerge, perhaps the best example being the Ḥabāḥiba, whose status seems to have been closely tied to office holding.[194] More important, when we look at those families with the longest staying power amongst the city's élite, reproducing themselves generation after generation, these appear to have had Marwānid origins. Thus, in the Banū Shaḥḥāj,[195] the Banū Jārūd (descendants of a *qāḍī*, al-Ḥārith b. al-Jārūd, whose family figures in the massacre of 133),[196] and the Banū Abī

[192] I follow Hopkins in seeing an association between administrative centralisation and political unification on the one hand, and social mobility on the other; see M. K. Hopkins, 'Elite mobility in the Roman empire', *Past and Present* 32 (1965), pp. 12–26.

[193] See Robinson, 'Al-Muʿāfā b. ʿImrān'.

[194] Descendants of ʿUbayd Allāh b. Ḥabḥāb, who would become Hishām's governor of Egypt and North Africa; see al-Azdī, *Taʾrīkh*, pp. 26ff., 149 and 172; Ibn ʿAbd al-Ḥakam, *Futūḥ Miṣr*, pp. 169, 217, 245 and 246; Severus b. al-Muqaffaʿ, *History of the Patriarchs of the Coptic Church of Alexandria*, III, ed. and trans. B. Evetts in *PO* 5 (1947), pp. 86f. See also Forand, 'Governors', p. 90; and N. Abbott, 'A new papyrus and a review of the administration of ʿUbaid Allāh b. al-Ḥabḥāb,' in G. Makdisi, ed., *Arabic and Islamic Studies in Honor of Hamilton A. R. Gibb* (Leiden, 1965), pp. 25ff.

[195] See chapter 7.

[196] See al-Azdī, *Taʾrīkh*, p. 149; Ibn Khurdādbih, *Masālik*, p. 95, note g; Juynboll, *Muslim Tradition*, p. 231 (for further literature).

Khidāsh,[197] we have families that had acquired their standing in the late Umayyad or early Abbasid periods, and retained it well into the tenth century.[198] The Banū ʿImrān and Ṣaddāmiyyūn may also qualify as tenth-century families with early Abbasid roots.[199]

[197] An Azdī family of learning that begins with Saʿīd b. al-ʿAlāʾ (Abū Khidāsh; d. 199/814–15), a *ḥadīth* transmitter who taught ʿAlī b. Ḥarb (al-Azdī, *Taʾrīkh*, p. 338). One grandson (Zayd) died in Malaṭya (*Taʾrīkh*, p. 363), and another, Muḥammad b. ʿAlī b. Abī Khidāsh, died while on *jihād* in Sumaysāṭ in 222/837; see Ibn Ḥajar, *Tahdhīb*, IX, p. 357 (citing al-Azdī); and al-Ṣafadī, *al-Wāfī bi'l-wafayāt*, IV, p. 106.

[198] All of these families are known to Ibn Ḥawqal, who visited the city a generation after al-Azdī's death, perhaps as late as 358/968; see Ibn Ḥawqal, *Ṣūrat al-arḍ*, pp. 215f.

[199] On the Banū ʿImrān, see Thomas of Marga, *Governors*, pp. 239ff./450ff.; on Abdūn al-Ṣaddāmī (who appears in 219/833), see al-Azdī, *Taʾrīkh*, p. 417.

FOUR

Christian élites in the Mosuli hinterland: the *shahārija*

I noted earlier that the province of al-Mawṣil fits the long-familiar Iraqi pattern, according to which non-Muslim indigenous élites levied taxes for a small Muslim/Arab ruling class claiming the exclusive right of sovereignty. In Iraq proper, the most prominent of these élites were the *dihqāns*, 'village headmen' who prospered for much of the seventh century, and whose star began to decline at the tail-end of that century, particularly as Arabisation and Islamicisation took hold.[1] In the province of Mosul, the village élite was topped by the *shahārija* (sing. *shahrīj*), and of these we know hardly more than did Theodor Nöldeke and Georg Hoffmann, both of whom wrote more than a century ago;[2] were it not for Morony's work on Iraq, Islamicists might have forgotten about them completely. Nöldeke defined the *shahrīg* of the Sasanian period as a regional official ('Oberhaupt eines Kreises'),[3] relying principally on the testimony of al-Yaʿqūbī, who glosses the *shahrīj* as *ra'īs al-kuwar*.[4] This gloss was in harmony with Nöldeke's understanding of the Middle Persian *shahr*, which he took to mean 'region' or 'district';[5] it also seemed to complement the testimony of both al-Masʿūdī, who places the *shahārija* just below the 'three great families' (*al-abyāt al-thalātha*) of the Sawād, but above the *dihqāns*,[6] and that of the ninth-century Nestorian Thomas of Marga, who reports that *shahārija* of his period collected tax revenues from the *dihqāns*.[7] For Nöldeke, just as the *dahīg* was responsible for the village (*dah*), so was the *shahrīg* said to have been responsible for the *shahr*. If our understanding of *shahr* has broadened considerably since Nöldeke's day,[8] his view continues to

[1] See Morony, *Iraq*, pp. 187, 190, 204.

[2] See T. Nöldeke's translation of al-Ṭabarī, *Geschichte der Perser und Araber zur Zeit der Sasaniden* (Leiden, 1879), pp. 446f.; Hoffmann, *Auszüge*, pp. 236ff.

[3] Nöldeke, *Geschichte der Perser*, p. 446. [4] Al-Yaʿqūbī, *Ta'rīkh*, I, p. 203.

[5] See Nöldeke, *Geschichte der Perser*, pp. 3, note 2, and 446, note 3; and also Barthold, *Historical Geography of Iran*, p. 152.

[6] Al-Masʿūdī, *Murūj al-dhahab wa-ma'ādin al-jawhar* (Beirut, 1979), I, p. 327.

[7] Thomas of Marga, *Governors*, pp. 152/311.

[8] Namely, empire, kingdom, satrap, region and province. See, for example, G. Widengren's comments on the *shahr*: 'On a donc l'impression d'une part que la terminologie n'a pas été absolument fixe' ('Recherches sur le féodalisme iranien', *Orientalia Suecana* 5 (1956), p. 140). See also E. Herzfeld, *Paikuli: Monument and Inscription of the Early History of the Sasanian Empire*

prevail in several quarters:[9] the *shahrīj* remains an official ('fonctionnaire') of the Sasanian state. This is true for Christensen, Widengren, Grignaschi and Morony.[10]

Below I shall have a few comments to make about the evidence upon which this conventional wisdom is based; but my main concern is to describe the *shahārija* in early Islamic Mosul, to say something about at least some of those 'faceless *'ulūj* and *naṣārā*',[11] in whom the Islamic tradition manifests only the most modest interest. The transformation of Christian Emesa of St Simeon the Fool (*fl.* mid-sixth century), with its publicans, slaves, prostitutes and taverns,[12] into the Umayyad Ḥimṣ of Yamanī tribesmen and their apocalyptic anxieties,[13] may be forever lost to us, but a fortuitous combination of sources allows us to say something about the fate of at least some Christians in the north. Of course, the point is also to say something about the state's relation to another élite, one very different from the *mdabbrānē* of the Byzantine west.

The *shahārija* of the north: geography and taxes

The Syriac tradition allows us to plot the *shahārija* in several towns in the early Islamic north, and we can be confident that they were concentrated in the heavily Nestorian lands to the east and south of the city of Mosul.[14] We can start with a toponym, Tall al-Shahārija. According to the conquest account recorded by al-Balādhurī,[15] 'Utba b. Farqad took control of both sides of the Tigris at Nineveh, and moved east into al-Marj (Margā), the inland region east of Mosul and north of the Greater Zāb; he then turned south, crossed the

(Berlin, 1924), II, p. 194; N. Pigulevskaya, *Les Villes de l'état iranien aux époques parthe et sassanide* (Paris, 1963), p. 128; and for the case of Fārs, R. N. Frye, *Sasanian Remains from Qasr-i Abu Nasr* (Cambridge, MA, 1973), pp. 3f., note 5.

9 Cf. the case of the *marzbān* in P. Gignoux, 'L'Organisation administrative sasanide: le cas du *Marzbān*', *JSAI* 4 (1984), p. 17.

10 A. Christensen, *L'Iran sous les Sassanides* (Copenhagen, 1944; second edn), p. 140; Widengren, 'Recherches', p. 144; G. Widengren, 'Iran, der große Gegner Roms: Königsgewalt, Feudalismus, Militärwesen', *Aufstieg und Niedergang der römischen Welt*: *Principat* 9:1 (Berlin and New York, 1974–), p. 280; M. Grignaschi, 'Quelques spécimens de la littérature sassanide conservés dans les bibliothèques d'Istanbul,' *JA* 254 (1966), pp. 31f. (in fact, Grignaschi has it both ways: al-Mas'ūdī's passage is taken to mean that the *shahārija* 'formaient une noblesse urbaine ayant le droit de préséance sur celle de la campagne'; at the same time, the *kātib al-kūra* is equivalent to the *shahrīj*, itself in turn equivalent to the *ostandār*: the *shahrīj* is a 'fonctionnaire' and 'il s'agissait d'un personnage assez élevé, nommé . . . directement par le Šāhensāh'); Morony, *Iraq*, p. 187 ('official in charge of a province'); cf. also A. A. Dehkhoda, *Loghat-nāma* (Teheran, 1994), p. 12889.

11 Crone, *Slaves*, p. 12.

12 For a brief overview, see C. Mango, *Byzantium: The Empire of New Rome* (New York, 1980), pp. 62f.

13 On the Ḥimṣī context of some late Umayyad apocalypticism, see W. Madelung, 'Apocalyptic prophecies in Ḥimṣ in the Umayyad age', *Journal of Semitic Studies* 31 (1986), pp. 141–85; and also Bashear, 'Apocalyptic and other materials on early Muslim–Byzantine wars'.

14 I use the words 'Nestorian' and 'concentrated' advisedly, since it is only during the late sixth and seventh centuries that the Church of the East embraced a strain of Antiochene Christology that could be accurately called Nestorian in character.

15 Al-Balādhurī, *Futūḥ*, pp. 333f.

river, and moved into Adiabene, where he conquered Ḥazza, which also lay just west of Irbil.[16] He is then said to have 'come to Tall al-Shahārija and al-Salaq'. Hoffmann identified the former as Tall Ḥibtūn, which, according to Fiey,[17] lay to the north along the Greater Zāb; Hoffmann does not provide any direct evidence for this identification.[18] If the Arabic al-Salaq is to be identified with the Syriac Salāk,[19] which lay to the east of Irbil, towards Azarbayjān, there may be grounds for locating Tall al-Shahārija somewhere between Irbil and al-Salaq, perhaps fairly close to the latter.[20] Well into the Islamic period we can place the *shahārija* in Kfarʿuzzēl, the Arabic Kafarʿizzā, which lay just to the east of Irbil.[21] The presence of *shahārija* in this town is attested for an earlier period by Thomas of Marga.[22]

There is thus some respectable evidence that the *shahārija* were present in ninth-century Adiabene in general and near the town of Ḥazza in particular, which appears to have had some administrative significance in the late Sasanian period.[23] How far south they reached in this period is less clear. The 'Life' of John of Dailam mentions two *shahrīgs*, one each from sites called 'A-r-b-d' and 'S-l-k',[24] and, as Brock has noted, both are difficult to locate. The first is probably related to a cluster of toponyms that include Ardābād and Darābād, but there is great confusion, since we have evidence for a Darābād in Adiabene as well as a Darābād in Bēt Garmē.[25] Similarly, we cannot say if 'S-l-k' points us in the direction of the present-day Kirkuk (in Bēt Garmē),[26] or Salāk (in Adiabene).[27] Here we might note that according to Īshōʿdnaḥ, Ḥnānīshōʿ built a monastery in the 'land (*atrā*) of S-l-k and D-i-b-r';[28] the second of these, given Syriac orthography, might very well be interpreted as 'R-b-d'. We can be more certain of *shahārija* presence north of the Greater Zāb, since Thomas of Marga also tells us that some *shahārija* came from Bēt

[16] The Muslim authorities were unable to locate Ḥazza with any precision; see, for example, Ibn Ḥawqal, *Ṣūrat al-arḍ*, p. 217; and al-Bakrī, *Muʿjam*, p. 441. On Ḥazza in general, see Fiey, *Assyrie chrétienne*, I.

[17] Fiey, *Assyrie chrétienne*, II, pp. 198ff.

[18] Hoffmann, *Auszüge*, p. 237. Yāqūt (*Muʿjam*, II, p. 193) only knows of a mountain called Jibtūn, which lay in (the province of) Mosul.

[19] See Fiey, *Assyrie chrétienne*, III, pp. 80f.

[20] The absence of Irbil in the conquest narratives is puzzling.

[21] See Ibn Ḥawqal, *Ṣūrat al-arḍ*, p. 217 (reproduced by al-Idrīsī, *Opus geographicum*, pp. 659f.); see also Fiey, *Assyrie chrétienne*, I, pp. 174ff.

[22] Thomas of Marga, *Governors*, pp. 142f./294f.; see also pp. 161/324f. and 199f./388. The *shahārija* were not, however, the only inhabitants of Kafarʿizzā, since a strong Nestorian presence, including a famous school, is described by Thomas of Marga (*Governors*, pp. 142f./295, 145/301f. and 174/349; see also Fiey, *Assyrie chrétienne*, I, p. 175). Budge's suggestion that the town was the seat of the bishop of Margā (*Governors*, II, p. 350 note 2) is disputed by Fiey (*Assyrie chrétienne*, I, p. 174 note 8).

[23] On Ḥazza, see Morony, *Iraq*, pp. 132f.; Fiey, *Assyrie chrétienne*, I, pp. 166ff.

[24] Brock, 'John of Dailam', pp. 187/163f.

[25] Fiey, *Assyrie chrétienne*, III, pp. 76ff.; Fiey, *Pour un Oriens Christianus Novus*, p. 73.

[26] Fiey, *Assyrie chrétienne*, III; Fiey, *Pour un Oriens Christianus Novus*, pp. 126f.

[27] Which is Brock's choice.

[28] See Īshōʿdnaḥ, *Le Livre de la Chasteté*, pp. 12/12; Chabot transliterates the second of these as 'Dībūr'. See also Fiey, *Assyrie Chrétienne*, III, p. 80.

Ṭḥūnē,[29] Kop,[30] and Ḥṭārā, which lay on the Khāzir river.[31] Finally, the anonymous *History* of Bēt Qoqa edited by Mingana identifies the wife of a *shahrīg* from Bā Nuhadrā, which lay to the north of the city of Mosul, along the Tigris.[32]

The geographic distribution of the *shahārija* is thus widespread in the north, and the presence of Tall al-Shahārija in al-Balādhurī's accounts suggests that they had already given their name to a settlement by the conquest period; even if one were inclined to dismiss al-Balādhurī's conquest testimony as late, Sayf (in al-Ṭabarī) also suggests that they came from the north, rather than from the south.[33] Indeed, in the relatively abundant Syriac testimony of the early Islamic period there are no signs that the *shahārija* were perceived as recent arrivals; to the contrary, Thomas suggests that they had deep roots, and this was the view – admittedly late – of Bar Bahlūl as well.[34] Finally, if one is inclined to embrace Nöldeke's speculative identification of another site associated with the *shahārija*,[35] we must push their presence in the north to the late sixth century – that is, well before the Muslim conquest.

What is striking is the Islamic-era presence of the *shahārija* in the north and their contrasting absence in the south: the *shahārija* seem to have been restricted to the eastern side of the Tigris in northern Iraq in general, and the early Islamic province of Mosul in particular. What this means is that they occupied the Iraqi periphery, and if we assume – as, I think, we should – that the conquests did not result in large-scale social dislocation, we can begin to understand the perseverance of the *shahārija* well into the ninth century.

To describe how they persevered, we need to take a closer look at the sources, and we can start with the 'Life' of John of Daylam. Although the 'Life' is hagiographic and therefore vulnerable to the standard critiques of the genre,[36] it is thoroughly local in character; moreover, the details – proper

[29] Thomas of Marga, *Governors*, pp. 161/324; Hoffmann, *Auszüge*, p. 238; and Fiey, *Assyrie chrétienne*, I, p. 267.

[30] Probably to be located in Margā as well; see Thomas of Marga, *Governors*, pp. 164/330.

[31] Thomas of Marga, *Governors*, pp. 393/666. The Khāzir is a tributary of the Greater Zāb, from which it breaks off about 20 kilometres from the Tigris, heading north towards Margā.

[32] See Mingana, ed., *Sources*, pp. 210/259; see Brock, 'Syriac sources', p. 26.

[33] Al-Ṭabarī, *Ta'rīkh*, I, pp. 2474f. (abridged by Ibn al-Athīr, *al-Kāmil*, II, pp. 523f.).

[34] Cf. Thomas of Marga's use of *ṭūhmā*, a term that can be rendered as 'race', 'stock', 'lineage' or 'descent'. See Thomas of Marga, *Governors*, pp. 393/666; Payne Smith, *Syriac Dictionary*, p. 168.

[35] See Nöldeke (*Geschichte der Perser*, p. 447) citing Theophylact of Simocatta, *History* (Stuttgart, 1972 reprint of de Boor, 1887) V. 8, 9 (Siraganon) ('Dorf[e] des Šahrīgān'); cf. M. and M. Whitby, *The History of Theophylact Simocatta: An English Translation with Introduction and Notes* (Oxford, 1986), p. 143 (translation: 'a certain village called Siraganon by its inhabitants') and p. 247 (location); and M. Whitby, *The Emperor Maurice and his Historian: Theophylact Simocatta on Persian and Balkan Warfare* (Oxford, 1988), p. 301 (map) and pp. 302f. (discussion). The secondary literature is concerned only with locating the site, which is conventionally located west of the southern shore of Lake Urmia; see Markwart, *Ērānšahr*, pp. 23f.

[36] For a discussion of this problem in West Syrian sources, see S. Harvey, *Asceticism and Society in Crisis: John of Ephesus and the Lives of the Eastern Saints* (Berkeley and Los Angeles, 1990), esp. pp. 34ff.

names and toponyms – suggest some authenticity, and Brock considers the 'Life' as 'generally reliable', counting the passage in question as historical.[37] The work survives in two forms: a West Syrian prose life, and an East Syrian verse panegyric; it is only in the latter that the relevant passage appears. The events recorded are likely to have occurred in the late seventh century.[38] It reads:

The Daylamites[39] set off again for the region[40] of Mosul and took people captive, including two men, members of the *shahrigan*, one, son of Gurya, the headman[41] of Arbad, whose name was Bahloi, the other, Behriya, son of Nuryād, the headman of Slokh. The blessed [John] saw them and recognized them as headmen from his own region, and so he bought the two of them from the Dailamites for 6000 [dīnārs]; he wrote off to their home country and they sent silver in the hands of their servants, six [thousand] pieces to ransom themselves, and six [thousand] for our master, making 12000 in all. Along with the *shahrigan* Bahloi and Behriya they went off home.[42]

It is significant that our passage is present in the East Syrian version and absent in the West Syrian, for it may reflect something of a Nestorian hagiographic *topos*, which was employed to demonstrate that the charisma and generosity of the Nestorian holy man extended beyond the faithful, even to those whose Christology, and perhaps social status as well, made them natural rivals to the Nestorians. Thus, according to one account, two of the *shahrīg*s, one named Naggārā and the other his son Maslamā, came to a holy man in the hope that he cure the latter.[43] Prescribed some *ḥnānā* – consecrated soil from saints' tombs – and an extended fast, Maslamā was cured. We read elsewhere that the leprous wife of a *shahrīg* from Bēt Nuhadrā visited another holy man for a cure.[44]

Although the text is intended to illustrate the selflessness of John, it says more. Most important, it makes plain that the *shahārija* were a recognisably discrete group of wealthy and landed headmen. This view is shared by Thomas of Marga, who remarks on their wealth,[45] and in at least one place makes clear its origin: the *shahārija* of Bēt Ṭhūnē are said to have owned

[37] See 'John of Dailam', p. 132.

[38] At any event, before 701, following Brock's summary; see 'John of Dailam', p. 181.

[39] The intrusion of Daylamites into the province of Mosul is noteworthy in this period, particularly since the text suggests that they did so with some frequency, and that they had the good sense to take the *shahārija* captive. Just who these 'Daylamites' were is difficult to say: perhaps the author has Kurds in mind.

[40] *Atrā*: generally 'land' or 'country', but also occasionally the administratively more precise 'province' as well.

[41] *Rīshā* ('head', 'chief'), probably equivalent to the 'village headmen' (*mārē qaryē*); elsewhere (ps.-Joshua, *Chronicle*, pp. 35/29), Wright translates 'landed proprietors'.

[42] Brock, 'John of Dailam', pp. 187/163f.

[43] See Thomas of Marga, *Governors*, pp. 393ff./666ff. Elsewhere Thomas refers to Arabs – both pre-Islamic and Muslim – as *ṭayyāyē*; in Naggārā and Maslama we probably have a pair of Arabising Persians, rather than Arab *shahārija*.

[44] See the *History* of Bēt Qoqa in Mingana, ed., *Sources*, pp. 210/259.

[45] Thomas of Marga, *Governors*, pp. 142f./294f. and 198f./386ff.

numerous villages.[46] It was also shared by the tenth-century encyclopaedist Bar Bahlūl. Here we read that the *shahārija* were *aʿyān aṣḥāb al-balad*, which, in the light of John of Daylam and Thomas of Marga, might safely be rendered as 'prominent landholders'. They are also called 'ancient people of high rank, settled folk' (*wa-hum al-qudamā' ahl al-martaba al-ʿāliya sukkān al-arḍ*), and 'exemplary and noble people' (*muthul al-qawm wa-nubl al-qawm*).[47] The wealth of the *shahārija* was also noted by Ibn Ḥawqal, who as a native of Nisibis may have known northern Mesopotamia better than most; as we have seen, the town (*madīna*) of Kafarʿizzā is said to have been inhabited by 'a group of *shahārija*, who are wealthy Christians' (*naṣārā dhū yasār*).[48]

The 'Life' of John of Daylam not only tells us that the *shahrīgān* were headmen; it also tells us that these headmen were taken captive, and returned only after the payment of a ransom. What lies behind these events is not only the apparent (and predictable) failure to maintain order, but more precisely the role these headmen played in local taxation. According to Thomas of Marga, while Māranʿemmeh was the Nestorian Metropolitan of Salāk (mid-eighth century), local *dihqān*s are said to have complained to him about the onerous taxation levied by the *shahārija*; the latter are said to have taken 'one half of the grain, wine, and nuts, and the "poll tax" (*ksef rīshā*)'.[49] Whether the revenues the *shahārija* collected entered the pockets of the Muslim élite with any regularity cannot be demonstrated with the evidence we presently have. And if we assume that the *shahārija* levied the taxes with some success – as we might, given their wealth – we unfortunately have no evidence for the coercive power that accompanied their claim to the revenues.[50] The evidence being so slim, we might rather take the account as a salutary reminder of how taxation, even in the middle of the eighth century, was as inefficient in asserting claims of sovereignty (Christians levied the taxes on Christians, and appeals for relief were made to Christian authorities) as it was in extracting revenues.

To Thomas of Marga we owe not only the best evidence for the *shahārija* in early Islam, but also a date for their eclipse in local taxation. The evidence is an *ex eventu* prophecy that he attributes to Māranʿemmeh, the Metropolitan of Salāk in the middle of the eighth century. As we have already seen, the *dahāqīn* had complained to him about the confiscatory tax practices of the *shahārija*, and he responded by offering some comforting words:

46 Thomas of Marga, *Governors*, pp. 161/324.

47 Bar Bahlūl, in Duval, ed., *Lexicon*, II, c. 1939. Hoffmann, *Auszüge*, p. 239, translates from the Syriac 'old established on the land' (*Landeingesessene*). The definition is also recorded by R. Payne Smith, *Thesaurus Syriacus* (Oxford, 1879–1901), II, p. 4077 ('indigenae, qui primi regionem incoluerunt, primates'), and it is likely that it stands behind Costaz's definition as well: 'noble of high rank, *sharīf dhū martaba ʿāliya*'; see L. Costaz, *Dictionnaire Syriaque–Français, Syriac–English Dictionary* (Beirut, 1963), p. 361.

48 Ibn Ḥawqal, *Ṣūrat al-arḍ*, p. 217.

49 Thomas of Marga, *Governors*, pp. 152/311f.

50 Had the Muslim garrison provided this coercion we might expect to hear of the *shahārija* in the Muslim sources, or lacking this, to hear of it in the Nestorian sources, since *shahārija*/Muslim co-operation would surely have been hard to resist for Nestorian polemicists. But of this we hear nothing.

My children: All of these villages will be taxed by the Arabs,[51] and all of these *shahrīgān* will leave. Then a man named Ḥ-T-M bar Ṣ-L-Ḥ will persecute and uproot them. All of you will be subjected to him, since as it is said, 'the wicked avenges the wicked, and God avenges them both.'[52]

The account concludes by noting that although the figure in question had not yet been born, the events transpired as Māranʿemmeh had prophesied. Neither Budge nor Hoffmann was able to identify this figure in order to make sense of the 'prophecy'.[53]

With the publication of Azdī's history of Mosul we can now do so. Al-Azdī's sources for this period in the history of his hometown are local, and they offer us an unparalleled view of one province in the early Abbasid period; while other sources have very little of any detail to say about Umayyad taxation in the province of Mosul, Azdī provides some very convincing details that demonstrate precisely how varied the tax administration was during the late second Islamic century. Thus, in 175/791 we are told that some districts were due the *rubʿ*, and others the *ʿushr*; meanwhile, tax administrators seem to have used the chronic Khārijite revolts as a convenient excuse for their inability to hand over the tax revenues. Hārūn's response was to attempt a systemisation of Mosuli taxation by summoning the local tax officials (who go unidentified); these were then instructed by Yaḥyā b. Khālid how to collect the *kharāj* in Nineveh, Marj, their adjoining territory, and the steppe-land (*barrīya*). The provincial officials are said to have resisted Baghdad's measures.[54]

What we seem to have here is an attempt to claim provincial revenues in an unprecedented way, and I suggest this because Azdī also provides evidence that a new form of coercion was being introduced in this period: the employment of local tribes to levy taxes. It is here that we come to the identity of Ḥ-T-M bar Ṣ-L-Ḥ. Ḥātim b. Ṣāliḥ, it turns out, was a member of the Banū Hamdān, and one of its most prominent clans, the Banū Ṣāliḥ. His son Rawḥ had been the first of this family to play a prominent role in Mosuli politics; after being put in charge of collecting the tribute (*ṣadaqa*) due from the Banū Taghlib, he was killed in the Hamdān–Taghlib battle that followed in 171/787. Ḥātim himself stayed in the background until 183/799 when he defeated a force led by Harthama b. Aʿyan; in so doing he emerged as the most powerful tribal chief in the city and its environs. After reaching a draw with another Abbasid force, this one led by Yazīd b. Mazyad al-Shaybānī, Ḥātim was granted one year's *kharāj* revenue by Hārūn; although the text is not precise, this revenue was apparently drawn from Ḥātim's stronghold of al-Salaq.[55] These revenues were thus drawn from the *shahārija* heartland.

[51] *Eshtqel*: see Payne Smith, *Syriac Dictionary*, p. 594. Budge, unaware of the issues lying behind the report, translates colourlessly: 'taken up'.

[52] Thomas of Marga, *Governors*, pp. 152/312.

[53] Thomas of Marga, *Governors*, pp. 152/312; Hoffmann, *Auszüge*, p. 238.

[54] Al-Azdī, *Ta'rīkh*, pp. 275f.

[55] For the accounts, see al-Azdī, *Ta'rīkh*, pp. 267ff.

Māranʿemmeh's prophecy and the passages from al-Azdī's *Taʾrīkh* thus provide us with a precious intersection of the Syriac and Islamic traditions. Certainly the two traditions perceive the events very differently: writing in the early tenth-century metropolis of Mosul, al-Azdī was at such a cultural distance from the largely Christian countryside that the *shahārija* were invisible; as far as he was concerned, life outside the city was dominated by immigrant Arab tribes. Similar things could be said about Thomas of Marga: unable to distinguish among Abbasid generals, their armies and their proxies, Thomas reduces them all to colourless *ṭayyāyē*. But having said this, we can be fairly certain about what happened: administrative reforms, coupled with (and largely effected by) the empowerment of local tribes, resulted in the first serious dislocation of Late Antique tax procedures in the hinterlands of Mosul, and this a full two generations after the Abbasid Revolution. Of course élites are resilient things: the *shahārija* may have relinquished their roles in the tax administration, but to judge from later sources (particularly Ibn Ḥawqal), they retained their land.

For all that the Marwānids and early Abbasids were concerned to establish a revenue system in the Jaziran west, we have seen that their efforts in the east do not seem to have penetrated into the hinterland, and certainly did not include the incorporation of this rural élite. The *asāwira* of Iraq had their military services to offer the Muslims, and one might infer from the premium-level stipends they received upon their conversion that these services were in high demand during the explosive conquest period;[56] since they were not landed, one might also infer that they played their hand extremely well: the longer they waited, the less they had to offer the caliphs. The *shahārija*, by contrast, were landed, and provided that the state eschewed both the dirty work of tax collection and a policy of rural confiscation, they had no incentive to assimilate. Moreover, unlike the *mdabbrānē* of the western Jazira, whose wealth presumably rested on land as well, the *shahārija* enjoyed the shared collective identity of their noble pedigree; possessing a (mythological) past secured them a future under the caliphs.

The eclipse of the *shahārija* during Hārūn's reign suggests another lesson about the state's relations with the north. Even now, at a time of unprecedented centralisation, the difficult task of rural coercion was delegated to locals, which, in the Mosuli hinterland, almost inevitably meant local tribes. Their eclipse, in other words, is no more to be explained by the ineluctable (and usually undefined) attraction to convert than it is by the imperial power of an absolutist Abbasid state. It is to be explained by the Abbasids' recognition that to make power effective in the north was to devolve it.

[56] On the *asāwira*, see Morony, *Iraq*, s.v.; M. Zakeri, *Sāsānid Soldiers and Early Muslim Society: The Origins of ʿAyyārān and Futuwwa* (Wiesbaden, 1995); and for their late conversion, Crone, *Slaves*, pp. 237f., note 362.

The *shahārija*: Christology and history

According to the evidence from the early Islamic period, the *shahārija* were located in a number of villages and towns of the province of Mosul, and there they seem to have been wealthy land owners whose properties had earned them local standing: the 'Life' of John of Dailam specifically identifies them as village headmen. It is as prominent land owners and village headmen – a landed gentry – that they played some kind of a role in what was probably a very loose tributary system of revenue extraction, and this during all of the Umayyad and into the early Abbasid periods. The site of Mosul changed beyond recognition under the early Marwānids, but its rural hinterland is a study of continuity. Indeed, it is in terms of continuity that confessional identity of the *shahārija* should also be discussed.

We have seen that Thomas of Marga offers the best evidence for the *shahārija*; here it should be noted that he describes them not because he had any special concern with the fiscal administration of the seventh century or patterns of land tenure. He is concerned with the *shahārija* because they had a distinctive Christology. The crucial passage concerns the activities of Māranʿemmeh as Nestorian bishop in Salāk, which lay east of Irbil; these activities took place during the third quarter of the eighth century. At this time the area remained full of Zoroastrians, and these Māranʿemmeh endeavoured to convert; he also tried to convert the *shahārija*, and he did so, it appears, because of their aberrant view of Christ. Indeed, Thomas of Marga hesitates to call them Christian, for they are, in his words, 'Christians in name [only]' (*ba-shmā kristiyānē*), regarding the Messiah as 'a mere man' (*barnāshā shḥīmā*). Their behaviour is repellent – they are said to have slept with nuns, berated holy men and engaged in orgies – and their heresy merits them a series of calamities: their village of Bēt Ṭḥunē is destroyed; their illegitimate bishop Rustām is killed; they are 'uprooted' by Ḥātim b. Ṣāliḥ.[57] Despite the efforts of local Nestorians, many persisted in their views, and those who converted to 'Nestorianism' did so by adjusting their Christology, professing: 'We believe that Jesus Christ is the Son of God, and that He is God.'[58]

Needless to say, the views Thomas attributes to the *shahārija* are difficult to interpret, not only because they derive from a hostile source, but also because they date from the Islamic period. Should we identify the *shahārija* as pragmatic Christians whose radically simplified Christology represents a doctrinal rapprochement to their new Muslim patrons? Or, rather, might they be Christians whose deviant view of Christ marks one end of the wide spectrum of Christologies available in the Late Antique region that would ultimately emerge as the province of Mosul? The former view has some merit. It has a

[57] Thomas of Marga, *Governors*, pp. 152f./311f., 161/324f., and 198ff./385ff.
[58] Thomas of Marga, *Governors* pp. 151/309f.

Palestinian analogue, where Qur'ānic Christology seems to have been known to the author of what Griffith calls the *Summa Theologiae Arabica*.[59] Closer to home, in Abbasid Adiabene, Wolfson argued that a Nestorian splinter group, which he identifies with Saadia's 'fourth sect' who 'assign to Jesus the position of a prophet only', is detectable in al-Shahrastānī's *Milal*;[60] the timing of this sect's appearance – the early Abbasid period – leads Wolfson to explain its Christology as an accommodation to the lean Christology of the sect's Muslim patrons.[61] A change in theological climate has also been argued by Crone, who has written that 'Islam made Judeo-Christianity a polemically viable position'.[62]

Wolfson's work demonstrates the late eighth- and ninth-century currency of a Christology that effaced Jesus' divinity; and it is even possible that his schismatics relate in some way to our *shahārija*. This said, in northern Mesopotamia the evidence for the theological and social pressure required to effect a christologial accommodation is weak; and in asserting Islamic influence Wolfson strings together a list of generalities,[63] none of which seems to apply to seventh-century Adiabene. Meanwhile, an argument for continuity is a strong one, and one should perhaps envision a process, whereby a privileged and administratively experienced group such as the *shahārija* did not so much fashion a new identity in order avoid doctrinal friction with their new patrons as retain and accentuate an old one.

Certainly conditions were such that we should expect continuity. The survival of paganism in the Jazira proper is illustrated by the well-known Ṣābi'a and, at least in the sixth century, the Qādishāyē.[64] Thomas of Marga himself attests to the popularity of Zoroastrianism in Salāk in the middle of the eighth

59 'The author of the *Summa* is taking issue with Christian people who, under the influence of the preaching of the Qur'an, were willing to say that the Messiah is simply a man.' See S. H. Griffith, 'The first Christian *summa theologiae* in Arabic: Christian *kalām* in ninth-century Palestine', in M. Gervers and R. J. Bikhazi, eds., *Conversion and Continuity: Indigenous Christian Communities in Islamic Lands Eighth to Eighteenth Centuries* (Toronto, 1990), p. 23.

60 See H. A. Wolfson, 'An unknown splinter group of Nestorians', in his *The Philosophy of the Kalam* (Cambridge, MA., 1976), pp. 337–49; see also H. A. Wolfson, 'Saadia on the Trinity and Incarnation', in M. Ben-Horin *et al.*, eds., *Studies and Essays in Honor of Abraham A. Neuman* (Leiden, 1962), pp. 565ff. For the passage in question, see al-Shahrastānī, *Kitāb al-Milal wa'l-niḥal* (London, 1842–6) I, p. 176.

61 Wolfson, 'Splinter group', pp. 343ff.

62 See P. Crone, 'Islam, Judeo-Christianity and Byzantine iconoclasm', *JSAI* 2 (1980), pp. 74f., who takes the account in 'Abd al-Jabbār (see S. M. Stern, 'Quotations from apocryphal gospels in 'Abd al-Jabbār', *Journal of Theological Studies* n.s. 18 (1967), p. 51) as an allusion to Jaziran Christians. Cf. Stern, ''Abd al-Jabbār's account of how Christ's religion was falsified by the adoption of Roman customs', *Journal of Theological Studies* n.s. 19 (1968), p. 135, note 4.

63 'We know that debates between Christians and Muslims on this Christological view had been going on ever since their first encounter. We know that Christians as a minority group in Muslim countries were not entirely impervious to Muslim influence. We know also that the Christian Arabic literature . . . had kept alive among Christians in Muslim countries a knowledge of the Ebionitic type of Christology of heretical Samosatenians, Arians, and Macedonians and also a knowledge of all the arguments in favor of it.' See Wolfson, 'Saadia on the Trinity', p. 567.

64 On the latter, see T. Nöldeke, 'Zwei Völker Vorderasiens', *ZDMG* 33 (1879), pp. 157ff.; ps.-Joshua, *Chronicle*, pp. 17/14; and ps.-Zacharias Rhetor, *Historia ecclesiastica*, I, pp. 92/63.

century.[65] In the countryside of northern Mesopotamia, where imperial pressure – be it Christian, Sasanian or Islamic – was attenuated, syncretism was probably the rule,[66] and 'heresy' endemic: Daniel of Ra'sal-ʿAyn railed against Marcionites in the middle of the sixth century;[67] and Msallyānē (Euchites) flourished among the monastic communities.[68] Northern Mesopotamia appears to have been something of an incubator for heresy, the Yazīdīs of the inaccessible mountains of Sinjār being only the most recent example of the predilection of Jaziran schismatics for the region's remoter areas.[69]

In paring Jesus' divinity down to prophecy, the *shahārija*'s heresy might be explained with reference to Jewish Christianity, particularly since we do hear of seventh-century conversions from Judaism to Christianity.[70] But problems abound. Leaving aside the imprecision of the category 'Judaeo-Christian',[71] we should remember that in matters of praxis there is no evidence for Judaeo-Christianity among the *shahārija*, and when it comes to locating influences on Aphrahat (d. c. 345), Peeters upbraids de Urbina for positing Jewish sources rather than Paulianist sympathisers.[72] Had the *shahārija* a Judaeo-Christian orientation, we might reasonably expect our Nestorian authors to call them Jews; after all, it took little to call one's opponent a Jew: Monophysites could call an Arab Muslim governor of Mosul a Jew,[73] and Nestorian sources could call Muslims in general the 'new Jews'.[74] There is rather more mileage in Peeters' view. Thus Wolfson, despite his own hesitation,[75] may have been correct in positing a connection between his deviant 'Nestorians' and the ideas

[65] See Thomas of Marga, *Governors*, pp. 149/307. John's life also alludes to Zoroastrians, and it speaks as well of those who 'worshipped trees'; see Brock, 'John of Dailam', pp. 137/146f., and 161.

[66] Thus John of Ephesus (*Lives of the Eastern Saints*, p. 236) writes of the peregrinations of Simeon the Mountaineer, who came across a village near Melitene in the early sixth century. The villagers identified themselves as Christians, but it was not a strain of Christianity that Simeon could identify: 'These men neither worship God like Christians, nor honour something else like pagans; and they are apostates against the one and against the other' (Brooks's translation).

[67] J. M. Fiey, 'Les Marcionites dans les textes historiques de l'Eglise de Perse', *Le Muséon* 83 (1970), pp. 183ff.; see also Īshōʿyahb III, *Liber epistularum*, pp. 282/203. Marcionites also appear in the East (Persia?) in the lifetime of the eighth-century Nestorian holy man Mār Shūbḥālīshōʿ; see Thomas of Marga, *Governors*, pp. 261/481.

[68] Thomas of Marga, *Governors*, pp. 51/91.

[69] For a recent work on the Yazīdīs, see J. S. Guest, *The Yezidis: A Study in Survival* (London, 1987). [70] Michael the Syrian, *Chronique* xi.xii (during Muʿāwiya's reign).

[71] See J. E. Taylor, 'The phenomenon of early Jewish-Christianity: reality or scholarly invention?', *Vigiliae Christianae* 44 (1990), pp. 313–34.

[72] See his review of de Urbina's *Die Gottheit Christi bei Afrahat* in *Analecta Bollandiana* 53 (1935), pp. 145f. In the Syriac heresiographical literature, Paul is said to have been influenced by Jews; see Barḥadbshabbā ʿArbāyā, *L'Histoire de Barḥadbešabba ʿArbaïa*, I, ed. and trans. F. Nau in *PO* 23 (1932), pp. 193f.

[73] Cf. the case of the Khathʿamī tribesman Mūsā b. Muṣʿab, who is a nefarious Jew to several Monophysite sources; on Mūsā, see chapter 7.

[74] See S. Griffith, 'The Prophet Muḥammad, his scripture and his message according to the Christian apologies in Arabic and Syriac from the first Abbasid century', in T. Fahd, ed., *La Vie du Prophète Mahomet: Colloque de Strasbourg, Octobre 1980* (Paris, 1983), pp. 121f.

[75] Wolfson himself suggested that a Paulianist Christology may have been 'floating around' among Nestorians in Iraq; see his 'Splinter group', p. 349.

attributed to Paul of Samosata, for there is good evidence that Paulianist strains of thought were embraced by some Nestorians before Islam.[76] The *Synodicon Orientale* tells us that the Nestorian synods of both 585 and 596 expressly criticise those who reject the divinity of Jesus Christ, and Īshōʿyab I singles out Paul of Samosata in particular.[77] In the middle of the seventh century Shahdost does the same, as did other Nestorian authorities as well.[78]

Certainly any argument for Paulianist influence on the *shahārija* is constructed of probabilities and inferences,[79] particularly since the charge of denying Jesus' divinity was thrown around recklessly in Late Antiquity, Paul of Samosata being invoked frequently.[80] But there are other reasons for seeing the issue as an intra-Nestorian affair. For one thing, identifying a Paulianist influence has the advantage of making some sense of Thomas of Marga's attitude, since a Paulianist view of Christ was at least occasionally foisted on Nestorius himself; as a result it became the practice of later Nestorian authors to distance themselves from Paulianists and those that resembled them.[81] For another, there is good evidence that the *shahārija* were subject to the authority of the Nestorian hierarchy – both formal and informal. When the *dihqān*s had complaints to make about the onerous taxation imposed by the *shahārija*, they took these complaints to the local Nestorian bishop, and when they wanted a cure, they went to the local Nestorian as well. The same point seems to be made in the legal judgments of Ḥnānīshōʿ, who was Nestorian Catholicos at the tail-end of the seventh century;[82] here we are mercifully

[76] The literature on Paul of Samosata, bishop of Antioch (c. 260–8), is large and continues to grow. For a summary of the literature, see F. W. Norris, 'Paul of Samosata: *Procurator Ducenarius*', *Journal of Theological Studies* n.s. 35 (1984), pp. 50–70. A general description can be found in J. N. D. Kelly, *Early Christian Doctrines* (San Francisco, rev. edn, 1978).

[77] Chabot, ed., *Synodicon Orientale*, pp. 134/395f. and 195/454. For a discussion of these and other passages, see S. Brock, 'The christology of the Church of the East in the synods of the fifth to early seventh centuries', in G. D. Dragas, ed., *Aksum-Thyateira: a Festschrift for Archbishop Methodios* (London, 1985), pp. 136ff.

[78] See L. Abramowski and A. Goodman, *A Nestorian Collection of Christological Texts* (Cambridge, 1972), II, pp. xxx, 7; see also the comments of ps.-Isaac of Nineveh (with a *terminus a quo* of 539/40), pp. 38 and 52f.; and the comments of Īshōʿyab II: L. Sako, *Lettre christologique du patriarche syro-oriental Īshōʿyabh II de Gdālā* (Rome, 1983), pp. 170/146. In addition to later Syriac heresiographers, Abū ʿĪsā al-Warrāq was aware of Paul's views; see D. Thomas, ed. and trans., *Anti-Christian Polemic in Early Islam: Abū ʿĪsā al-Warrāq's 'Against the Trinity'* (Cambridge, 1992), pp. 70f.

[79] Late and circumstantial evidence can connect the region of Mosul to Paul, when Antiochenes of his day are said to have been brought to Iraq in the wake of Shāpūr's conquests; see the *Histoire nestorienne*, I (1), ed. and trans. A. Scher in *PO* 4 (1908), p. 221; and G. Bardy, *Paul de Samosate: Etude historique* (Louvain, 1929), pp. 240f. According to the account, Shāpūr settled the captives in the 'lands of Iraq, al-Ahwāz, Fārs, and in the towns (*mudun*) that his father [Ardashīr] built.'

[80] See, for example, D. S. Wallace-Hadrill, *Christian Antioch: A Study of Early Christian Thought in the East* (Cambridge, 1982), p. 70.

[81] Abramowski and Goodman, *Nestorian Collection*, II, p. xxxi; G. Chediath, *The Christology of Mar Babai the Great* (Kottayam, 1982), p. 82.

[82] On Ḥnānīshōʿ (d. 699–700), see Baumstark, *Geschichte*, p. 209; and I. Ortiz de Urbina, *Patrologia syriaca* (Rome, 1965), pp. 150f.

delivered out of the literary sources onto the firmer ground of documentary material. The passage in question concerns a petition that had been presented to the Catholicos by an abbot named Qardag; the latter appealed to Ḥnānīshōʿ to have him restore to the unidentified 'monastery of Abraham' some properties that had earlier been granted to a certain Qardōyā (or Qardōnā), whose descendants had taken control of the land following his death.[83] The account is interesting for several reasons, particularly for the light it throws on patterns of land tenure in seventh-century monasteries. But the crucial point to make here is that although the Syriac terms *shahrīg* or *shahrīgān* are not used, Sachau argued that the descendants of Qardōyā should be identified as such. As Sachau noted, the group must be Christian, not only because they practised baptism, but also because the abbot was given a Christian burial; most importantly, they are also said to have 'lightened the tax load' of the monastery, which may have been located in the *shahārija* heartland of Adiabene.[84] If we accept Sachau's argument, the account can serve to reinforce the impression left by both Thomas of Marga and the 'Life' of John of Dailam. Here the *shahārija* do not appear to have had any separate ecclesiastical hierarchy; similarly, there is no evidence that in praxis they were distinguishable from their Nestorian neighbours.

The *shahārija* of the Sasanian period

To recapitulate: the *shahārija* of the Islamic period were a landed gentry of the Mosuli hinterland, who reflect the shallow reach of city-based power, along with the slow pace of change throughout the seventh, eighth and ninth centuries more generally: retaining a hand in the tax administration until the early ninth century, and their wealth and identity until well into the tenth, they represent the élite layer of that proportionally huge (and largely silent) collection of (mostly) Christian communities, in which early Muslim administrators manifested no interest, but upon whose revenues the Abbasid state came increasingly to rely. If Cameron is correct that the end of Late Antiquity came only with the 'rolling out of Islam like a great carpet over tracts of Christian soil' – a metaphor which might be replaced by Brown's image of the Church ('an archipelago of little islands of "centrality" scattered across an "unsown sea" of almost total indifference') – the end came late indeed.[85] To say something more about continuity, it remains to relate the Islamic-period *shahārija* of the north to those of Sasanian Iraq.

If the *shahārija* of early Islamic Mosul were a landed gentry, what of the view (first proposed by Nöldeke) that they were functionaries of the Sasanian

[83] See Sachau, *Syrische Rechtsbücher*, II, pp. 6ff. (text and translation) and 182f. (commentary).

[84] Sachau, *Syrische Rechtsbücher*, II, pp. 182f.

[85] See A. Cameron's review article of Patlagean, 'Late Antiquity – the total view', *Past and Present* 88 (1980), p. 135; and P. Brown, 'The saint as exemplar in Late Antiquity', *Representations* 1 (1983), p. 9.

state? Here we must take account of the striking fact that the enormous increase of material evidence made available since Nöldeke's day has so far failed to yield a single *shahrīg*. Now we might not expect them to appear in the inscriptions, which have otherwise proved a valuable resource for administrative history;[86] but one might reasonably expect something in the vast corpus of seals and seal impressions, many of which include Christian themes,[87] and which can serve as a valuable corrective to the Arabic literary sources.[88] Indeed, it is on the basis of the evidence from the seals that R. Gyselen has concluded that the *shahārija* were not imperial officials, but rather representatives of the *dihqāns*; it is the *shahrab*, in her view, that was the 'haut fonctionnaire envoyé par le gouvernement', not the *shahrīg*, the literary sources having confused the two.[89] The argument is one from silence, but it must be correct, at least for the period well covered by the seals (i.e. from the middle of the sixth century). The literary ground is predictably slippery, but it offers some tentative support for Gyselen's conclusions, and suggests that the *shahārija* had emerged as a rural aristocracy by the late Sasanian period.

To be sure, al-Masʿūdī had a wealth of Sasanian material at his fingertips, both primary and secondary in nature,[90] and the titles attributed to him suggest that he did something with the material.[91] His predecessor al-Yaʿqūbī also had an interest in things Sasanian, and he seems to have had access to pre-Islamic material as well.[92] The relevant passage in al-Yaʿqūbī appears at the tail-end of a longer discussion of Sasanian administration and genealogy,[93]

86 See, for example, Gignoux, 'L'Organisation administrative', pp. 9ff. (discussing the *marzbāns*, who appear only infrequently).

87 See, for instance, S. Shaked, 'Jewish and Christian seals of the Sasanian period', in Rosen-Ayalon, ed., *Studies in Memory of Gaston Wiet*, pp. 17–31.

88 R. Göbl (*Die Tonbullen vom Tacht-e Suleiman* (Berlin, 1976), p. 89) calls them 'eine selbständige und unabhängige Quelle für die Rekonstruktion der spätsāsānidischen *notitia dignitatum*'. For several examples, see P. Gignoux and R. Gyselen, *Sceaux sasanides de diverses collections privées* (Louvain, 1982), pp. 15f.

89 See R. Gyselen, *La Géographie administrative*, p. 28. Her view is seconded by R. Frye in his review in *JAOS* 113 (1993), p. 287. Cf. V. F. Piacentini, '*Madīnalshahr, qaryaldeh, nāḥiyalrustāq*. The city as political–administrative institution: the continuity of a Sasanian model', *JSAI* 17 (1994), pp. 99, note 19 ('The *shahrij* was a nobility with a predominantly urban base, superior to the *dehkan*, which at the time of Khosrōv I was made up of the small country nobility') and also 101.

90 Such as, for example, passages from the Pahlavi *Letter of Tansar*; on this, see M. Boyce, ed. and trans., *The Letter of Tansar* (Rome, 1968), p. 3. For al-Masʿūdī on the pre-Islamic period, see T. Khalidi, *Islamic Historiography: The Histories of al-Masʿūdī* (Albany, 1975), pp. 90ff.; T. Khalidi, *Arabic Historical Thought in the Classical Period* (Cambridge, 1994), pp. 131ff.; L. Marlow, *Hierarchy and Egalitarianism in Islamic Thought* (Cambridge, 1997), pp. 66ff. (for the reception of Sasanian material); and M. Springberg-Hinsen, *Die Zeit vor dem Islam in arabischen Universalgeschichten des 9. bis 12. Jahrhunderts* (Würzberg, 1989), pp. 35ff.

91 E.g. his *Kitāb al-Taʾrīkh fī akhbār al-umam min al-ʿarab waʾl-ʿajam*; see Yāqūt, *Irshād al-arīb ilā maʿrifat al-adīb* (Leiden and London, 1907–13), V, p. 149.

92 See Christensen, *L'Iran*, pp. 62 and 71; A. A. Duri, *The Rise of Historical Writing among the Arabs*, ed. and trans. L. I. Conrad (Princeton, 1983), pp. 64f.; Khalidi, *al-Masʿūdī*, pp. 82f.; Khalidi, *Arabic Historical Thought*, pp. 115ff.; Springberg-Hinsen, *Die Zeit vor dem Islam*, pp. 29ff.

93 Al-Yaʿqūbī, *Taʾrīkh*, I, pp. 200ff.

the first half of which addresses the reforms of Khusraw I (r. 531–79), in particular the appointment of the four *ispahbadh*s over the 'Four Quarters' of the empire. If we stick to the conventional dating of these reforms, the material here can date from no earlier than the middle or late sixth century.[94] This section is then followed by a discussion of social hierarchy that is very different in character; it is here that the *shahrīj* is glossed as the *raʾīs al-kuwar*. The passage starts at the top (the *shāhanshāh*), continues through the high administration, clergy, and lower administrative levels; the language is not of administrative geography, but rather one of equivalence between the Sasanian and Islamic states.[95] Here al-Yaʿqūbī seems to have been working directly from a list of terms that he did not fully understand: the glosses throughout this section are vague,[96] and since he had already worked out that the *ispahbadh* was *al-raʾīs*, and that the *marzbān* was the *raʾīs al-balad*, his gloss of the *shahrīj* as the *raʾīs al-kuwar* might best be regarded as an educated guess,[97] perhaps one intended to reconcile contrasting material from the pre- and post-reform periods; indeed, in Christensen's view, this second section is based on fifth-century material.[98]

Al-Yaʿqūbī's testimony is at best inconclusive; al-Masʿūdī, meanwhile, describes the *shahārija* in what should now be very familiar terms: they occupy an aristocratic rank. The relevant section reads:

> We also discussed in our book called the *Akhbār al-zaman*[99] accounts of the four dynasties; the canals that each of their kings dug; the peerless cities they built; their kings' views and opinions; many of their judgments on the élites and the subject populations (*fī khawāṣṣihā wa-ʿawāmmihā*); the genealogies of the royal cavalry and those who commanded the royal cavalry in times of war; the genealogies of those wise men and ascetics who gained fame during their reigns; the genealogies of the *marāziba*; the descendants of the four levels mentioned above, along with the branching out of genealogical lines, and the dispersal of their offspring.[100] We also described the three [great] families whom *kisrā* made the foremost nobility of the Sawād of Iraq, and who remain well known as such among present-day inhabitants of the Sawād; the nobles of the Sawād [who come] after the three families in rank, viz. the *shahārija*, whom Īraj made the nobility of the Sawād; and the second level after the *shahārija*, viz. the

94 On Khusraw's reforms, see Christensen, *L'Iran*, pp. 364ff.; M. Grignaschi, 'La riforma tributaria di Hosrō I e il feudalesimo sassanide', *Atti del Convegno Internazionale sul Tema: La Persia nel Medioevo* (Rome, 1971), pp. 87–147; Morony, *Iraq*, pp. 27f.; and more recently, K. Schippmann, *Grundzüge der Geschichte des sasanidischen Reiches* (Darmstadt, 1990), pp. 52ff.

95 Thus, *kisrā shāhanshāh* = *malik al-mulūk*; cf. Morony (*Iraq*, p. 27): 'Arabic literature tends to heighten the impression that Islamic institutions were of Sasanian origin by anachronistically describing the Sasanians in contemporary ninth and tenth-century terms.'

96 Thus *buzurgfarmadhār* is glossed as *mutaqallad al-umūr*.

97 The manuscript itself reads 'al-sh-h-r-n-h', and Houtsma presumably emended it in the light of Nöldeke's translation of al-Ṭabarī, which had appeared only four years earlier, and which he acknowledges on the previous page (202, note o). On the single manuscript – and all of its copyist's errors – on which Houtsma had to rely, see Nöldeke's review in *ZDMG* 38 (1884), esp. p. 159.

98 Christensen, *L'Iran*, pp. 518ff. (following Stein).

99 On this work, see the author's description (*Murūj*, I, p. 9) and A. Shboul, *Al-Masʿūdī and his World* (London, 1979), pp. 68ff.

100 *Tashaʿʿub ansābihim wa-tafarruq aʿqābihim*.

dahāqīn, who are the descendants of Wakhart b. Farwāk b. Siyāmuk b. Narsī b. Kayūmarth, the king.[101]

What we have before us is thus an extended citation from a now lost work; even so, the character of the original is clear enough. Behind the narrative lies a static and idealised vision of Sasanian society whose principal feature was a cultural superiority that was at once geographically bounded (to Iran) and religiously sanctioned (by Zoroastrianism),[102] and according to which social power was genetically based. As far as the *shahārija* are concerned, the crucial name is obviously that of Īraj, a legendary figure in the mythology of the Sasanian dynasty;[103] he is frequently said to have been one of the three sons of Afrīdūn, who, according to legend, divided his empire among the three.[104] Īraj, who also was known as Īrān,[105] thus gave his name to Īrānshahr; and although this included Iranian lands in general (Fārs, al-Jibāl and Khurāsān),[106] its centre is said to have been Iraq; thus al-Aṣmaʿī identifies the pre-Islamic name of al-ʿIrāq as Īrānshahr,[107] and elsewhere we read that Iraq was known as the 'heart of Īrānshahr'.[108] In connecting the *shahārija* with Īraj our source thus anchors the former in a mythology of Iranian beginnings. Since we read elsewhere that Īr also gave his name to an unidentified people who traced their genealogy back to him,[109] it is reasonable to see in all of this the construction of a pseudo-genealogy, one that not only credits the *shahārija* with an aristocratic pedigree, but also safely anchors them in the heart of the Iranian motherland.[110]

Aristocratic status was thus grounded in a mythological past; and with the Sasanian state having been decapitated in Islamic Iraq, it was left to a predominantly rural aristocracy to preserve (and re-interpret, presumably according to its own interests) Sasanian political and cultural traditions, in the short

101 Al-Masʿūdī, *Murūj*, I, pp. 326f. (on the royal genealogies, see pp. 260ff.)
102 See the discussion in Cook and Crone, *Hagarism*, pp. 42f. On a Sasanian 'static world' posited 'in some typically élitist ideological aspects', see G. Gnoli, *The Idea of Iran: an Essay on its Origins* (Rome, 1989), p. 165.
103 See, for example, al-Masʿūdī, *Murūj*, I, pp. 265f.; Boyce (ed.), *The Letter of Tansar*, p. 63; A. Christensen, *Les Kayanides* (Copenhagen, 1931), p. 62; Ibn Khurdādhbih, *Masālik*, p. 15; al-Thaʿālibī, *Ghurar akhbār mulūk al-Furs* (Paris, 1900), pp. 41ff.; Ḥamza al-Iṣfahānī, *Taʾrīkh*, p. 33; and, of course, Firdawsī, *Shāhnāma* (Costa Mesa and New York, 1988–), I, index.
104 According to a much later source, Afrīdūn's reign lasted 500 years; see al-Ghazālī's *Ghazālī's Book of Counsel for Kings*, trans. F. R. C. Begley (London, 1964), p. 48.
105 See, for example, al-Masʿūdī, *Murūj*, I, p. 279.
106 Thus Yāqūt, *Muʿjam*, I, p. 417; for this account and some commentary, see also C. Barbier de Meynard, *Dictionnaire géographique, historique et littéraire de la Perse* (Paris, 1861), pp. 63f.
107 See al-Jawālīqī, *al-Muʿarrab* (Cairo, 1969), p. 279.
108 Yāqūt, *Muʿjam*, I, pp. 417f.; Qudāma b. Jaʿfar, *Kitāb al-Kharāj*, p. 159.
109 One pseudo-etymology has al-ʿIrāq derive from Īrān, itself derived from Īr, who, according to Qudāma's informant(s), was the name given to 'a people designated by Īr b. Afrīdūn b. Waywanjahān (?) b. Ushahanj (?) b. Fīrūzān b. Siyāmuk b. Narsī b. Jayūmart'. See Qudāma b. Jaʿfar, *Kitāb al-Kharāj*, p. 159. The overlapping tail of the genealogical chain takes on added significance in the light of the poetry I translate below.
110 Cf. the geographic claims made by the earliest Sasanians' use of the term *Īrānshahr*; on this, Gnoli, *The Idea of Iran*, p. 137.

run channelling them to imperial historians such as al-Ṭabarī, al-Masʿūdī and al-Yaʿqūbī, in the long run (and in markedly persianophile political circumstances) producing *Shāhnāmēs*. In the meantime, with the disappearance of the state institutions that helped anchor these ranks in place, social movement was just short of frenetic. This is made particularly clear in some panegyric poetry preserved by Abū al-Faraj al-Iṣfahānī.[111] The poet in question, a certain Abū al-Asad, Nubāta b. ʿAbd Allāh al-Ḥimmānī, is said to have found favour with al-Fayḍ b. Abī Ṣāliḥ (d. 173/789) some time during Hārūn's reign.[112] The poem in question praises one courtier, Ḥamdūn b. Ismāʿīl,[113] at the expense of another, ʿAlī b. Yaḥyā al-Munajjim,[114] of the very famous Munajjim family.[115] The relevant lines read as follows:

> A fine thing God has made! I knew you before your [pl.] wealth,
> when you were still in sailors' shorts.
> Hardly a year passed before I saw you walking in silk,[116] Qūhistān
> garments, and in the luxury of life.[117]
> While, in the winter sun, your women were still crying at desert
> pigeons under the *dawwālī* dates.
> And then they started to strut in Iraqi brocade and in fineries
> of dark silks,[118]
> Forgetting [the toil] of picking thorny *ḥulāwā* plants from their
> beds, and of carrying *kushūth* clover in baskets.
> So much so, that when they came into wealth, they claimed (lying):
> 'We are the *shahārīj*, the descendants of the *dihqāns*!'
> Were I to get near you, my prick would be in the ass of Sāsān's
> mother, or a mule's would be stuck up Shīrīn's.
> If the lowest in rank and most vile among them is asked [of his

[111] *Al-Aghānī*, XIV, pp. 135f. The passage was first noted by al-Ṭabarī's editors, but it has been ignored since. See the *Introductio, glossarium, addenda et emendanda* to al-Ṭabarī (Leiden, 1901), p. cccxviii (where the *shahārija* are glossed as *magnates Persici*).

[112] His panegyric of al-Fayḍ appears not only in *al-Aghānī*, but also in al-Jahshiyārī, *Wuzarāʾ*, p. 164. On al-Fayḍ, see D. Sourdel, *Le vizirat ʿabbaside* (Damascus, 1959–60) I, pp. 111f., where he is understandably cautious about the course of his career.

[113] See I. Guidi's index to *al-Aghānī*, *Tables alphabétiques du Kitâb al-Aġânî* (Leiden, 1900), p. 311.

[114] For some of the vast material on ʿAlī b. Yaḥyā, see Ibn al-Nadīm, *Kitāb al-Fihrist* (Beirut, 1988 reprint of R. Tajaddud's Tehran, 1971 edn), esp. p. 160; al-Khaṭīb al-Baghdādī, *Taʾrīkh Baghdād*, XII, pp. 121f.; Ibn Khallikān, *Wafayāt al-aʿyān*, I, pp. 350f.; III, pp. 373f.; and VI, p. 201; al-Marzubānī, *Muʿjam al-shuʿarāʾ* (Cairo, 1960), pp. 141f.; al-Qālī, *al-Amālī* (Cairo, 1926), I, p. 229; Ibn Abī Uṣaybiʿa, *ʿUyūn al-anbāʾ fī ṭabaqāt al-aṭibbāʾ* (Beirut, reprint of N. Riḍā's 1965 edn), p. 283; al-Qifṭī, *Taʾrīkh al-ḥukamāʾ* (Leipzig, 1903), pp. 117 and 128f.

[115] On the Munajjim family, see M. Fleischammer, 'Die Banu al-Munajjim', *Wissenschaftliche Zeitschrift der Martin-Luther Universität* 12 (1963) (not available to me), pp. 215ff.; and S. M. Stern, 'Abū ʿĪsā Ibn al-Munajjim's Chronography', in S. M. Stern *et al.*, eds., *Islamic Philosophy and the Classical Tradition* (Festschrift for R. Walzer) (Oxford, 1972), pp. 437ff.

[116] There is no trace here of the odium attached by the pious to wearing silk; for examples, see A. J. Wensinck, *A Handbook of Early Muhammadan Tradition* (Leiden, 1927), pp. 45f.

[117] *Al-līnī*, which, following the editor's suggestion, may also be construed on the pattern of the preceding (*al-Qūhī*), that is, a kind of fabric from a village located between Mosul and Nisibis; but the existence of this village seems to be attested no earlier than Yāqūt's time; see Yāqūt, *Muʿjam*, IV, p. 375.

[118] Black silks, according to al-Jāḥiẓ (*Kitāb al-Bukhalāʾ* (Beirut, 1983) II, p. 5), seem to have been emblematic of first-generation Arabised Christians from Jundaysābūr.

pedigree] he responds by boasting: I am the son of Shūbīn,
And he says: 'Kisrā granted me [lands], and made me his heir. Who then could outboast or would make an enemy of me?'
Who shall tell Kisrā, (who is now in hell), of the claim of the Nabīṭ, (the progeny of devils),
Who claim that you fathered them, just as the lizard claims [ludicrously] to be of the sperm of the fish?

The poem is valuable in a number of ways. Whatever its precise date, it supplies our earliest evidence (the early or mid-ninth century) for the presence of *shahārija* in Islamic Iraq; it thus confirms al-Masʿūdī's passing comment that Sasanian aristocratic distinctions remained alive in middle Abbasid Iraq, a view attested elsewhere too.[119] More importantly, it demonstrates exactly what one should already know, namely that aristocratic status, far from being fixed by genetic make-up, was asserted and argued.[120]

In the episode described by our poet, *shahrīj* status is signalled by emblematically Persian clothing, but this seems to be only one ingredient in a larger cluster of cultural symbols of persianophile *adab*. ʿAlī b. Yaḥyā's *adab* appears to have been proverbial,[121] a fact acknowledged by his contemporary Aḥmad b. Abī Ṭāhir Ṭayfūr,[122] and the *shahārija* appear elsewhere as paragons of Sasanian court culture. Thus we read in a passage attributed by al-Ḥuṣrī (d. 413/1022) to al-Ḥasan b. Sahl, al-Maʾmūn's secretary (d. 236/850), that there are ten ingredients to *adab*, three of which, lute (*ḍarb al-ʿūd*), chess (*luʿb al-shaṭranj*), and polo playing (*luʿb al-ṣawālij*) are called 'shahr[ī]jāniyya'.[123] There are similar accounts elsewhere.[124] It is only natural that al-Ḥasan and

[119] See al-Yaʿqūbī, *Taʾrīkh*, I, p. 178.

[120] Cf. the Arabic verb *tadahqana* ('to fashion oneself a *dihqān*').

[121] It may be that in having one foot in, and one foot outside, Arabic letters, ʿAlī aroused some resentment (cf. the case of al-Sarakhsī in Ibn Abī Uṣaybiʿa, *ʿUyūn al-anbāʾ*, pp. 293f.). ʿAlī was a poet, panegyrist and critic, and he was also an important conduit for the entrance of Greek learning into Arabic, commissioning translations of Galen and Hippocrates by Ḥunayn b. Isḥāq, Isḥāq b. Ḥunayn and others; his personal library is said to have been so filled with foreign learning that it attracted the likes of Abū Maʿshar; (see, *inter alia*, Yāqūt, *Irshād al-arīb*, V, pp. 459ff.; and G. Bergsträsser, *Ḥunayn ibn Isḥāq über die syrischen und arabischen Galen-Übersetzungen* (Leipzig, 1925), 10, 12, 28, 30, 45 and 51). One report traces ʿAlī's genealogy to an administrator in Ardashīr's time; see al-Marzubānī, *Muʿjam al-shuʿarāʾ*, p. 141.

[122] See Ibn ʿAbd Rabbihi, *al-ʿIqd al-farīd* (Beirut, 1983), II, pp. 262f.; and Yāqūt, *Irshād al-arīb*, V, p. 459. Note as well that Ibn al-Nadīm counts a *risāla* to ʿAlī b. Yaḥyā among Aḥmad b. Abī Ṭāhir Ṭayfūr's works; see his *Fihrist*, p. 163.

[123] Al-Ḥuṣrī, *Zahr al-ādāb* (Cairo, 1969) I, p. 155. The passage was first noted by I. Goldziher, *Mohammedanische Studien* (Halle, 1890), I, p. 168, note 2, where he translates *luʿb al-ṣawālij* as 'das Spiel mit Wurfspiessen' (followed by his translators: *Muslim Studies* I, p. 155, note 3).

[124] Cf. the version preserved by Aḥmad b. Jaʿfar b. Shādhān in his *Kitāb Adab al-wuzarāʾ* (Leiden ms. 1942), on which see P. de Jong and M. J. de Goeje, *Catalogus codicum orientalium Bibliothecae Academiae Lugduno Batavae* (Leiden, 1866), IV, pp. 197–8, as cited by M. Enger in his 'Notizen, Correspondenzen und Vermischtes ueber das Vezirat', *ZDMG* 13 (1859), p. 243, note 1. On Abū Bakr b. Shādhān (or Abū ʿAlī b. Shādhān), see E. Kohlberg, *A Medieval Muslim Scholar at Work: Ibn Ṭāwūs and his Library* (Leiden, 1992), pp. 99f. The account is credited to al-Ḥasan's brother, al-Faḍl b. Sahl (d. 202/818, identified by his sobriquet '*dhū al-riʾāsatayn*'), and here al-Faḍl identifies three ingredients as typically 'shahraḥbiyya' (presumably derived from the *shahrab*): geometry, medicine and astrology (*al-nujūm*); three others, chess, lute and polo playing, are now 'Anūshirwāniyya'.

his brother al-Faḍl b. Sahl, sons of a Zoroastrian father, would be cited as authorities.[125]

A provisional explanation for the survival of the *shahārija* in the north and their disappearance in the south is thus as follows. *Pace* Hoffmann, the *shahārija* were already in place in the north (as well as in the south) at the time of the conquest, occupying an aristocratic rank, one perhaps generated in the wake of Khusraw's reforms.[126] There, where the Sasanian state had a relatively weak institutional hold,[127] they seem to have prospered, their assimilation to local norms (perhaps) being signalled by their (sixth or seventh-century?) conversion to a strain of Nestorian Christianity, one that reinforced an identity distinct from that of the *dihqān*s. In the south, where the Muslim presence was considerably more concentrated, and the pace of change considerably quicker, their fate was altogether different. In a cultural milieu where Arabs were considered ill-fit for tax collection,[128] it was the *dihqāns* who appeared as the administrators of choice.[129] Into this very broad category the *shahārija* disappeared.[130]

125 On al-Ḥasan b. Sahl and his brother al-Faḍl, see *EI*² s.vv. (Sourdel) and Sourdel, *Le vizirat ʿabbaside*, esp. I, pp. 196ff. Accounts concerning al-Faḍl's Persian credentials go unquestioned by Sourdel (*EI*², p. 731: 'it is unquestionable that he [al-Faḍl] was the most Iranian of the viziers of the ʿAbbāsid court: imbued with very ancient traditions which he set out to promote in the cultural field'), whereas Crone senses polemics stemming from al-Ma'mūn's designation of ʿAlī al-Riḍā: see *Slaves*, p. 257, note 604. In addition to the literature cited therein, note that his ability to translate a letter from Persian into Arabic is said to have caused wonder (al-Jahshiyārī, *Wuzarā'*, p. 230).

126 Cf. the *Encyclopaedia Iranica*, s.v. *dehqān*.

127 We lack any attestation for a *shahrab* in Nōd Ardashīragān, and the highest imperial appointee attested is the *āmārgar*, whose responsibilities seem to have been flexible; see Gyselen, *La Géographie administrative*, pp. 35f., 56, 78f., figures 17 and 20. One imagines that on the eve of the conquests, Sasanian administration was overwhelmingly military in character; certainly there is no shortage of evidence for *marzbān*s (see, for example, the *Life* of Samuel in Palmer, *Monk and Mason*, microfilm 1, VIII and IX, where John of Ephesus is also noted).

128 Al-Jahshiyārī, *Wuzarā'*, p. 28. Bedouins, in particular, were seen as simpletons who were hopelessly unqualified for fiscal matters. See, for examples, al-Dīnawarī, *Akhbār*, p. 115 (according to which the idea of appointing a bedouin (*aʿrābī*) in the tax bureau is presented as absolutely preposterous); al-Ṭabarī, *Ta'rīkh*, II, p. 1470; and al-Yaʿqūbī, *Ta'rīkh*, II, p. 279.

129 In phraseology intended to evoke a Qur'ānic parallel, Abū Mūsā al-Ashʿarī is given to say of a *dihqān* that 'he has his religion and I have his secretarial skills' (*la-hu dīnuhu wa-lī kitābatuhu*); see Ibn Qutayba, *ʿUyūn al-akhbār*, I, p. 43. For more examples, see J. Juda, *Die sozialen und wirtschaftlichen Aspekte der Mawālī in frühislamischer Zeit* (Tübingen, 1983), pp. 115ff.

130 Cf. Morony, *Iraq*, p. 205 ('In lower Iraq, all surviving Persian notables tended to be treated as *dahāqīn*, although the distinction between those who lived in town and those who lived in the countryside survived').

FIVE

Islam in the north: Jaziran Khārijism

Unlike a history of the city of Mosul, a history of the settled communities of the Marwānid Jazira cannot be written; and of all the problems, perhaps the most elusive concerns the (usually) slow processes of conversion, acculturation and assimilation, by which an Arabian language of monotheist reform was transformed into a rhetoric of territorial rule.[1] Now one conventionally explains problems such as these with reference to the character of our source material, which says so little about the Late Antique world in which early Muslims settled.[2] This is of course true; but it must also be said that the material generally reflects the prevailing character of early Muslim belief, when Muḥammad's (apparent) marriage of ethnicity and creed had not yet been been dissolved. The tradition held that Jews and Christians had no place in the *jazīrat al-ʿarab* (the Arabian Peninsula),[3] but there were no such restrictions in the Jazira: as long as they paid the *jizya*, Jaziran Christians simply did not matter. Accounts of the conversion of a deracinated tribesman such as Ṣuhayb b. Sinān – the most famous of all early Jaziran/Byzantine Christians – predictably say more about the Shuʿūbiyya controversies of the second and third Islamic centuries than they do about the Jazira itself.[4]

By contrast, the experience of immigrant tribesmen did leave an authentic mark on our sources, and one that can actually tell us something about non-urban élites. As far as the north is concerned, we know something about how the tribes responded to Islamic rule for two interrelated reasons. First, pastoral tribesmen of this and all periods (at least until the introduction of the aeroplane) were a problem for the state. The geography of the Jazira – steppe

1 Cf. A. Cameron, *Christianity and the Rhetoric of Empire* (Berkeley and Los Angeles, 1991); P. Brown, *Power and Persuasion in Late Antiquity* (Madison, 1992).

2 Cf. I. Lapidus ('The conversion of Egypt to Islam', *Israel Oriental Studies* 2 (1972), p. 248): 'The history of conversion to Islam, in Egypt or elsewhere, remains a suprisingly obscure subject on which Arabic sources almost never comment.'

3 The idea is most frequently expressed in the *ḥadīth* 'No two religions shall come together in the Arabian Peninsula' (*lā-yajtamiʿ dīnān fī jazīrat al-ʿarab*); thus Ibn Abī Shayba, *Muṣannaf*, VII, p. 635.

4 See Goldziher, *Muslim Studies*, II, p. 128; and for more sources, Robinson, 'al-Muʿāfā b. ʿImrān', p. 119, note 79.

land infrequently interrupted by river valleys and mountain ranges to the north and east – insulated it from all but the most exceptional projections of state power; and aside from seasonal inundations, the yield of its rain-fed agriculture was too modest to attract administrators' attention. Generally speaking, the region was always liminal, the preserve of pastoral groups that moved in and out of alliances with urban élites, for the most part even outside Mann's 'extensive penumbra', where imperial 'control' is out of the question, and where subject populations only grudgingly acknowledge 'certain niceties of compliance'.[5] The second reason we know something of these tribesmen is that many chose a mode of belief – Khārijism – in the name of which they rebelled, and of which the authorities quite reasonably came to disapprove; in other words, rather than being merely restive tribesmen, they were regarded by the state as revolutionary tribesmen.

The Khārijites saw themselves as reformers, rather than revolutionaries; they clearly possessed a political programme, and this is why they are only explicable within the politicised Jazira of the Marwānid period: there is no certain evidence of pre-Marwānid Khārijites, and indeed we should hardly expect any, since there were no local state structures against which the Khārijite tribesmen might revolt.[6] By contrast, in the wake of the Second Fitna we have the beginning of an almost unbroken string of rebels: Ṣāliḥ b. Musarriḥ and Shabīb b. Yazīd; Bisṭām/Shawdhab;[7] Bahlūl b. Bishr/Kuthāra;[8] Suḥārī b. Shabīb;[9] Saʿīd b. Bahdal;[10] Bisṭām al-Shaybānī;[11] al-Ḍaḥḥāk b. Qays;[12]

[5] M. Mann, *The Sources of Social Power I: A History of Power from the Beginning to AD 1760* (Cambridge, 1986), p. 26. On pastoralism in conditions such as these, see M. Rowton, 'Urban autonomy in a nomadic environment', *JNES* 32 (1973), pp. 201–15; and M. Rowton, 'Enclosed nomadism', *JESHO* 17 (1975), pp. 1–30.

[6] The rebellions of Maṭar b. ʿImrān and Faḍāla b. Sayyār seem to have preceded Ṣāliḥ b. Musarriḥ's, but apparently only just; see al-Balādhurī, *Ansāb*, Reis. 598 fols. 45a–b and 51b–52a; al-Ṭabarī, *Taʾrīkh*, II, p. 893. Sakīn (Sukayn?) al-Jamalī may qualify as well (al-Balādhurī, *Ansāb*, Reis. 598, fol. 52a).

[7] Disagreement about whether his revolt broke out in the Jazira or in the Sawād (in Jūkhā) may stem from differing views on administrative geography. See al-Ṭabarī, *Taʾrīkh*, II, pp. 1347f. and 1375ff.; al-Azdī, *Taʾrīkh*, pp. 6f.; the anonymous *ʿUyūn*, III, p. 47; al-Balādhurī, *Ansāb*, Reis. 598, fols. 43b (which puts him among Ṣāliḥ's men) and 83a–85a; Ibn al-Athīr, *al-Kāmil*, V, pp. 45ff.; Bar Hebraeus, *Chronicon syriacum*, p. 120 (=Budge, *Chronography*, p. 111).

[8] Sometimes pointed Buhlūl; see al-Ṭabarī, *Taʾrīkh*, II, pp. 1622ff.; al-Balādhurī, *Ansāb al-ashrāf*, vib (Jerusalem, 1993), pp. 95ff.; al-Yaʿqūbī, *Taʾrīkh*, II, p. 387; the anonymous *ʿUyūn*, III, pp. 109ff.; Ibn al-Athīr, *al-Kāmil*, V, pp. 209ff.

[9] Al-Ṭabarī, *Taʾrīkh*, II, pp. 1633f.; al-Balādhurī, *Ansāb*, VIb, p. 102; Ibn al-Athīr, *al-Kāmil*, V, p. 213.

[10] Al-Ṭabarī, *Taʾrīkh*, II, pp. 1897f.; al-Balādhurī, *Ansāb*, Reis. 598, fol. 116a–b; Michael the Syrian, *Chronique* xi.xii; *Chronicle of 1234*, I, pp. 316/247; Khalīfa b. Khayyāṭ, *Taʾrīkh*, pp. 242 and 245; al Azdī, *Taʾrīkh*, pp. 60 and 67. The latter two sources read Baḥdal.

[11] Al-Ṭabarī, *Taʾrīkh*, II, pp. 1897f.; al-Balādhurī, *Ansāb*, Reis. 598, fol. 180a–b; Khalīfa b. Khayyāṭ, *Taʾrīkh*, p. 248; Michael the Syrian, *Chronique*, xi.xxi; *Chronicle of 1234*, I, pp. 316/246f.

[12] Al-Ṭabarī, *Taʾrīkh*, II, years 127, 128, 129; al-Balādhurī, *Ansāb*, Reis. 598, fols. 180b–184b; Khalīfa b. Khayyāṭ, *Taʾrīkh*, pp. 245ff.; Ibn Qutayba, *al-Maʿārif*, pp. 369 and 412; al-Azdī, *Taʾrīkh*, pp. 67ff.; al-Yaʿqūbī, *Taʾrīkh*, II, pp. 404f.; the anonymous *ʿUyūn*, III, pp. 159f.; Ibn al-Athīr, *al-Kāmil*, V, pp. 334ff.; Theophanes, *Chronicle*, AM 6236 and AM 6237; Agapius, *Kitāb al-ʿUnwān*, pp. 515ff.; *Zuqnin Chronicle*, pp. 190f./146; *Chronicle of 1234*, I, pp. 319ff./249ff.; Elias of Nisibis, *Opus chronologicum*, p. 171.

al-Khaybarī;[13] and Shaybān b. ʿAbd al-ʿAzīz.[14] What is more, their strength appears to have grown during the Marwānid period. Whereas support for early Marwānid rebellions such as Shabīb's numbered in the hundreds, al-Ḍaḥḥāk, according to one report, could pass through Mosul and pick up three thousand tribesmen;[15] whereas Ṣāliḥ b. Musarriḥ would start his rebellion by raiding the region of Dārā and Nisibis, sending the townsfolk to shelter,[16] by 126/743 Bisṭām could openly court, and duly receive, permission to enter Nisibis and Mosul.[17] Little wonder then that so many held the Jazira to be incorrigibly Khārijite:[18] it seems that the longer the Marwānids ruled the Jazira, the more attractive Khārijism became to its tribesmen.

In what follows I shall try to understand why the Jazira acquired this reputation, focusing on the movement(s) led by the first great Khārijites of the north, Ṣāliḥ b. Musarriḥ and Shabīb b. Yazīd. As Muslim Arabs, these tribesmen qualified for membership in the ruling élite; indeed, some Khārijites even seem to have distinguished themselves in the army – that is, the main institution in which Arabs could retain or promote their status. To anticipate my argument in question form: why and in what circumstances did they rebel, abandoning the presumptive status that came with membership in the army, to re-acquire it through piety?

Origins

Although it was once thought perfectly straightforward to locate the origins of Khārijism in the events of ʿAlī's caliphate, it has become clear that we can no more assume an early monolithic unity from which the Khārijites are said to have 'broken off' than we can accept an early date (the *tafarruq* of 64/683) for the clear division of these Khārijites into their constituent subdivisions, Ibāḍī, Ṣufrī, Azraqī, etc.[19] The (relatively late) Islamic sources generally identify

[13] Al-Azdī, *Taʾrīkh*, pp. 71f.; al-Ṭabarī, *Taʾrīkh*, II, pp. 1938ff.; al-Yaʿqūbī, *Taʾrīkh*, II, p. 405; the anonymous *ʿUyūn*, III, p. 160; Ibn al-Athīr, *al-Kāmil*, V, pp. 348ff.; Agapius, *Kitāb al-ʿUnwān*, pp. 520f.

[14] See al-Azdī, *Taʾrīkh*, pp. 72f.; Khalīfa b. Khayyāṭ, *Taʾrīkh*, pp. 252f.; al-Ṭabarī, *Taʾrīkh*, II, pp. 1940f.; Agapius, *Kitāb al-ʿUnwān*, p. 521; the anonymous *ʿUyūn*, III, pp. 160f.; Ibn al-Athīr, *al-Kāmil*, V, pp. 353ff.; *Chronicle of 1234*, I, pp. 322/251f. Khārijite rebellions were also a prominent feature of northern Mesopotamia during the early Abbasid period, producing figures such as al-Mulabbad, ʿAbd al-Salām b. Hāshim, al-Ḥasan b. Mujālid, al-Faḍl b. Saʿīd, Khurāsha b. Sinān and al-Walīd b. Ṭarīf. For a review, see L. V. Vaglieri, 'Le vicende del Ḫarigismo in epoca abbaside', *Rivista degli studi Orientali* 24 (1949), pp. 31–44.

[15] See al-Ṭabarī, *Taʾrīkh*, II, pp. 1898f.

[16] See al-Ṭabarī, *Taʾrīkh*, II, p. 887; al-Balādhurī, *Ansāb*, Reis. 598, fol. 43b. The only detailed account of the reception of settled Christians to Shabīb's rebellion concerns the village of al-Batt; for this, see below.

[17] See al-Balādhurī, *Ansāb*, Reis. 598, fol. 180a.

[18] See al-Ashʿarī, *Maqālāt al-islāmiyyīn* (Istanbul, 1929) I, p. 128; Ibn Qutayba, *ʿUyūn al-akhbār*, I, p. 204; al-Ṭabarī, *Taʾrīkh*, III, p. 1142; Ibn al-Faqīh, *Kitāb al-Buldān*, p. 315.

[19] See Wansbrough, *The Sectarian Milieu*, pp. 124f.; J. Wilkinson, 'The early development of the Ibāḍī movement in Baṣra', in Juynboll, ed., *Studies on the First Century of Islamic Society*, p. 143; K. Lewinstein, 'Making and unmaking a sect: the heresiographers and the Ṣufriyya', *SI* 76 (1992), pp. 77f.; K. Lewinstein, 'The Azāriqa in Islamic heresiography,' *BSOAS* 54 (1991), especially pp. 261ff.

Jaziran Khārijites as Ṣufrīs,[20] but the (relatively early) Syriac sources consistently use the terms *ḥrōrī* and *ḥrōrāyē* (Ar. *ḥarūrī*/*ḥarūriyya*), thus adding some weight to Lewinstein's scepticism about the existence of a discrete Ṣufrī subsect in this early period.[21] Such is the case not only for the *Chronicle of 1234* that preserves parts of Dionysius' history, but for other sources for whom direct reliance on Islamic historical material is more difficult to demonstrate, such as the *Chronicle of 819* and the *Zuqnin Chronicle*. Since the *Zuqnin Chronicle* also describes in some detail a *ḥarūrī* named ʿAtīq, who does not seem to be attested in the Arabic sources,[22] it is hard to argue that this material is entirely derivative. To the objection that the Syriac historians were ignorant of Islamic sectarian vocabulary, one can note that the source used by Michael the Syrian and the anonymous author of the *Chronicle of 1234* quite clearly is familiar with Khārijite sub-sects. Khalīfa's, al-Ṭabarī's and al-Balādhurī's sources all call Bisṭām a Bayhasī,[23] that is, presumably, that he is said to have belonged to the Khārijite sub-sect of the Bayhasiyya;[24] in the Syriac tradition Bisṭām is connected to the Bayhasiyya as well.[25] Similarly, our Syriac source knows of Saʿīd b. Bahdal as the chief of the 'Murgāyē',[26] a term which must be related to the Khārijite sub-sect of the Murjiʾat al-Khawārij.[27]

The Syriac evidence thus supports two conclusions. First, an argument from the silence of Dionysius, at least as he is preserved in the later Syriac chronicles, suggests that the term 'Ṣufrī', unlike 'Bayhasiyya' and 'Murjiʾat al-Khawārij',[28] did not circulate widely within northern Mesopotamia; had it had any real resonance, our Edessan source would have used it.[29] Second, although accounts that identify Ṣāliḥ b. Musarriḥ as the first Ṣufrite to rebel must cause some unease,[30] we can still attach some sectarian identity to Ṣāliḥ,

[20] See the relatively early example in Ibn Qutayba, *al-Maʿārif*, p. 410, according to which Ṣāliḥ b. Musarriḥ and Shabīb b. Yazīd were the leadership (*raʾs*) of the Ṣufriyya; and al-Ashʿarī, *Maqālāt al-islāmiyyīn*, I, p. 118.

[21] See Lewinstein, 'Making and unmaking', esp. pp. 77ff.

[22] *Zuqnin Chronicle*, pp. 174f./132.

[23] Khalīfa b. Khayyāṭ, *Taʾrīkh*, p. 248; al-Ṭabarī, *Taʾrīkh*, II, p. 1897f.; al-Balādhurī, *Ansāb*, Reis. 598, fol. 180a.

[24] On the the Bayhasiyya, see al-Ashʿarī, *Maqālāt al-islāmiyyīn*, I, pp. 113ff.; Ibn Ḥazm, *Kitāb al-Faṣl fī al-milal waʾl-ahwāʾ waʾl-niḥal* (Riyadh, 1982), V, p. 54.

[25] *Chronicle of 1234*, I, pp. 316/247; Michael the Syrian, *Chronique*, xi.xxi.

[26] *Chronicle of 1234*, I, pp. 316/247; Michael the Syrian, *Chronique*, xi.xxi.

[27] See al-Ashʿarī, *Maqālāt al-islamiyyīn*, I, p. 123.

[28] And, just as *The Chronicle of 1234*'s curious use of the term *rāfeṭē* (Ar. *rawāfiḍ*) (I, pp. 296/231) suggests that its meaning was much broader in the early period than the Islamic sources give one to believe (see Conrad, 'Theophanes', pp. 40f.), the Syriac use of these other terms may be of some help in identifying their early meanings as well. This is particularly the case for the Bayhasiyya/Ṣufriyya overlap detected by Lewinstein, 'Making and unmaking'.

[29] The terms *khārijī*/*khawārij* are never used to describe the figures with whom we are presently concerned, and when the term *khārijī* finally does appear in the Christian tradition, its usage is radically degraded: thus Elias of Nisibis, writing in the early eleventh century, describes as a *khārijī* a pre-Islamic rebel in the time of Constantine (the Syriac term used in the bilingual text is *ṭrōnā*, 'tyrant'); see his *Opus chronologicum*, p. 98; F. Delaporte translates simply 'le tyran'; see *La chronographie de Mar Elie Bar Šinaya* (Paris, 1910), p. 64. Cf. a Karaite parallel in M. Cook, '"Anan and Islam: the origins of Karaite scripturalism', *JSAI* 9 (1987), p. 182.

[30] Al-Ṭabarī, *Taʾrīkh*, II, p. 880.

Shabīb and those 'Ḥarūrīs' who followed in their footsteps.[31] In other words, these figures were not parochial bandits, dressed by the late and urban literary tradition in the garb of religious revolutionaries. These were warrior saints who did have a programme; and they were bandits only in the sense that they were drawn from the same surplus of rural leadership that produces banditry, many of whose techniques they employed with considerable success. Shabīb shares a number of features of a Hobsbawmian bandit, including his local status, his modest numbers, his appearance on the state's periphery, the presence of millenarian currents in the air, and, finally, his background as a soldier;[32] but in moving beyond the confines of the Jaziran steppe, he had horizons far broader than a bandit's. An appetite for (merely) material interests could have been satisfied within Mosul, where the Tigris valley offered ample opportunity to raid caravans, small settlements and other tribes.[33] Khārijism, from this perspective, is the Islamic form of that politicised and revolutionary edge of social action towards which banditry, given the appropriate conditions, can move.

Of course, one hardly needs the Syriac evidence to see that the Khārijites had a programme and a tradition; the Arabic sources make plain the existence of a local tradition of Khārijism that had its origins in Ṣāliḥ b. Musarriḥ's rebellion, and at the core of which was a programme of pious activism. Thus we read that no Ṣufrī would rebel without first visiting and cutting his hair at Ṣāliḥ's tomb, which is said to have been located somewhere in the region around Mosul;[34] and as late as 168/784, a Khārijite would rebel in his name.[35] Meanwhile, Suḥārī b. Shabīb followed in his father's footsteps, rebelling in 119/737;[36] and al-Ḍaḥḥāk b. Qays eulogised Bahlūl b. Bishr.[37] What to call this

[31] In the words of the Zuqnin chronicler, 'In the year 1047, ʿAtīq rebelled (*mrad*) and went out to Ḥrōrism'; see the *Zuqnin Chronicle*, pp. 174f./132; and cf. al-Ḍaḥḥāk (*Zuqnin Chronicle*, pp. 190f./146).

[32] For the typology, see E. J. Hobsbawm, *Bandits* (London, 1969); and *Primitive Rebels* (Manchester, 1971), pp. 13–29.

[33] For an example, see al-Ṭabarī, *Taʾrīkh*, II, p. 933 (where he makes off with *kharāj* revenues).

[34] See Ibn Durayd, *Kitāb al-Ishtiqāq*, p. 133; al-Baghdādī (attrib.), *Kitāb al-Milal wa'l-niḥal* (Beirut, 1970), p. 75; Ibn Qutayba, *al-Maʿārif*, p. 410. For another example of tomb visiting in early Islam, see the case of Ṣafwān b. al-Muʿaṭṭal of the Banū Sulaym, who was buried in Shimshāṭ; see Khalīfa b. Khayyāṭ, *Ṭabaqāt* (Damascus, 1966), II, p. 817; and Lecker, *The Banū Sulaym*, pp. 91f. (on Ṣafwān). On the Late Antique precedents for saint worship in general, see I. Goldziher, 'On the veneration of the dead in paganism and Islam', in *Muslim Studies*, I, pp. 209–38; P. Brown, *The Cult of the Saints* (Chicago, 1981), pp. 69ff. For hair-cutting, see the literature cited by van Ess, *Theologie*, II, p. 461, note 8; it is presumably a rite of separation, symbolising the Khārijites' *hijra*, but see S. M. Olyan, 'What do shaving rites accomplish and what do they signal in biblical ritual contexts?', *Journal of Biblical Literature* 117 (1998), pp. 611–22.

[35] Thus Yasīn al-Tamīmī, who rebelled in 168/784, 'was of the view of those Khārijites who argue for Ṣāliḥ b. Musarriḥ' (*yarā raʾy al-khawārij alladhīna yaqūlūna bi-Ṣāliḥ*) (editor amends the text to yield *yaqūlūna bi-raʾy Ṣāliḥ*). See al-Azdī, *Taʾrīkh*, pp. 251f.; and cf. Ibn al-Athīr, who had a copy of this part of Azdī's *Taʾrīkh* on his desk (*wa-kāna yamīl ilā maqālat Ṣāliḥ b. Musarriḥ*) (*al-Kāmil*, VI, p. 78).

[36] See al-Ṭabarī, *Taʾrīkh*, II, pp. 1633f.; Ibn al-Athīr, *al-Kāmil*, V, p. 213.

[37] Al-Ṭabarī, *Taʾrīkh*, II, p. 1627.

tradition is difficult to say, but if we should neither assume *ḥarūrī* nor exclude *khārijī*,[38] the poetry suggests that the preferred term was *al-shurāt*: as we shall see, this term is central to Ṣāliḥ b. Musarriḥ's views on rebellion, and what draws together the poetry composed in honour of Ṣāliḥ, Bahlūl b. Bishr, Bisṭām/Shawdhab, Suḥārī b. Shabīb and Saʿīd b. Bahdal, is precisely their pious fatalism: they (or their men) 'sold themselves' for God, sacrificing this world for the next.[39]

Sāliḥ b. Musarriḥ and Shabīb b. Yazīd

The local tradition of Khārijism seems to have begun with Ṣāliḥ b. Musarriḥ, who is said to have raised his rebellion in Ṣafar 76/May 695, taking riding animals from imperial authorities (sometimes identified as Muḥammad b. Marwān, and other times left unidentified) in Dārā and then raiding in the area of Nisibis, Dārā and Sinjār. After defeating an army sent by Muḥammad b. Marwān, Ṣāliḥ's men crossed the Tigris, and in the village of al-Mudabbaj they were defeated by an army led by al-Ḥārith b. ʿUmayra; Ṣāliḥ was killed and was succeeded by Shabīb b. Yazīd.[40] By the standards of Jaziran Khārijites who followed, Ṣāliḥ's rebellion was therefore less than impressive; nor does it appear that his significance lay in any original thinking.[41] It rather lay in his ability to inspire and move.

At least in part he was inspired by piety: according to Abū Mikhnaf, he was 'an ascetic and obedient man, sallow-faced, pious' (*kāna Ṣāliḥ rajul nāsik mukhbit muṣfarr al-wajh ṣāḥib al-ʿibāda*);[42] and according to al-Haytham b. ʿAdī, he was counted among 'those Khārijites who practised obedience [to

[38] Of course the term came to be used polemically, thus overshadowing the more positive Qur'ānic usage; see below, where *khurūj* is contrasted with *quʿūd*; and cf. the lines ascribed to ʿImrān b. Ḥiṭṭān (*la-qad zāda'l-ḥayāta ilayya bughḍan/wa-ḥubban li'l-khurūji Abū Bilāli*) in I. ʿAbbās, *Shiʿr al-Khawārij* (Beirut, n.d.), p. 16; the poem is also included in T. Nöldeke, *Delectus veterum carminum arabicorum* (Berlin, 1890), p. 90.

[39] The poetry is conveniently compiled in ʿAbbās, *Shiʿr*. For Ṣāliḥ, see p. 62 (*sharā nafsahu li'llāh*); for Bahlūl, p. 73 (*man kāna yakrahu an yalqā manīyatahu/fa'l-mawtu ashhā ilā qalbī min al-ʿasali*); for Ṣuḥārī, p. 73 (*innanī shārin bi-nafsī li-rabbī*); for Bisṭām [Shawdhab], pp. 70f.; and for Saʿīd b. Bahdal, p. 82 (*idhā raḥala al-shārūna*). Note too that Maṭar b. ʿImrān belongs to the same tradition; thus al-Balādhurī, *Ansāb*, Reis. 598, fol. 52a (*bāʿa li'llāh nafsahu*).

[40] For overviews of Ṣāliḥ and Shabīb's rebellion, see A. A. Dixon, *The Umayyad Caliphate 65–86/684–705* (London, 1971), pp. 182ff. (using both al-Ṭabarī and the relevant parts of al-Balādhurī's *Ansāb* in manuscript); J. Wellhausen, *Die religiös-politischen Oppositionsparteien im alten Islam*, trans. R. C. Ostle as *The Religio-political Factions in Early Islam* (Amsterdam, 1975), pp. 69ff.; Morony, *Iraq*, pp. 475ff.; van Ess, *Theologie*, II, pp. 460–4. F. Brünnow (*Die Charidschiten unter den ersten Omayyaden: Ein Beitrag zur Geschichte des ersten islamischen Jahrhunderts* (Leiden, 1884), pp. 48f.) could not avail himself of the appropriate volume of al-Ṭabarī, and therefore relied almost exclusively on Ibn al-Athīr.

[41] Thus al-Ashʿarī (*Maqālāt al-islāmiyyīn*, p. 118) identifies 'the followers (*aṣḥāb*) of Ṣāliḥ' as a Khārijite sub-sect, despite the fact that he cannot credit Ṣāliḥ with having articulated a doctrine of his own (*lam yuḥdith Ṣāliḥ qawl tafarrada bi-hi*).

[42] Al-Ṭabarī, *Taʾrīkh*, II, p. 881. This – his face made 'sallow' (*muṣfarr*) from constant devotion – provides one explanation for the term 'Ṣufriyya' itself. See Lewinstein, 'Making and unmaking', pp. 79f.; M. Fierro, 'Al-Aṣfar', *SI* 77 (1993), pp. 178ff.

God], and out of humility he never raised his head' (*min makhābīt al-khawārij wa-kāna lā yarfa' ra'sahu khushū'an*).[43] Piety is a common enough feature among Khārijites;[44] what appears to have made Ṣāliḥ noteworthy was the quality of his preaching. We read that he taught his students how to recite the Qur'ān and what it meant (*yuqri'uhum al-Qur'ān wa-yufaqqihuhum*). One traditionist, Qabīṣa b. 'Abd al-Raḥmān, even kept a record of his sermons, excerpts of which he passed on to Abū Mikhnaf's teachers.[45] The passage in question is interesting for a number of reasons, not the least of which is that if we take it as authentic, it is the earliest substantial piece of religious discourse we possess from the Jazira – Khārijite or otherwise.[46] A particularly interesting passage is as follows:

I charge you with fear of God (*ūṣīkum bi-taqwā Allāh*),[47] abstinence (*zuhd*) in this world, desire for the next, frequent remembrance (*dhikr*) of death, separation from the sinners (*fāsiqīn*), and love for the believers. Indeed, modesty (*zahāda*) in this world makes [God's] servant desirous of what is God's (*fīmā 'ind Allāh*) and empties his body for obedience to God; frequent remembrance of death makes one fearful of God, so that one entreats him and submits to him (*yastakīn lahu*). Departure from the sinners is a duty (*ḥaqq*) on all believers; God said in his Book: 'Do not pray over any of them who dies, ever, nor stand at his grave; they denied God (*kafarū*) and his messenger, and they have died sinners.'[48]

The sermon then turns to standard Khārijite concerns: the Prophet, Abū Bakr and 'Umar all ruled according to God's book and the Sunna; 'Uthmān did not, and was killed for it; we disassociate ourselves from 'Alī and his party because of his decision to arbitrate (in the wake of Ṣiffīn). And for Ṣāliḥ disassociation means active rebellion, rather than Qumranic seclusion:

So prepare yourself – may God have mercy on you – to fight (*jihād*) against these enemies aligned [against Islam] (*al-aḥzāb al-mutaḥazzaba*) and the oppressive leaders of error, and to go out from the transient to the eternal world, and to join our believing, resolute brothers who have sold this world for the next, and who have expended their wealth, seeking to please God in the hereafter.[49]

The language of the sermon is thoroughly allusive. It evokes Qur'ān 4:95, 9:46 and 9:83, (among others), which contrast *jihād* and *khurūj* with *qu'ūd*, and the first makes it clear that God reserves the higher reward for those who fight (*faḍḍala Allāh al-mujāhidīn bi-amwālihim wa-anfusihim 'alā al-qā'idīn ajran*

[43] Al-Balādhurī, *Ansāb*, Reis. 598, fol. 43b.
[44] E.g. 'Imrān b. Ḥiṭṭān, 'Abd Allāh b. Maḥūz, and Qaṭarī b. Fujā'a: see al-Baghdādī, *al-Farq bayn al-firaq* (Cairo, n.d.), p. 93; al-Shahrastānī, *Milal* I, p. 90; al-Dīnawarī, *al-Akhbār*, pp. 284ff; F. Gabrieli, 'La poesia Ḫārigita nel secolo degli Omayyadi', *Rivista degli Studi Orientali* 20 (1943), p. 352.
[45] See al-Ṭabarī, *Ta'rīkh*, II, pp. 882ff.
[46] Cf. van Ess, *Theologie* II, p. 461.
[47] Part of the stock formulary of early Islamic epistles; see M. Cook, *Early Muslim Dogma* (Cambridge, 1981), pp. 6f.
[48] The quotation is from Qur'ān 9:84.
[49] Al-Ṭabarī, *Ta'rīkh*, II, p. 883. On this rendering of *aḥzāb*, see A. F. L. Beeston and L. I. Conrad, 'On some Umayyad poetry in the *History* of al-Ṭabarī', *JRAS* 3.3 (1993), p. 205.

ʿaẓīman).[50] The final passage also echoes Qur'ān 9:20[51] and 4:100,[52] and fuses asceticism and revolution: family and possessions are transient, and are to be sacrificed for everlasting life in the hereafter.[53] In alluding to the Qur'ān, Ṣāliḥ thus imports a Prophetic paradigm into the late first-century Jazira: tribesmen of Ṣāliḥ's day are to follow the example of those believing tribesmen of Muḥammad's day, who actively fought on the Prophet's behalf against the unbelievers.[54] Insofar as it can be interpreted as polemics for activist, rather than quietist, Khārijism, it also suggests the presence of the latter – quietist Khārijites who were content to remain in what the activists described as *dār al-kufr*; and for those who do not accept his call, Ṣāliḥ recommended that they be killed.[55] In this, and in his call for *hijra*, Ṣāliḥ thus appears to conform to what the classical tradition would hold to be Azraqī doctrines; there can be no doubt, however, that *hijra* clearly had a place in the (non-Azraqī) Jazira.[56]

Ṣāliḥ is thus subversive in that he recycles elements of Qur'ānic piety and activism to turn them back on the Umayyad élite, which was itself busy defining the Prophet's legacy in terms sympathetic to Umayyad rule. It is thus radical only in that it was becoming increasingly reactionary, particularly as the state turned away from *jihād* and *hijra* during the late Umayyad period; this, at least in part, may help explain the growing popularity of Khārijism.[57] No doubt some of his message struck familiar chords among local settled Christians. Morony has related Ṣāliḥ's asceticism and fatalistic piety to Ephrem and Isaac of Nineveh;[58] and charismatic piety was not entirely unfamiliar to pastoralists of the Syro-Mesopotamian steppe: in the *Life* of John the Arab, we have a fourth-century Christian analogy,[59] and no less an authority than Peter Brown has spoken of the 'Beduinization of the

[50] 'God has preferred in rank those who struggle with their possessions and their selves over the ones who sit at home' (so Arberry).

[51] 'Those who believe, and have emigrated, and have struggled in the way of God with their possessions and their selves are mightier in rank with God' (Arberry).

[52] 'Whoso emigrates in the way of God will find in the earth many refuges and plenty; whoso goes forth from his house an emigrant to God and His Messenger, and then death overtakes him, his wage shall have fallen on God; surely God is All-forgiving, All-compassionate' (Arberry).

[53] See also the poetry credited to Suḥarī b. Shabīb (al-Ṭabarī, *Ta'rīkh*, II, p. 1634), and Bisṭām's words to his men as he realises his fate (al-Ṭabarī, *Ta'rīkh*, II, p. 1378). Cf. Qur'ān 4:74.

[54] Among the Azāriqa the parallel was occasionally made explicit; see the words of an unidentified Azraqī, *li-annā al-yawm bi-manzilat al-muhājirīn bi'l-Madīna*; see al-Ashʿarī, *Maqālāt al-islāmiyyīn*, I, pp. 88f.

[55] See the account in al-Ṭabarī, *Ta'rīkh*, II, p. 886.

[56] Thus, according to al-Haytham b. ʿAdī, 'They [the authorities] were loath to kill a Khārijite in the Jazīra or Syria for fear that the Khārijites would take it as *dār al-hijra*' (al-Balādhurī, *Ansāb*, Reis. 598, fol. 51b (with a variant on f. 52b)). The passage presumably means that the death of a Khārijite rebel in the province would draw other Khārijites to the place where he died, which they would then turn into a Khārijite camp. Cf. the *Zuqnin Chronicle*, pp. 174f./132, where ʿAtīq's withdrawal into the desert is described as typically Arab.

[57] On the significance of *jihād* in the early period, see P. Crone, 'The first-century concept of *Hiğra*', *Arabica* 41 (1994), pp. 352–87; and K. Y. Blankinship, *The End of the Jihâd State: The Reign of Hishâm Ibn ʿAbd al-Malik and the Collapse of the Umayyads* (Albany, 1994).

[58] Morony, *Iraq*, pp. 476f.

[59] See Brock, 'Some monasteries on Mount Izla', p. 10 (John appears as a fierce horseman, sending bedouin raiders to the hills).

ascetic life'.[60] One might also be inclined to relate Ṣāliḥ's ideas to the millenarian anxieties of the late seventh century, which are reflected in the late seventh- and early eighth-century apocalypses, and which seem to have produced messiah figures at the beginning of the eighth century (in Mardīn),[61] and at its end (in Mosul).[62] All of this said, Ṣāliḥ fits a Late Antique pattern only as much as Muḥammad does; more precisely, inasmuch as Muḥammad's movement can be described as millenarian, so too can Ṣāliḥ's.[63]

For all that Ṣāliḥ was a reflective ascetic, one who could offer a programme and who could inspire, his career as a rebel was short lived and spectacularly unsuccessful. Credit for transforming Ṣāliḥ's dispiriting failure into inspirational martyrdom probably belongs to Shabīb b. Yazīd al-Shaybānī, whom the tradition gives the role of reconstituting Ṣāliḥ's rebellion; in fact, the tradition appears so keen to knot the historical memory of the two men that questions can be raised about what actually happened.

It is primarily to Abū Mikhnaf, as preserved in al-Ṭabarī, that we owe the standard account, which has as its chief feature a single, continuous rebellion, begun by Ṣāliḥ and reconstituted by Shabīb.[64] Now the Syriac sources know only of Shabīb, and this silence is significant only because it is shared by several reports within the Islamic tradition; this is true not only of those less detailed,[65] but of extended ones, such as those found in the relatively early al-Balādhurī,[66] Ibn Aʿtham,[67] and the relatively late Ibn Khallikān.[68] In these accounts Shabīb rebels on his own, for reasons of his own. To the objection that Abū Mikhnaf's report is corroborated by Ibn Qutayba and Khalīfa b. Khayyāṭ,[69] one need only note that both are vague, and that neither can convincingly join Ṣāliḥ with Shabīb. In fact, the same could be said of Abū Mikhnaf himself. We have a purported exchange of letters between the two men, but this serves only to establish Shabīb's impatient activism ('But if you want to postpone that day, inform

[60] See Brown, 'The rise and function of the holy man', pp. 83ff.

[61] The accounts are confused in several particulars; see Michael the Syrian, *Chronique* xi.xix; the *Chronicle of 1234*, I, pp. 308/240; Theophanes, *Chronicle*, AM 6213; Agapius, *Kitāb al-ʿUnwān*, p. 504; and also the *Zuqnin Chronicle*, pp. 173/131. The event was first discussed by J. Starr, 'Le mouvement messianique au début du viii siècle', *Revue des Etudes Juives*, n.s. 52 (1937), pp. 81–92.

[62] On Mārūtā, see the *Chronicle of 819*, ed. A. Barsaum and trans. J.-B. Chabot as *Chronicon anonymum and annum domini 819 pertinens* (Paris, 1920 and 1937; *CSCO* 81 and 109), I, pp. 19/13; the *Chronicle of 846*, pp. 237/179f.; the *Zuqnin Chronicle*, pp. 282f./224f. and 287ff./229ff.

[63] In this regard, I have learned much not only from a classic (P. Worsley, *The Trumpet Shall Sound: A Study of 'Cargo' Cults in Melanesia* (New York, 1968, second edn), but also from T. A. Diacon, *Millenarian Vision, Capitalist Reality* (Durham, NC and London, 1991).

[64] The account begins at al-Ṭabarī, *Ta'rīkh*, II, p. 881; Hishām b. Muḥammad al-Kalbī cites Abū Mikhnaf for the same report in al-Balādhurī, *Ansāb*, Reis. 598, fol. 43b. Abū ʿUbayda shares Abū Mikhnaf's view (al-Balādhurī, *Ansāb*, Reis. 598, fol. 47a) (but has no details), and so too the secondary literature (Wellhausen, *Religio-political Factions*, pp. 69ff., and Dixon, *The Umayyad Caliphate*, p. 182).

[65] See al-Yaʿqūbī, *Ta'rīkh*, II, p. 328.

[66] Al-Balādhurī, *Ansāb*, Reis. 598, fol. 44b (citing al-Kalbī).

[67] Ibn Aʿtham, *Futūḥ*, VII, pp. 84f.

[68] Ibn Khallikān, *Wafayāt al-aʿyān*, II, pp. 454ff.

[69] Dixon, *The Umayyad Caliphate*, p. 182.

me; people die in the morning and in the evening, and I cannot be sure that fate will not cut me off'), and reinforce Ṣāliḥ's leadership ('You will be the *shaykh* of the Muslims').[70] We also have a dramatic battle scene, in which Shabīb heroically delivers the remnants of Ṣāliḥ's forces, and which serves to establish Shabīb's claim to succeed the fallen Ṣāliḥ.[71]

There are, then, both alternatives to, and seams within, Abū Mikhnaf's reconstruction, and it might be suggested that his account should be read primarily in the light of Khārijite polemics about succession, which provided figures on whom to hang doctrinal variations.[72] Noting that Ṣāliḥ's rebellion preceded Shabīb's,[73] al-Haytham b. ʿAdī pointedly remarks that the Khārijites confused serial rebellion with succession: 'The Khārijites believe that when one of them rebels, and then another, the second was following the first';[74] as far as al-Haytham is concerned, the rebellions were separate. It might further be suggested that claims made by those in favour of Shabīb's succession multiplied over time, since they appear in at least two different forms;[75] certainly intrusions into the narrative of Shabīb's final battle suggest that those polemicising against his succession were active.[76] Meanwhile, the alternative to Abū Mikhnaf's reconstruction – positing two distinct rebellions, one led by Ṣāliḥ

[70] Al-Ṭabarī, *Ta'rīkh*, II, pp. 884f. On the literary function of correspondence in the conquest accounts, see Noth/Conrad, *Early Arabic Historical Tradition*, pp. 76ff.

[71] Al-Ṭabarī, *Ta'rīkh*, II, pp. 891f.

[72] See al-Baghdādī's account of Ṣāliḥ and Shabīb (*Farq*, p. 110), in which Ṣāliḥ is said to have opposed the Azāriqa, and Shabīb is said to disagree with Ṣāliḥ on the right of women to the imamate. For another example, see Lewinstein, 'The Azāriqa', pp. 257f.

[73] According to al-Ashʿarī, (*Maqālāt al-islāmiyyīn*, I, pp. 120f.), Ṣāliḥ and Dāwūd (b. al-Nuʿmān al-ʿAbdī?; see al-Balādhurī, *Ansāb*, Reis. 598, fol. 51a–b) were among those Khārijites about whom there was no report of any rebellion (*mimman lam yudhkar annahu kharaja*), or to whom no *madhhab* was credited (*wa-lā la-hu madhhab yuʿraf bi-hi*) (cf. al-Shahrastānī, *Milal*, I, p. 95). However, the passage is quickly followed by another, which states that in fact Ṣāliḥ and Dāwūd did participate in a 'single revolt' (*kharja*), which is said to have taken place near the end of their lives, and 'which is not the famous one' (*thumma kānat la-humā fī ākhir ayyāmihimā kharja laysat bi'l-mashhūra*). If the Dāwūd in question is to be identified as Dāwūd b. al-Nuʿmān, the two could not have participated in the same revolt, since Dāwūd's is dated to 86 or 87. The meaning of this last phrase is obscure, but a *kharja* presumably stands in contrast to an extended rebellion (*khurūj*), and a following passage, which explains the origin of a group called the al-Rājiʿa, presumably refers to the *kharja*. Here Shabīb is nowhere to be seen.

[74] *Wa'l-khawārij yarawna man kharaja minhum thumma kharaja baʿdahu ākhar anna al-thānī tabiʿa al-awwal* (al-Balādhurī, *Ansāb*, Reis. 598, fol. 45a). Cf. the deliberations that took place in early Ramaḍān of year 120, when Khārijites in the north were forced to choose between Saʿīd b. Bahdal and Abū Karib: they chose to follow the former, on the grounds that he had rebelled before the latter, and Abū Karib promptly renounced his claims to leadership; precisely the same procedure is then followed when Saʿīd comes across Shaybān b. ʿAbd al-ʿAzīz (see Khalīfa b. Khayyāṭ, *Ta'rīkh*, p. 242). Indeed, there was predictable confusion surrounding the rebellions of Bisṭām, Shaybān b. ʿAbd al-ʿAzīz, Saʿīd b. Bahdal and al-Ḍaḥḥāk b. Qays, all four having broken out within a period of four years.

[75] Abū Mikhnaf (see al-Ṭabarī, *Ta'rīkh*, II, pp. 891f.; al-Balādhurī, *Ansab*, Reis. 598, fol. 45b) suggests that Shabīb had to persuade Ṣāliḥ's supporters of his leadership, whereas other sources (Ibn Qutayba, *al-Maʿārif*, p. 410; al-Baghdādī, *Farq*, p. 110) have it that Ṣāliḥ appointed Shabīb. An account reported by a variety of authorities cited by al-Balādhurī (*Ansāb*, Reis. 598, fol. 47a) has Shabīb receive the *bayʿa*.

[76] Thus, even in the heat of battle Maṣqala b. Muhalhil interrogates Shabīb on his opinion of Ṣāliḥ, and when Shabīb equivocates, Maṣqala abandons his cause; see al-Ṭabarī, *Ta'rīkh*, II, p. 967.

and another by Shabīb – can explain why al-Shahrastānī connects Shabīb's followers with the Bayhasiyya, rather than with the Ṣufriyya,[77] and also why two separate labels, the *shabībiyya* and the *ṣāliḥiyya*, survived.[78]

Whatever the precise relation between Ṣāliḥ and Shabīb, we can be sure that the latter's reputation rested primarily on his spectacular successes against the Umayyads. He cut an impressive figure,[79] and this in large part because he was an extremely able guerrilla. Khārijite forces were typically small,[80] and at its start, Ṣāliḥ's numbered barely over a hundred men.[81] During the course of his campaigns their numbers eventually did increase, but only moderately; we read that they numbered 181(?), 800, and finally, 1,000.[82] Meanwhile, Umayyad forces are consistently said to have been larger, often ten times their size,[83] and yet these still balked at meeting Shabīb head on.[84] Given the size of his forces, Shabīb hardly posed a threat to the Umayyad state, and in ruling territory he showed no real interest. Rather, he fought and moved, leading his men to a series of spectacular victories through Nahrawān, al-Madā'in, Kufa, up the Tigris and back again to Kufa, Anbār, and finally Khūzistān, constantly proving himself against stronger and stronger Umayyad forces, and never (it appears) giving any thought to securing the territory won;[85] his seems to have been a programme of humiliation rather than conquest. How else are we to understand accounts of his first raid of Kufa, when he pounded al-Ḥajjāj's palace with his club, stormed the mosque to lead his band in prayer, and left town in the morning?[86] In Geertz's sense, Shabīb was 'insolent';[87] and his insolence can be

[77] Al-Shahrastānī, *Milal*, I, p. 95; noted by Lewinstein, 'Making and unmaking', p. 80. More than a century ago Brünnow noted the curious participation of Ṣufrites – purported, in his words, to be the least 'fanatical' of all sects – in Shabīb's rebellion; see his *Charidschiten*, p. 49.

[78] According to al-Baghdādī (*Farq*, pp. 109f.), the Shabībiyya are also known as the Ṣāliḥiyya.

[79] Many have noted this (Wellhausen, *Religio-political Factions*, 75; van Ess, *Theologie*, II, p. 461 ('colourful personality'), but no one has made much of it.

[80] Even allowing, of course, for some fidgeting with the numbers for narrative effect. W. M. Watt has estimated early Khārijite numbers in several publications; for a useful summary, see his *Islam and the Integration of Society* (London, 1961), pp. 98f.

[81] Al-Ṭabarī, *Ta'rīkh*, II, p. 887.

[82] Al-Ṭabarī, *Ta'rīkh*, II, pp. 890, 935, 942 and 949.

[83] For example, ʿAdī b. ʿAdī b. ʿUmayra, the first Umayyad general sent out after Ṣāliḥ, is credited with a force of 1,000 men; see al-Ṭabarī, *Ta'rīkh*, II, p. 887. For a review of all the numbers in al-Ṭabarī's account, see Wellhausen, *Religio-political Factions*, pp. 70f.

[84] See the comments of Saʿīd b. Mujālid to the cowardly Kufans in al-Ṭabarī, *Ta'rīkh*, II, p. 908.

[85] Much later, when Sulaymān b. Hishām had joined up with the Khārijites, now under the leadership of Shaybān b. ʿAbd al-ʿAzīz, he seems to have sensed that their tactics could never lead to the victory he envisaged: 'When one of you is victorious in battle, he goes and tries to have himself killed, and does so!' (*thumma yastaqtil wa-yuqtal*). Sulaymān would have had them dig in and secure their victory. See al-Ṭabarī, *Ta'rīkh*, II, p. 1943.

[86] Al-Ṭabarī, *Ta'rīkh*, II, pp. 917f.; al-Balādhurī, *Ansāb*, Reis. 598, fol. 46a; al-Yaʿqūbī, *Ta'rīkh*, II, p. 328. Shaban puts a somewhat lighter spin on this and other events, calling them 'practical jokes', but he understood that their significance was that they were public and symbolic challenges to Umayyad authority. See his *Islamic History*, pp. 107f.

[87] 'Every serious charismatic threat that ever arose in Alawite Morocco took the form of some local power-figure's laying claim to enormous baraka by engaging in actions – *siba*, literally, "insolence" – designed to expose the weakness of the king by showing him up as unable to stop them.' See C. Geertz, 'Centers, kings, and charisma: reflections on the symbolics of power', in J. Ben-David and T. N. Clark, eds., *Culture and its Creators: Essays in Honor of Edward Shils* (Chicago, 1977), p. 168.

seen most clearly in an account Ibn al-Kalbī thought worthwhile to report concerning Shabīb's reaction to al-Ḥajjāj's forces, which were bearing down on him:

When the fighting force (*al-nās*) was defeated and he withdrew behind the bridge, al-Ḥajjāj's cavalry pursued him. The narrative continues:[88] he [Shabīb] began to nod off, so I said to him: 'O Commander of the Faithful, turn and look behind you!' He turned around blithely (*ghayr muktarith*) and leaned over, nodding off again. They were getting close to us, so we [all] said: 'O Commander of the Faithful, they are getting close to you!' By God, he turned around blithely, and began to nod off again. Al-Ḥajjāj then sent a message to his cavalry, [ordering] them: 'Leave him [to burn] in God's fire.'[89]

Wellhausen explained Shabīb's indifference in the light of his army's defeat and the death of his wife Ghazāla,[90] but this strikes me as a bit precious; the point here, as elsewhere,[91] is to illustrate Shabīb's fearless bravado; it is, after all, as an 'illustrious horseman and mighty champion' that an early Syriac source knows him.[92] The inspiration for this material may be Shabīb's heroic exploits as retold by Muslims; it may be the memory of local Christians, who held him in high regard as well. We read that in the village of al-Batt, which was located 'on the borders (*tukhūm*) of the [region] of Mosul',[93] Shabīb stayed in the townspeople's church; and there they hailed him as a Hobsbawmian bandit-avenger: 'May God make you prosper! You are merciful to the weak and those who are subject to the *jizya* (*ahl al-jizya*). Those whom you rule can speak to you and make appeal to you about what befalls them; you then consider them and shield them [from retribution] (*takuff ʿanhum*).'

Umayyad agents, meanwhile, represent the loathsome authority of the state, whose power of retribution puts fear in villagers' hearts:

But these people are tyrannical (*jabābira*); they will not be spoken to, and they do not accept a plea (*ʿudhr*). By God, if news reaches them that you are staying in our church, they will kill us when you leave (if you are so fated). We beseech you (*fa-in ra'ayt*), stay next to the village [that is, do not enter it], so that you do not create for them a grievance (*maqāl*) against us.[94]

[88] (*Qāla*); the source of the narrative is a Khārijite named Aṣghar. The passage includes several more narrative interjections, which are best left untranslated.

[89] Al-Ṭabarī, *Ta'rīkh*, II, p. 961. The passage (among others) is reproduced in Ibn Abī al-Ḥadīd, *Sharḥ nahj al-balāgha* (Beirut, 1964), II, p. 92 (for a similar example, see *ibid*, II, p. 75).

[90] Wellhausen, *Religio-political Factions*, p. 73.

[91] Another example is the battle of Qaṭīṭiyā (al-Ṭabarī, *Ta'rīkh*, II, pp. 908f.; the toponym is problematic), where Shabīb responds to the Umayyad forces surrounding him by calmly finishing his meal and then bursting through the siege.

[92] See the *Chronicle of 819*, I, pp. 14/9.

[93] There appears to have been some confusion about this location. Yāqūt (*Muʿjam*, I, p. 488) knows of two such places, one in the district of Baghdad, 'near Rādhān', and the other near Baʿqūbā. Rowson's suggestion that the latter is intended in this passage (*The History of al-Ṭabarī*, vol. XXII, *The Marwānid Restoration*, trans. E. Rowson (Albany, 1989), p. 84, note 335), is corroborated by al-Muqaddasī (*Aḥsan al-taqāsīm*, pp. 54 and 115), where Batt is counted among the districts of Sāmarrā'. The location does not appear in al-Azdī.

[94] Al-Ṭabarī, *Ta'rīkh*, II, p. 934. Incidents such as this shed some light on the curious Khārijite indulgence of the *ahl al-dhimma*; see Wellhausen, *Religio-Political Factions*, p. 21; Lewinstein, 'The Azāriqa', p. 263, note 80.

Here it bears emphasising that Jaziran Khārijism cannot be characterised as a recrudescence of tribalism; it clearly tapped into a reservoir of anti-Umayyad sentiment that transcended Shaybānī (or other tribal) grievances. As a Shaybānī chief,[95] Shabīb was presumably part of a structure of status and privilege that gave him access to Shaybānī tribesmen, and if kinship is taken to operate most effectively at the lowest levels of segmentation, we might suspect that much of Shabīb's strength was drawn from tribesmen of his lineage, the Banū Murra b. Hammām b. Murra b. Dhuhl;[96] but on at least one occasion he is said to have disregarded kinship ties and killed a member of the Murra b. Hammām,[97] and we know that participation in his insurrection was not limited to Shaybānīs – or even Arabs for that matter: some joined for the spoils or out of desperation,[98] while others joined for revenge.[99]

Causes and consequences

It should be clear enough that Shabīb's reputation stems from his charisma and bravado, rather than any signal contribution to Khārijite thought. The precise connections between his movement and that of his precedessor Ṣāliḥ b. Musarriḥ remain murky, Abū Mikhnaf's reconstruction in this regard being particularly problematic, especially since in tying Shabīb to Ṣāliḥ, he also effaced any clear sense of why Shabīb rebelled. In what follows I shall argue that the omission is crucial, for insofar as the events of Shabīb's rebellion can be recovered, they suggest that the context was an army context: what led Shabīb to rebel was the elimination of his name from the *dīwān*.[100] In other

[95] Cf. the probably legendary exchange between Shabīb and Rawḥ b. Zinbā', in which Shabīb responds to Rawḥ's question about his pedigree: '[I am] a man of the Banū Shaybān and one of the Banū Murra; I possess a chiefly lineage, power, and command authority among my kinsmen' (*wa-lī sharaf wa-qadr wa-ṭā'a fī qawmī*); see Ibn A'tham, *Futūḥ*, VII, p. 84. Cf. the very similar report in al-Baghdādī, *Farq*, p. 110, which comes on the authority of anonymous historians (*aṣḥāb al-tawārīkh*), and where Shabīb claims to have a large Shaybānī following. Both accounts have 'Abd al-Malik ignorant of Shabīb's *nasab*, and both have Shabīb vowing to teach the caliph a lesson he will not forget. On the Shaybān in early Islam, see also M. al-'Ubaydī, *Banū Shaybān wa-dawruhum fī al-ta'rīkh al-'arabī wa'l-islāmī ḥattā maṭla' al-'aṣr al-rāshidī* (Baghdad, 1984).

[96] On Shabīb's descent, see Ibn Ḥazm, *Jamhara*, pp. 326f.; al-Balādhurī, *Ansāb*, Reis. 598, fol. 44b; and Ibn al-Kalbī, *Ǧamhara*, II, p. 552. In addition to Shabīb, the Banū Murra b. Hammām b. Murra b. Dhuhl produced another Khārijite, Hudba (Ḥurayth b. Iyās b. Hanzala b. al-Ḥārith) (Ibn Ḥazm, *Jamhara*, p. 326), perhaps to be identified with al-Balādhurī's Hudba al-Ṭā'ī (*Ansāb*, Reis. 598, fol. 44b).

[97] Al-Ṭabarī, *Ta'rīkh*, II, p. 975.

[98] Abū Mikhnaf (al-Ṭabarī, *Ta'rīkh*, II, p. 941) reports that Shabīb was joined by 'many people pursuing worldly goods, along with people whom al-Ḥajjāj was pursuing for money or [other] claims' (*tibā'āt*). Among these was al-Ḥurr b. 'Abd Allāh b. 'Awf, who had earned al-Ḥajjāj's wrath by retaliating against two *dihqān*s; he renounced the rebellion after Shabīb's death, and/or, according to a more revealing passage, after al-Ḥajjāj had explicitly granted amnesty to those in al-Ḥurr's circumstances (that he did so suggests that al-Ḥurr's case was one of many). Cf. the rebellion led by al-Khirrīt b. Rāshid in Wilkinson, 'Early development', pp. 128f.

[99] Thus Salāma b. Sayyār of the Taym Shaybān enrolled to avenge the death his brother Faḍāla; see al-Ṭabarī, *Ta'rīkh*, II, pp. 892f.; and 'Abbās, *Shi'r*, pp. 66ff.

[100] For bandits as marginal figures (including former soldiers), see Hobsbawm, *Bandits*, p. 27.

words, having lost the élite status conferred upon members of the *dīwān*, Shabīb sought to regain it through other means: he, and other Khārijites of the tradition, sought to preserve that mixture of piety, reformist monotheism and pastoralist muscle that had fuelled Muḥammad and his original community, and which, in the Jazira of the late first century, was rapidly dissolving under Marwānid pressure.

Shabīb was literally and figuratively a child of holy war.[101] Like so many immigrant tribesmen, his background was the conquests: his father, Yazīd b. Nuʿaym, had been among those who emigrated to Kufa;[102] and it is presumably from Kufa that he participated in Salmān b. Rabīʿa al-Bāhilī's raids on the northern frontiers, which took place during the reign of ʿUthmān.[103] On one of these he found a wife named Jahīza, who gave birth to Shabīb in either 25 or 26/645–6 in the northern Mosuli town of Sātīdamā; the birth itself is subject to legendary frills,[104] but the sequence of events is perfectly ordinary. Shabīb then followed in his father's footsteps. According to al-Kalbī, he led night-time raids against the Kurds (*wa-kāna Shabīb ṣāḥib fatk wa-ghārāt wa-kāna yubayyit al-akrād*), having received a stipend after gaining the age of majority (*kāna Shabīb fī al-dīwān furiḍa la-hu ḥīna adraka*).[105] Elsewhere we read that he enrolled Salāma b. Sayyār, having known him earlier because the two had together been 'on the muster roll (*dīwān*) and in the raids (*maghāzī*).'[106]

Al-Balādhurī offers two versions of the events leading up to Shabīb's rebellion. In the first, which is credited to al-Kalbī, Shabīb's name is dropped from the *dīwān* 'because of the length of his absence and his staying away from the inspection of the muster masters' (*wa-qad kāna ismuhu saqaṭa min al-dīwān li-kathrat ghaybatihi wa-takhallufihi ʿan al-iʿtirāḍ ʿalā al-ʿurrāḍ*).[107] As far as the narrative itself is concerned, his absence is to be explained by his spiritual journey, which eventually took him to Kufa, where he met Ṣāliḥ b. Musarriḥ. After learning the news, Shabīb is said to have gone to the caliph ʿAbd al-Malik, enrolling intermediaries to speak on his behalf to restore his stipends and rations;[108] but the caliph refused, on the grounds that the Bakr and Tamīm

[101] Note too that it is tempting to see in Ṣāliḥ's *kunya* (b. Musarraḥ – a common enough reckoning, on which see van Ess, *Theologie*, II, p. 460) an allusion to his father's military background; on *s-rr-ḥ*, 'to dispatch soldiers', see the *glossarium* to al-Ṭabarī, *Ta'rīkh*, p. ccxv; and R. Dozy, *Supplément aux dictionnaires arabes* (Leiden and Paris, 1927; second edn), I, p. 646a.

[102] Ibn Ḥazm, *Jamhara*, pp. 327.

[103] On these, see Caetani, *Annali dell'Islam*, VII, pp. 167f.

[104] In particular, the birth scene of Shabīb, on which see Wellhausen's comments, *Religio-political Factions*, p. 74 and note 16. For the river (and mountain) of Sātīdamā, see Yāqūt, *Muʿjam*, II, p. 552 and III, p. 7.

[105] Al-Balādhurī, *Ansāb*, Reis. 598, fol. 44b.

[106] Al-Ṭabarī, *Ta'rīkh*, II, pp. 892f.

[107] Al-Balādhurī, *Ansāb*, Reis. 598, fol. 45a. On some of the terminology, see C. E. Bosworth, 'Recruitment, muster and review in medieval Islamic armies', in V. J. Parry and M. E. Yapp, eds., *War, Technology and Society in the Middle East* (London, 1975), pp. 70ff.; and on *takhalluf* in this and other senses, see Bonner, *Aristocratic Violence*, pp. 32ff.

[108] According to an account of Umayyad Egypt, stipend levels were determined by the caliph himself; see W. Hoenerbach, 'Zur Heeresverwaltung der ʿAbbāsiden', *DI* 29 (1950), p. 262.

were 'tribes of great evil' (*ḥayyān kathīr sharruhumā*).[109] The second report, which is credited to al-Haytham b. ʿAdī, offers us a much more schematic version of the same events: the Marwānids did not grant the Bakr and Tamīm of Syria a stipend, so Shabīb rebelled in order to get it.[110] Ibn Aʿtham al-Kūfī offers another variant: here the influential courtier Rawḥ b. Zinbāʾ al-Judhāmī functions as Shabīb's intermediary with ʿAbd al-Malik.[111] The text suffers from a lacuna, and ʿAbd al-Malik's response seems to anticipate the events that follow: 'I am loathe to grant a stipend to anyone of the people . . . in Syria, because they follow the Khārijite view' (*innī la-akrah an afriḍ li-aḥad min ahl . . . bi'l-Shām farḍ li-anna raʾyahum raʾy al-khawārij*).[112]

Needless to say, the reports are difficult to interpret. Ibn Aʿtham's seems altogether the least promising, particularly since it suggests that once a Khārijite, always a Khārijite; in practice, Marwānid policies were more considerably more realistic.[113] Nor do I set much stock by a sequence that endows Shabīb with Khārijite – or, indeed, even serious spiritual – inclinations before his name was dropped from the *dīwān*: as we have seen, the Hajj narrative must be taken as an attempt to equip him with ascetic qualifications, thereby connecting him more securely to the pious Ṣāliḥ b. Musarriḥ. Meanwhile, the dialogue with ʿAbd al-Malik (or Rawḥ) works best if Shabīb is an army commander with a tribal following, and if one has ʿAbd al-Malik see in him nothing more than another free-loading tribesman, one who felt entitled to a stipend without earning it properly – that is, by campaigning. In short, I see nothing wrong in interpreting Shabīb as a disgruntled commander who, having been dropped (for whatever reason) from the army rolls, embraced Khārijism as a result. Since at least one later rebel, Bahlūl b. Bishr, was clearly an army commander of some real distinction,[114] and another, Shabīb's son Suḥārī, was perhaps one too,[115] there may be grounds for positing a general

[109] Al-Balādhurī, *Ansāb*, Reis. 598, fol. 45a; al-Ṭabarī (*Taʾrīkh*, II, pp. 881f.) may have had access to a version of the story, but he chose to follow Abū Mikhnaf's main account.

[110] *Lā yafriḍūn li-Bakr wa-lā li-Tamīm bi'l-Shām fa-kharaja Shabīb yaṭlub al-farīḍa* (al-Balādhurī, *Ansāb*, Reis. 598, fol. 45a.).

[111] On Rawḥ, see Crone, *Slaves*, pp. 99f.; I. Hasson, 'Le chef judhāmite Rawḥ b. Zinbāʿ', *SI* 77 (1993), p. 115ff.; and the account in al-Balādhurī, *Ansāb*, Reis. 598, fol. 52a.

[112] Ibn Aʿtham, *Futūḥ*, VII, pp. 84f.

[113] In at least one case, the authorities were content to accept rank-and-file *khawārij* into the army: after their leader's death, the remnants of Bisṭām al-Shaybānī's force thus enrolled in Marwān's mobile security force (*rawābiṭ*) (see al-Ṭabarī, *Taʾrīkh*, II, p. 1898; these men may have earlier been on the *dīwān*). Since the main responsibility of the Mosulī *rawābiṭ* seems to have been to fight Khārijites (see al-Azdī, *Taʾrīkh*, pp. 195, 251, and 257f.; al-Balādhurī, *Ansāb*, III, p. 249), their experience would have been especially valuable. On the *rawābiṭ*, see chapter 7.

[114] According to a tradition attributed to Abū ʿUbayda and al-Madāʾinī, Hishām wrote to the governor of Mosul (at this point, al-Walīd b. Talīd), ordering him to send a commander named Kuthāra against the Khārijite; the governor, no doubt exasperated, responded: 'The rebel *is* Kuthāra!' See al-Ṭabarī, *Taʾrīkh*, II, pp. 1625f.; al-Balādhurī, *Ansāb*, VIb, pp. 96f. (*wa-kāna min ahl al-dīwān maʿrūf bi-shujāʿa*); and the anonymous *ʿUyūn al-ḥadāʾiq*, III, p. 110.

[115] According to al-Madāʾinī, Suḥārī b. Shabīb rebelled because Khālid al-Qasrī refused his demand for a stipend; see al-Balādhurī, *Ansāb*, VIb, p. 102; cf. al-Ṭabarī, *Taʾrīkh*, II, pp. 1633f.

pattern, according to which Jaziran Khārijite leaders were often drawn from the army's rolls.[116] Insofar as Khārijite leaders were drawn from the *dīwān*, the state thus produced its own opposition.

Why would disgruntled commanders go Khārijite? And why did they have any appeal? As far as individual commanders are concerned, to be dropped from the *dīwān* was to lose élite status, one which is signalled by the rewards that warfare brought, and this not only for service on the frontier: ʿAbd al-Malik is reported to have rewarded ʿAnaza tribesmen who had killed an earlier rebel, Faḍāla b. Sayyār, by granting more of them stipends,[117] and Khālid al-Qasrī offered supplementary stipends to those who killed Bahlūl's men.[118] But if one fell out with the state's authorities, one's options narrowed considerably: sedentarisation presumably meant a drop in status and thus a drop out of politics altogether, and similarly brigandage or mercenary work.[119] Khārijism, by contrast, held out the prospect of both continued employment and high status in warfare legitimised by the piety and holiness of those prosecuting it. Meanwhile, for tribesmen of lesser or diminished standing, Khārijite religiosity could be called upon to trump the inherited status of those from (traditionally) more distinguished lineages.[120]

Here it bears remembering that the choice to go Khārijite entailed no conversion or transformation of belief. According to the vision of Ṣāliḥ b. Musarriḥ, to embrace *shārī* Khārijism was to reassert a primeval, conquest-era Muslim identity that had been abandoned by the Umayyads. To Khārijite eyes, it was the Umayyads who were innovating, and the innovation lay in the state's shutting down of *hijra* and *jihād*, a *ḥadīth*-driven programme that took institutional form in the professionalisation of caliphal armies, armies in which they no longer had a place. To historians' eyes, these ideological and institutional changes mark nothing less than the state's attempt to monopolise legitimate violence, while the Khārijites' showy raids represent an attempt to demonstrate the tribesmen's continuing right to commit the sacral violence that God had made incumbent upon all Muslims.[121] The late eighth-century *Zuqnin Chronicle* tells us that Arabs had settled in the Jazira, and among these sedentarising Arabs there is no sign of revolution.

[116] Cf. the examples of Qaṭarī b. Fujāʾa and Ḥamdān b. Ḥamdūn b. al-Ḥārith.

[117] *Wa-faraḍa la-hum wa-lam takun la-hum farāʾiḍ qabl dhālika illā qalīla* (al-Ṭabarī, *Taʾrīkh*, II, p. 893; I owe my understanding of this passage to P. Crone).

[118] Al-Ṭabarī, *Taʾrīkh*, II, p. 1624.

[119] As, for example, the *ṣaʿālīk* of the northern frontiers; see A. Pertusi, 'Tra storia e leggenda: akritai e ghâzi sulla frontiera orientale di Bisanzio', *Actes du XIVe Congrès International d'Etudes Byzantines* (Bucharest, 1974), pp. 248ff.; see also al-Azdī, *Taʾrīkh*, pp. 279 and 386.

[120] Cf. M. Hinds, 'Kufan political alignments and their background in mid-seventh century AD', *IJMES* 2 (1971), p. 347, an article which is reprinted in Bacharach, *et al.*, eds., *Studies in Islamic History*, pp. 1–28. Such may very well have been the case for Shabīb himself; see F. M. Donner, 'The Bakr b. Wāʾil tribes and politics in northeastern Arabia on the eve of Islam', *SI* 51 (1980), pp. 5–38, where it is argued that the Banū Muḥallim were the most powerful Shaybānī lineage on the eve of Islam.

[121] Cf. C. Tilly, 'War making and state making as organised crime', in P. B. Evans, D. Rueschemeyer and T. Skocpol, eds., *Bringing the State Back in* (Cambridge, 1985), pp. 172ff.

Together Ṣāliḥ and Shabīb thus bequeathed to the Jazira a potent model, a heady fusion of pastoralist muscle and theatrical asceticism that attracted opportunistic tribesmen throughout the eighth century; their appeal lay in their ability to exemplify the virtues that the Umayyads were leaving behind. A single pattern now held (temporarily interrupted by the rebellion of al-Ḍaḥḥāk b. Qays, in the midst of civil war), one that produced small warrior bands whose historiographic coverage far outstrips their political significance. Scenes of real violence never appear, and the skirmishes have a ritualised quality: these tribesmen were restive communities of saints out to show up the Umayyads rather than revolutionaries intent on their destruction. Thus when Bisṭām rebelled in 100/718, his men numbered under a hundred, and similarly Bahlūl b. Bishr, whose numbers may have been a bit higher; with Saʿīd b. Bahdal the numbers increase (perhaps to 500), anticipating al-Ḍaḥḥāk's. Their strength lay not in numbers, but rather in the inspirational piety of their leadership, God-fearing heroes such as Hudba al-Yashkurī (Bisṭām's *ibn ʿamm*), Muqātīl b. Shaybān, and al-Rayyān b. ʿAbd Allāh;[122] Bahlūl himself is said to have spent much of his time praying (*wa-kāna yataʾallah*), and very little of it eating.[123] Tribes such as the Yashkur might occasionally supply a leader;[124] but the Shaybān retained pride of place,[125] particularly three extensions of the Muḥallim b. Dhuhl, each of which could claim one Khārijite apiece: the Thaʿlaba b. Muḥallim (Sakīn), the ʿAmr b. Muḥallim (Baṭīn), and the Rabīʿa b. Muḥallim (al-Ḍaḥḥāk b. Qays).[126]

This tradition lasted two generations; despite the continuity of Shaybānī leadership, the pattern breaks with al-Ḍaḥḥāk b. Qays. His was a large rebellion from the start, numbering in the thousands;[127] and in this he anticipates the movement led by al-Walīd b. Ṭarīf al-Shaybānī in 178–9/794–5 when, according to some sources, the rebels numbered 16,000 and violence was real.[128] No doubt al-Ḍaḥḥāk's army was large because he paid it well: a monthly stipend of 120 dirhams for his riders, 100 for his footsoldiers and 80

[122] See the obituaries in al-Ṭabarī, *Taʾrīkh*, II, pp. 1376ff.

[123] Al-Ṭabarī, *Taʾrīkh*, II, p. 1622.

[124] In addition to Hudba and al-Rayyān b. ʿAbd Allāh, there was Shaybān b. ʿAbd al-ʿAzīz; see al-Ṭabarī, *Taʾrīkh*, II, pp. 1943ff. Cf. the case of al-Khaṭṭār, a converted Christian, in al-Balādhurī, *Ansāb*, Reis. 598, fol. 51a.

[125] It has long been observed that the Shaybān, in the words of L. V. Vaglieri, represented the 'hard core' support for the Khārijites in the north; see *EI²*, s.v. 'Khāridjites', cc. 1075–6; and Wellhausen, *Religio-political Factions*, p. 75.

[126] When Bahlūl b. Bishr (a Shaybānī) defeated Ḥawshab b. Yazīd b. Ruwaym (a Shaybānī commander of al-Ḥajjāj's *shurṭa*), the latter responded by explicitly appealing for clemency on the basis of their shared kinship: *nashadtuka biʾl-raḥim fa-innī jāniḥ mustajīr* (al-Ṭabarī, *Taʾrīkh*, II, p. 1625; on Ḥawshab, see Ibn al-Kalbī, *Ǧamhara*, II, p. 332; al-Balādhurī, *Ansāb* Reis. 598, fol. 48a). Note as well that one of Abū Mikhnaf's informants was a tribesman of the Banū Muḥallim (al-Ṭabarī, *Taʾrīkh*, II, p. 886).

[127] For the figures of 3,000 to 4,000 men, see al-Balādhurī, *Ansāb*, Reis. 598, fol. 180b; and the anonymous *ʿUyūn*, III, p. 159. Later, the figures jump even higher.

[128] On al-Walīd, see al-Ṭabarī, *Taʾrīkh*, III, pp. 631ff.; al-Azdī, *Taʾrīkh*, pp. 281ff.; al-Yaʿqūbī, *Taʾrīkh*, II, pp. 495f.; *Chronicle of 1234*, II, pp. 6f./4; Michael the Syrian, *Chronique*, xii.iii.

for his muleteers.[129] Al-Ḍaḥḥāk's paid army, his striking of coins,[130] and finally, his appeal to the city folk of Mosul all suggest that Jaziran Khārijism of Ṣāliḥ's and Shabīb's variety was now on the wane. Khārijites were no longer seeking to show up the Umayyads; having experienced two generations of Umayyad rule, they sought to rule for themselves.

[129] For the salaries, see al-Ṭabarī, *Ta'rīkh*, II, p. 1939. Cf. Hobsbawm, *Bandits*, p. 74 ('It is therefore a mistake to think of bandits as mere children of nature roasting stags in the greenwood. A successful brigand chief is at least as closely in touch with the market and the wider economic universe as a small landowner or prosperous farmer.')

[130] On these, see chapter 7.

SIX

Massacre and narrative: the Abbasid Revolution in Mosul I

If chapter 3 demonstrates anything, it is that a history of Marwānid Mosul is in large measure a rewriting of al-Azdī's tenth-century *Ta'rīkh al-Mawṣil*, a work whose virtues were recognised by a historian as accomplished as al-Masʿūdī,[1] but which never seems to have enjoyed much popularity outside its native city.[2] This is in stark contrast to the abundant use later historians made of the author's *ṭabaqāt* work,[3] and suggests that the problem was the relatively narrow field of study rather than the quality of his scholarship. A number of *rijāl* specialists could – and did – benefit from a local compilation of *ḥadīth* transmitters,[4] and it is probably as a *rijāl* specialist that al-Azdī was known, having studied under *ḥadīth* experts such as Muḥammad b. Aḥmad b.

[1] Al-Masʿūdī, *Murūj*, I, p. 16.

[2] That the second part was available in thirteenth-century Mosul is clear from the *Kāmil* of Ibn al-Athīr (d. 1232) (see Forand, 'Governors', pp. 103f.). Ibn al-Athīr could not have used the Chester Beatty manuscript, since it was copied in Rabīʿ II of 654/13 May 1256 (see the *Ta'rīkh*, pp. 5ff. of the *muqaddima*); but his text could very well have belonged to the same tradition, since his abundant use of the work for second-century material is interrupted in years 124 and 152 – that is, precisely the same years absent from the Chester Beatty manuscript. There is no sign of the work in Ibn al-Ṭiqṭaqā's *al-Fakhrī*, which was written in Mosul in 1302; then again, there is little reason to think that there should have been.

[3] For the confusion between the oft-cited *ṭabaqāt* work and the annalistic history (both are frequently called *ta'rīkhs*), see Robinson, 'al-Muʿāfa b. ʿImrān', pp. 115f. I am inclined to think that the account identified by A. Elad ('Two identical inscriptions from Jund Filasṭīn from the reign of the ʿAbbāsid caliph, al-Muqtadir', *JESHO* 35 (1992), p. 311), which he suggests came from the annalistic work, rather comes from the *ṭabaqāt*, but neither case can presently be proven; the same may be true of material relating to Yaḥyā b. Yaḥyā al-Ghassānī (Rotter, 'Fulūs', p. 175, note 34). The *ṭabaqāt* work was apparently no slim volume, since al-Azdī's entry on al-Muʿāfā b. ʿImrān was more than twenty leaves long (thus al-Dhahabī, *Tadhkirat al-ḥuffāẓ*, p. 287; cf. al-Azdī, *Ta'rīkh*, p. 301).

[4] That the work was indeed organised by *ṭabaqāt* is made clear by al-Khaṭīb al-Baghdādī (*Ta'rīkh Baghdād*, VIII, p. 33) among others. In the first of these would have been placed conquest figures such as ʿUtba b. Farqad, ʿAbd Allāh b. al-Muʿtamm, ʿArfaja b. Harthama and Ṣuhayb b. Sinān, the latter a companion and tribesman of the Namir b. Qāsiṭ from the area of Nineveh (see Ibn Ḥajar, *Tahdhīb*, IV, pp. 438f., who cites al-Azdī). The latest entry I have found concerns Ibrāhīm b. ʿAlī b. Ibrāhīm, who died in 306/918, producing a *terminus post quem* for the composition of the work (al-Khaṭīb al-Baghdādī, *Ta'rīkh Baghdād*, VI, p. 132).

Abī al-Muthannā (d. 277/890),[5] ʿUbayd b. Ghannām (d. 297/908),[6] and Muḥammad b. ʿAbd Allāh al-Muṭayyan (d. 298/910),[7] having transmitted the *Kitāb al-Taʾrīkh wa-asmāʾ al-muḥaddithīn wa-kunāhum* of Muḥammad b. Aḥmad al-Muqaddamī (d. 301/913),[8] and, finally, having taught *rijāl* experts such as Ibn Jumayʿ (d. 402/1012).[9] Meanwhile, among non-Mosulis only modern historians seem to have thought much of the city history proper: scholars in the west have known of the annalistic history since the late nineteenth century,[10] but it was only edited in 1967, on the basis of a *unicum* in the Chester Beatty Library.[11] The work deserves a full study in its own right; here I limit myself to some modest *Quellenforschung*, along with some marginally more imaginative speculation about how one set of passages might have been understood.

The material consulted by al-Azdī for the eighth century can be reconstructed only with difficulty.[12] For 'imperial' history he drew on many of the same sources that lie behind al-Balādhurī's and al-Ṭabarī's treatment of the period, e.g., al-Madāʾinī, Abū Maʿshar, al-Haytham b. ʿAdī and ʿUmar b.

[5] Apparently the uncle of the more celebrated Abū Yaʿlā al-Mawṣilī (on whom see H. Schützinger, 'Abū Yaʿlā al-Mauṣilī. Leben und Lehrerverzeichnis (*Kitāb al-Muʿǧam*),' *ZDMG* 131 (1981), pp. 281–96); see al-Dhahabī, *Siyar aʿlām al-nubalāʾ*, XIII, pp. 139ff.; Ibn al-Athīr, *al-Kāmil*, VII, p. 439 (which reads Aḥmad b. Muḥammad).

[6] Al-Dhahabī, *Siyar aʿlām al-nubalāʾ*, XIII, p. 558.

[7] The literature on Muḥammad b. ʿAbd Allāh (sometimes pointed al-Muṭayyin) is large; see al-Dhahabī, *Siyar aʿlām al-nubalāʾ*, XIV, pp. 41f.; Ibn Abī Yaʿlā, *Ṭabaqāt al-ḥanābila* (Cairo, 1952), I, pp. 300f.; Ibn al-Nadīm, *Fihrist*, p. 287; Sezgin, *GAS*, I, p. 163 (with further bibliography).

[8] C. Rieu, *Supplement to the Catalogue of the Arabic Manuscripts in the British Museum* (London, 1894), pp. 406f. (617). On al-Muqaddamī, *muḥaddith* and *qāḍī* of Baghdad, see Sezgin, *GAS*, I, pp. 165f. To judge from several reports preserved by Ibn al-ʿAdīm, *Bughya*, pp. 1843, 2164, 2568, 2813, 2839, 3900f., 3986, 4020 and 4117, al-Azdī also transmitted some historical material from al-Muqaddamī.

[9] Author of a *Muʿjam al-shuyūkh* (Beirut, 1985), in which al-Azdī appears at least once (p. 379; see also al-Dhahabī, *Siyar aʿlām al-nubalāʾ*, XV, pp. 386f.); on Ibn Jumayʿ, see Sezgin, *GAS*, I, pp. 220f.

[10] See F. Wüstenfeld, *Die Geschichtschreiber der Araber und ihre Werke* (Göttingen, 1882), p. 36 (113). In his first volume (1898) Brockelmann knew of the work, thanks to Wüstenfeld (*GAL*, I, p. 138), but by the first *Supplementband* (1937; p. 210) he had come to be familiar with the Chester Beatty MS, excerpts from a Cairo copy having been published in the interim by Yūsuf Sarkīs, 'Nubdhatān min *Taʾrīkh al-Mawṣil*', *Lughat al-ʿArab* 6 (1928), pp. 112ff. S. Ṣāʾigh had thought the work lost when he wrote his own history, which was published in 1923 (*Taʾrīkh al-Mawṣil*, I, p. 6).

[11] For a description of the manuscript, see A. J. Arberry, *The Chester Beatty Library: A Handlist of the Arabic Manuscripts* (Dublin, 1955), I, p. 11 (3030); see also L. ʿAbd al-Badīʿ, *Fihris al-makhṭūṭāt al-muṣawwara*, II.i (Cairo, 1956), p. 74. The edition is generally sound, even if criticisms can be made; see C. F. Robinson, 'A local historian's debt to al-Ṭabarī: the case of al-Azdī's *Taʾrīkh al-Mawṣil*', in H. Kennedy, ed., *al-Ṭabarī: A Muslim Historian and his Work* (Princeton, forthcoming); and A. Elad, 'The siege of al-Wāsiṭ (132/749): some aspects of ʿAbbāsid and ʿAlīd relations at the beginning of ʿAbbāsid rule', in M. Sharon, ed., *Studies in Islamic History and Civilization in Honour of Professor David Ayalon* (Leiden, 1986), p. 71, note 64.

[12] The only detailed study of al-Azdī and his sources was made by his editor, A. Ḥabība, 'A Study of Abū Zakariyā's Work', Ph.D. thesis (University of Cambridge, 1965); the results were published in the introduction to the *Taʾrīkh*, pp. 21ff. (of the *muqaddima*).

Shabba; he also consulted at least two works that survive to our day: Khalīfa b. Khayyāṭ's and al-Ṭabarī's histories.[13] Of course for Mosuli history these authorities had little to offer, but al-Azdī could also draw on a local tradition of *ḥadīth* and *akhbār* scholarship; this seems to have matured in the early third/ninth century,[14] particularly with Ibn ʿAmmār (d. 242/856)[15] and ʿAlī b. Ḥarb (d. 265/879),[16] and, to judge from the surviving section of al-Azdī's *Ta'rīkh*, could clearly reach back to the very beginning of the second century. Unless the first part of the *Ta'rīkh* is recovered, we shall never know how deeply into the first century it extended; but al-Azdī's reliance on Iraqi authorities to describe the conquest of Mosul suggests that it broke off some time in the Sufyānid period.[17] The reliance of the pre-eminent historian of Mosul on non-Mosuli authorities for conquest material is not without some significance.

The local tradition of history that did develop took at least two forms. From the brief and annual entries identifying the city's governors and *qāḍīs*, one can infer the presence of at least one fairly prosaic list (and probably two), which might have been produced as early as the middle of the second century;[18] that al-Azdī frequently concedes his confusion in dating the accession of new governors may also be taken to suggest that this list was organised by caliphal reigns.[19] More important than this lean prosopographical material are the

[13] Many of the sources are discussed by Ḥabība in his introduction; for al-Azdī and al-Ṭabarī, see Robinson, 'A local historian's debt to al-Ṭabarī'.

[14] By the end of the second century, Mosul had produced at least three *ḥadīth* scholars of note: al-Muʿāfā b. ʿImrān (d. 185/801; see Robinson, 'Al-Muʿāfā b. ʿImrān'); al-Qāsim b. Yazīd al-Jarmī (d. 194/809; see al-Dhahabī, *Siyar aʿlām al-nubalā'*, IX, pp. 281ff.; al-Mizzī, *Tahdhīb al-kamāl*, XXIII, pp. 360ff.; Ibn Ḥajar, *Tahdhīb*, VIII, pp. 241f.); and Ibrāhīm b. Mūsā al-Zayyāt (d. 205/820; see al-Bukhārī, *Kitāb al-ta'rīkh al-kabīr* (Hyderabad, 1941–70), I, p. 327; al-Mizzī, *Tahdhīb al-kamāl*, II, p. 219; and al-Azdī, *Ta'rīkh*, pp. 358f.), where Ibrāhīm is put among the first Mosuli scholars to travel in order to hear *ḥadīth*. All three seem to have had only local significance; the tradition, it appears, was still nascent.

[15] To the sources cited in Robinson, 'Al-Muʿāfā b. ʿImrān', p. 119, note 86 one can add Ibn Manẓūr, *Mukhtaṣar ta'rīkh madīnat Dimashq*, XXII, pp. 283f. (Ibn ʿAmmār transmitting on the authority of al-Muʿāfā b. ʿImrān).

[16] See Robinson, 'al-Muʿāfā b. ʿImrān', p. 119, notes 88 and 89. It is presumably figures such as Ibn ʿAmmār and ʿAlī b. Ḥarb whom al-Azdī has in mind when he mentions (*Ta'rīkh*, p. 25) 'those Mosulis knowledgeable in history' (*man yaʿlam al-sīra min ahl al-Mawṣil*).

[17] Here I assume that the material at his disposal for his annalistic history was no better than that for his *ṭabaqāt*, in which he not infrequently made use of Sayf b. ʿUmar and his *Kitāb al-Ridda wa'l-futūḥ* (thus Ibn al-Athīr, *Usd al-ghāba*, III, pp. 263f. and 401; Ibn Ḥajar, *al-Iṣāba*, VI, p. 221), al-Haytham b. ʿAdī (Ibn Ḥajar, *al-Iṣāba*, VI, p. 379 (al-Azdī is here called 'Abū al-Muʿāfā')), and Abū ʿUbayda (Ibn Ḥajar, *al-Iṣāba*, VI, p. 412).

[18] On lists such as these, see F. Rosenthal, *A History of Muslim Historiography* (Leiden, 1968), pp. 162f.; J. Schacht, *The Origins of Muhammadan Jurisprudence* (Oxford, 1950), pp. 100ff.; and Crone, *Slaves*, p. 214, note 102.

[19] For examples of his confusion, and also of his efforts to establish a chronology, see the *Ta'rīkh*, pp. 217, 222, 224, 307f. There is no evidence in Mosul for the second-century amplification of lists into larger historical works, a common enough feature of Iraqi learning of the time; see, for examples, the *Kitāb Wulāt al-Kūfa*, *Kitāb Quḍāt al-Kūfa wa'l-Baṣra*, and *Kitāb Umarā' Khurāsān wa'l-Yaman* of al-Haytham b. ʿAdī (d. 822); see Ibn al-Nadīm, *Fihrist*, p. 112; and further, S. Leder, *Das Korpus al-Haiṯam ibn ʿAdī* (Frankfurt am Main, 1991), pp 197ff. The numismatic evidence is spotty, since few of the coppers are dated, and we shall see that the coins can both corroborate and complement al-Azdī's record.

reports credited to local authorities, which appear in growing frequency and detail in the early sections of the work. Thus already during the governorship of al-Ḥurr b. Yūsuf, al-Azdī drew on Muḥammad b. al-Muʿāfa b. Ṭāwūs, that rare Mosuli whose learning was exported in the late second or early third century;[20] but still al-Azdī's knowledge of the early Marwānid period seems thin, and it is generally limited to the building activities of the period; for material relating to someone as significant as the Khārijite Shawdhab, al-Azdī can do no more than draw from the same pool of traditions on which al-Ṭabarī also drew.[21] By 128/746, a date marked by the revolt of the Khārijites al-Ḍaḥḥāk b. Qays al-Shaybānī and Shaybān b. ʿAbd al-ʿAzīz,[22] things have improved considerably; we now have clear evidence for an authentic tradition of local history.[23] The account, which is credited to Hārūn b. al-Ṣaqr b. Najda, grandson of one of Yazīd b. ʿAbd al-Malik's commanders and son of the commander of the city's *rawābiṭ*,[24] contains real local colour, and is clearly independent of the authorities who lie behind al-Ṭabarī's informants.[25] Hārūn's account is one of the first to reflect the considerable patrimony of local history produced by a network of scholars and élites that recorded – and to a very large degree, made – Mosuli history in the early Abbasid period. The availability of local history from this period may explain the shape of al-Azdī's work.[26]

In the Third Civil War and Abbasid Revolution, al-Azdī thus had an opportunity to show this learning off to great effect; but since he was now faced with events as controversial as they were decisive in the city's history, we face a problem of our own. Whereas no reconstruction of the city's eighth-century growth would collapse with a redating of al-Ḥurr b. Yūsuf's accession, or, for that matter, with the discovery of another Umayyad *fals*, the city's passage from Umayyad to Abbasid rule is fraught with a wide variety of difficulties.[27] To chart this passage we need to look in some detail at al-Azdī's collection of accounts, which together represent one of the first sustained pieces of narrative in his work. In what follows I examine these reports in order to reach some tentative conclusions about al-Azdī, the local Mosuli historical tradition, and, in the following chapter, the causes of the massacre itself.[28]

[20] See below, note 34. [21] Al-Azdī, *Taʾrīkh*, pp. 6f.; cf. al-Ṭabarī, *Taʾrīkh*, I, pp. 1347f.
[22] Al-Azdī, *Taʾrīkh*, pp. 73f. [23] Cf. Crone, *Slaves*, p. 11.
[24] See al-Azdī, *Taʾrīkh*, pp. 7, 152 (where al-Ṣaqr is credited with *rithāʾ* in honour of massacre victims), 203f., and 217.
[25] Al-Azdī, *Taʾrīkh*, p. 73 (the account is transmitted on the authority of Muḥammad b. Aḥmad b. Abī al-Muthannā, whose interests therefore extended beyond *ḥadīth*).
[26] Thus the twenty-five years between 101 and 125 are edited in fifty-three pages, while the decade between 125 and 135 is covered in *ca.* one hundred pages.
[27] On some of the historiographical problems of the Revolution, see Elad, 'The siege of al-Wāsiṭ', pp. 75ff.; and J. Lassner, *Islamic Revolution and Historical Memory: An Inquiry into the Art of ʿAbbāsid Apologetics* (New Haven, 1986).
[28] The fullest discussions of the massacre seem to be F. ʿUmar, *al-ʿAbbāsiyyūn al-awāʾil* (Baghdad, 1973), I, pp. 76ff., and S. Daywahchī, *Taʾrīkh al-Mawṣil* (Baghdad, 1982), pp. 57ff.; see also Forand, 'Governors', pp. 91ff.

Some themes

The beginning of the massacre section is signalled by an uncredited account of al-Saffāḥ's appointment of his brother Yaḥyā b. Muḥammad as governor of Mosul;[29] it is followed by three views, each credited to local authorities, on the circumstances or causes of the massacre. The main narrative section now follows:[30] in the main, it is composed of *akhbār* of local provenance, intended either to record the circumstances that led to the massacre or describe the dreadful events in some detail. Many of the latter make compelling reading, and indicate the significance attached by al-Azdī to eye-witness reports; they also suggest the existence in the ninth and early tenth century of a fairly deep reservoir of vivid and partisan local history. A final section then follows;[31] at turns elegiac, caustic and apocalyptic, it serves to recapitulate and bring the collection of narratives to a close. It is fair to say that virtually all of this would have been lost were it not for al-Azdī; it is also certain that the impact of the material, concentrated as it is in one section in the annalistic *Ta'rīkh*, is far greater than it would have been in the *ṭabaqāt* work.

If al-Azdī is to be credited for saving the material from oblivion, he did so as a historian, rather than ethnographer or archaeologist. Despite the immediacy – indeed even the intimacy – of several accounts, what we have in the main is not a transcription of oral tradition, but polished episodes of local history, chosen and transmitted by learned authorities. Well over a half of all the accounts can be traced to three sources. The first is the family of al-Muʿāfā b. Ṭāwūs, an authority whose expertise on Mosuli history was recognised outside the city.[32] Of Ṭāwūs little can be said.[33] Al-Muʿāfā himself claimed to have impressed Ibrāhīm b. al-ʿAbbās, governor of Mosul in 194/809, with his grotesque flattery; he also fathered a son, Muḥammad, who transmitted massacre accounts on his authority, and Muḥammad's son, Muḥassin (or Muḥsin), did so as well.[34] The second source is Muḥammad b. Aḥmad b. Abī al-Muthannā, whom we know to be one of al-Azdī's teachers and a leading figure in late third/ninth-century Mosuli learning in general: according to an anecdote preserved by al-Dhahabī, Muḥammad was second only to ʿAlī b. Ḥarb among Mosuli *ḥadīth* transmitters in the middle of the third century.[35] The third source is the family of Bakkār b. Shurayḥ, son of one of the massacre's victims, an early Abbasid *qāḍī* and member of one of Mosul's leading

[29] Al-Azdī, *Ta'rīkh*, p. 145: 5. [30] Al-Azdī, *Ta'rīkh*, p. 146: 15.

[31] Al-Azdī, *Ta'rīkh*, p. 151: 3.

[32] Thus, al-Balādhurī *Futūḥ*, pp. 180 and 332 (conquest-era material); al-Balādhurī, *Ansāb*, III, p. 281 (massacre).

[33] A problematic anecdote (al-Azdī, *Ta'rīkh*, p. 16) seems to suggest that Ṭāwūs's father was alive during ʿUmar b. Hubayra's governorship of the city (c. 102/720), while Ṭāwūs himself is said (*Ta'rīkh*, p. 252) to have been a (younger) contemporary of Harthama b. Aʿyan, apparently thrice governor of Mosul (years 168/784, 182/798 and 185/800).

[34] Al-Azdī, *Ta'rīkh*, pp. 147ff. and 319f.

[35] Al-Dhahabī, *Siyar aʿlām al-nubalā'*, XIII, pp. 140f.

families; a son and a grandson transmitted several accounts to al-Azdī, one of which takes place in their ancestral home.[36] In addition to these three principal sources of material, several other accounts are related on the authority of anonymous *shaykhs*; by this we are to understand the 'learned men of Mosul'.

As far as the form of this local tradition is concerned, we can only presume that it was mixed, with the mixture heavily favouring written transmission. On the one hand, al-Azdī confesses to having forgotten some early Abbasid material,[37] which, if accepted at face value, suggests that at least some of his material was not written. On the other hand, the conventional terms of transmission (e.g. *ukhbirtu*, *ḥuddithtu*) frequently disguise the use of some written materials;[38] another part of the *Ta'rīkh* makes it clear that al-Azdī possessed a book of reports he had compiled (orally) from Muḥammad b. Aḥmad b. Abī al-Muthannā;[39] and he frequently cites the work of ʿAlī b. Ḥarb in written form.[40] Among his written material he used a variety of what we would now call 'secondary' sources, some of which were anonymous 'books' and 'histories',[41] as well as 'primary' sources, the latter drawn in part from an archive of documents to which he, as *qāḍī* of the city, apparently enjoyed free access. These included, *inter alia*, correspondence between imperial and provincial authorities preserved by the Banū al-Jārūd,[42] as well as *iqṭāʿ* texts preserved by members of the Banū Shaḥḥāj. In fact, al-Azdī's handling of the latter suggests a genuine interest in securing reliably authentic documents. We read, for example, that Masrūr b. Muḥammad b. Ḥamdawayh b. Masrūr al-Shaḥḥājī produced for al-Azdī the original letter from al-Saffāḥ granting the first portion of an *iqṭāʿ* to Wā'il b. al-Shaḥḥāj (who is occasionally called Wā'il al-Shaḥḥājī); the text was copied *verbatim*, and includes the name of the

36 The report is translated below, p. 134.

37 Concerning Ismāʿīl b. ʿAlī, al-Azdī writes that 'I heard Muḥammad b. al-Muʿāfā b. Ṭāwūs say this several times (*marāran*), but I did not memorize the figures who provided its *isnād*'; see al-Azdī, *Ta'rīkh*, p. 156.

38 For comments, see Sezgin, *GAS*, I, pp. 77f.; S. Günther, *Quellenuntersuchungen zu den 'Maqātil aṭ-Ṭālibiyyīn' des Abū'l-Farağ al-Iṣfahānī (gest. 356/967)* (Hildesheim and Zürich, 1991), esp. pp. 25ff.; cf. al-Azdī, *Ta'rīkh*, p. 237 for a written collection of *ḥadīth* cited without an *ijāza*.

39 For one clear instance of *gehörte Überlieferung*, see al-Azdī, *Ta'rīkh*, p. 154. Elsewhere (p. 85), the editor emends 'my book' (*kitābī*) to 'a book' with insufficient reason, the text in question presumably being one of the author's personal notebooks; cf. G. Schoeler ('Die Frage der schriftlichen oder mündlichen Überlieferung der Wissenschaften im frühen Islam', *DI* 62 (1985), pp. 201–30); and the *Ta'rīkh*, p. 237.

40 Al-Azdī, *Ta'rīkh*, pp. 279, and 313 (use of ʿAlī b. Ḥarb), and 30f. ('Alī transmitting the text of a letter).

41 Thus, an 'old book' concerning the Ibāḍiyya (al-Azdī, *Ta'rīkh*, p. 113), perhaps several books with material on Sāmarrā' (p. 416), an anonymous 'history' (p. 5), Muḥammad b. Abī Dāwūd's (clearly historical) 'book' (p. 322), and, finally, *al-Ta'rīkh al-Hāshimī* (p. 239), which might be identified as one of the Hāshimī histories noted by al-Masʿūdī (*Murūj*, I, p. 15), rather than the epitome of al-Ṭabarī written by Muḥammad b. Sulaymān al-Hāshimī (Ibn al-Nadīm, *Fihrist*, p. 291).

42 For letters, see al-Azdī, *Ta'rīkh*, pp. 199f. (a letter to the city's *qāḍī* al-Ḥārith b. Jārūd, assigning responsibility over the *kharāj* to the latter), and 214 (a letter written by al-Manṣūr to the city's governor, Ismāʿīl b. ʿAlī, concerning taxation, retained by al-Ḥārith b. Jārūd, who passed it on to his sons). On the position of the *qāḍī* in the early Abbasid city, see chapter 7.

scribe, its date (Jumādā II, 136; no day provided), the location of the caliph's stamp (the bottom), and his *ʿalāma* ('signature sign') at the top.[43]

As history of the most local variety, the massacre section reflects the degree to which élite Mosuli families, whose grandfathers experienced the massacre, and whose grandsons related and recorded it, managed to conflate the two: massacre history, here written by an Azdī member of the religious establishment, was the experience of Mosuli élite families, the city's response being represented by the response of its leading men. The purpose was thus in part to preserve the fading memory of those local worthies who were brutally executed; no fewer than three overlapping lists are included, and in several cases it is clear that the figures in question were no longer widely known.[44] But the purpose of local history extended beyond underlining the political leadership of notable families, particularly since their stewardship of the city was so catastrophically inglorious; it also functioned to memorialise pious men who died pious deaths, who faced Abbasid brutality with courage and forbearance. When the oddly named ascetic Maʿrūf b. Abī Maʿrūf and his anonymous son are presented before Muḥammad b. Ṣūl for beheading, he retains sufficient composure to respond with morbid wit:

The mounted soldiers and cavalry surrounded the mosque, and they started to send the men out [of the mosque] to execute them. The first to be sent out were Maʿrūf b. Abī Maʿrūf and his son, and when Ibn Ṣūl told him to 'stick your neck out' (*umdud ʿunqaka*), he responded 'I will not help you to defy God' (*mā kuntu bi'lladhī uʿīnuka ʿalā maʿṣīyat Allāh*).[45]

We shall see that the indiscriminate character of much of this violence, along with the deliberate murder of non-combatants, was impressive to a great number of historians, Christian and Muslim alike; but it is naturally in al-Azdī that they are described in the greatest detail. When Yaḥyā b. Muḥammad inquires about a curious noise, and is told that it 'is the wailing of the women whose men have been killed', he orders that the women and children should be killed too; 'men, children, and women were killed for three successive days'. A grandson relates, on the authority of his grandfather, that 'eighty men, women and children were killed in our house; men, women and children were being killed'.[46]

[43] Al-Azdī, *Ta'rīkh*, p. 158. See also pp. 24 and 171, the latter recording what remains of this *iqṭāʿ*, and where it is made plain that Masrūr took a copy of the original as well, which al-Azdī himself copied, vouching for its authenticity because of its age, seal marks, and script (*fa-wajadtuhu dāllan ʿalā ṣidqihi bi-ʿitqihi wa-khawātīmihi wa'l-khuṭūṭ allatī fīhi*). See also p. 289, where Masrūr produces another *iqṭāʿ* letter, this written by the city's *qāḍī*, Ismāʿīl b. Ziyād, to Wā'il's son ʿIsār; rather than copying it *verbatim*, our author merely summarises its contents.

[44] Thus Aḥmad b. ʿAbd al-Raḥmān (al-Azdī, *Ta'rīkh*, pp. 146f.) must identify two of the victims (ʿAlī b. Nuʿaym and Khāqān b. Yazīd al-Raḥabī) as forefathers of present-day families; and Khāqān and Shurayḥ b. Shurayḥ are also identified as the eponyms of well-known city monuments. One of Bakkār's sons (*Ta'rīkh*, p. 153) also identifies several of the victims as *sharīf*s, as well as the *imām* of the congregational mosque.

[45] Al-Azdī, *Ta'rīkh*, pp. 147f.; cf. p. 153. This, and all other massacre translations, are deliberately loose. On Maʿrūf b. Abī Maʿrūf, see van Ess, *Theologie*, II, p. 467.

[46] Al-Azdī, *Ta'rīkh*, p. 148 (both reports).

It is also in al-Azdī that the events are related with some real pathos. In this, and the account that follows, the prose is spare and the syntax simple; it actually suggests genuine oral history.

I was only a young boy in the year of the massacre. Fearing for my safety, my mother took me into one of our apartments, where she hid me in the garbage.[47] She then sat down aside my little brother, who was asleep in his cradle. Four of Yaḥyā's soldiers then entered, and told my mother to get to her feet and give them everything [of value] that we had. So she gave them everying she had – jewellery, household goods, and the like. But after they had taken these things, one of the soldiers ran his sword into her belly, killing her. Later, after they had left, the baby woke up and began to cry. I felt for him, and I climbed out of my hiding place in the garbage, and sprinkled a few drops of water in his mouth. I soon heard another sound, so I returned to my spot. But then he woke up again, this time in a fright, as the sun had begun to shine into the apartment. And he kept on crying and tossing, so much so that he fell out of his cradle onto our mother's belly. I was now too scared to get out to help him, so he kept tossing in the blood and entrails until he died.[48]

It is not just the victims who describe the brutality. We read that a *ḥadīth* transmitter, on pilgrimage at the Kaʿba, happened upon someone who had participated in the massacre, and who was doing penance for his actions. The latter then recalls when he entered one of the houses of the city:

I came upon a man, his wife, and their two sons. I killed the man, telling his wife that I would kill her sons too if she didn't give me whatever she had of value. So she gave me some dinars and provisions. When I repeated my threat, and she said she had nothing else to give me, I killed the two boys. Finally, I told her I'd kill her too if she didn't come up with something. When she saw that I was serious, she told me to take pity, and that she did have something that the boys' father had entrusted to her. So she gave me a gilded coat of mail, the likes of which I had never seen. I began to turn it over, wondrous at its beauty, and there, written in gold, were the following words:

> When the amir and his two retainers commit tyranny
> And the earthly judge exceeds all limits in passing judgment
> Woe, woe, woe upon the earthly judge from the heavenly judge.

I dropped the sword and shuddered. From there I came directly here.[49]

Accounts of the indiscriminate slaughter of non-combatants were thus impressive testimonials; but they were a double-edged sword. On the one hand, they were damning evidence of brutality and blood lust on the part of the Abbasids and their Khurāsānī army; this probably explains why, as we shall see in some detail, the theme appears in the Syrian-written Christian tra-

[47] The editor points *shukhaym* (*shakhama*, 'to spoil, putrify'); see Ibn Manẓūr, *Lisān al-ʿarab* (Beirut, 1956), XII, p. 320.

[48] Al-Azdī, *Taʾrīkh*, p. 148. In the case of ʿAmr b. al-Sakan (al-Balādhurī, *Ansāb*, vii/i, p. 158), one can identify by name the commander in charge of Yaḥyā b. Muḥammad's *shurat*.

[49] Al-Azdī, *Taʾrīkh*, p. 152. The three figures are presumably al-Saffāḥ, Yaḥyā b. Muḥammad and Muḥammad b. Ṣūl. A variant ('the amir and his two scribes') is provided by Ibn ʿAsākir, *Taʾrīkh madīnat Dimashq*, LXIV, p. 367.

dition almost immediately, and perhaps also why the events are altogether absent, or mentioned only in passing, in some otherwise very thorough works of Islamic historiography. On the other hand, the accounts also highlight the utter failure on the part of the Mosuli élite to anticipate, prevent, or even respond to the violence. Indeed, accounts that have the élite accept the Abbasids' cynical invitation to the Manqūsha palace, where they were promptly slaughtered, may be taken to suggest some credulity – and perhaps too a fair share of hubris; there certainly can be no question that the reports, taken together, make plain the élite's failure to resist the Abbasid violence once it was under way.

It is not just that scenes of resistance are conspicuously absent, while those of pious resignation appear and reappear, nor that only one tradition – and perhaps an aberrant one at that – has a single member of the élite, al-Maʿmar (or Muʿammar) b. Ayyūb al-Hamdānī, escape to fight another day.[50] It is also that reports of those who did resist are especially telling. Although the congregational mosque was thronging with Mosulis, it was left to a *mawlā* of the Ṭamathān to fight back: 'Only one of the people of Mosul whom Ibn Ṣūl encircled [around the mosque] put up a fight, a *mawlā* of the Ṭamathān. He prised off the supports of the *minbar* and fought them until he was killed.'[51] The role played by Mosuli women makes a particularly striking contrast to the failure of Mosuli men to resist. In one account the role reversal is explicit; here discharging a man's responsibility means wearing a man's clothes:

> I was only a young boy when I entered the *dār* of al-Ṣabāḥ b. al-Ḥusayn al-Muzanī on the fourth or fifth day of the massacre of the Mosulis. There his daughter, girded in a loincloth, wearing a turban,[52] and holding her father's sword in her hand, was slain, having killed four of Yaḥyā b. Muḥammad's men; she had a wound on her head and her thigh.[53]

Men are to defend the honour of women; but in the midst of the massacre, women must defend themselves. According to a family tradition reported by Aḥmad b. Bakkār, an aunt named Maḥḍa was the last family member left alive in the house: 'The Khurāsāniyya entered our *dār*, and one of them said "Let's take this one."[54] To this she responded: "No way, you son of a bitch. The likes of me will never be taken." So he struck her with his sword, killing her.'[55] Finally, it is a woman who calls Yaḥyā b. Muḥammad to account:

[50] Al-Azdī, *Taʾrīkh*, p. 147. Cf. the accounts in Ibn Ḥazm (*Jamhara*, p. 21), which has 400 survivors.

[51] Al-Azdī, *Taʾrīkh*, p. 147. 'Ṭamathāniyīn' is not pointed in the MS, and I cannot improve upon this reading. [52] That is to say, dressed for battle. [53] Al-Azdī, *Taʾrīkh*, p. 149.

[54] *Hādhihi nasbīhā*; the English is intended to express the ambiguity of the Arabic.

[55] *Ibid.* For other honourable women taken into captivity, cf. the story of the crypto-Khārijite Yazīd b. Abī Muslim, who claims to have killed a fellow Khārijite only because al-Ḥajjāj threatened to enslave his daughters (al-Mubarrad, *al-Kāmil*, (Leipzig, 1892), p. 346); Juwayriya's father claimed that his daughter, as an *imrāʾa karīma*, was not to be taken into captivity (thus Khalīfa b. Khayyāṭ, *Taʾrīkh*, p. 36).

On the fourth day [of the massacre] Yaḥyā b. Muḥammad went riding around Mosul, led by men with lances and swords unsheathed. A woman from the house of al-Ḥārith b. Jārūd blocked his way, and took hold of the bit of his horse. His men moved towards her in order to kill her, but he stopped them and gave her leave to speak. So she asked him 'Aren't you of the Banū Hāshim? Aren't you the Prophet's cousin? Doesn't it outrage you that the Zanj are raping Arab women?'[56]

The next day Yaḥyā is said to have ordered the execution of the 4,000 Zanj. The role of the Zanj here, particularly when seen in the light of other accounts, suggests that the ethnicity of the rapists was nearly as significant as the act itself.[57] And if, in narrative terms, rape has a metaphorical role ('the triumph of pure belief over infidelity'),[58] here it is horribly inverted: the new *dawla* may have brought the Banū Hāshim to power, but it did so at a terrible cost to Arab Islam.

In sum, the accounts offer an implicit critique of the Mosuli élite alongside a detailed record of Abbasid excess. The accounts also propose a reconstruction of the confusing events. It is to al-Azdī's reconstruction that we should now turn; we thus turn from themes to form.

Responsibility and narrative

The section opens in understated fashion: 'In this year [AH 133] Yaḥyā b. Muḥammad b. ʿAlī b. ʿAbd Allāh b. al-ʿAbbās killed the people of Mosul; there is a difference of opinion about why.'[59] According to the first of these, the massacre was sparked by an accident involving a local woman and a Khurāsānī soldier; the woman, who was standing on a rooftop, is said to have spilled some mallow (*khiṭmiyya*)[60] on a soldier passing below; the account becomes vague – perhaps even corrupt – but a crowd seems to have formed, and the ensuing tumult led Yaḥyā b. Muḥammad to set the soldiers against the townsmen. The second view, which is attributed to the same figure, Aḥmad b. ʿAbd Allāh al-Saʿdī, is briefer, and simply reads: 'The cause of their killing was their inclination (*mayl*) towards the Umayyads.' According to the third explanation, it was the city folk's refusal to accept the caliph's appointment of Muḥammad b. Ṣūl and their embrace of an unidentified Azdī/Muhallabī that set the terrible train of events into motion: al-Saffāḥ has the Muhallabī killed and sends Yaḥyā b. Muḥammad to the city with 12,000 men; he makes his quarters in the *qaṣr al-imāra* and prohibits Muḥammad b. Ṣūl from entering

[56] Al-Azdī, *Taʾrīkh*, p. 149.

[57] According to al-Yaʿqūbī's uncredited account (*Taʾrīkh*, II, pp. 428f.), the Abbasids arrived with 4,000 *Khurāsānī* soldiers, and Yaḥyā b. Muḥammad 'killed 18,000 people of pure Arab stock (*min ṣalīb al-ʿarab*)'. See G. Rotter, *Die Stellung des Negers in der islamisch-arabischen Gesellschaft bis zum XVI. Jahrhundert* (Bonn, 1967), pp. 131ff.

[58] See J. S. Meisami's review of S. P. Stetkevych, *Abū Tammām and the Poetics of the ʿAbbāsid Age* in the *Journal of Arabic Literature* 25 (1994), p. 69.

[59] Al-Azdī, *Taʾrīkh*, pp. 145: 10–146: 14.

[60] This was presumably used as a balm, hair softener, or (following the editor's suggestion) a cleanser of some sort.

the city, instructing him to set up his quarters in al-Ḥurr's *qaṣr*; a month later twelve Mosulis are executed; the people of the city go into open rebellion; an amnesty is promised to all those who gather at the congregational mosque; troops posted at the doors of the mosque massacre those who respond.

Since all three explanations begin with variations on the same phrase (i.e. *kāna sabab dhālika*; *sabab qatlihim*; *sabab qatl ahl al-Mawṣil*) the section has a somewhat staged effect; and the impression is compounded by the anomalous character of the third explanation, which is really no explanation at all, but rather a reconstruction of the events that triggered the massacre. In fact, it turns out that there is no real controversy to speak of. Thus a tradition credited to Aḥmad b. Bakkār brings together the first and second interpretations: the real cause of the massacre was their 'inclination towards the Umayyads and their hatred of the Abbasids', and the evidence adduced is the mallow incident, now with a crucial addition that the Khurāsānī soldier considered the 'accident' to have been intentional.[61] Umayyad sympathies and hostility against the Abbasids similarly underlie the tradition that immediately follows, which fuses the second and third interpretations: the city's Umayyad sympathies are said to have concerned Yaḥyā b. Muḥammad so much that he thought it best to beat them to the punch.[62]

The political allegiances of the élite are less at issue in al-Azdī's account than is the precise course of events; this explains not only the anomalous character of the third explanation, but why all three are preceded by the following, which sports no *isnād*. Here al-Azdī speaks directly:

> In this year (133 AH) Abū al-ʿAbbās appointed his brother, Yaḥyā b. Muḥammad, governor of Mosul, to where he proceeded from Kufa. Before him Muḥammad b. Ṣūl had been governor, and he [Muḥammad] remained [in the city] with him (*aqāma maʿahu*) [even after Yaḥyā's arrival]. He proceeded to Mosul with 12,000 horsemen and foot soldiers – according to some accounts (*fīmā dhakarū*) – and he then set up his quarters in the *qaṣr al-imāra*, which adjoins the congregational mosque, ordering Muḥammad b. Ṣūl to set up his quarters in al-Ḥurr b. Yūsuf's *qaṣr*, i.e. the Manqūsha, and forbidding him from setting up quarters within the city proper (*nafs al-madīna*) and from passing beyond its walls [into the city].[63]

Any alert reader immediately asks himself two related questions. Why did Muḥammad b. Ṣūl, now dismissed from his post, remain in Mosul? And what is the significance of his taking up residence outside the city, in the Manqūsha palace? In prefacing the three explanations with this account al-Azdī has thus done us the favour of tipping his narrative hand: an adequate accounting of the massacre turns on where Yaḥyā b. Muḥammad and Muḥammad b. Ṣūl were, and what they were doing.

A full reconstruction emerges only reluctantly. A first glimpse comes in an account transmitted by al-Saʿdī (account 'A').[64] After listing several of the

[61] Al-Azdī, *Ta'rīkh*, p. 150: 1–5. [62] Al-Azdī, *Ta'rīkh*, p. 150: 6–16.
[63] Al-Azdī, *Ta'rīkh*, p. 145: 6–10. [64] Al-Azdī, *Ta'rīkh*, pp. 146: 15–147: 11.

victims by name, the report continues: 'He [i.e. Muḥammad b. Ṣūl] sent them (*baʿatha bi-hā*) [?] to Yaḥyā b. Muḥammad; the people of the city rebelled against him (*wathaba bi-hi*).' As the additional bracketing indicates, this part of the report is too elliptical to be fully meaningful on its own: the reader is ignorant of what was sent, and how whatever was sent caused the townsfolk to rebel.[65] The crucial information – that what was sent were some notables' severed heads – appears only in an ensuing account, in a report credited to Muḥammad b. al-Muʿāfā (account 'B').[66] There we read that Ibn Ṣūl 'had those Mosulis who had accepted [?] enter the Manqūsha (*adkhala Ibn Ṣūl man qabila min ahl al-Mawṣil al-Manqūsha*)', where they were promptly killed; 'He then sent the heads in covered serving dishes to Yaḥyā b. Muḥammad, the people [of the city] not knowing anything [of the victims' fate] or of what was in them.[67] When they [i.e. the heads] reached Yaḥyā, he ordered him [Muḥammad b. Ṣūl] to massacre the people.' Thus, to understand account 'A', we need account 'B', which tells us what was sent to Yaḥyā b. Muḥammad. But to understand a crucial passage in account 'B' we still need to recall information introduced by Muḥammad al-Muʿāfā earlier, to the effect that Muḥammad b. Ṣūl had summoned the city's élite to the palace (*thumma daʿāhum daʿwa*); only in this way can we understand the phrase 'those Mosulis who had accepted [i.e. the invitation]'.

Explaining the interdependency of these accounts takes us back into the ninth century. The following is al-Balādhurī's account of the massacre.

> As for Yaḥyā b. Muḥammad b. ʿAlī b. ʿAbd Allāh, the caliph Abū al-ʿAbbās appointed him governor of Mosul; he put its population to the sword and razed its city walls. The Mosulis were of three kinds: Khārijites, thieves and merchants.[68] Then Yaḥyā's crier announced the Friday prayer, so all the people gathered together. He then ordered that they all be killed, among them being merchants. Muḥammad b. Ṣūl had been the governor of Mosul before him; he then became his [Yaḥyā's] deputy. Now Muḥammad b. Ṣūl had been killing the Mosuli notables at night, and throwing their corpses into the river, but when Yaḥyā became governor, he ordered him to attack them openly (*falammā waliya Yaḥyā amarahu bi-mukāshafatihim*);[69] his appointment took place in year 133. Because of their evil, the people of Mosul were called the Khazars of the Arabs. Al-Manṣūr [then] appointed Yaḥyā governor of Armenia.[70]

[65] Thus the editor (al-Azdī, *Taʾrīkh*, p. 147 note 4) feels compelled to explain (*ay bi-ruʾūs al-ḍaḥāyā*), adducing the report that follows. On its own the text is entirely opaque.

[66] Al-Azdī, *Taʾrīkh*, pp. 147: 14–148: 8.

[67] The manuscript reads *fī aṭbāqin wa-makābbin* (sg. *makibba*, 'cover', 'covering'); see M. Ullmann, *Wörterbuch der klassichen arabischen Sprache* (Wiesbaden, 1970–), I, p. 16. It almost goes without saying that delivering severed heads was the favoured method of proving that executions had actually taken place; for other examples, see al-Dīnawarī, *Akhbār*, p. 255; and al-Yaʿqūbī, *Taʾrīkh*, II, p. 324.

[68] Cf. Yaḥyā b. Yaḥyā al-Ghassānī's comment to ʿUmar II, which is preserved by al-Azdī in Ibn Ḥajar, *Tahdhīb*, XI, p. 300.

[69] So reads Duri, but one might read 'when he became governor, their fate came to light' (*falammā waliya Yaḥyā inkashafa amruhum*), following al-Muʿāfā's report as transmitted by al-Azdī.

[70] Al-Balādhurī, *Ansāb*, III, p. 281.

By the standard of al-Azdī, the account is not only mistaken, but noticeably garbled: in part this is because it apparently conflates the events of the massacre with those of a generation later,[71] and in part because it suffers from an interpolation of anti-Mosuli polemics ('The Mosulis were of three kinds . . . Because of their evil . . .'), doubtlessly intended to set Abbasid actions in a more favourable (or at least explicable) light. The principal features of an earlier narrative – in which the appointments of Muḥammad b. Ṣūl and Yaḥyā b. Muḥammad were prominent, and where the killing took place in two stages – remain discernible, however; and it is to be credited to one of the two Mosuli authorities who are cited for the accounts that immediately follow, namely al-Muʿāfā b. Ṭāwūs (transmitting on the authority of his father), and Abū al-Faḍl al-Anṣārī (105/723–186/801), a mediocre *ḥadīth* transmitter and *qāḍī* of Mosul.[72] Considering the relative significance of the two men in the local tradition, one assumes that it was al-Muʿāfā who provided al-Balādhurī (directly or indirectly) with the report. In any event, al-Balādhurī was clearly drawing on the same vein of local tradition upon which al-Azdī himself drew, and which dates from at least three generations before the *Taʾrīkh al-Mawṣil.*

With this in mind, we can return to al-Azdī's narrative. How are we to understand its apparent 'intertextuality'? It may be suggested that our Mosuli historian disassembled what had been a single, continuous account produced by al-Muʿāfā b. Ṭāwūs much earlier, with an apparent loss of coherence as a result; this was common enough practice, al-Ṭabarī himself compiling in the same fashion.[73] It may also be that he drew together separate strands originally composed for an audience that already knew the details, i.e. that members of the élite had been invited to the Manqūsha palace, and that their severed heads were then sent on to Yaḥyā b. Muḥammad; the account appears wanting only to those unfamiliar with the events. In either case, al-Azdī's narrative was dangerously close to running off the rails, and it is not long before the confusion is eliminated and the one issue left outstanding – how precisely did the beheadings spark the revolt? – resolved.

A full accounting of the events of the massacre finally appears on page 150 of the printed edition; it is equipped with what can only be called a transparently apologetic *isnād*: 'Someone else, whose knowledge in the matter concerned I trust, informed me, on the authority of old *shaykh*s whom he described as having repeated this in his presence, that . . .' After defeating Marwān II, ʿAbd Allāh b. ʿAlī approaches the city, and the people of Mosul, apparently under the leadership of the last Umayyad governor, Hishām b. ʿAmr, greet ʿAbd Allāh, proclaiming their allegiance to the Abbasids. ʿAbd

[71] Namely, Hārūn's suppression of al-ʿAṭṭāf b. Sufyān's rebellion in 176/792, when the walls *were* razed; see al-Azdī, *Taʾrīkh*, p. 279.

[72] See al-Azdī, *Taʾrīkh*, p. 304; Ibn Ḥajar, *Tahdhīb*, V, pp. 126f. (citing al-Azdī's *Ṭabaqāt*); al-Ṣafadī, *al-Wāfī biʾl-wafayāt*, XVI, p. 637; al-Dhahabī, *Mīzān al-iʿtidāl* (Cairo, 1325), II, p. 19.

[73] See Stefan Leder, 'Features of the novel in early historiography – the downfall of Xālid al-Qasrī', *Oriens* 32 (1990), pp. 76ff.

Allāh then appoints Yaḥyā b. Muḥammad over Mosul, making Muḥammad b. Ṣūl his deputy (*khalīfa*). However, Yaḥyā becomes fearful of a rebellion, and orders Muḥammad b. Ṣūl to execute some of the city's élite after inviting them 'with a show of respect and honour'. Muḥammad sends their heads to Yaḥyā, but 'the matter is uncovered' (*inkashafa al-khabar*) – the *datum* heretofore missing – and the people rebel. With this report alongside the others, the sequence of events is now – at last – relatively clear: Muḥammad b. Ṣūl had invited the city's notables to the Manqūsha palace, where he killed most of them; although their heads were carried to Yaḥyā under cover, word leaked out that the killing had taken place; the city folk rebelled as a result; a grant of amnesty was announced to those who came to the congregational mosque; the massacre then followed. The account therefore ties together all of the issues left unresolved: the relationship between the Umayyad defeat and the earliest Abbasid administration in Mosul in general, and between Yaḥyā b. Muḥammad and Muḥammad b. Ṣūl in particular, and, finally, the execution of the notables and the massacre of the city's populace.

Now the preceding is not intended merely to demonstrate that reading narratives of the Abbasid Revolution is hard work, although we can never be reminded of this enough.[74] It is rather to describe how one historian handled the *khabar* format, which, whatever its genetic links with *ḥadīth*, seems (at least to western ears) to muffle the historian's voice. The challenge faced by al-Azdī was in fashioning a narrative of events that was at once faithful to the principles of *khabar* historiography, based on the moving eyewitness testimony at his disposal and, of course, coherent. Narrative authority always lay in authorial distance from the subject matter to hand; to argue was to select and arrange, to lead the reader – circuitously but deliberately – to an adequate accounting of the events. Convention thus allowed him to anticipate the three explanations by setting the topographical scene, but not to take credit for the last word on what actually happened. Here al-Azdī's handling of the *isnād* is striking. 'Someone whose knowledge in the matter concerned I trust informed me, on the authority of old *shaykhs* whom he described as having repeated this in his presence, that . . .'[75] seems to be as close as we come to 'I would argue . . .'. For one is unavoidably struck by the report's extreme concision and schematic treatment of the events; it does not so much tell a story as recapitulate one, filling in the one hole left in the continuous narrative created by the succession of accounts.[76] The only meagre details – a few victims' names – were presumably derived from other reports, as was the manifestly anachronistic assertion that 'the city was Umayyad'; this was probably inspired by the more restricted and careful view articulated by named authorities, who had explained the killing as a result of the city's

[74] This is a point made quite clear by Lassner, *Islamic Revolution and Historical Memory*.

[75] Al-Azdī, *Ta'rīkh*, p. 150.

[76] We read, for example, that 'the matter [i.e. of the severed heads] was uncovered' (*inkashafa al-khabar*) but we learn nothing of the circumstances of this crucial turn of events.

inclination (*mayl*) towards the Umayyads.[77] As we shall see, it cannot be accurate.

So much for the mechanics of narrative; a more ambitious reading of the text is as follows. According to al-Azdī, the massacre of 133 was on the one hand meaningless,[78] and on the other explicable in political terms: the Mosulis 'were strong and resistant, and the land (*balad*) was Umayyad'; Yaḥyā b. Muḥammad could thus credibly anticipate rebellion, and beat them to the punch. One is tempted to sense in this representation of Umayyad history a prescription for a more prudent conduct of city politics vis-à-vis the Ḥamdānids; political views of a controversial character, in our author's opinion, were best left unexpressed. Following Muḥammad b. al-Muʿāfā b. Ṭāwūs's reconstruction, whose characteristic feature is the Mosulis' rejection of a Khathʿamī governor in favour of an Azdī, a tenth-century reader (or listener) might also conclude that kinship should have only a secondary role to play in city politics; for while Azdī tribal arrogance had set the terrible chain of events into motion, it was left to a lowly *mawlā* of an obscure Azdī lineage (the Ṭamathān) to resist.

Diffusion, transmission and evidence for other reconstructions

In addition to al-Azdī and al-Balādhurī, accounts of the massacre can also be found in the works that follow. Much could be said about these accounts;[79] I shall focus only on the earlier sources.

1) Anonymous, *Zuqnin Chronicle* (ca. 775), II, pp. 206/160
2) Agapius of Manbij (ca. 950), *Kitāb al-ʿUnwān*, p. 532
3) Anonymous, *Chronicle of 1234* (final redaction in the late twelfth century), I, pp. 338f./264
4) Khalīfa b. Khayyāṭ (239/854), *Taʾrīkh*, p. 269
5) al-Balādhurī (279/892), *Ansāb al-ashrāf*, III, p. 281
6) al-Yaʿqūbī (283/897), *Taʾrīkh*, II, pp. 428f.
7) Ibn Ḥazm (456/1064), *Jamharat ansāb al-ʿarab*, p. 21
8) Ibn ʿAsākir (571/1176), *Taʾrīkh madīnat Dimashq*, LXIV, p. 367

[77] Al-Azdī, *Taʾrīkh*, p. 145.

[78] Thus neither al-Saffāḥ nor al-Muʿtaḍid, when questioned why the killing took place, can supply an answer; see al-Azdī, *Taʾrīkh*, p. 151; Ibn Ḥazm, *Jamhara*, p. 21.

[79] *Pace*, C. E. Bosworth, *al-Maqrīzī's 'Book of Contention and Strife' concerning the Relations between the Banū Umayya and the Banū Hāshim* (Manchester 1980), p. 140, al-Maqrīzī does not follow Ibn al-Athīr *verbatim*. Rather, he based his account on Ibn al-Athīr's, supplementing it with Ibn Ḥazm's (or one very similar to it), the latter's being betrayed not only by the anomalous appearance of Ibrāhīm b. Yaḥyā, but also the number of those who fled (400) and the killing of cocks and dogs. Meanwhile, aside from the numbers, al-Nuwayrī seems to have followed Ibn al-Athīr quite closely, and indeed he may have had a better copy of the *Kāmil* than we have; for whereas the present editions have the very curious *yalī ʿalaynā mawlā al-Khathʿam wa-akhrajahu* (*al-Kāmil*, V, p. 443; cf. Leiden, 1871, V, pp. 340f.), al-Nuwayrī (apparently correctly) reads *lā yalī ʿalaynā mawlā li-Khathʿam*.

9) Ibn al-Athīr (629/1232), *al-Kāmil fī al-ta'rīkh*, V, pp. 443f.
10) al-Nuwayrī (732/1332), *Nihāyat al-arab fī funūn al-adab*, XXII, pp. 58f.
11) Ibn Khaldūn (808/1406), *Ta'rīkh* (Būlāq, 1284), III, p. 177
12) al-Maqrīzī (845/1442), *Kitāb al-Nizā' wa'l-takhāṣum fīmā bayna Banī Umayya wa-Banī Hāshim* (Cairo, 1998), pp. 99f.; trans. C. E. Bosworth, *al-Maqrīzī's 'Book of Contention and Strife concerning the Relations between the Banū Umayya and the Banū Hāshim'* (Manchester, 1980), pp. 92f. (translation) and 139f. (commentary)

How quickly, and in what form, did reports of the massacre spread? Of one date we can be fairly certain: by 775, news of Abbasid massacres in Iraq had reached the monastery of Zuqnin, north of Āmid. There, an anonymous monk wrote in 1063 of the Seleucid era (751/2) 'the Persians returned [!] to the land [i.e. Iraq] with great armies, and they fought and defeated everyone who met them in battle. They committed a great massacre amongst the Arabs (*ṭayyāyē*) of Mosul and 'Aqūlā (Kufa).[80] They massacred the old along with the young.'[81]

Events of the revolutionary period have quite clearly been telescoped, and one might be inclined to replace Kufa with Wāsiṭ or perhaps al-Ḥīra; but there is no question that a faint echo of the events in Mosul had travelled west very quickly. If news of the massacre appeared almost immediately, there is no attempt to assign responsibility.

Of another date we can be less certain. After mentioning the caliph's appointments in other provinces, the compiler of the *Chronicle of 1234* offers the following:

And he put his brother Yaḥyā in charge over all of Athūr,[82] Mawṣil and Nineveh. When Yaḥyā took charge of Mawṣil, he rounded up many of Mawṣil's notables (*rīshānē*) in a mosque, and [there] he killed them. Others fled and went into hiding. One of Yaḥyā's commanders, whose name was Ibn Faḍl, was present there, and he tricked thirty of the city's notables, with whom Yaḥyā was angry. He took them to an underground chamber, as if he were hiding them in order to intercede on their behalf. He [then] went up to them one after the other, and cut them down like sheep. He put their heads on platters, covered them with cloths, and sent them to Yaḥyā. Those who saw them, understood them to be something precious. When Yaḥyā saw them, out of gratitude he rose, kneeled down and prayed.[83] He immediately ordered that all of their families be killed. With swords drawn, they went out and mercilessly killed wives, virgins, young men and infants. This Yaḥyā committed unspeakable evils in Mawṣil.[84]

80 I translate in the plural, despite the singular verb. It is tempting to translate 'they put to the sword'. 81 *Zuqnin Chronicle*, pp. 206/160.

82 The toponym, favoured in the Syriac tradition, did survive in Arabic too: see al-Bakrī, *Mu'jam*, 108; cf. al-Muqaddasī, *Aḥsan al-taqāsīm*, pp. 136ff. (*iqlīm aqūr*).

83 Cf. al-Nuwayrī, *Nihāyat al-arab*, XXII, pp. 49 (al-Saffāḥ prostrating himself when he receives the head of Marwān); and al-Ya'qūbī, *Ta'rīkh*, II, p. 317 (where 'Abd al-Malik prostrates himself after receiving the head of Muṣ'ab b. al-Zubayr – and is almost beheaded himself as a result). 84 *Chronicle of 1234*, I, pp. 338f./264.

The account is impressive in a number of ways, and I shall take full advantage of it below. But what is its provenance? As the title indicates, in its present form the *Chronicle of 1234* is quite late, indeed late enough for one of its redactors to have integrated al-Azdī's (or al-Muʿāfā's) text into an earlier layer of the chronicle, which for this period was composed principally of the now-lost history of the Patriarch Dionysius of Tell Maḥrē (d. 845).[85] This is unlikely, however. It is hard to see how al-Azdī's history, which seems to have been lost to the entire Islamic historiographic tradition outside of Mosul, somehow remained accessible to a Christian Edessan writing in Syriac; in any case, had a later redactor used al-Azdī (or al-Muʿāfā) here, we might expect him to have used him elsewhere.[86] On the other hand, Dionysius clearly had access to good material on the eighth century.[87] But where did Dionysius find it? It is conceivable that Dionysius himself drew on an Arabic account of the massacre,[88] but the burden of proof must lie with those who would argue against the anonymous chronicler's use of Theophilus of Edessa (d. 785), whose historical work ended in the period of the Revolution itself. For while the argument against Theophilus must posit an Arabic intermediary available to the Christian Edessan, the argument in favour of Theophilus can turn to Revolution accounts in Agapius of Manbij's tenth-century *Kitāb al-ʿUnwān*, in the midst of which Agapius explicitly acknowledges Theophilus as his source.[89] And there we read the following:

He [ʿAbd Allāh b. Muḥammad] appointed Yaḥyā b. Muḥammad governor of Mosul and its dependencies. When Yaḥyā b. Muḥammad entered Mosul, he ordered that the Arabs of Mosul, along with their chiefs (*al-ruʾasā*), gather in the congregational mosque, and that they be slaughtered all together (*ʿalā dam wāḥid*); he killed children and women [too]. The Arabs were overwhelmed by this calamity;[90] shame and ignominy blanketed them. The Banū Hāshim increased their oppression, making the *kharāj* ever more onerous, and seizing the money of all the Arabs.[91]

85 On Dionysius in the *Chronicle of 1234*, see Abouna's introduction to his translation of the second volume, *Chronicle of 1234*, II, p. ix; Palmer, *Seventh Century*, pp. 85ff.; Conrad, 'Syriac perspectives', pp. 34f.; and Conrad, 'The conquest of Arwād', pp. 325ff.

86 That the anonymous Edessan chronicler was using an Arabic source for accounts in Mosul in 232/847 – that is, after Dionysius's history had come to a close – is betrayed by the use of *hijrī* dating; see the *Chronicle of 1234*, II, pp. 39/28 (noted by Abouna, p. x).

87 The quality of Dionysius' material on the early Abbasids struck Abramowski, *Dionysius von Tellmahre*, pp. 57f., but he came to no firm conclusions about its provenance.

88 On Dionysius' use of Arabic material for conquest history, see R. Hoyland, 'Arabic, Syriac and Greek historiography in the first Abbasid century: an inquiry into inter-cultural traffic', *Aram* 3 (1991), pp. 219ff.; and on Dionysius' sources in general, Palmer, *Seventh Century*, pp. 95ff. I once suggested that this may explain the massacre account (see my review of Palmer, *Seventh Century* in *JRAS* 3, 5 (1995), p. 99).

89 Theophilus lived until 785, but since his chronicle came to a close in the revolutionary period, one presumes that he wrote very early in the 750's; see Conrad, 'The conquest of Arwād', pp. 331f.

90 *Fa-ghashiyat al-ʿarab ʿind dhālika al-kaʾba.*

91 Agapius, *Kitāb al-ʿUnwān*, p. 532.

The account betrays Agapius' fingerprints,[92] tipping the scales in favour of Theophilus' authorship of the account. For 'Athūr, Mosul and Nineveh' he translated *al-Mawṣil wa-mā yalīhā*; he preserved mention of the congregational mosque, but telescoped Theophilus' longer account concerning Ibn Faḍl (Ibn Ṣūl) into a single sentence; he then turned to stock material (also available to Michael the Syrian) relating Abbasid overtaxation.

If the preceding is accepted, the *Chronicle of 1234* offers near contemporaneous testimony on the massacre, presumably drawn from oral accounts that circulated in the immediate aftermath of the Revolution; it thus demonstrates that many of the essentials of al-Azdī's reconstruction were already established within a decade or two of the events, and documents the continuous transmission of controversial material from the middle of the eighth until the early tenth. If the argument for Theophilus' authorship is not accepted, we can still add two more Christian accounts (in addition to that of the *Zuqnin Chronicle*) to the respectable list of Arabic accounts recounting the massacre. In the early period, these included Khalīfa b. Khayyāṭ, who holds Yaḥyā b. Muḥammad responsible (this in year 134), and al-Yaʿqūbī, who knows quite a bit more: that the Mosulis rebelled against an (anonymous) governor, leading the caliph to send his brother Yaḥyā with 4,000 Khurāsānīs; that those killed included Arabs, their slaves and *mawālī*; and, finally, that the killing was in some way related to the Friday prayers. Given the spread of reports, it is impossible to escape the conclusion that the omission of any mention of the massacre in al-Ṭabarī's *Ta'rīkh* was deliberate.[93]

What Theophilus, al-Balādhurī and al-Yaʿqūbī cannot do is corroborate al-Azdī in precise detail. Indeed, the account in the *Chronicle of 1234* departs from the reconstruction proposed by al-Azdī in one crucial respect. Whereas al-Azdī's sources state that the city élite were invited to the Manqūsha palace, where they were executed, the *Chronicle of 1234* explicitly states that they were rounded up in the mosque; some were killed there, and others later killed in the 'underground chamber',[94] which is presumably to be taken to mean the *dār al-imāra*, which we know to have adjoined the congregational mosque. In fact, there seems to have been some real confusion about the location and actions of Muḥammad b. Ṣul, and where the city notables were killed; as we have already seen, these are the very issues that al-Azdī tried so hard to settle. That Muḥammad b. Ṣūl was present at the mosque is made

[92] On Agapius' handling of the common source (=Theophilus), see Conrad, 'The conquest of Arwād', pp. 328f.

[93] Cf. S. Moscati's comments ('Le massacre des Umayyades dans l'histoire et dans les fragments poétiques,' *Archiv Orientální* 18 (1950), p. 92): 'L'histoire de Ṭabarī, qui est sans aucun doute la plus longue et la plus importante de celles dont on dispose pour cette période, nous étonne par son laconisme au suject du carnage des Umayyades.' For more examples, see Elad, 'The siege of al-Wāsiṭ', p. 78; H. Kennedy, *The Early Abbasid Caliphate* (London, 1981), p. 216; and Madelung, *Succession*, pp. 331f.

[94] The difference, it might be noted here, may be the *coup de grâce* against an argument that posits al-Azdī (or one of his sources) as a source for the *Chronicle of 1234*.

SEVEN

Massacre and élite politics: the Abbasid Revolution in Mosul II

From the accounts recorded by al-Balādhurī, al-Azdī, and the *Chronicle of 1234*, we can piece together a detailed picture of the events of the massacre; in al-Balādhurī and al-Azdī we also have evidence for the reconstructions that prevailed in the city during the ninth century; and in al-Azdī's we can also see in some detail how one tenth-century historian argued his case. This said, we are hard put to discern any convincing causes for the massacre, much less the larger political context into which the dreadful events are to be placed. In large part this is because the *Ta'rīkh* is of a piece with other examples of Abbasid historiography, in which revolutionary accounts so frequently propose a deceptively narrow range of action: politics is figured as a zero–sum game, where hostility to the Abbasids meant sympathy for the Umayyads, and *taswīd* forced *tabyīḍ*: things are quite literally black and white. But Aḥmad b. ʿAbd Allāh al-Saʿdī's wild assertion that the city folk were Umayyad is precisely that: Umayyad sympathy cannot be squared with the evidence. Nor can one hold with Forand that the massacre 'must have stemmed from serious opposition to the ʿAbbāsid revolution'.[1] The Mosulis were not counter-revolutionaries, and if the ferocious violence of 133 is typical enough of revolutionary periods, the massacre can be compared neither to the Terror nor to mere *chouannaries*.

Things are predictably more complex. On the one hand, the Mosulis were anything but Umayyad loyalists, for we know that the élite had grown receptive to Khārijite overtures, indeed enthusiastic enough to risk Umayyad wrath by receiving Khārijite rebels into the city with open arms. The city's first direct contact with Khārijism seems to date from about 100/718, when Shawdhab appeared in al-Ḥazza, eventually making his way to Mosul, where he killed the city's governor; Rotter is probably correct that he controlled the city for several months.[2] Clearer sympathy for the Khārijites may be signalled as early as 118/736, with the rebellion of the Shaybānī commander Bahlūl b. Bishr.[3] Certainly he had strong ties to the city: one infers from an anecdote that he

[1] Forand, 'Governors', p. 92.
[2] See al-Balādhurī, *Ansāb*, Reis. 598, fol. 84b; al-Ṭabarī, *Ta'rīkh*, II, pp. 1348ff.; Rotter, 'Fulūs', p. 176. [3] So argues Rotter, 'Fulūs', pp. 184f.

was a commander in Mosul's garrison, known personally by al-Walīd b. Talīd,[4] and one report has men from the Mosul and Jaziran armies following him into rebellion.[5] Seven years later, Bisṭām al-Shaybānī marched first to Nisibis, where he secured the loyalty of the city's inhabitants; he then turned towards Mosul, where he settled in the northern outskirts of the city, apparently doing the same.[6] When Saʿīd b. Bahdal rebelled shortly thereafter, he too marched on Mosul; the city folk paid him allegiance and prudently requested that he continue on.[7] They feared the Marwānid response.

Months later, and now deeper into the civil war, the Mosulis went so far as to invite al-Ḍaḥḥāk b. Qays al-Shaybānī into the city. The Khārijite had little trouble defeating a Shaybānī commander delegated by Marwān II to defend it,[8] and he proceeded to mint a large issue of coins.[9] The invitation to al-Ḍaḥḥāk had apparently come from partisans (*aṣḥāb*) of Shaybān b. ʿAbd al-ʿAzīz, who eventually succeeded him.[10] Shaybān himself, on the run from Marwān II's forces, not unreasonably chose to make his stand in Mosul, since the city folk had welcomed him there; according to al-Azdī's source, 'they were on his side', and it was thanks to the city's supply of provisions that he managed to hold out for as long as a year.[11] In fact, the city's support for Shaybān's cause so enraged Marwān II that he is given to swear: 'When I defeat the Mosulis, I will kill their fighting men (*muqātilatahum*) and enslave their offspring!' (*dhurrīyatahum*).[12] That it was left to the Abbasids to carry out a threat made by the last Umayyad may have struck at least some of al-Azdī's readers as ironic; in any event, the city's history during the last Umayyad civil war does not recommend an interpretation of the massacre that turns on Umayyad sympathies.

Unlike Marwān II's Qaysī commanders who had everything to lose with the defeat of their patron–caliph,[13] the Mosulis were thus anything but Umayyad loyalists; and, on the grounds that one's enemy's enemies are one's (potential) friends, we might suspect some common cause between the city folk and the Abbasids. Indeed, some Mosulis are said to have had some Shīʿite credentials: we are told that Zayd b. ʿAlī wrote to the Mosulis in 121/738 appealing for

[4] Al-Ṭabarī, *Taʾrīkh*, II, pp. 1625f.; al-Balādhurī, *Ansāb*, Reis. 598, fol. 133a.

[5] De Goeje and de Jong, eds., *Fragmenta*, p. 110.

[6] See al-Madāʾinī as preserved by al-Balādhurī, *Ansāb*, Reis. 598, fol. 180a–b.

[7] Khalīfa b. Khayyāṭ, *Taʾrīkh*, p. 242.

[8] See al-Ṭabarī, *Taʾrīkh*, II, pp. 1938f.; Ibn al-Athīr, *al-Kāmil*, V, p. 349; the anonymous *ʿUyūn*, III, p. 159; al-Azdī, *Taʾrīkh*, p. 69.

[9] Rotter, 'Fulūs', p. 191; C. Wurtzel, 'The coinage of the revolutionaries in the late Umayyad period', *Museum Notes* 23 (1978), pp. 190f. The Mosuli *fulūs* also mention what appears to be another Khārijite, Zuhayr b. ʿAlqama; see Rotter, 'Fulūs', pp. 194f. and Wurtzel, 'Coinage', p. 191.

[10] Al-Ḍaḥḥāk's popularity was such that Marwān thought it useful to parade his severed head around the cities of the Jazira; see al-Ṭabarī, *Taʾrīkh*, II, p. 1940.

[11] Al-Azdī, *Taʾrīkh*, pp. 72ff. [12] Al-Azdī, *Taʾrīkh*, p. 74.

[13] For an overview, see Bonner, *Aristocratic Violence*, pp. 45ff. For Syria after the Abbasid Revolution, see P. M. Cobb, 'White Banners: Contention in ʿAbbāsid Syria, 750–877' (Ph.D. thesis, University of Chicago, 1997), esp. pp. 94ff.

their support.[14] Certainly the city folk's reception of the victorious Abbasid army is presented positively in our sources: accounts have the last Umayyad governor, Hishām b. ʿAmr, shut the city gates in Marwān II's face,[15] and the city embrace the Abbasids with alacrity.[16] The accounts – dating as they do from the early Abbasid period – must raise suspicions; for just as the Mosulis may have tried to dispel any concern for lingering Umayyad loyalties by putting into circulation accounts that have Hishām b. ʿAbd al-Malik's estates vandalised in the wake of the Revolution,[17] so too they may have outfitted themselves with a more savoury revolutionary experience. But insofar as official Abbasid propaganda can be culled from the surviving material in the *Akhbār al-dawla al-ʿAbbāsiyya*, it too held that the city was fertile ground for the *daʿwa*, at least in part because of Marwān II's hostility towards the Mosulis.[18] Moreover, Wāʾil b. al-Shaḥḥāj, a member of one of Mosul's leading families, responded pragmatically to the events of the Revolution, and his reward came in the form of a valuable land grant.[19] In short, if the evidence undermines al-Saʿdī's view that the Mosulis were unreconstructed Umayyads, it also undermines Forand's view that they were squarely opposed to the Revolution.

One imagines that there was more than one response to Marwān II's defeat on the Zāb, local members of the Umayyad family and their dependants arguing a pro-Marwānid line ('better the devil you know than the devil you don't . . .'), those with Kufan and/or Shīʿite sympathies arguing the Abbasid case; no doubt the situation was very confusing, the defeat having come as a shock to the Mosulis. In any event, it is obvious enough that the argument was won by those who felt the city could not afford the risk in harbouring a desperately weakened Marwān II. This, in view of very recent events (the Battle

14 See al-Azdī, *Taʾrīkh*, p. 44; Ibn Aʿtham, *Futūḥ*, VIII, pp. 115f. (what purports to be a letter from Zayd b. ʿAlī to 'the people of Mosul and the rest of the Jazira') and also 126; al-Ṭabarī, *Taʾrīkh*, II, p. 1685; al-Iṣfahānī, *Maqātil al-ṭālibiyyīn* (Cairo, 1949), p. 135.

15 Thus al-Ṭabarī, *Taʾrīkh*, III, p. 47; al-Azdī, *Taʾrīkh*, p. 133; al-Masʿūdī, *Murūj*, IV, p. 86 (where it is the people of the city who refuse Marwān, seeing that authority had slipped from his hands); al-Nuwayrī, *Nihāyat al-arab*, XXII, p. 47.

16 In addition to the following note, see also the anonymous *Akhbār al-dawla al-ʿAbbāsiyya*, pp. 355ff. The Mosul cavalry is said to have been among the forces that pursued Marwān II all the way to Egypt (al-Ṭabarī, *Taʾrīkh*, III, p. 46; al-Azdī, *Taʾrīkh*, p. 158).

17 Al-Azdī, *Taʾrīkh*, p. 172. This may reflect long-suppressed resentment towards Hishām, rather than enmity towards the dynasty itself: we have already seen that one source has Marwān II order the destruction of Hishām's Euphrates estates (Agapius, *Kitāb al-ʿUnwān*, p. 517), and Yazīd III had pledged to refrain from extravagant building projects (al-Ṭabarī, *Taʾrīkh*, II, p. 1835). If the incident did occur, the mob was perhaps turning against not only the Umayyad caliph who had ushered in a policy of *enrichessez-vous*, but also the city's élite which had benefited so spectacularly.

18 A hostility, as we have already seen, that is echoed in al-Azdī as well; see the anonymous *Akhbār al-dawla al-ʿAbbāsiyya*, pp. 221 (where Muḥammad b. Ṣūl appears as one of the seventy *dāʿīs*), pp. 355 and 378; and also the anonymous *Taʾrīkh al-khulafāʾ* (Moscow, 1967), fols. 207b, 279b and 280a. On these two sources, see E. Daniel, 'The anonymous "History of the Abbasid Family" and its place in Islamic historiography', *IJMES* 14 (1982), pp. 420ff.

19 On this grant, see below, note 42.

of the Zāb), in addition to longer term concerns (the city's very rocky relations with the Marwānids, particularly Marwān II's threat), was the prudent thing to do. It is thus all the more surprising then that the city folk promptly chose to challenge Abbasid authority on the first matter of any real consequence: the appointment of a permanent governor. Now it is true that the reports offer something short of a full accounting of the events: the Muhallabī candidate is never named, and in rejecting the Khathʿamī appointee, the Mosulis are given to bluster: 'A *mawlā* of the Khathʿam to be our amir – it just won't do!' (*mā narḍā an yakūn amīrunā mawlan li-Khathʿam*). But if it is impossible to know whether the purported indignation is to be explained by the lower status of the non-Arab *mawlā*,[20] or rather the ancient bad blood between the Azd and Khathʿam,[21] there is no reason to doubt the course of events itself.

A variety of sources put Muḥammad b. Ṣūl at the Battle of the Zāb,[22] and one imagines that he lingered in the north before moving to Mosul, this after the victorious Abbasid army had already been welcomed into the city. As far as the Abbasids were concerned, the Mosulis had thus accepted Abbasid rule; and in resisting the appointment of Muḥammad b. Ṣūl, they were in open rebellion. The local candidate was promptly dispatched, and the city rewarded with a new governor, now accompanied by a Khurāsānī garrison; the number assigned to this force – 12,000 – is manifestly topological, but there is no reason to doubt that it was large.[23] The 'rebellion' was then answered in textbook fashion – the execution of those held responsible – and one might reasonably infer that Yaḥyā was ultimately responsible for executing the notables as well as for the massacre that followed, since presumptive Abbasid sensitivities did not stop the historical tradition from associating him with the killing.[24] Undated coins struck in Yaḥyā's name survive – our earliest evidence for Abbasid rule in the

20 As argued by Crone, *Slaves*, p. 244, note 428; see also A. Elad, 'Aspects of the transition from the Umayyad to the ʿAbbāsid caliphate', *JSAI* 19 (1995), p. 126, note 172. Muḥammad b. Ṣūl may have been a *mawlā*, but his father had been the *ṣāḥib* of Jurjān (see *EI²* s.v. 'al-Ṣūlī', to which can be added the anonymous *ʿUyūn*, III, p. 21). Note as well that two generations later (and in very different circumstances), another *mawlā*, the well-travelled al-Ḥasan b. Jamīl, served without any apparent objection; see al-Azdī, *Taʾrīkh*, p. 294; al-Ṭabarī, *Taʾrīkh*, III, p. 749; and, for his Abbasid career in general, N.D. Nicol, 'Early Abbasid Administration in the Central and Eastern Provinces, 132–218 AH/750–833 AD,' (Ph.D. thesis, University of Washington, 1979), pp. 39f.

21 See *EI²*, s.v. 'Azd'; al-Ṭabarī, *Taʾrīkh*, I, p. 1731; and, as already noted, ʿAlī's Khathʿamī governor was killed by Taghlibī tribesmen (Ibn al-Athīr, *al-Kāmil*, III, p. 380). For the enduring significance of antipathies such as these in Mosul as late as 197/812, when Hamdānīs refused to acknowledge the governorship of a (Rabīʿa) Taghlibī, see al-Azdī, s.a.; more generally, see E. Landau-Tasseron, 'The sinful wars: religious, social and historical aspects of *ḥurūb al-fijār*', *JSAI* 8 (1986), pp. 51ff.

22 Al-Ṣūlī, *Ashʿār awlād al-khulafāʾ wa-akhbāruhum* (London, 1936), p. 299 (which reads Abū ʿAwn b. Muḥammad b. Ṣūl); see also al-Ṭabarī, *Taʾrīkh*, III, pp. 45ff.; Ibn al-Jawzī, *al-Muntaẓam* (Beirut, 1993), VII, p. 302. After leaving Mosul he appears as governor of Armenia and Azarbayjān, but the historical record is less than clear; see Bonner, *Aristocratic Violence*, pp. 52ff.; and, for more details, Nicol, 'Early Abbasid Administration', pp. 89f.

23 See Conrad, 'The conquest of Arwād', p. 355.

24 So it is argued by Khalīfa b. Khayyāṭ, al-Yaʿqūbī and Ibn ʿAsākir; and in having Ibn Ṣūl send the severed heads to Yaḥyā, al-Azdī certainly implies that the Abbasid was in charge.

north;[25] one imagines that Muḥammad b. Ṣūl had no time to strike any of his own. More important, the list of those executed clearly suggests that the Mosulis' rebellion had broad support among the élite. Among those killed one finds tribesmen of noble lineages (*sharīfs*), some of whom fathered long-lived Mosuli families (e.g. Shurayḥ b. Shurayḥ, al-ʿUrāhim b. al-Mukhtār, ʿAlī b. Nuʿaym al-Ḥimyarī, and Waththāq b. al-Shaḥḥāj), landed *mawālī* (Khāqān (or Tarkhān) b. Yazīd al-Raḥabī,[26] the forefather of a dynasty of *muṣaḥḥiḥūn*), men of property and standing (e.g. al-Ṣabāḥ b. al-Ḥusayn), and, finally, men of learning and piety (the *imām* of the city's congregational mosque, his son, and the ascetically inclined traditionist Maʿrūf b. Abī Maʿrūf). It is impossible to know if the indiscriminate slaughter of (non-combatant) city folk that followed these executions was deliberate, somehow intended to teach the Mosulis the lesson promised them by Marwān II, but it is tempting to conclude that the town's establishment was held collectively responsible for ejecting the Khathʿamī and nominating the Muhallabī in his place.

Deliberate lesson or dreadful accident, the Mosulis had a short memory, and continued to flirt with rebels and rebellion. Memories were still fresh in 754, when al-Mulabbad, joined by local Khārijites, headed for the city in what seems to have been an unsuccessful attempt to court the city's support.[27] Not so a decade later, when in 765 the Hamdānī Khārijite Ḥassān b. Mujālid al-Mawṣilī rebelled in the nearby town of Bāfakhkhārā, defeating al-Ṣaqr b. Najda and the *rawābiṭ* dispatched against him. That the movement enjoyed the support of the Mosuli élite is made clear in al-Manṣūr's response: 'The people of Mosul agreed to terms (*sharaṭū*) according to which they would not rebel against me; if they did, they would forfeit life and property.'[28] Unfortunately, the terms are not described, but it is striking enough that the provincials had a hand in setting them. A generation later, in 176/792, the Mosulis were once again led into rebellion, this time by al-ʿAṭṭāf b. Sufyān, a local commander and land owner. Al-ʿAṭṭāf imprisoned tax agents, levying taxes on his own; and it was only some very delicate negotiations that saved the city's élite from Hārūn's wrath and a repeat of the events of 132.[29]

The late Umayyad and early Abbasid history of Mosul thus features several instances of rebellion; and, considering how the world had changed from the

[25] Thus H. Lavoix, *Catalogue des monnaies musulmanes de la Bibliothèque Nationale* (Paris, 1887), p. 458 (1627); and N. Lowick, *Early ʿAbbāsid Coinage: A Type Corpus*, ed. E. Savage (London, 1996), p. 329. See also the anonymous *Akhbār al-dawla al-ʿAbbāsiyya*, p. 234 (where Yaḥyā is called the *ṣāḥib al-Mawṣil*).

[26] On the titles 'Khāqān' and 'Ṭarkhān', see C. E. Bosworth and G. Clauson, 'al-Xwārazmī on the peoples of Central Asia', *JRAS* (1965), pp. 9ff.

[27] As it happened, he managed to defeat the city's governor, now identified as ʿAbd al-Ḥamīd b. Ribʿī; see al-Balādhurī, *Ansāb*, III, p. 150; al-Azdī, *Taʾrīkh*, p. 166; Crone, *Slaves*, pp. 174f. In the same year, one of the few notables to survive the massacre, the Azdī ʿUthmān b. ʿAbd al-Aʿlā, is said to have rebelled in Syria; after defeating an army sent by ʿAbd Allāh b. ʿAlī from Ḥarrān, it seems he was himself defeated by another, led by Ḥumayd b. Qaḥṭaba (al-Azdī, *Taʾrīkh*, p. 164). One wonders what his motives were.

[28] On the movement, see al-Azdī, *Taʾrīkh*, pp. 203ff.; and Ibn al-Athīr, *al-Kāmil*, V, pp. 484f.; on the town, see Fiey, *Assyrie chrétienne*, II, p. 490 (the village is 11 km south of Mosul).

[29] On al-ʿAṭṭāf and his rebellion, see below.

740s to the 790s, one might conclude that there was something about the political culture of Mosul itself that explains the pattern. It seems that after two generations of urban growth, the city had generated a political dynamic of its own, one driven by a wilful city élite. Of course city élites are as old as cities themselves; nor is there anything new in writing their histories.[30] What makes the Mosuli case worth describing is our source material, which allows us a glimpse of local politics as the rules of imperial–provincial relations were being written. In other words, even if courting Umayyad rebels, repudiating an Abbasid candidate and raising the standard of rebellion do not add up to bids for provincial independence on the part of the Mosulis, they certainly reflect an ambivalence about what precisely the terms of caliphal–provincial relations should be: the 'politics of notables' would come to Mosul, but it did not come naturally.[31] It thus remains to say something more about the city's élite and its relations with the caliphate in the decades following the massacre.

The city élite and its politics

When the Marwānids came to Mosul, they came to a Kufan garrison that had lain outside a Sufyānid sphere of influence radiating east from Syria; a Kufan *appanage* where social power seems to have been held by conqueror families with lingering Kufan ties, the settlement had yet to acquire any distinct political meaning, nor its settlers any clear identity as Mosulis. In appropriating Mosul, both literally (purchasing land and appointing kinsmen as governors) and symbolically (building and consuming in kingly fashion), the Marwānids began to lodge the emerging city into a network of family and, as imperial institutions came to take hold, state interests too: as al-Azdī's chronicle tells us, by Hishām's reign it had become conventional that some proportion of Mosuli revenue be sent to Syria; and although it is impossible to measure how much reached the caliph, that any did at all was only possible because of a nascent bureaucracy. In building and investing on such a scale, the Marwānids thus tapped into the site's economic potential, and this, in turn, set in motion forces towards a political parochialism well suited to the city's liminal position on the northern edge of settled Iraq. Indeed, it was on a balance of provincial revenues that the city élite seems to have measured the competing possibilities of rebellion and loyalty.

By the second third of the eighth century, Mosul had developed a political culture of its own; to be a Mosuli now meant something. The best example is the Umayyad family of Yūsuf b. Yaḥyā b. al-Ḥakam; it illustrates how, over the course of two generations of urban growth, Syrian kinsmen loyal to the ruling house could devolve into Mosuli provincials. Yūsuf himself served as

[30] For useful comments on urbanism in the Near East, see M. Bonine, 'From Uruk to Casablanca: perspectives on the urban experience of the Middle East', *Journal of Urban History* 3 (1977), pp. 141–80.

[31] On these, see B. Shoshan, 'The "Politics of Notables" in medieval Islam', *Asian and African Studies* 20 (1986), pp. 179–215.

governor during at least part of ʿAbd al-Malik's reign (65–85/685–705), his son al-Ḥurr from about 108 to 113 (727–32), and his grandson Yaḥyā b. al-Ḥurr for a short time in 113 or 114 (732), before the appointment of al-Walīd b. Talīd.[32] Yaḥyā seems to have inherited his father's authority in the city, and probably never received a caliphal appointment; when al-Walīd arrived, he stepped down without resisting.[33] As al-Azdī puts it, 'al-Ḥurr b. Yūsuf's governorship of Mosul for Hishām, the length of his tenure, that *al-Manqūsha* was his dwelling, his descendants, clients, and estates – [all] this is well known and widely acknowledged'.[34] The family's success was in part based on its ties with the Marwānid family, which were tightened through marriage, Āmina bt. Yaḥyā (al-Ḥurr's aunt) and Umm Ḥakīm (his sister) marrying Hishām.[35] But in equal measure their position came to be based on property: al-Ḥurr had built the city's most fabulous Marwānid palace, and at his death his son Yaḥyā is said to have inherited this *qaṣr*, houses (*dūr*), inns (*fanādiq*), and agricultural estates (*ḍiyāʿ*); an area of Mosul bore the name 'al-Ḥurr'.[36]

By the early 750s, al-Ḥurr's family appears to have been more Mosuli than Umayyad. If it is less than surprising that upon his appointment as governor in 134/751 Ismāʿīl b. ʿAlī ordered the execution of Yaḥya b. al-Ḥurr, the anecdote that records the event is striking: it has Ismāʿīl envy Yaḥyā for his continued wealth and flattering retinue. The fate of his properties illustrates how much pull the family retained in the early Abbasid city. Against the wishes of the Mosulis, a *mawlā* of the family appears to have made a claim for ownership, going so far as to marry into the family. At some point, Ismāʿīl himself requested that al-Manṣūr grant him the lands, which he did; but family members then descended upon Baghdad, and they successfully argued that the lands should be returned, a judgment naturally disputed by Ismāʿīl's family.[37] At this point the line between local and imperial interests had become very much blurred: Ismāʿīl was now busy sinking roots of his own, building a mosque, bath and *funduq*; and after his nine-year governorship, these roots were deep enough for him to attempt (in the event, unsuccessfully) to resist

[32] Al-Azdī, *Taʾrīkh*, pp. 24f.; Ibn Ḥazm, *Jamhara*, p. 110; Rotter, 'Fulūs', p. 167.

[33] Thus al-Azdī, *Taʾrīkh*, p. 33, where Yaḥyā is described as *mawlā mā kāna abūhu mawlāhu*; see also Rotter, 'Fulūs', p. 180, note 60. Another son, Salāma (or Salma) b. al-Ḥurr, was a poet of some local reputation and died at the hands of al-Ḍaḥḥāk, while another, ʿUbayd Allāh, fought alongside ʿAbd Allāh b. Marwān b. Muḥammad; see al-Azdī, *Taʾrīkh*, p. 29; Ibn Ḥazm, *Jamhara*, p. 110.

[34] Al-Azdī, *Taʾrīkh*, p. 25.

[35] Al-Azdī, *Taʾrīkh*, p. 24; al-Balādhurī, *Ansāb*, VIb, pp. 2 and 104.

[36] Yāqūt, *Muʿjam*, II, p. 239. Local tradition seems to locate al-Ḥurr's tomb in the mosque of Nabī Jirjis; see the *Guide Book to the Mosul Museum*, p. 9.

[37] Abū Jaʿfar, we are told (al-Azdī, *Taʾrīkh*, p. 157), had known al-Ḥurr during the Umayyad period. The status of these lands remained a muddle until Hārūn's reign, when al-Ḥurr's family was finally dislodged; see also Lassner, *Shaping of ʿAbbāsid Rule*, p. 24; and J. Lassner, 'Did the caliph Abu Jaʿfar al-Manṣur murder his uncle ʿAbdallah b. ʿAli, and other problems within the ruling house of the ʿAbbasids', in Rosen-Ayalon, ed., *Studies in Memory of Gaston Wiet*, p. 75 (where the massacre is explained by the Mosulis' 'residual sympathies to the Umayyad cause'). For other examples of Abbasid confiscations, see Elad, 'Aspects of the transition', pp. 94f.; Lassner, *Shaping of ʿAbbāsid Rule*, p. 256, note 12.

removal, and for a brother and a son to rule after him.[38] To say that Ismāʿīl intended secession in 142/759 would be going too far; but in his family one might fairly detect another example of a dynastic pattern typical of Mosul in the eighth century: al-Walīd b. Talīd had been followed in the governorship by his nephew Abū Quḥāfa (121/739–126/743),[39] much as Yaḥyā and al-Ḥurr had followed Yūsuf b. Yaḥyā al-Ḥakam.

There is no evidence that the Umayyads understood that they bore responsibility for creating the monster of Mosuli restiveness; it was left to the Abbasids to understand that to rule Mosul, one had to patronise the city élite. In the short term, this meant rewarding those Mosulis who had turned on the Umayyads and mending fences with families that had lost members in the massacre; in the long term, it meant putting into place institutions and offices that empowered and implicated local élites in an imperial project. Indeed, insofar as effective empires secure tribute less through outright coercion or force than by nurturing communities of interest, by creating 'habits of obedience' or 'hierarchies of dominance and deference',[40] the Abbasids were as effective as the Marwānids were ineffective. The Mosulis shut their gates on Marwān II not simply because he had been routed by the Abbasids; he was shut out because of a systematic failure on the part of the Marwānids to rule on terms acceptable to the city élite.

A principal short-term beneficiary of Abbasid policy was Wāʾil b. al-Shaḥḥāj, who rallied the people of the city to ʿAbd Allāh b. ʿAlī shortly after his defeat of Marwān II; some of his brothers then joined him in pursuing the last Umayyad.[41] It seems that al-Saffāḥ first granted Wāʾil a *qaṣr* along with a parcel of land, and that three years later, al-Manṣūr added more land adjacent to the first parcel. Both *qaṭīʿa*s were prime real estate, located in the southern outskirts of the city (*bi-rabaḍ madīnat al-Mawṣil al-asfal*); the property, previously owned by Hishām b. ʿAbd al-Malik and members of the Umayyad house after him, had been confiscated as *ṣawāfī* land by the Abbasids.[42] Wāʾil

[38] I.e., ʿAbd al-Ṣamad b. ʿAlī (162–3/778–80) and Aḥmad b. Ismāʿīl b. ʿAlī (c. 165/781) (at the beginning of Ismāʿīl's tenure he was something like thirty-one years old). Aḥmad b. Ismāʿīl enjoyed a very favourable reputation among the people of the city, and of some interest is an account relating the death of the holy man Ibn Wishāḥ al-Mawṣilī. Aḥmad, in his capacity as leader of public worship, officiated at the funeral, and the account suggests a *Fortleben* of Syrian Christian piety: the villagers, we read, took away soil from his tomb, with which they would bless themselves at home (al-Azdī, *Taʾrīkh*, pp. 246f.).

[39] See Forand, 'Governors', p. 91; Rotter, 'Fulūs', pp. 180ff.

[40] I borrow 'habits of obedience' from L. Stone, *The Causes of the English Revolution 1529–1642* (New York, 1972), p. 21 and throughout; and 'hierarchies of dominance and deference' from D. Cannadine and S. Price, eds., *Rituals of Loyalty: Power and Ceremonial in Traditional Societies* (Cambridge, 1987), p. 2. 'Force' and 'power' have been much discussed terms among Romanists (thus J.C. Mann's review of Luttwak, 'Power, force and the frontiers of the Empire,' *Journal of Roman Studies* 69 (1979), pp. 175f.), but surprisingly little has been said on the Islamic side of things.

[41] Al-Azdī, *Taʾrīkh*, pp. 158f.

[42] Al-Azdī, *Taʾrīkh*, pp. 171f. On this meaning of *ṣawāfī*, see the *Glossarium* to al-Ṭabarī, *Taʾrīkh*, s.v. *ṣāfā*, and for a full discussion, M. J. Kister, 'The Battle of Ḥarra: some socio-economic aspects', in Rosen-Ayalon, ed., *Studies in Memory of Gaston Wiet*, pp. 41ff.

b. al-Shaḥḥāj's experience was unexceptional, and forms part of a larger pattern of Abbasid indulgence of a resilient Mosuli élite of notable families. Yaḥyā b. Muḥammad himself was dismissed in 135/752, we are told, because of the massacre and his poor conduct; he was replaced by Ismāʿīl b. ʿAlī, who paid bloodwit to the victims' families and pledged that he would listen to the Mosulis' grievances and treat them well. Two years later he relocated the markets that had been devastated by the massacre, built a new mosque, and, for the entirety of his governorship, retained provincial revenues within Mosul, rather than sending them on to Kufa; in al-Azdī's words, 'people returned to the city and Ismāʿīl improved its condition'.[43] When news of al-Mulabbad's revolt in 137/154 reached al-Manṣūr, he counselled Ismāʿīl to deal gently with the Mosulis: their loyalty, it appears, was still to be bargained for.

The Abbasids curried favour with the city élite not only by granting land and retaining the taxes within the province; they also distributed leading positions within the city's administration. The eponym of the Shaḥḥājī clan, Shaḥḥāj b. Widāʿ al-Azdī, had commanded a force of 2,000 men for Yazīd II against the Khārijite Shawdhab in 101/719–20; an anecdote preserved by Ibn al-ʿAdīm makes it clear that the family already owned lands in the Marwānid period.[44] He died in battle, having left a number of sons, and the unfortunate Waththāq aside, these prospered well beyond the period of the Abbasid Revolution. In 146/763–4, nearly ten years after having received his land grant, Wāʾil appears as the chief of either the *shurṭa* or the *ḥarb*; in 180/796–7, properties were registered in the name of his son ʿIsār; as late as 202/817, grandchildren are mentioned in al-Azdī's *Taʾrīkh*.[45]

Another Mosuli family, the Shurayḥids, also successfully steered their way through the *Sturm und Drang* of the Revolution. Of Shurayḥ b. ʿUmar (ʿAmr) al-Khawlānī, their eponym, we know nothing,[46] but his son Shurayḥ b. Shurayḥ was among those killed in the massacre, and was memorialised in a *rithāʾ* as the Azdis' 'beauty and support, without whom the Qaḥṭān are powerless'.[47] Another son, Bakkār b. Shurayḥ, served as *qāḍī* of the city from 153/769 until his death in 163/779, having appointed his own *locum tenens* in the interim.[48] Another son, al-Muʿāfā b. Shurayḥ, was a prominent city politician and leader

[43] Al-Azdī, *Taʾrīkh*, pp. 156ff.

[44] Al-Ṭabarī, *Taʾrīkh*, II, p. 1376; al-Azdī, *Taʾrīkh*, p. 7. There is some confusion about pointing the name: Ibn Ḥawqal (*Ṣūrat al-arḍ*, p. 216), reads Banī Shakh[kh]āj, and Ibn al-ʿAdīm (*Bughya*, p. 4187), no doubt following Ibn ʿAsākir (*Taʾrīkh madīnat Dimashq*, XX, p. 142), Saḥāj al-Mawṣilī. [45] Al-Azdī, *Taʾrīkh*, pp. 197, 289, 339f., 346 and 348.

[46] Nor can we be sure about the identity of the father. One candidate is the Hamdānī Shīʿite ʿAmr b. Salama (d. 85/704; see al-Ṭabarī, *Taʾrīkh*, III, p. 2524; al-Dhahabī, *Siyar aʿlām al-nubalāʾ*, III, p. 524; Ibn Ḥajar, *Tahdhīb*, VIII, pp. 42ff.; al-Rāzī, *Jarḥ*, V, p. 235). If so, the *nisba* would be geographic rather than tribal, Hamdānī Khawlānīs being far from uncommon (for one example, see al-Samʿānī, *Kitāb al-Ansāb* (Hyderabad, 1982), V, p. 235). Of course, the Azd–Hamdān rivalry argues against this ʿAmr, and other candidates are the Kufan *qāḍī* ʿAmr b. Salama (Abū Qurra), and the notable of al-Ḥajjāj's time (ʿAmr b. Salama); see Ibn al-Kalbī, *Ǧamhara*, II, p. 183. [47] Al-Azdī, *Taʾrīkh*, p. 153.

[48] Namely, ʿAbd al-Ḥamīd b. Abī Rabāḥ; on Bakkār's tenure, see the *Taʾrīkh*, pp. 217ff.

in the *ʿaṣabiyyāt* of the late second century.[49] Several grandsons seem to have withdrawn from politics into the world of scholarship, some providing al-Azdī with invaluable accounts about Mosuli politics in the late second and early third centuries.[50] This is not the only Mosuli family that understood that scholarship was one of the best ways to retain élite status in an Abbasid commonwealth of learning.

While al-Manṣūr was patronising the city élite, his governors were trying to insinuate themselves into it. We have already seen that Ismāʿīl b. ʿAlī sank roots in the city, and so too did Hishām b. ʿAmr, who served as the last Umayyad governor of the town, had a second term under the Abbasids, and after whose brother a *qaṣr* was named.[51] Another example is provided by Mūsā b. Muṣʿab, who is not infrequently confused in the sources with another Mūsā with experience in the north (and Egypt too), Mūsā b. Kaʿb.[52] The confusion is understandable: Mūsā b. Kaʿb enjoyed a celebrated Abbasid pedigree, while Mūsā b. Muṣʿab possessed only local (if spectacular) infamy among Syriac communities: the author of the *Zuqnin Chronicle*, who describes Mūsā's rapacious taxing, goes as far as to identify him as the fulfilment of prophecy in Proverbs and as the anti-Christ,[53] while others appeal to another venerable *topos*, branding him a Jew.[54] Mūsā's murky background may also have contributed to the confusion: we have only a vague report about his family's origins in Palestine, along with a somewhat more sure account regarding his father's experience as

[49] See the *Taʾrīkh*, pp. 217, 222, 224ff., 229, 232, 237, 242, 244 (Bakkār); and 227, 249, 276, 286, 296, and 345 (Muʿāfā).

[50] See al-Azdī, *Taʾrīkh*, pp. 126 and 132 (Muḥammad b. al-Muʿāfā), 276 (ʿAbd al-Ṣamad b. al-Muʿāfā), and 286 (Aḥmad b. al-Muʿāfā).

[51] See al-Azdī, *Taʾrīkh*, p. 76. Al-Azdī says nothing of Hishām's Abbasid role in the city, which is attested only in the copper coinage of 145/762 (*ʿāmil al-amīr Jaʿfar b. amīr al-muʾminīn*); see Rotter, 'Fulūs', pp. 196f.; Lavoix, *Catalogue des monnaies musulmanes*, p. 459 (1629); Tübingen AM2 D5, AM2 D6 and AM2 E1 (I am indebted to S. Album for sharing his Tübingen list); Lowick, *Early ʿAbbāsid Coinage*, p. 331; cf. American Numismatic Society (hereafter ANS) 1971.316.203. Year 145 produced several issues in Mosul. On Hishām's Abbasid career, see Crone, *Slaves*, pp. 167f.

[52] A Tamīmī *naqīb* who fought under ʿAbd Allāh b. ʿAlī at the Zāb, and garrisoned at Ḥarrān with a force of 3,000 men, served as the first governor of the Jazira; see al-Azdī, *Taʾrīkh*, pp. 26, 128f., 248 and 253; Khalīfa b. Khayyāṭ, *Taʾrīkh*, pp. 263 and 271ff.; al-Ṭabarī, *Taʾrīkh*, III, pp. 39, 56 and 521; al-Kindī, *Kitāb al-umarāʾ wa-kitāb al-quḍāh* (Leiden and London, 1912), pp. 106ff.; al-Balādhurī, *Ansāb*, III. I follow here Crone (*Slaves*, p. 186), who sees only one Mūsā b. Kaʿb, unlike Cahen ('Fiscalité', p. 137 note 7) and Forand ('Governors', p. 94), who distinguish between two. Al-Azdī's Mūsā b. Kaʿb (unattested numismatically) is a mistake for Mūsā b. Muṣʿab.

[53] *Zuqnin Chronicle*, pp. 252f./198.

[54] The idea first appears in the *Chronicle of 813* (ed. and trans. E. W. Brooks as *Fragmenta chronici anonymi auctoris ad annum domini 813 pertinentia* (Louvain, 1905–7; *Chronica Minora* III of *CSCO* 5–6, pp. 248/188); see also the *Chronicle of 819*, I, pp. 20/14; the *Chronicle of 846*, pp. 248/188; and Michael the Syrian, *Chronique*, xi.xxvi. It eventually crossed over into the secondary literature, both European (Hage, *Kirche*, p. 74; Fiey, *Mossoul*, p. 24; Fiey, *Chrétiens syriaques*, p. 25, where he more guardedly cites Michael the Syrian), and Arab (ʿUmar, *al-ʿAbbāsiyyūn*, II, p. 171). Cf. Paul 'the Jew', the fourth-century Chalcedonian patriarch of Antioch who was guilty of overtaxing too (Michael the Syrian, *Chronique*, ix.xvi). For some background, see Olster, *Roman Defeat, Christian Response, and the Literary Construction of the Jew*.

a pragmatic secretary of Marwān II. After the defeat of the last Umayyad, Muṣʿab is said to have secured a pardon from ʿAbd Allāh b. ʿAlī, and thus began an unrecorded but speedy social climb: his son Mūsā is counted as the suckling brother of al-Mahdī.[55]

Appointed governor of a unified north by about 769, Mūsā set to taxing the region with exceptional zeal, a project whose devastating effects are recorded by Christian historians in lugubrious detail. There can be no doubt that many of these were serious indeed, particularly when combined with famine;[56] even so, for all its dreadful details, the *Zuqnin Chronicle*'s striking portrait of Mūsā tells something less than a full story. For one thing, compared to the Umayyad precedent, a harsh taxation regime was probably as old as Abbasid rule itself;[57] for another, while the *Zuqnin Chronicle* has Mūsā do the caliph's dirty work, he was almost continually in and out of Abbasid hot water, and this precisely because he was given to lining his own pocket with the region's taxes.[58] It may be that his role in Monophysite/Nestorian competition for favour, as much as his enthusiasm for taxing, explains why he was vilified in the Monophysite tradition. For if, according to the *Zuqnin Chronicle*, he turned away delegation after delegation of West Syrians seeking relief, we read in a Nestorian source that Mūsā's secretary, one Abū Nūḥ al-Anbārī, favoured the 'Christians' (*naṣārā*: read Nestorians), and exempted Timothy from tribute;[59] similarly, reports of Monophysite persecution under al-Mahdī contrast sharply with Ḥnānīshōʿ's generous comment in a document written in 775.[60]

Whatever his attitude towards the Monophysites, Mūsā ruled the unified north from the east; a large issue of copper coins puts him in Balad in 155/771–2,[61] and the literary testimony puts him seven *farsakh*s away in

[55] See al-Ṭabarī, *Taʾrīkh*, III, p. 46; al-Azdī, *Taʾrīkh*, pp. 126 and 225f. (Mūsā b. Muṣʿab b. Sufyān b. Rabīʿa); and Crone, *Slaves*, p. 193. In Mālik b. ʿAbd Allāh al-Khathʿamī (al-Balādhurī, *Futūḥ*, p. 191), we have another northern Khathʿamī with roots in Palestine. One expressed even the most modest sympathy with the Umayyads at great peril in the north; thus Harthama b. Aʿyan was taken to task for referring to Umayyad caliphs as 'leaders' (*aʾimma*; al-Azdī, *Taʾrīkh*, p. 252), but Umayyad origins among Abbasid bureaucrats were not at all rare (see Elad, 'Aspects of the transition', pp. 113f.).

[56] For a discussion of the evidence from the *Zuqnin Chronicle* (index, s.v. 'Moïse Bar Muṣʿab'), see Cahen, 'Fiscalité'.

[57] See, for examples, Michael the Syrian, *Chronique*, xi.xxv; Agapius, *Kitāb al-ʿUnwān*, p. 546; Bar Hebraeus, *Chronicon syriacum*, pp. 124f. (=Budge, *Chronography*, p. 115); Elias of Nisibis, *Opus chronologicum*, p. 181.

[58] Thus he was arrested and dismissed on more than one occasion, and his move from Mosul to Egypt came on the heels of new charges of tax irregularities; see the accounts in al-Azdī, *Taʾrīkh*, pp. 224, 227 and 248f.; cf. al-Ṭabarī, *Taʾrīkh*, III, p. 381.

[59] The passage mistakenly reads 'Abū Mūsā b. Muṣʿab'; see Mārī b. Sulaymān, *Kitāb al-Majdal*, p. 71. On Abū Nūḥ, see G. Graf, *Geschichte der christlichen arabischen Literatur*, II (The Vatican, 1947), p. 118.

[60] For an overview of the West Syrian sources, see Fiey, *Mossoul*, p. 24; Fiey, *Chrétiens syriaques*, pp. 26ff. and 34f.; and S. Moscati, 'Nuovi studi storici sul califfato di al-Mahdī', *Orientalia* n.s. 15 (1946), pp. 167ff.; for Ḥnānīshōʿ, see Chabot, ed., *Synodicon Orientale*, p. 245/516.

[61] See Lavoix, *Catalogue des monnaies musulmanes*, p. 425 (1564); Tübingen AL4 A2; ANS 1917.216.10 and 1980.106.2; and Lowick, *Early ʿAbbāsid Coinage*, p. 329.

Mosul, where his principal concern must have been the city's élite: not only was he an agent of the caliphate, he also owned an estate that had to be looked after.[62] There too he was caught up in confessional squabbles, these between Monophysites and Muslims over church construction; he sided with the Muslims.[63] In addition to renovating the city's congregational mosque, he adorned Mosul with a mosque that took his name.[64] Decisions such as these might be taken as signals of good will to the city's religious establishment;[65] what is clearer is that Mūsā was saddled with his singularly unpopular Khathʿamī kinship, and this he tried to overcome by marriage and patronage. Thus he married his daughter to the notable al-Muʿāfā b. Shurayḥ, and employed so many local Khawlānī Yamanīs that he acquired their *nisba*; in fact, when he was transferred to the governorship of Egypt (where he was just as unpopular), a coterie of 1,000 Mosulis is said to have followed him in tow, so dependent were they on his patronage.[66]

Caliphs and governors alike were thus accommodating to the Mosulis, and here it bears repeating that the parties negotiating the city's position in the empire were three (caliphs, governors and city élite), rather than two (the state and the city élite); the experience of Ismāʿīl b. ʿAlī is enough to show that governors and caliphs were occasionally at odds with each other, and that from their rivalries the city folk stood to profit. Governors' horizons were presumably low and short term; as far as the caliphs were concerned, the long-term future clearly lay in a political symbiosis between province and empire, one in which local élites had a role to play.

In the case of Mosul, the pattern is signalled not only by the experience of notable families and governors, but by institutional evidence, namely, the *rawābiṭ* (militia) and the *qāḍī* (city judge). Both institutions appeared during the reign of al-Manṣūr, when efforts to mend local fences were at their keenest. For the Mosulis who occupied them, these positions offered local status, access to caliphal benefits and (occasionally) a crucial role in city politics. For the caliphs, the offices functioned as channels for the flow of patronage and favour (from Baghdad to Mosul), as well as of information (from Mosul to Baghdad or Kufa) about local affairs, in this case especially valuable when it was independent of the governors. The two institutions also seem to have ensured some continuity amidst the fairly regular circulation of these governors; a short term of office was the price they paid for Ismāʿīl b. ʿAlī's audacity in 142/759.

The caliphs generally ruled with a light hand, coercive power coming into play in eighth-century Mosul for a handful of purposes: levying taxes in the hinter-

62 See the account in al-Azdī, *Taʾrīkh*, pp. 248f.

63 For the account, see chapter 1.

64 The renovation of the congregational mosque was recorded in an inscription that al-Azdī read, and the new mosque was apparently frequented by our historian; see the *Taʾrīkh*, pp. 147, 225 and 248.

65 Certainly al-Walīd's building and investment in Umayyad Syria are said to have endeared him to the Syrians (thus de Goeje and de Jong, eds., *Fragmenta*, p. 11).

66 Al-Azdī, *Taʾrīkh*, pp. 249 and 253; and on Mūsā's tenure in Egypt, al-Kindī, *Kitāb al-umarāʾ*, esp. pp. 134ff.

land required the occasional show of force, and as far as the pastoralists were concerned, its more frequent exercise as well; public order within the city had to be maintained; Khārijites also had to be held in check, since they could threaten the rural *kharāj*. According to al-Azdī's entry for the year 145/762, the first two of these responsibilities lay in the hands of the governor, the third in the hands of the chief of the *rawābiṭ*, a term denoting precisely the fast-moving, mounted force required on the steppe, and one which local tribesmen could most effectively provide:[67] 'It was the custom (*rasm*) that in Mosul there be a governor (*wālī*) who had sole authority over public worship (*ṣalāt*), policing (*maʿūna*) and collecting the land tax (provided the latter was added to his duties), and a chief of the *rawābiṭ*), who alone was responsible for battling the Khārijites. According to some, he was under the command of the governor.'[68] Responsibilities and loyalties were predictably more elastic than al-Azdī's prescription would suggest: the chief of the *rawābiṭ* could reappear as the chief of the *shurṭa*, and he was sometimes charged with collecting the pastoralists' tribute (*ṣadaqāt*).[69]

Although its origins are less than clear,[70] by 142/759 the *rawābiṭ* had been established in Mosul, now under the leadership of Ibn Mishkān; he is said to have led a force of 2,000, and its size seems to have grown over time.[71] Foreigners (such as Ḥarb b. ʿAbd Allāh al-Rāwandī) might occupy the leadership,[72] but just as frequently it fell to locals such as al-Ṣaqr b. Najda al-Azdī and Rawḥ b. Ḥātim b. Ṣāliḥ al-Hamdānī; Wāʾil b. al-Shaḥḥāj, described as the chief of the *shurṭa*, may qualify here as well.[73] As we have already seen, Wāʾil was favoured by al-Manṣūr, while Rawḥ belonged to a Hamdānī family that would vie with the Azd for leadership in the city during Hārūn's reign.[74]

67 The term (in both the singular and plural) appears earlier, in connection with Marwān II (al-Ṭabarī, *Taʾrīkh*, II, p. 1945: 30,000 (!) *rawābiṭ* sent to reinforce Ibn Dubāra, who was battling Shaybān b. ʿAbd al-ʿAzīz) and al-Manṣūr (al-Balādhurī, *Futūḥ*, pp. 209f.: a *rābiṭa*, here composed of men on the *dīwān*, is stationed in Bāb al-Lān). For a minimalist definition, see al-Khawārizmī, *Mafātīḥ al-ʿulūm* (Leiden, 1895), p. 119 ('bedouins who possess riding animals'); see also Kennedy, 'Central government', pp. 30f. (who was the first to discern their significance in local politics).

68 Al-Azdī, *Taʾrīkh*, p. 195. The enumeration seems to correspond to the relatively simple Umayyad pattern (thus al-Walīd b. Talīd, who is put in charge of *ṣalāt*, *aḥdāth* and *kharāj*) rather than to the increasingly differentiated Abbasid one; for an example of a tripartite division of responsibilities (Ḥamza b. Mālik al-Khuzāʿī over the *ḥarb* and *ṣalāt*, Manṣūr b. Ziyād over the *kharāj* and *ṣadaqāt*, and Abū Nuʿaym over the *rawābiṭ*), see al-Azdī, *Taʾrīkh*, pp. 257f.

69 See al-Azdī, *Taʾrīkh*, pp. 194ff. (Ḥarb b. ʿAbd Allāh in charge of the *rawābiṭ* and *shurṭa*), and 268 (the Hamdānī Rawḥ b. Ḥātim b. Ṣāliḥ, following the editor's suggestion at note 2, often called the chief of the *rawābiṭ*, collects the pastoralists' tribute); cf. also Ibn al-Athīr, *al-Kāmil*, VI, p. 113.

70 They appear already by the time of al-Mulabbad's rebellion; see al-Balādhurī, *Ansāb*, III, p. 249 (where Ismāʿīl is appointed governor of Mosul and sends an unidentified commander leading the *rābiṭat al-Mawṣil* against al-Mulabbad); cf. al-Ṭabarī, *Taʾrīkh*, III, p. 120 (Jaziran *rawābiṭ* are dispatched against al-Mulabbad), and al-Azdī, *Taʾrīkh*, p. 166 (who supplies Ibn Mishkān's name, cryptically adding that Ibn Mishkān *kāna ʿāmil ʿalā al-Jazīra aw baʿḍihā*).

71 Al-Azdī, *Taʾrīkh*, pp. 177 and 194 (2,000) and 268 (4,000).

72 Al-Azdī, *Taʾrīkh*, pp. 194f.

73 Al-Azdī, *Taʾrīkh*, pp. 177, 197, 203 and 268.

74 The scion of the family was Ḥātim b. Ṣāliḥ; his brother (Ḥasan), son (Rawḥ) and nephew (al-Ḥusayn b. al-Zubayr) all played parts in the city's history; see al-Azdī, *Taʾrīkh*, s.vv.

Al-Ṣaqr b. Najda also belonged to a prominent family, producing two sons of note; one composed poetry, while the other transmitted historical material to al-Azdī, at least once on his father's authority.[75] As a Mosuli, the chief of the local militia possessed some leverage in the balance of local and imperial politics: the army garrisoned in the city (usually called the *ḥarb*) went on far-flung campaigns,[76] and was in any case ultimately dependent on the caliph for its pay; but this militia rarely strayed too far and, loyal (one presumes) to the patronage of its chief,[77] it could provide decisive support. An illustration appears in Ismāʿīl b. ʿAlī's ill-fated attempt to resist dismissal in favour of Mālik b. al-Haytham al-Khuzāʿī, dated by al-Azdī in 142/759. It seems that Ismāʿīl tried to enlist the support of the Tamīmī Ibn Mishkān, the chief of the *rawābiṭ*, at this point said to be 2,000 men strong; but al-Manṣūr, having caught wind of the plan, called on the latter's loyalty, and Ismāʿīl's support quickly disintegrated.[78] To be the chief of the *rawābiṭ* could thus mean being a king-maker; occasionally it led to the governorship. The career path may be signalled as early as 114/732, when al-Walīd b. Talīd, Muḥammad b. Marwān's *ṣāḥib shurṭa*, became governor. There is no clear evidence that Rawḥ b. Ḥātim also served as governor, although his cousin ʿAlī b. al-Ḥasan came to rule the city during the civil war between al-Amīn and al-Maʾmūn; but there is clear evidence that al-Ṣaqr b. Najda did, since his name appears on several (undated) copper coins. They appear to demonstrate that *de jure* authority could devolve to locals well before the civil war, when Abbasid authority had effectively collapsed, leaving power in the hands of local chieftains.[79]

If appointing the commander of the *rawābiṭ* was a bone of contention between the caliph and the governor, appointing the *qāḍī* seems to have remained the prerogative of the caliph alone. Whereas local figures often appear in the leadership of the *rawābiṭ*, the position of the *qāḍī* they fill as a general rule. The arrangement suggests that the power of patronage was too potent for the caliphs to leave to the governors; it also suited the *qāḍī*s (and the local élite whom they so frequently represented) because it gave them access to Baghdad, while it insulated them from the consequences of the relatively frequent turnover amongst the governors. Traces of the procedure appear frequently enough, such as when complaints about ʿAbd Allāh b. Khalīl were

75 See al-Azdī, *Taʾrīkh*, pp. 70, 84, 129, 327 and 395.

76 An example is Ḥarb b. ʿAbd Allāh, who died fighting the Khazars in 147/764 (al-Azdī, *Taʾrīkh*, p. 201).

77 Nowhere are we told how its members were paid, but from what we know elsewhere (Løkkegaard, *Islamic Taxation*, p. 187), one might infer that the *maʿūna* was supported by local levies.

78 See al-Azdī, *Taʾrīkh*, pp. 177f.

79 See ANS 0000.999.5396 and 1949.163.43; Tübingen AM2 F2; Lavoix, *Catalogue des monnaies musulmanes*, p. 462 (1635); H. Nützel, *Katalog der orientalischen Münzen* (Berlin, 1898–1902), I, p. 369 (2265 and 2266). One can speculate that he governed in 152/769, a year for which al-Azdī (and, following him, Ibn al-Athīr) is silent. It was presumably through a process of elimination that E. von Zambaur (*Manuel de généalogie et de chronologie pour l'histoire de l'Islam* (Hanover, 1927), p. 36) arrived at year 147.

taken directly to Hārūn in 188/804.[80] In Mosul, as elsewhere, we find that familiar confluence of property and education that produced long-lived dynasties of learning in many Islamic cities;[81] and, to judge by the very frequent appearance of Mosuli *qāḍīs* as *ḥadīth* transmitters, the office had something of a role to play in the nascent *ḥadīth* industry of the second-century town.[82]

The evidence regarding the *qāḍīs*' responsibilities once again shows that al-Azdī's description of the city's administration in 145/762 is schematic at best, because two years later the fisc was in the *qāḍī*'s, rather than the governor's, hands.[83] No doubt this is why the *qāḍī* in question, al-Ḥārith b. Jārūd, came into possession of correspondence between al-Manṣūr and the city's governor Ismāʿīl b. ʿAbd Allāh al-Qasrī, the latter now in charge of the *kharāj*; the caliph's letter is clearly based on detailed knowledge of city affairs, and describes what appears to have been widespread corruption.[84] *Qāḍīs* with fiscal expertise (and tax records to hand) must have given pause to governors inclined towards embezzling; *qāḍīs* appointed by caliphs certainly ensured some stability in the administration of the city, since they generally served much longer terms than the governors. While a local notable such as Bakkār b. Shurayḥ served two terms as *qāḍī* over approximately ten years, Mosul had no fewer than six governors; a governor might be forced from office, but the *qāḍī* remained in place.[85] The conspicuous exception to the pattern is supplied by Ismāʿīl b. Ziyād al-Duʾalī, who, implicated in the rebellion of al-ʿAṭṭāf b. Sufyān, was dismissed in 180/796: appointed by the caliph, his sympathies still lay with the townspeople.[86]

[80] Al-Azdī, *Taʾrīkh*, p. 306; on Mosuli *qāḍīs*, see also Kennedy ('Central government', pp. 29ff.), and Juynboll, *Muslim Tradition*, p. 231 (for a partial list).

[81] Examples are Maʿmar b. Muḥammad, the forefather of a distinguished jurist, Bakkār b. Shurayḥ of a Shurayḥid family that produced at least four *ḥadīth* transmitters, al-Ḥārith b. Jārūd, eponym of the Banū Jārūd and, finally, the family of al-Muʿāfā b. ʿImrān. Cf. the case of Nishapur in Bulliet, *Patricians*, pp. 64f.

[82] Probably the best examples are those of Abū Faḍl al-Anṣārī (see above, chapter 6, note 72), and al-Ḥasan b. Mūsā al-Ashyab (above, chapter 1, note 60), but see also ʿAbd Allāh b. Kurz al-Fihrī in al-Dhahabī, *Taʾrīkh al-Islām* (Beirut, 1990), XI, p. 216 (which has further bibliography).

[83] Al-Azdī, *Taʾrīkh*, pp. 199 and 202. On the many hats worn by early *qāḍīs*, see D. G. Dannhauer, *Untersuchungen zur frühen Geschichte des Qāḍī-amtes* (Bonn, 1975), pp. 36ff.; and I. Bligh-Abramski, 'The judiciary (*Qāḍīs*) as a governmental-administrative tool in early Islam', *JESHO* 35 (1992), pp. 43ff.

[84] It also reflects a fiscal administration consisting of tax agents (*ʿummāl*), scribes, 'assistants' (*aʿwān*; cf. al-Ṭabarī, *Taʾrīkh*, II, p. 1732), and officials who confirmed the fineness of the coinage given in payment (*qasāṭīr*); see al-Azdī, *Taʾrīkh*, pp. 214f.; and on Ismāʿīl and his family, Crone, *Slaves*, pp. 102f.

[85] For two very different examples (Maʿmar b. Muḥammad and al-Ḥasan b. Mūsā al-Ashyab), see al-Azdī, *Taʾrīkh*, index; and Kennedy, 'Central government', p. 29. The stability of the post of the *qāḍī* in the midst of political tumult is certainly not unique to Mosul; for a later example, see R. Mottahedeh, 'Administration in Būyid Qazwīn', in D. S. Richards, ed., *Islamic Civilization 950–1150* (Oxford, 1973), pp. 35f.

[86] Thus al-Azdī's *Taʾrīkh*, pp. 274 and 288; Kennedy's view that none of the city's *qāḍīs* was dismissed 'for obviously political reasons' ('Central government', p. 29) must be qualified accordingly. Ismāʿīl's high regard in the city – he is called 'ascetically inclined, of good character' – contrasts with his sorry academic reputation outside it (see Juynboll, *Muslim Tradition*, p. 231).

In fact, al-ʿAṭṭāf's rebellion marks the end of a century-long pattern of Mosuli politics; it reflects the continued restiveness of the Mosuli élite on the one hand, and the ultimate success of the Abbasids' accommodating policies on the other. As an Azdī tribesman, land owner and commander of some repute, al-ʿAṭṭāf was no doubt a member of that élite, in the eyes of the Mosulis less a rebel than a local politician cobbling together a coalition.[87] In addition to the *qāḍī*, Ismāʿīl b. Ziyād al-Duʾalī, this coalition included al-Muʿāfā b. Shurayḥ, the son of Shurayḥ b. Shurayḥ (massacre victim), brother of Bakkār b. Shurayḥ (former *qāḍī*), and son-in-law of Mūsā b. Muṣʿab, along with two land owners, Bīrawayh and Muntaṣir, who were expressly excluded from the general amnesty called by Hārūn: thousand-dīnār bounties were put on their heads, and their lands, along with al-ʿAṭṭāf's, were confiscated. The 'rebellion', which lasted perhaps as long as two years, apparently featured no violence worthy of note: the governor, who at this point was either Muḥammad b. al-ʿAbbās or ʿAbd al-Malik b. Ṣāliḥ, was simply pushed aside, al-ʿAṭṭāf usurping all effective authority. In al-Azdī's words, 'he was in control of everything' (*ghālib ʿalā al-amr kullihi*), by which we should understand all the powers invested by the caliph in his governors.[88]

More light is shed on the movement by the accounts of Hārūn's reimposition of direct control over the city. Al-ʿAṭṭāf, leading a force of 4,000 men, marched first to the town of Marj Juhayna,[89] whereupon the town's *shuyūkh* and *ʿulamāʾ* requested that he continue on; Hārūn himself marched to al-Ḥadītha, which lay on the opposite (eastern) side of the Tigris. Al-ʿAṭṭāf then turned tail for Armenia, which left the Mosulis desperately vulnerable to the caliph, who had sworn in the meantime to kill every Mosuli he set eyes on. The Mosulis acted quickly to avert disaster, sending a delegation to meet the caliph in Marj Juhayna. Its members were apparently chosen with some care, and almost certainly with the knowledge that Abū Yūsuf would represent Hārūn in the negotiations; along with those city worthies (*wujūh*) whom we might expect, it included prominent members of the city's religious establishment (*mā kāna bi-hā min ahl al-ʿilm*), such as Abū al-Faḍl al-Anṣārī, a *faqīh* and traditionist who later served as Hārūn's *qāḍī*, Mūsā b. Muhājir (d. 201/816), who had studied under Sufyān al-Thawrī and Shuʿba b. al-Ḥajjāj, and two other *faqīh*s, Saʿd and ʿAtīq; the latter had studied under Abū Yūsuf himself.[90] The delegation duly met with Abū Yūsuf, who was not only an Anṣārī himself, but an Anṣārī predisposed towards the Mosulis (*kāna māʾil ilā ahl al-Mawṣil*); after convincing Hārūn of their deep piety, he concocted an ingenious *ḥīla* in order to extricate the caliph from his oath.

[87] Thus al-Azdī (*Taʾrīkh*, pp. 279f.) has him 'form an alliance' (*taḥālafa*), which Ibn al-Athīr (*al-Kāmil*, VI, p. 140, dated a year later), writing in a very different time, construes as 'rebel' (*khālafa*); cf. al-Balādhurī, *Futūḥ*, p. 332; al-Dīnawarī, *Akhbār*, p. 386; Forand, 'Governors', pp. 96f. [88] Al-Azdī, *Taʾrīkh*, p. 280. [89] See Fiey, *Assyrie chrétienne*, I, p. 227.

[90] For the account, see al-Azdī, *Taʾrīkh*, pp. 284ff. On Mūsā, see the *Taʾrīkh*, p. 341; and on ʿAtīq, see Ibn Abī al-Wafāʾ, *al-Jawāhir al-muḍiyya* (Cairo, 1979), II, pp. 513f. (here citing al-Azdī's *Ṭabaqāt*).

The story is typical Abū Yūsuf, who was notorious for his *ḥiyal*; still, there can be no doubt that the Mosulis pulled all available strings, in this case academic strings that intertwined Mosuli and Kufan learning. The Mosulis lost their city walls – according to one report, amnesty was granted to all those who razed sections of the wall adjacent to their homes, while another says that the caliph undertook the demolition himself – but apparently little else. Among the ringleaders, only al-Muʿāfā b. Shurayḥ was caught, and even he managed to secure favourable terms by requesting the intervention of 'those Yamanī tribesmen (*al-Yamaniyya*) who were with him [i.e. Hārūn]', here identified as al-Ḥasan b. Qaḥṭaba, ʿAbd Allāh b. Mālik (b. al-Haytham) al-Khuzāʿī, and the brother of this last, Ḥamza. The three could intercede on al-Muʿāfā's behalf because they combined Abbasid credentials with northern connections. Al-Ḥasan had been a deputy *naqīb*, and had campaigned and served as governor in Armenia; his brother Ḥumayd, also a deputy *naqīb*, had served in the Jazira and Mosul.[91] ʿAbd Allāh and Ḥamza were the sons of Mālik b. al-Haytham al-Khuzāʿī, *naqīb* and popular governor of the city 142–45/759–62, and they had served in the city's administration too.[92]

Mosul's walls, built and renovated by the Marwānids, had enclosed and protected a city élite generated by social forces the Marwānids had themselves put into motion by transforming the Kufan garrison into a Umayyad city; as Wickham has said of a political culture that produced even more vigorous civic identities, 'the first thing that defined a city was its walls'.[93] These now had to be razed, having come to symbolise under the Abbasids the city's reluctant integration into the empire.[94] It is difficult to think that the point at issue was anything other than the fate of the provincial revenues that had paid for these walls, local expectations having been formed during the heady days of Hishām's caliphate and al-Ḥurr b. Yūsuf's governorship, when exploding revenues were spent locally. This can explain the city's marriage of convenience with northern Khārijites, who cut revenues off from imperial agents, in addition to the appeal of al-ʿAṭṭāf's programme, which called for ignoring the governor, imprisoning the tax officials and levying taxes anew; it can also explain why retaining local revenues figures in al-Manṣūr's accommodating policies and in the popularity of Ismāʿīl b. ʿAlī, who carried them out. In any case, with the walls levelled, the town was now open not only to the caliphs' armies, but to a new pattern of politics dominated by local pastoralists with city ties,

[91] See al-Azdī, *Taʾrīkh*, p. 117; Khalīfa b. Khayyāṭ, *Taʾrīkh*, p. 285 (governor of the Jazira); Crone, *Slaves*, p. 188.

[92] Ḥamza was in charge of the *ṣalāt* and *ḥarb* of the city in 169/785, and his brother ʿAbd Allāh followed in his footsteps in 173/789; see al-Azdī, *Taʾrīkh*, pp. 258 and 281; Crone, *Slaves*, p. 181. ʿAbd Allāh's son, al-Muṭṭalib, would himself serve as governor in 196/811 (al-Azdī, *Taʾrīkh*, p. 325).

[93] C. Wickham, *Early Medieval Italy: Central Power and Local Society, 400–1000* (Totowa, 1981), p. 82.

[94] Kennedy ('Central government', p. 31) suggests that the *rawābiṭ* were disbanded by Hārūn as well.

rather than city notables proper. Mosul's fate would continue to be determined as much by local forces as imperial ambitions, but these now came from the steppe. Thus, when the caliphate fell into crisis during the civil war between al-Amīn and al-Ma'mūn, a tribal élite dominated by Azdīs and Hamdānīs took direct control, anticipating the Ḥamdānids of a century later. The pattern was striking to al-Azdī himself:

> When imperial authority (*amr al-sulṭān*) weakened, and the protection [it provided] declined, the people of Mosul rallied around ʿAlī b. al-Ḥasan al-Hamdānī so that he would take control of the region and protect its outlying districts (*li-yushrif ʿalā amr al-balad wa-yaḥūṭ aṭrāfahu*). From this time until the passing of the Banū al-Ḥasan, they would admit an appointed governor only if they found him satisfactory, and all the while they remained in control.[95]

ʿAlī b. al-Ḥasan should in no way be taken for a rebel: far from challenging Abbasid authority, tribal figures such as ʿAlī filled a vacuum of effective political power as Abbasid authority collapsed; they negotiated with caliphs and knew the unwritten rules of local politics, according to which the caliphs left the city to its bipolar élite, provided that it professed loyalty to the caliphs. Mosulis would continue to flirt with Khārijites, but a new pattern had emerged.[96]

[95] Al-Azdī, *Taʾrīkh*, p. 324.

[96] For examples, see al-Azdī, *Taʾrīkh*, pp. 343ff.

Conclusion

This has been a book about social power on the periphery of the nascent Islamic state, but whereas much has been said about the periphery, relatively little has been said about the state. It might therefore be useful to conclude by making some general comments about the evolution of the caliphate, particularly those features upon which the history of the north sheds some light.

The point is not simply to redress any perceived imbalance in the literature. For one thing, imperial views have long had their way in the field, leaving local history with a great deal of catching up to do; at best, this is just one instalment in what one might hope to be a larger programme of research. For another (and more important) thing, it is hard to make anything other than a simplistic distinction between local and metropolitan views, for by the time that the provincials began to speak for themselves, they were finding (or had already found) a place in a commonwealth of dynasties: it is not accidental that al-Azdī appears alongside the Ḥamdānids, or that Ibn ʿAbd al-Ḥakam appears alongside the Ṭūlūnids. Nor is it accidental that the normative form of local history writing came to be the biographical dictionary, rather than the annalistic chronicle; for whereas the latter potentially had to handle any number of sensitive issues (e.g. rebellion and heresy), the former offered a retrospective filiation of learning that tied province to metropolis, and anchored regional forms of classical Sunnism to the wellspring of the Prophet himself.

Local historians are of course distinctive and invaluable; much of the present book is unthinkable in the absence of al-Azdī's book. But even an annalistic work such as al-Azdī's says almost as much about the Abbasids' enormous success in establishing a commonwealth of culture, learning and politics as it does about local affairs.[1] When al-Azdī describes the negotiations and aftermath of al-ʿAṭṭāf b. Sufyān's rebellion, he records not only the final episode of old-style Mosuli rebelliousness, but how this great Abbasid success played out in his native city: as (caliphally appointed) *qāḍī*, writing in the (Iraqi-generated) genre of annalistic history under the (caliphally sanctioned) Ḥamdānids, he records how the Mosulis secured clemency by appealing to

[1] For a very different evaluation of local historiography, see Bulliet, *View*, p. 10.

familiar members of the Abbasid legal and military élite, individuals under whom they had studied and served. Administration and the expectation that taxes were to be sent to Baghdad made Mosul part of the Abbasid empire; but no less important in tying province to capital was a network of learning, which emerged during the second century as the study of *ḥadīth* began to crystallise. The caliphs and *ʿulamāʾ* may frequently have disagreed, but in the long run the relation was symbiotic: it is hard to see how caliphal law could have provided as effective an integrating force for the empire as the catholic *sharīʿa*, based as it was upon the personal transmission of a finite body of knowledge and a uniform set of skills. The politics of Sībawayhī's grammar are unmistakably Abbasid;[2] local history writing reflects the robustness of the Abbasid commonwealth as much as it records it.

The Abbasids thus overcame Umayyad regionalism by establishing an imperial administration and by fostering the *sharīʿa* too; but this is the end of the story. A wilful Mosuli élite had been born as the Marwānids transformed the garrison into a city, purchasing land, investing in infrastructure, and safeguarding their investments by appointing kinsmen to the governorship; a recognisable politics of notables had emerged after the massacre, as the Abbasids came to terms with the doggedly local character of social power. Both stages are secondary, reflecting an imperialist's understanding of the land and its usufruct. Early Islamic history was determined as much by the consequences of the conquests as the opportunities they presented. The Sufyānids had sat atop what was a very loose tributary state; theirs was a conquest machine only slowly running down, and it took the catastrophe of the Second Fitna (683–92) to persuade those born outside Arabia – many of whom had first matured in the midst of the First Fitna – that ruling the Fertile Crescent meant abandoning the Arab kinship state that had formed in the wake of the conquests. For in social terms, Islam seems to have meant *jihād* and conquest led by commanders and caliphs, themselves instruments of God's providential will; as such, it was a language of political integration spoken from above, and whatever Muḥammad's understanding, those following him thought it restricted to the highest social register – Arab tribesmen.

The exclusivity and insularity of the ruling élite determined a great deal of first-century history. The state apparatus remained in Arabia and Arabised Syria, while outside its social boundaries were reinforced and institutionalised: only reluctantly did garrisons yield to garrison cities, and these, divided into tribal *khiṭaṭ*, were intended to exclude non-Arabs, to recreate in microcosm tribal arabias in subject lands, and to give physical expression in the provinces to the *dīwān*, the depository of non-Arab revenues to which only (Arab) tribesmen-soldiers had access; in urbanism as such, early Muslims evinced little interest. In a political arena as circumscribed as this, the right to

[2] Cf. R. Kraster, *Guardians of Language: The Grammarian and Society in Late Antiquity* (Berkeley and Los Angeles, 1988).

rule seems to have been a claim of paternalistic authority rather than lordship over the land, and it was expressed in gestures rather than grand spectacles.[3] *Bayʿa*s and *waṣīya*s could be elaborate,[4] but as a rule they were on a small scale, and in this they reflect not only their origins amongst Arabian and Syrian tribesmen, but also the (largely) peripatetic life of caliphs circulating amongst the *ashrāf*. When Marwānid princes built themselves palaces and hunting lodges, they deposited for us archaeological evidence of a striking cultural fusion at work in the early eighth century; but through it all, they seem to have kept their reception halls small and their aversion to city life intact.

So Sufyānid attitudes did not disappear with ʿAbd al-Malik. The so-called 'fiscal rescript' of ʿUmar II (r. 717–20), for example, documents the élite's continuing anxiety about the political consequences of assimilation and conversion.[5] But in other respects Marwānid change was fundamental and far-reaching. Most important, political discourse now came to be directed at the non-Muslim subjects of an emerging territorial state, the Dome of the Rock providing what is certainly the most impressive example: one does not erect a building as glorious and assertive as this simply to accommodate local pilgrims. Whatever its efficacy, the iconography of early Marwānid coinage, which was the subject of intense experimentation from around 72–7, must have been similarly intended not only for the inspection of the Arab élite, but also for the hands of at least some of its subjects; suppressing images emblematic of Christian/Byzantine rule (e.g. crosses), no less than building atop the Temple Mount, signals a new rhetoric of rule. In building and striking, the Marwānids thus began to lay imperial claims – permanent, justified, increasingly 'natural' claims – over subjects and lands, a project only completed by the Abbasids during the century that followed, when Arabs, now with several generations of settlement behind them, began to yield taxes themselves, and Muslim historians, now rubbing shoulders with Christian and Jewish élites in

[3] Cf. the very public character of imperial victory celebrations in M. McCormick, *Eternal Victory: Triumphal Rulership in Late Antiquity, Byzantium, and the Early Medieval West* (Cambridge, 1986), pp. 100ff.; J. L. Nelson, *Politics and Ritual in Early Medieval Europe* (London and Ronceverte, 1986), pp. 239ff. (inaugurations, annointings); see also S. R. F. Price, *Rituals and Power: The Roman Imperial Cult in Asia Minor* (Cambridge, 1984). For the adoption of Christian themes in ceremony more generally, see Cameron, 'Images of authority'.

[4] On *bayʿa*s in the *sīra*, see U. Rubin, *The Eye of the Beholder: The Life of Muḥammad as Viewed by the Early Muslims* (Princeton, 1995), s.v.; of the many striking *bayʿa* accounts from the Umayyad period, see al-Balādhurī, *Ansāb*, IVb (Jerusalem, 1938), pp. 58f. (of Ibn al-Zubayr), and the succession events choreographed by Rajāʾ b. Ḥaywa, which are discussed in detail in C. E. Bosworth, 'Rajāʾ ibn Ḥaywa al-Kindī and the Umayyad caliphs', *Islamic Quarterly* 16 (1972), pp. 36–80. To have witnessed one was no small thing (thus the obituary of ʿAbd Allāh b. Shajara al-Saksakī in Ibn ʿAsākir, *Taʾrīkh madīnat Dimashq*, XXXIV, p. 133). On the *bayʿat al-hijra* and the *bayʿa ʿarabiyya*, see Kister, 'Land, property and *jihād*', pp. 279ff. See also M. Bravmann, '*Bayʿah* "homage": a proto-Arab (south-semitic) concept', *DI* 45 (1969), pp. 301–5 (reprinted in *The Spiritual Background of Early Islam* (Leiden, 1972), pp. 213–19); E. Tyan, *Institutions du droit public musulman* (Paris, 1954–7), I, pp. 315ff.; R. P. Mottahedeh, *Loyalty and Leadership in an Early Islamic Society* (Princeton, 1980), esp. pp. 50ff.; M. J. Rahman, 'The oath of allegiance', *Islamic Culture* 8 (1934), pp. 258ff.

[5] H. A. R. Gibb, 'The fiscal rescript of ʿUmar II', *Arabica* 2 (1955), pp. 1–16.

the cities of Iraq, reconstructed a past useful to the present. That Marwānid caliphs still balked at promoting the most powerful of all methods of political integration – conversion – says more about the extraordinary persuasiveness of Muḥammad's fusion of ethnicity and monotheism than it does about their enthusiasm for empire building.

Much of this is reflected in the north. To be more precise: the provincial history of the Umayyad and early Abbasid north can be described as the impact and absorption of state power projected from the centre, the two being determined by local traditions and geography.

We can begin with the post-conquest Jazira. Here, in the absence of a garrison – indeed, in the absence of much Muslim settlement at all – there is no provincial history to speak of. Tribute was occasionally imposed, but systematic taxation had still to appear, and effective authority – religious and civil – remained in the hands of Christian authorities. The region may have been crowned by a string of (slowly tarnishing) Late Antique cities, but these were shunned; even in the Marwānid and Abbasid periods, well after direct rule had been imposed, many would remain predominantly Christian. Caliphs certainly built in the region, occasionally (and temporarily) endowing it with some political significance, but even so, the sites – Hishām's Ruṣāfa, Marwān II's Ḥarrān, al-Manṣūr's al-Rāfiqa, and finally Hārūn's al-Raqqa – were all intended as military or administrative centres, and all manifest an unease with established (read: Christian) urban life. In this they resemble Sufyānid Mosul; unlike Abbasid Mosul, however, these cities had the misfortune of being on the wrong side of the steppe, distant from the booming economy of early Abbasid Iraq.

In contrast to Iraq, the Jazira's significance lay principally in the tribal manpower generated on its steppe, and it was among the tribes, rather than in the cities, that early Muslims showed some interest. In part the threat may have been ideological, in the Taghlibs' fusion of (Monophysite) monotheism and Arab pastoralism; certainly the proximity of the steppe to Umayyad Syria meant it was worth the caliphs' efforts to project some influence towards the east. In the Marwānid period, the state would funnel much of this manpower into caliphal armies (particularly Qaysīs), but some spilled over, pooling into small opposition movements (Khārijites) that resisted the changes imposed upon the state by the consequences of conquest. Exemplifying the fading virtues of the early community, Khārijite heroes had some appeal, but they were swimming against a very strong current, and the inexorable drift towards settlement, combined with the area's proximity to caliphal armies, conspired against their long-term survival.

In the short term, the belated imposition of state hegemony in the Jazira meant the preservation of effective political authority by urban élites; in the long term, the conquests' prime beneficiary among the Christians was probably the institution of the Church. With the withdrawal of Byzantine civil administration (including all the religio-political *dirigisme* that it entailed) and its replacement by Islamic hegemony that was as aloof as it was indifferent to Christian belief, the Church not only gained autonomy from the state, but it lost its only rival (also the state) for the services of privileged families.[6] The result was a hardy and durable Christian identity that was symbolised by Church authorities, many of who wrote their community's past: whatever his literary skills, Dionysius of Tell Maḥrē wrote conquest history not as a professional historian, but as a patriarch-historian.[7] Here the contrast between northern and southern Iraq is striking. Both were home to prosperous Christian communities, led by worldly and wealthy church authorities; but whereas in the south, where Abassid rule, urbanism and 'Hellenising pluralism' were at their most concentrated,[8] Christians gradually assimilated to the ruling faith, those of the north, where Muslim rule was belated and always tenuous, remained considerably more stubborn. It is in the north that the *shahārija* retained their privilege well into the tenth century. Of course some urban élites did succumb to the attractions of imperial patronage in Iraq, even conversion; the Ṣābi' family of Ḥarrān, which produced historian after historian in the tenth and eleventh centuries, is the clearest example. But that they did so only gradually, and, moreover, that the south failed to produce the likes of the Ṣābi's, illustrates the distinctiveness of the north.

In the east, where the Tigris initially locked Mosul into an Iraqi political orbit, things were different. Ḥijāzī Muslims here, as elsewhere, founded garrisons rather than cities, and the site served an essentially administrative and military purpose for the Kufans, governed as it was by Kufan chiefs, and colonised deliberately (as frontiers generally are) also by Kufans; the anchor line was cut only at the end of the century, by which time Mosul had ceased to function as a frontier garrison. Syrian hegemony was now introduced (almost certainly for the first time), some (much?) of the city becoming demesnial lands, a trend that would continue, and perhaps even intensify, during the early Abbasid period. The break from the Kufan past was also signalled by new administrative patterns and a new style of settlement; Mosul was now emphatically Marwānid, its Syrian-inspired élite foundation sending the Kufan *miṣr* into obsolescence. One imagines that property was increasingly commoditised in the early Marwānid period; certainly it became more valuable, particularly as the Marwānids and their kinsmen invested heavily, having recognised that the site was favourable in economic, as well as administrative terms. The managed programme of building was apparently intended to exploit this potential for the benefit of the Marwānid family; but it also set in motion forces that ultimately subverted Marwānid rule in the city: the Mosulis not only fell in with Khārijites, but abandoned Marwān at the first opportunity. It was left to the Abbasids to promote a community of interest that made notables out of recalcitrant provincials.

[6] On the Byzantine background, see Haldon, *Byzantium in the Seventh Century*, pp. 387ff.
[7] On the vitality of the Church in a later period, see Kawerau, *Die jakobitische Kirche.*
[8] I borrow the phrase from Crone and Cook, *Hagarism*, p. 84.

From this perspective, the Umayyads' failure can be linked to the Abbasids' success, and the experience of the city of Mosul contrasted to that of the Jaziran steppe.

The tribal élite of early Islam was notoriously fractious, and although the grievances were frequently material, the language of political opposition was thoroughly moral and reformist; when opponents of the state (such as the Khārijites) seceded, they did so only temporarily, in order to return as revolutionaries. The Mosulis, by contrast, were pragmatic, their aims utterly parochial, and their marriage to eighth-century Khārijites one of convenience, rather than conviction: they rejected Umayyad rule not because the Umayyads failed to make a compelling claim for the caliphate, but because they failed to accommodate their ambitions. A peripatetic court, which generally steered clear of cities, and a bare-bones bureaucracy, which relied on non-Muslims and *mawālī*, were the natural result of the conquering tribesmen's spectacular victories, and it is true that the system could sometimes offer spectacular rewards to the client who was either opportunistic or just plain lucky.[9] But the aristocratic exclusivity of Umayyad rule, based as it was on a tribal model of politics that offered only limited opportunities for social advancement, had less and less appeal to emerging city élites, since it failed to offer a predictable path for incomers, or the promise of systematic return for the investment of patiently acquired professional skills, be they bureaucratic or academic. This helps to explain why the Arabs of the Jaziran steppe were the Umayyads' most dogged loyalists during the first years of Abbasid rule, while those of Mosul abandoned Marwān II at the first opportunity.

Unlike the Umayyads, the Abbasids understood the political consequences of sedentarisation and assimilation, and that empire building required more than just symbols of Islamic hegemony and fair coinage: they understood that it required mobilising loyalty, rather than patronising favourites, and that the call had to take place in the cities. The professionalisation of the military was thus completed, culminating in the slave armies of the ninth century. The explosion of bureaucratic culture opened up more avenues for social climbers, exceptional Marwānid *mawālī* such Ṣāliḥ b. ʿAbd al-Raḥmān and Rajāʾ b. Ḥaywa becoming the Abbasid rule. Meanwhile, Christian, Jewish and Muslim élites began to exchange ideas, all coming to hold (unequal) stakes in a state committed to economic and political patterns that underpinned urban life. In time, the *sharīʿa* itself would emerge, a body of law predicated upon a trans-regional academic culture organised around a more or less uniform set of institutions and skills; it was through

[9] A particularly good example concerns Khālid al-Qasrī and Ziyād b. ʿUbayd Allāh; the latter had the good fortune of being outside Hishām's court when the former exited, having been given his first prime appointment; see al-Balādhurī, *Ansāb*, vib, pp. 158ff. When one's luck turned, appeals to loyalty through *ṣuḥba* could go unheeded; see, for example, al-Yaʿqūbī, *Taʾrīkh*, II, p. 353 (Mūsā b. Nuṣayr and Ṭāriq b. Ziyād, his *mawlā*).

these skills that city élites could reproduce themselves, forming the backbone of the Abbasid commonwealth. In Mosul, the first representative of this learning died in 205/820,[10] during the Indian summer of the caliphate's political unity.

[10] Abū Yaḥyā Ibrāhīm b. Mūsā al-Zayyāt; see al-Azdī, *Ta'rīkh*, pp. 358f.

Bibliography

Primary sources

Islamic

ʿAbd al-Razzāq al-Ṣanʿānī, *Tafsīr* (Riyadh, 1989)
Abū Shāma, ʿAbd al-Raḥmān b. Ismāʿīl, *Kitāb al-Rawḍatayn fī akhbār al-dawlatayn* (Cairo, 1287)
Abū ʿUbayd, al-Qāsim b. Sallām, *Kitāb al-Amwāl* (Cairo, 1968)
Abū Yūsuf, Yaʿqūb b. Ibrāhīm, *Kitāb al-Kharāj* (Būlāq, 1302; Cairo, 1927; Beirut and Cairo, 1985)
Abū Zurʿa al-Dimashqī, *Taʾrīkh* (Damascus, 1980)
Anon., *Akhbār al-dawla al-ʿAbbāsiyya* (Beirut, 1971)
Akhbār majmūʿa (Beirut, 1981)
Kitāb al-ʿUyūn waʾl-ḥadāʾiq fī akhbār al-ḥaqāʾiq, vol. III ed. M. de Goeje and P. de Jong as *Fragmenta Historicorum Arabicorum* (Leiden, 1869); vol. IV (Damascus, 1973)
Taʾrīkh al-khulafāʾ (Moscow, 1967)
al-Ashʿarī, Abū al-Ḥasan ʿAlī, *Maqālāt al-islāmiyyīn* (Istanbul, 1929)
al-Azdī, Yazīd b. Muḥammad, *Taʾrīkh al-Mawṣil* (Cairo, 1967)
al-Baghdādī, ʿAbd al-Qāhir, *al-Farq bayn al-firaq* (Cairo, n.d.)
(attrib.), *Kitāb al-Milal waʾl-niḥal* (Beirut, 1970)
al-Bakrī, Abū ʿUbayd ʿAbd Allāh, *Muʿjam mā istaʿjama min asmāʾ al-bilād waʾl-mawāḍiʿ* (Cairo, 1951)
al-Balādhurī, Aḥmad b. Yaḥyā, *Ansāb al-ashrāf*: MS Reisülkuttap 598; vol. I (Cairo, 1959); vol. III (Wiesbaden/Beirut, 1978); vol. IVa (Jerusalem, 1971); vol. IVb (Jerusalem, 1938); vol. V (Jerusalem, 1936); vol. V (Beirut, 1996); vol. VIb (Jerusalem, 1993); vol. VII/I (Beirut, 1997); vol. XI (Greifswald, 1883, ed. as *Anonyme Arabische Chronik*)
Futūḥ al-buldān (Leiden, 1866)
al-Bayḍāwī, ʿAbd Allāh b. ʿUmar, *Tafsīr* (Cairo, n.d.)
al-Bukhārī, Muḥammad b. Ismāʿīl, *Kitāb al-Taʾrīkh al-kabīr* (Hyderabad, 1941–70)
al-Dhahabī, Shams al-Dīn Muḥammad b. Aḥmad, *Mīzān al-iʿtidāl* (Cairo, 1325)
Siyar aʿlām al-nubalāʾ (Beirut, 1982)
Tadhkirat al-ḥuffāẓ (Hyderabad, 1958)
Taʾrīkh al-Islām (Beirut, 1990)

al-Dīnawarī, Abū Ḥanīfa, *al-Akhbār al-ṭiwāl* (Leiden, 1888)
al-Fasawī, Abū Rifāʿa, *Kitāb Badʾ al-khalq wa-qiṣaṣ al-anbiyāʾ*, ed. R. G. Khoury as *Les légendes prophétiques dans l'Islam* (Wiesbaden, 1978)
Firdawsī, *Shāhnāma* (Costa Mesa and New York, 1988–)
al-Ghazālī, *Ghazālī's Book of Counsel for Kings*, trans. F. R. C. Begley (London: Oxford University Press, 1964)
Ḥamza al-Iṣfahānī, *Taʾrīkh sinī mulūk al-arḍ wa'l-anbiyāʾ* (Petropoli, etc., 1844)
al-Harawī, ʿAlī b. Abī Bakr, *Kitāb al-Ishārāt ilā maʿrifat al-ziyārāt*, trans. J. Sourdel-Thomine as *Guide des lieux de pèlerinage* (Damascus, 1957)
al-Ḥimyarī, Ibn ʿAbd al-Munʿim, *al-Rawḍ al-miʿṭār fī khabar al-aqṭār* (Beirut, 1975)
al-Ḥuṣrī, Ibrāhīm b. ʿAlī, *Zahr al-ādāb* (Cairo, 1969)
Ibn ʿAbd al-Ḥakam, ʿAbd al-Raḥmān b. ʿAbd Allāh, *Futūḥ Miṣr wa'l-Maghrib* (Cairo, 1995)
Ibn ʿAbd Rabbihi, Aḥmad b. Muḥammad, *al-ʿIqd al-farīd* (Beirut, 1983)
Ibn Abī al-Ḥadīd, *Sharḥ nahj al-balāgha* (Beirut, 1964)
Ibn Abī Shayba, ʿAbd Allāh b. Muḥammad, *al-Muṣannaf* (Beirut, 1989)
Ibn Abī Uṣaybiʿa, Aḥmad b. al-Qāsim, *ʿUyūn al-anbāʾ fī ṭabaqāt al-aṭibbāʾ* (Beirut reprint of Nizār Riḍā edn, 1965)
Ibn Abī al-Wafāʾ, ʿAbd al-Qādir b. Muḥammad, *al-Jawāhir al-muḍiyya* (Cairo, 1979)
Ibn Abī Yaʿlā, Abū al-Ḥusayn Muḥammad b. Muḥammad, *Ṭabaqāt al-ḥanābila* (Cairo, 1952)
Ibn al-ʿAdīm, Kamāl al-Dīn, *Bughyat al-ṭalab fī taʾrīkh Ḥalab* (Damascus, 1988)
Zubdat al-ḥalab min taʾrīkh Ḥalab (Damascus, 1951)
Ibn ʿAsākir, ʿAlī b. al-Ḥasan, *Taʾrīkh madīnat Dimashq* (Beirut, 1998)
Ibn Aʿtham al-Kūfī, *Kitāb al-Futūḥ* (Hyderabad, 1968–75)
Ibn al-Athīr, ʿIzz al-Dīn, *al-Kāmil fī al-taʾrīkh* (Beirut, 1965; Leiden, 1871)
al-Taʾrīkh al-bāhir fī al-dawla al-atābakiyya (Baghdad, 1963)
Usd al-ghāba (Būlāq, 1871)
Ibn al-Azraq al-Fāriqī, Aḥmad b. Yūsuf, *Taʾrīkh Mayyāfāriqīn wa-Āmid* (MS BM OR 5803)
Ibn Baṭṭūṭa, Muḥammad, *Riḥla* (Beirut, 1975)
Ibn Durayd, Muḥammad b. al-Ḥasan, *Kitāb al-Ishtiqāq* (Göttingen, 1854)
Ibn al-Faqīh al-Hamadhānī, *Kitāb al-Buldān* (Leiden, 1885; Bibliotheca Geographorum Arabicorum 5)
Ibn Ḥajar al-ʿAsqalānī, Aḥmad b. ʿAlī, *al-Iṣāba fī tamyīz al-ṣaḥāba* (Cairo, 1977)
Lisān al-mīzān (Hyderabad, 1331)
Tahdhīb al-tahdhīb (Hyderabad, 1327)
Ibn Ḥanbal, Aḥmad b. Muḥammad, *Masāʾil* (Beirut, 1981)
Ibn Ḥawqal, Abū al-Qāsim, *Ṣūrat al-arḍ* (Leiden, 1939; Bibliotheca Geographorum Arabicorum 2)
Ibn Ḥazm, Abū Muḥammad ʿAlī, *Jamharat ansāb al-ʿarab* (Cairo, 1977)
Kitāb al-Faṣl fī al-milal wa'l-ahwāʾ wa'l-niḥal (Riyadh, 1982)
Ibn Hishām, ʿAbd al-Malik, *al-Sīra al-nabawiyya*, ed. M. al-Saqqā (Beirut, many reprints); trans. A. Guillaume as *The Life of Muhammad* (Oxford, 1955)
Ibn Ḥubaysh, ʿAbd al-Raḥmān b. Muḥammad, *Kitāb al-Ghazawāt* (Cairo, 1987)
Ibn al-Jawzī, Abū al-Faraj ʿAbd al-Raḥmān, *al-Muntaẓam* (Beirut, 1993)
Ibn Jubayr, *Riḥla* (Leiden and London, 1907)
Ibn Jumayʿ, Muḥammad b. Aḥmad, *Muʿjam al-shuyūkh* (Beirut, 1985)

Ibn al-Kalbī, Hishām, *Ğamharat al-nasab: Das genealogische Werk des Hišām Ibn Muḥammad al-Kalbī*, ed. Caskel (Leiden, 1966)
Ibn Khallikān, Shams al-Dīn Muḥammad, *Wafayāt al-aʿyān* (Beirut, 1977)
Ibn Khurdādhbih, ʿUbayd Allāh b. ʿAbd Allāh, *Kitāb al-Masālik wa'l-mamālik* (Leiden, 1889; Bibliotheca Geographorum Arabicorum 6)
Ibn Manẓūr, Jamāl al-Dīn Muḥammad, *Lisān al-ʿarab* (Beirut, 1956)
Mukhtaṣar taʾrīkh madīnat Dimashq (Damascus, 1988)
Ibn Miskawayh, Aḥmad b. Muḥammad, *Tajārib al-umam* (London, 1922)
Ibn al-Muqaffaʿ, ʿAbd Allāh, *Risāla fī al-ṣaḥāba,* ed. and trans. C. Pellat as *Conseilleur du calife* (Paris, 1976)
Ibn al-Nadīm, Muḥammad b. Isḥāq, *Kitāb al-Fihrist* (Beirut, 1988 reprint of Riḍā Tajaddud's Tehran, 1971 edn)
Ibn Qutayba, ʿAbd Allāh b. Muslim, *al-Maʿārif* (Cairo, fourth printing, 1981)
ʿUyūn al-akhbār (Cairo, 1925)
Ibn Saʿd, Abū ʿAbd Allāh Muḥammad, *Kitāb al-Ṭabaqāt al-kubrā* (Leiden, 1905–40)
Ibn Shaddād, ʿIzz al-Dīn, *al-Aʿlāq al-khaṭīra fī dhikr umarāʾ al-Shām wa'l-Jazīra (taʾrīkh Lubnān wa'l-Urdunn wa-Filasṭīn)* (Damascus, 1962)
Ibn al-Ṭiqṭaqā, Muḥammad b. ʿAlī, *al-Fakhrī* (Paris, 1895)
Ibn Zanjawayh, Ibn Mukhlid, *Kitāb al-Amwāl* (Riyadh, 1986)
al-Idrīsī, Abū ʿAbd Allāh Muḥammad, *Opus geographicum* (Rome, 1984)
al-Iṣfahānī, Abū al-Faraj, *Kitāb al-Aghānī* (Cairo, 1984)
Maqātil al-ṭālibīyīn (Cairo, 1949)
al-Iṣfahānī, Abū Nuʿaym, *Ḥilyat al-awliyāʾ* (Cairo, 1938)
al-Iṣtakhrī, Ibrāhīm b. Muḥammad, *Kitāb Masālik al-mamālik* (Leiden 1870; Bibliotheca Geographorum Arabicorum 1)
Jāḥiẓ, ʿAmr b. Baḥr, *Kitāb al-Bukhalāʾ* (Beirut, 1983)
Kitāb al-Tabaṣṣur bi'l-tijāra (Cairo, 1966)
al-Jahshiyārī, Muḥammad b. ʿAbdūs, *Kitāb al-Wuzarāʾ wa'l-kuttāb* (Cairo, 1938)
al-Jawālīqī, Mawhūb b. Aḥmad, *al-Muʿarrab* (Cairo, 1969)
Khalīfa b. Khayyāṭ, *Ṭabaqāt* (Damascus, 1966)
Taʾrīkh (Beirut, 1995)
al-Khaṭīb al-Baghdādī, *Taʾrīkh Baghdād* (Cairo, 1931)
al-Khaṭīb al-Tibrīzī, Yaḥyā b. ʿAlī, *Sharḥ al-qaṣāʾid al-ʿashr* (Aleppo, 1969)
al-Khawārizmī, Muḥammad b. Aḥmad, *Mafātīḥ al-ʿulūm* (Leiden, 1895)
al-Kindī, Muḥammad b. Yūsuf, *Kitāb al-umarāʾ wa-kitāb al-quḍāh* (Leiden and London, 1912)
al-Maqdisī, Abū Naṣr al-Muṭahhar, *Kitāb al-Badʾ wa'l-taʾrīkh* (Paris, 1918)
al-Maqrīzī, Aḥmad b. ʿAlī, *Kitāb al-Nizāʿ wa'l-takhāṣum fīmā bayna Banī Umayya wa-Banī Hāshim* (Cairo, 1988); trans. C. E. Bosworth as *Al-Maqrīzī's 'Book of Contention and Strife concerning the Relations between the Banū Umayya and the Banū Hāshim'* (Manchester: Journal of Semitic Studies, monograph 3, 1980)
al-Marzubānī, Abū ʿUbayd Allāh, *Muʿjam al-shuʿarāʾ* (Cairo, 1960)
al-Masʿūdī, al-Ḥasan b. ʿAlī, *Kitāb al-Tanbīh wa'l-ishrāf* (Leiden, 1894; Bibliotheca Geographorum Arabicorum 8)
Murūj al-dhahab wa-maʿādin al-jawhar (Beirut, 1979)
al-Minqarī, Naṣr b. Muzāḥim, *Waqʿat Ṣiffīn* (Cairo, 1981)
al-Mizzī, Abū al-Ḥajjāj Yūsuf, *Tahdhīb al-kamāl fī asmāʾ al-rijāl* (Beirut, 1992)
al-Mubarrad, Muḥammad b. Yazīd, *al-Kāmil* (Leipzig, 1892)

al-Muqaddasī, Muḥammad b. Aḥmad, *Aḥsan al-taqāsīm fī ma'rifat al-aqālīm* (Leiden, 1877; Bibliotheca Geographorum Arabicorum 3)
al-Muttaqī al-Hindī, *Kanz al-'ummāl* (Hyderabad, 1945–75)
Nu'aym b. Ḥammād, Abū 'Abd Allāh, *Kitāb al-Fitan* (Mecca, 1991 (?))
al-Nuwayrī, Aḥmad b. 'Abd al-Wahhāb, *Nihāyat al-arab fī funūn al-adab* (Cairo, 1923–)
al-Qālī, Abū 'Alī Ismā'īl, *al-Amālī* (Cairo, 1926)
al-Qāsim b. Sallām, *Kitāb al-Amwāl* (Cairo, 1353)
Qazwīnī, Zakariyā b. Muḥammad, *Kitāb 'Ajā'ib al-makhlūqāt*, ed. F. Wüstenfeld as *Kosmographie* (Göttingen, 1848)
al-Qifṭī, 'Alī b. Yūsuf, *Ta'rīkh al-ḥukamā'* (Leipzig, 1903)
Qudāma b. Ja'far, *Kitāb al-Kharāj wa-ṣinā'at al-kitāba* (Baghdad, 1981)
al-Qushayrī, Abū 'Alī Muḥammad, *Ta'rīkh al-Raqqa* (Damascus, 1998)
al-Rāzī, Ibn Abī Ḥātim, *Kitāb al-Jarḥ wa'l-ta'dīl* (Beirut reprint of Hyderabad, 1953 edn)
al-Ṣābi', Hilāl, *Kitāb Tuḥfat al-umarā' fī ta'rīkh al-wuzarā'* (Leiden, 1904)
al-Ṣafadī, Khalīl b. Aybak, *al-Wāfī bi'l-wafayāt* (Leipzig, Istanbul and Beirut, 1931–)
al-Sam'ānī, 'Abd al-Karīm b. Muḥammad, *Kitāb al-Ansāb* (Hyderabad, 1982)
al-Shābushtī, 'Alī b. Muḥammad, *al-Diyārāt* (Beirut, 1986 reprint of 'Awwād edn, Baghdad, 1951)
al-Shahrastānī, Muḥammad b. 'Abd al-Karīm, *Kitāb al-Milal wa'l-niḥal* (London, 1842–6)
al-Shaybānī, Muḥammad b. al-Ḥasan, *Sharḥ kitāb al-siyar al-kabīr* (Cairo, 1960)
al-Ṣūlī, Muḥammad b. Yaḥyā, *Akhbâr ar-Râdî billâh*, trans. M. Canard (Algiers, 1946)
Ash'ār awlād al-khulafā' wa-akhbāruhum (London, 1936)
al-Ṭabarī, Muḥammad b. Jarīr, *Kitāb Ikhtilāf al-fuqahā'* (Leiden, 1933)
Ta'rīkh al-rusul wa'l-mulūk (Leiden, 1879–1901), including *Introductio, glossarium addenda et emendanda*; sections trans. T. Nöldeke as *Geschichte der Perser und Araber zur Zeit der Sasaniden* (Leiden, 1879) and E. Rowson as *The Marwānid Restoration*, vol. XXII of *The History of al-Ṭabarī* (Albany, 1989); Bal'amī's Persian version translated by H. Zotenberg as *Chronique de Abou Djafar-Mohammed-ben-Yezid Tabari* (Paris, 1958, reprint of 1867–74)
al-Tha'ālibī, 'Abd al-Malik b. Muḥammad, *Ghurar akhbār mulūk al-Furs* (Paris, 1900)
al-Thaqafī, Abū Isḥāq, *Kitāb al-Ghārāt* (Beirut, 1987)
al-'Umarī, Ibn Faḍl Allāh, *Masālik al-abṣār* (Cairo, 1924)
al-'Umarī, Yasīn b. Khayr, *Munyat al-udabā' fī ta'rīkh al-Mawṣil al-ḥadbā'* (Mosul, 1955)
(ps.)-Wāqidī, Muḥammad b. 'Umar, *Futūḥ al-'Irāq*, MS Cod. Arab. CXXXVII, Königliche Bibliothek, Copenhagen
Futūḥ al-Jazīra, Libri Wakedii de Mesopotamiae expugnatae historia (Göttingen, 1827)
Futūḥ al-Shām (Calcutta, 1854)
Geschichte der Eroberung von Mesopotamien und Armenien, trans. B. G. Niebuhr and A. D. Mordtmann (Hamburg, 1847)
Ta'rīkh futūḥ al-Jazīra wa'l-Khābūr wa-Diyār Bakr wa'l-'Irāq (Damascus, 1996)
al-Warrāq, Muḥammad b. Hārūn, *Radd 'alā al-thalath firaq min al-Naṣārā*, ed. and trans. D. Thomas as *Anti-Christian Polemic in Early Islam: Abū 'Īsā al-Warrāq's 'Against the Trinity'* (Cambridge, 1992)

al-Yaʿqūbī, Aḥmad b. Abī Yaʿqūb, *Kitāb al-Buldān* (Leiden, 1892; Bibliotheca Geographorum Arabicorum 8); trans. G. Wiet as *Le Pays* (Cairo, 1937)
Taʾrīkh (Leiden, 1883)
Yāqūt, Ibn ʿAbd Allāh al-Rūmī, *Irshād al-arīb ilā maʿrifat al-adīb* (Leiden and London, 1907–13)
Muʿjam al-buldān (Leipzig, 1866–73)
al-Zayyāt, Isḥāq b. al-Ḥasan, *Dhikr al-aqālīm* (Barcelona, 1989)

Christian

Agapius (Maḥbūb) of Manbij, *Kitāb al-ʿUnvān, histoire universelle*, II (ii), ed. and trans. A. A. Vasiliev in *PO* 8 (1912)
ʿAmr b. Mattā, *Kitāb al-Majdal*, ed. and trans. H. Gismondi in *Maris Amri et Slibae De patriarchis Nestorianorum commentaria* (Rome, 1896–9)
Anon., *Chronicle of 724*, ed. and trans. E. W. Brooks as *Chronicon miscellaneum ad annum domini 724 pertinens* (Louvain, 1904; *Chronica Minora* II of *CSCO* 3–4)
Chronicle of 813, ed. and trans. E. W. Brooks as *Fragmenta chronici anonymi auctoris ad annum domini 813 pertinentia* (Louvain, 1905–7; *Chronica Minora* III of *CSCO* 5–6)
Chronicle of 819, ed. A. Barsaum and trans. J.-B. Chabot as *Chronicon anonymum ad annum domini 819 pertinens* (Paris, 1920 and 1937; *CSCO* 81 and 109)
Chronicle of 846, ed. E. W. Brooks and trans. J.-B. Chabot as *Chronicon ad annum domini 846 pertinens* (Paris, 1904; *Chronica Minora* II of *CSCO* 3–4)
Chronicle 1234, ed. and (Latin) trans. J.-B. Chabot as *Chronicon anonymum ad annum Christi 1234 pertinens* (Paris, 1916, 1920, 1937, and Louvain, 1974; *CSCO* 81–2, 109 and 354 (Fr. trans. A. Abouna))
Histoire nestorienne (*Chronique de Séert*), ed. and trans. A. Scher in *PO* 4 (1908), 7 (1911) and 13 (1919)
History of Bēt Qoqa, ed. A. Mingana in *Sources syriaques* (Mosul, 1907)
Khuzistan Chronicle, ed. and trans. I. Guidi as *Chronicon anonymum* (Paris, 1903: in *Chronical Minora* I of *CSCO* 1–2); German trans. and commentary T. Nöldeke, 'Die von Guidi herausgegebene syrische Chronik uebersetzt und commentiert', *Sitzungsberichte der kaiserlichen Akademie der Wissenschaften*, Phil.-Hist. Klasse, 128 (1893), 1–48
Maronite Chronicle, ed. E. W. Brooks and trans. J.-B. Chabot as *Chronicon maroniticum* (Paris, 1904; *Chronica Minora* II of *CSCO* 3–4)
Zuqnin Chronicle (vol. II), ed. J.-B. Chabot as *Incerti auctoris chronicon anonymum pseudo-Dionysianum vulgo dictum II* (Paris and Louvain, 1933 and 1989; *CSCO*, 104 and 507 (trans. R. Hespel)); partially ed. and trans. J.-B. Chabot as *Chronique de Denys de Tell-Maḥré* (Paris, 1895)
Barḥadbshabba ʿArbāyā, *L'Histoire de Barḥadbešabba*, ed. and trans. F. Nau in *PO* 23 (1932)
Bar Hebraeus, *Chronicon ecclesiasticum*, ed. and trans. J. B. Abbeloos and T. J. Lamy (Paris and Louvain, 1872–7)
Chronicon syriacum, ed. P. Bedjan (Paris, 1890); trans. E. A. Wallis Budge as *The Chronography of Gregory Abu'l-Faraj . . . Known as Bar Hebraeus* (Oxford, 1932)
Taʾrīkh mukhtaṣar al-duwal (Beirut, 1983 reprint of Salhani's edn of 1890)
Denha, *Histoire des divins actions de saint Mar Marouta l'ancien* in the *Histoires d'Aḥoudemmeh et de Marouta*, ed. and trans. F. Nau in *PO* 3 (1909)

Elias of Nisibis, *Opus chronologicum*, ed. by E. W. Brooks (Paris, 1910; *CSCO* 62); French trans. F. Delaporte as *La chronographie de Mar Elie Bar Šinaya* (Paris, 1910)
Eutychius, *Das Annalenwerk des Eutychios von Alexandrien*, ed. and trans. M. Breydy (Louvain, 1985; *CSCO* 471–2)
Gabriel of Qarṭmīn, *Life*, ed. and trans. A. Palmer in *Monk and Mason on the Tigris Frontier* (Cambridge, 1990), microfiche
Īshōʿyahb III, *Išōʿyahb patriarchae III Liber epistularum*, ed. and trans. R. Duval (Paris, 1904 and 1905; *CSCO* 11–12)
Īshōʿdnaḥ, *Le Livre de la Chasteté*, ed. and trans. J.-B. Chabot (Rome, 1896; Mélanges d'Archéologie et d'Histoire 16, 1896)
John of Ephesus, *Lives of the Eastern Saints*, I, ed. and trans. E. W. Brooks in *PO* 17 (1923)
John of Fenek, *Ktābā d-rīsh mellē*, ed. and partially trans. A. Mingana in *Sources Syriaques* (Mosul, 1907); partial trans. S. P. Brock, 'North Mesopotamia in the late seventh century: Book XV of John Bar Penkāyē's *Rīš Mellē*', *JSAI* 9 (1987), 57–74
ps.-John the Less, *The Gospel of the Twelve Apostles*, ed. and trans. J. R. Harris (Cambridge, 1900)
John Moschus, *Le Pré Spirituel*, trans. M.-J. R. de Journel (Paris, 1946)
ps.-Joshua, *The Chronicle of Joshua the Stylite*, ed. and trans. W. Wright (Cambridge, 1882); trans. A. Luther, *Die syrische Chronik des Joshua Stylites* (Berlin and New York, 1997)
Mārī b. Sulaymān (attrib.), *Kitāb al-Majdal*, in *Maris Amri et Slibae De patriarchis Nestorianorum commentaria*, ed. and trans. H. Gismondi (Rome, 1896–9)
Mārūtā of Maipherqaṭ, *The Canons Ascribed to Mārūtā of Maipherqaṭ*, ed. and trans. A. Vööbus (Louvain, 1982; *CSCO* 439–40)
ps.-Methodius, *Die syrische Apokalypse des Pseudo-Methodius*, ed. and trans. G. J. Reinink (Louvain, 1993; *CSCO* 540–1)
Michael the Syrian, *Chronique de Michel, patriarche jacobite d'Antioche 1166–1199*, ed. and trans. J.-B. Chabot (Paris, 1899–1924)
Narsai, *Homilae et carmina*, ed. A. Mingana (Mosul, 1905)
Nikephoros, *Brevarium historicum*, ed. and trans. C. Mango as *Nikephoros Patriarch of Constantinople Short History* (Washington, DC, 1990)
Procopius, *History of the Wars*, ed. and trans. H. B. Dewing (London and New York: Loeb, 1914–40)
Rabban Hormizd, *The Histories of Rabban Hôrmîzd the Persian and Rabban Bar-Idtâ*, ed. and trans. E. A. Wallis Budge (London, 1902)
Sabrīshōʿ, *Life*, ed. A. Mingana in *Sources syriaques* (Mosul, 1907)
Samuel, *Life*, ed. and trans. A. Palmer in *Monk and Mason on the Tigris Frontier* (Cambridge, 1990), microfiche
Sebeos (attrib), *Histoire d'Héraclius par l'évêque Sebéos*, trans. F. Macler (Paris, 1904)
Severus b. al-Muqaffaʿ, *History of the Patriarchs of the Coptic Church of Alexandria*, III, ed. and trans. B. Evetts in *PO* 5 (1947)
Simeon of the Olives, *Life*, ed. P. Dolabani in *Maktabzabnē d-ʿumrā qaddīshā d-Qarṭmīn* (Mardīn, 1959)
Theophanes Confessor (attrib.), *The Chronicle of Theophanes Confessor*, trans. C. Mango and R. Scott (Oxford, 1997)
Theophylact of Simocatta, *History* (Stuttgart, 1972 reprint of C. de Boor's 1887 edn);

trans. M. and M. Whitby as *The History of Theophylact Simocatta: An English Translation with Introduction and Notes* (Oxford, 1986)

Thomas of Marga, *The Book of Governors*, ed. and trans. E. A. Wallis Budge (London, 1893)

ps.-Zacharias Rhetor, *Historia ecclesiastica Zachariae Rhetori vulgo adscripta*, ed. and trans. E. W. Brooks (Paris, 1919, 1921, 1924; *CSCO* 83–4, 87–8)

Secondary literature

ʿAbbās, I., *Shiʿr al-khawārij* (Beirut: Dār al-Thaqāfa, n.d.)

Abbott, N., *The Ḳurrah Papyri from Aphrodito in the Oriental Institute* (Chicago: University of Chicago Press, 1938)

'A new papyrus and a review of the administration of ʿUbaid Allāh b. al-Ḥabḥāb', in Makdisi, ed., *Arabic and Islamic Studies*, 21–35

ʿAbd al-Badīʿ, L., *Fihris al-makhṭūṭāt al-muṣawwara* II.i (Cairo: Maṭbaʿat Dār al-Kutub al-Miṣriyya, 1956)

Abel, A., 'Un *Ḥadīṯ* sur la prise de Rome dans la tradition eschatologique de l'Islam', *Arabica* 5 (1958), 1–14

Abiade, M., *Culture et education arabo-islamiques au Šām pendant les trois premiers siècles de l'Islam* (Damascus: L'Imprimerie du Ministère de la Culture et de l'Orientation Nationale, 1981)

Abramowski, L. and A. Goodman, *A Nestorian Collection of Christological Texts* (Cambridge: Cambridge University Press, 1972)

Abramowski, R., *Dionysius von Tellmahre, jakobitische Patriarch von 818–845* (Leipzig: F. A. Brockhaus, 1940)

Adams, R. M., *Land behind Baghdad: A History of Settlement on the Diyala Plains* (Chicago: University of Chicago Press, 1965)

al-Albānī, M. N., *Fihris makhṭūṭāt Dār al-Kutub al-Ẓāhiriyya* (Damascus: Majmaʿ al-Lugha al-ʿArabiyya, 1970)

Alexander, P. J., 'Medieval apocalypses as historical sources', *American Historical Review* 73.4 (1968), 997–1018; reprinted in his *Religious and Political Thought in the Byzantine Empire* (London: Variorum, 1987)

The Oracle of Baalbek: The Tiburtine Sibyl in Greek Dress (Washington, DC: Dumbarton Oaks, 1967)

Algaze, G., 'Habuba on the Tigris: archaic Nineveh reconsidered', *JNES* 45 (1986), 125–35

Arberry, A. J., *The Chester Beatty Library: A Handlist of the Arabic Manuscripts* (Dublin: E. Walker, 1955)

The Koran Interpreted (London: Allen & Unwin, 1955 and New York: Macmillan, 1955)

Arzoumanian, Z., 'A critique of Sebēos and his *History of Heraclius*, a seventh-century Armenian document', in Samuelian, ed., *Classical Armenian Culture*, 68–78

Ashtor, E., *A Social and Economic History of the Near East in the Middle Ages* (London: Collins, 1976)

Athamina, K., 'Arab settlement during the Umayyad caliphate', *JSAI* 8 (1986), 185–207

Atti del Convegno Internazionale sul Tema: La Persia nel Medioevo (Rome: Accademia Nazionale dei Lincei, 1971)

Ayalon, D., 'Regarding population estimates in the countries of medieval Islam', *JESHO* 28 (1985), 1–19

Bacharach, J., 'Marwanid Umayyad building activities: speculations on patronage', *Muqarnas* 13 (1996), 27–44

Bacharach, J., L. I. Conrad and P. Crone, eds., *Studies in Early Islamic History* (Princeton: Darwin Press, 1996)

Badger, G. P., *The Nestorians and their Rituals* (London: Joseph Masters, 1852)

al-Bakhit, M. A., and I. ʿAbbās, eds., *Proceedings of the Second Symposium on the History of Bilād al-Shām during the Early Islamic Period up to 40 AH/640 A.D.* (Amman: University of Jordan Press, 1987)

al-Bakhit, M. A. and R. Schick, eds., *Bilād al-Shām during the Abbasid Period (132 AH/750 AD–451 AH/1059 AD): Proceedings of the Fifth International Conference on the History of Bilād al-Shām* (Amman: Lajnat Taʾrīkh Bilād al-Shām, 1992)

Ball, W., 'The Upper Tigris area: new evidence from the Eski Mosul and North Jazira projects', in Bartl and Hauser, eds., *Continuity and Change*, 415–27

Barbier de Meynard, C., *Dictionnaire géographique, historique et littéraire de la Perse* (Paris: L'Imprimerie Impériale, 1861)

Bardy, G., *Paul de Samosate: Etude historique* (Louvain: Spicilegium sacrum Lovaniense, 1929)

Barthold, W., *An Historical Geography of Iran*, trans. S. Soucek and ed. with an introduction by C. E. Bosworth (Princeton: Princeton University Press, 1984)

Bartl, K., 'Tell Sheikh Hasan: a settlement of the Roman-Parthian to the Islamic period in the Balikh valley/northern Syria', *Archéologie Islamique* 4 (1994), 5–17

Bartl, K. and S. R. Hauser, eds., *Continuity and Change in Northern Mesopotamia from the Hellenistic to the Early Islamic Period* (Berlin: Dietrich Reimer Verlag, 1996; Berliner Beiträge zum Vorderen Orient 17)

Barton, J., *Oracles of God: Perceptions of Ancient Prophecy in Israel after the Exile* (London: Darton, Longman & Todd, 1986)

Bashear, S., 'Apocalyptic and other materials on early Muslim–Byzantine wars: a review of Arabic sources', *JRAS* 3, 1 (1991), 173–207

Arabs and Others in Early Islam (Princeton: Darwin Press, 1997)

'Muslim apocalypses and the hour: a case-study in traditional reinterpretation', *Israel Oriental Studies* 13 (1993), 75–99

Bates, M., 'Byzantine coinage and its imitations, Arab coinage and its imitations: Arab-Byzantine coinage', *Aram* 6 (1994), 381–403

'The dirham mint of the northern provinces of the Umayyad caliphate', *Armenian Numismatic Journal* 15 (1989), 89–112

'History, geography and numismatics in the first century of Islamic coinage', *Revue Suisse de Numismatique* 65 (1986), 231–261

Baumstark, A., *Geschichte der syrischen Literatur* (Bonn: A. Marcus & Weber, 1922)

Bayless, W., 'Synesius of Cyrene: a study of the role of the bishop in temporal affairs', *Byzantine Studies/Etudes Byzantines* 4 (1977), 147–56

Beeston, A. F. L. and L. I. Conrad, 'On some Umayyad poetry in the *History* of al-Ṭabarī', *JRAS*, 3.3 (1993), 191–206

Bell, G., *Amurath to Amurath* (London: W. Heinemann, 1911)

Ben-David, J. and T. N. Clark, eds., *Culture and Its Creators: Essays in Honor of Edward Shils* (Chicago: University of Chicago Press, 1977)

Bergsträsser, G., *Ḥunayn ibn Isḥāq über die syrischen und arabischen Galen-Übersetzungen* (Leipzig: F. A. Brockhaus, 1925)
Bidawid, R. J., *Les Lettres du patriarche nestorien Timothée I* (The Vatican: Biblioteca Apostolica Vaticana, 1956)
Bisheh, G., 'From castellum to palatium: Umayyad mosaic pavements from Qasr al-Hallabat in Jordan', *Muqarnas* 10 (1993), 49–56
Bivar, A. D. H., 'Cavalry equipment and tactics on the Euphrates frontier', *Dumbarton Oaks Papers* 26 (1972), 271–91
Blankinship, K. Y., *The End of the Jihâd State: The Reign of Hishâm Ibn ʿAbd al-Malik and the Collapse of the Umayyads* (Albany: State University of New York Press, 1994)
Blau, J., *A Grammar of Christian Arabic* (Louvain, 1966; CSCO 267)
Bligh-Abramski, I., 'The judiciary (*qāḍīs*) as a governmental-administrative tool in early Islam', *JESHO* 35 (1992), 40–71
de Blois, F., 'The Iftikhāriyān of Qazvīn', in Eslami, ed., *Iran and Iranian Studies*, 13–23
Bloom, J., *Minaret: Symbol of Islam* (Oxford: Oxford University Press, 1989)
Bonine, M., 'From Uruk to Casablanca: perspectives on the urban experience of the Middle East', *Journal of Urban History* 3 (1977), 141–80
Bonner, M., *Aristocratic Violence and Holy War: Studies in the Jihad and the Arab–Byzantine Frontier* (New Haven: American Oriental Society, 1996)
Bosworth, C. E., 'Abū ʿAbdallāh al-Khwārazmī on the technical terms of the secretary's art', *JESHO* 12 (1969), 113–64
'Rajā' ibn Ḥaywa al-Kindī and the Umayyad caliphs', *Islamic Quarterly* 16 (1972), 36–80
'Recruitment, muster and review in medieval Islamic armies', in Parry and Yapp, eds., *War, Technology and Society*, 59–77
Bosworth, C. E. and G. Clauson, 'al-Xwārazmī on the peoples of Central Asia', *JRAS* (1965), 2–12
Boyce, M., ed. and trans., *The Letter of Tansar* (Rome: Istituto Italiano per il Medio ed Estremo Oriente, 1968)
Bravmann, M. M., '*Bayʿah* "homage": a proto-Arab (south-semitic) concept', *DI* 45 (1969), 301–5; reprinted in his *The Spiritual Background of Early Islam* (Leiden: E. J. Brill, 1972), 213–19
'The state archives in the early Islamic period', *Arabica* 15 (1968), 87–9; reprinted in his *The Spiritual Background of early Islam*, 311–14
Brett, M., 'The way of the nomad', *BSOAS* 58 (1995), 251–69
Brock, S. P., 'Christians in the Sasanid Empire: A Case of Divided Loyalties,' in Mews, ed., *Religion and National Identity*, 1–19
'The Christology of the Church of the East in the synods of the fifth to early seventh centuries', in Dragas, ed., *Aksum-Thyateira*, 125–42
'The Fenqitho of the monastery of Mar Gabriel in Tur ʿAbdin', *Ostkirchliche Studien* 28 (1979), 168–82
'Notes on some monasteries on Mount Izla', *Abr-Nahrain* 19 (1980/1981), 1–19
'Syriac historical writing: a survey of the main sources', *Journal of the Iraqi Academy* 5 (1979–80), 1–30 (English section)
'A Syriac Life of John of Dailam', *Parole de l'Orient* 10 (1981–2), 123–89

'Syriac sources for seventh-century history', *Byzantine and Modern Greek Studies* 2 (1976), 17–36

'Syriac views on emergent Islam', in Juynboll, ed., *Studies on the First Century of Islamic Society*, 9–22

Brock, S. P. and S. A. Harvey, *Holy Women of the Syrian Orient* (Los Angeles and London: University of California Press, 1987)

Brockelmann, K., *Geschichte der arabischen Literatur* (Weimar, Leipzig and Leiden: E. J. Brill, 1898–1949)

Lexicon syriacum (Hildesheim: Georg Olms, 1966; reprint of 1928 edn)

Brown, P., *The Cult of the Saints* (Chicago: University of Chicago Press, 1981)

Power and Persuasion in Late Antiquity (Madison: University of Wisconsin Press, 1992)

'The rise and function of the holy man in Late Antiquity', *Journal of Roman Studies* 61 (1971), 80–101; reprinted in his *Society and the Holy in Late Antiquity* (Berkeley: University of California Press, 1982)

'The saint as exemplar in Late Antiquity', *Representations* 1 (1983), 1–25

Brünnow, F., *Die Charidschiten unter den ersten Omayyaden: Ein Beitrag zur Geschichte des ersten islamischen Jahrhunderts* (Leiden: E. J. Brill, 1884)

Brunt, P. A., 'The Revenues of Rome' (review article), *Journal of Roman Studies* 71 (1981), 161–72

Bulliet, R., *The Camel and the Wheel* (Cambridge, MA: Harvard University Press, 1975)

Islam: The View from the Edge (New York: Columbia University Press, 1994)

The Patricians of Nishapur (Cambridge, MA: Harvard University Press, 1972)

Caetani, L., *Annali dell'Islam* (Milan: U. Hoepli, 1905–26)

Cahen, C., 'Fiscalité, propriété, antagonismes sociaux en Haute-Mésopotamie au temps des premiers ʿAbbāsides d'après Denys de Tell-Mahré', *Arabica* 1 (1954), 136–52

Calder, N., *Studies in Early Muslim Jurisprudence* (Oxford: Clarendon Press, 1993)

Cameron, A., *Christianity and the Rhetoric of Empire* (Berkeley and Los Angeles: University of California Press, 1991)

'The eastern provinces in the seventh century AD: Hellenism and the emergence of Islam', in Said, ed., *Hellenismos*, 278–313

'The history of the image of Edessa: the telling of a story', in C. Mango and O. Pritsak, eds., *Okeanos: Essays Presented to Ihor Ševčenko on his Sixtieth Birthday by his Colleagues and Students* (Cambridge, MA: Harvard University Press, 1983; Harvard Ukranian Studies 7), 80–94

'Images of authority: élites and icons in late sixth-century Byzantium', *Past and Present* 84 (1979), 3–35

'Late Antiquity – the total view' (review article), *Past and Present* 88 (1980), 129–35

Cameron, A., ed., *The Byzantine and Early Islamic Near East III: States, Resources and Armies* (Princeton: Darwin Press, 1995)

Cameron, A. and L. I. Conrad, eds., *The Byzantine and Early Islamic Near East I: Problems in the Literary Source Material* (Princeton: Darwin Press, 1992)

Canard, M., *Histoire de la dynastie des H'amdanides de Jazîra et de Syrie* (Algiers: Imprimeries 'la Typo-litho' et Jules Carbonel, 1951)

Canivet, P. and J. P. Rey-Coquais, eds., *La Syrie de Byzance à l'Islam*, Actes du

Colloque International, 11–15 Septembre 1990 (Damascus: Institut Français de Damas, 1992)
Cannadine, D. and S. Price, eds., *Rituals of Loyalty: Power and Ceremonial in Traditional Societies* (Cambridge: Cambridge University Press, 1987)
Caton, S., *'Peaks of Yemen I Summon': Poetry as Cultural Practice in a North Yemen Tribe* (Berkeley and Los Angeles: University of California Press, 1990)
Chabot, J.-B., ed. and trans., *Synodicon orientale ou recueil de synodes nestoriens* (Paris: Imprimerie Nationale, 1902)
Chamberlain, M., *Knowledge and Social Practice in Medieval Damascus, 1190–1350* (Cambridge: Cambridge University Press, 1994)
Chediath, G., *The Christology of Mar Babai the Great* (Kottayam: Oriental Institute of Religious Studies, 1982)
Christensen, A., *L'Iran sous les Sassanides* (Copenhagen: E. Munksgaard, 1944; second edn)
Les Kayanides (Copenhagen: A. F. Host & Son, 1931)
Claude, C., *Die byzantinische Stadt im 6. Jahrhundert* (Munich: Beck, 1969)
Cobb, P. M., 'White Banners: Contention in 'Abbāsid Syria, 750–877', Ph.D. thesis (University of Chicago, 1997)
Conrad, L. I., 'The conquest of Arwād: a source-critical study in the historiography of the early medieval Near East', in Cameron and Conrad, eds., *The Byzantine and Early Islamic Near East I*, 317–401
'Epidemic disease in central Syria in the late sixth century: Some new insights from the verse of Ḥassān ibn Thābit', *Byzantine and Modern Greek Studies* 18 (1994), 12–58
'A Nestorian diploma of investiture from the *Tad̲kira* of Ibn Ḥamdūn: the text and its significance', in al-Qāḍī, ed., *Studia Arabica et Islamica*, 83–104
'Die Pest und ihr soziales Umfeld im Nahen Osten des frühen Mittelalters', *DI* 73 (1996), 81–112
'The *quṣūr* of medieval Islam: some implications for the social history of the Near East', *al-Abḥāth* 29 (1981), 7–23
'Syriac perspectives on Bilād al-Shām during the Abbasid period,' in al-Bakhit and Schick, eds., *Bilād al-Shām During the Abbasid Period*, 1–44
'Theophanes and the Arabic historical tradition: some indications of intercultural transmission', *Byzantinische Forschungen* 15 (1988), 1–44
Cook, M., "Anan and Islam: the origins of Karaite scripturalism', *JSAI* 9 (1987), 161–82
'An early Islamic apocalyptic chronicle', *JNES* 52 (1993), 25–9
Early Muslim Dogma (Cambridge: Cambridge University Press, 1981)
'The Heraclian dynasty in Muslim eschatology', *al-Qanṭara* 13 (1992), 3–23
Muhammad (Oxford: Oxford University Press, 1983)
'The opponents of the writing of tradition in early Islam', *Arabica* 44 (1997), 437–530
Cook, M. and P. Crone, *Hagarism: The Making of the Islamic World* (Cambridge: Cambridge University Press, 1977)
Costaz, L., *Dictionnaire Syriaque–Français, Syriac–English Dictionary* (Beirut: Imprimerie Catholique, 1963)
Creswell, K. A. C., *A Short Account of Early Muslim Architecture*, rev. and supp. J. W. Allan (Adershot: Scolar, 1989)

Crone, P., 'The first-century concept of *Hiğra*', *Arabica* 41 (1994), 352–87
'Islam, Judeo-Christianity and Byzantine iconoclasm', *JSAI* 2 (1980), 59–95
Meccan Trade and the Rise of Islam (Princeton: Princeton University Press, 1987)
Slaves on Horses: The Evolution of the Islamic Polity (Cambridge: Cambridge University Press, 1980)
'Two legal problems bearing on the early history of the Qur'ān', *JSAI* 18 (1994), 1–37
'Were the Qays and Yemen of the Umayyad period political parties?', *DI* 71 (1994), 1–57
Dagron, G. 'Le christianisme dans la ville byzantine', *Dumbarton Oaks Papers* 31 (1977), 1–25
Dalley, S., 'Nineveh after 612 BC', *Altorientalische Forschungen* 20 (1993), 134–47
Daniel, E. 'The anonymous "History of the Abbasid Family" and its place in Islamic historiography', *IJMES* 14 (1982), 419–34
Dannhauer, D. G., *Untersuchungen zur frühen Geschichte des Qāḍī-amtes* (Bonn: Friedrich-Wilhelms Universität, 1975)
al-Daywahchī, S., 'al-Jāmiʿ al-umawī fī al-Mawṣil', *Sumer* 6 (1950), 211–19
'Khiṭaṭ al-Mawṣil fī al-ʿahd al-umawī', *Sumer* 7 (1951), 222–34
'Qalʿat al-Mawṣil fī mukhtalif al-ʿuṣūr', *Sumer* 10 (1954), 94–111
'Sūr al-Mawṣil', *Sumer* 3 (1947), 117–28
Ta'rīkh al-Mawṣil (Baghdad: al-Majmaʿ al-ʿIlmī al-ʿIrāqī, 1982)
Degen, E., 'Die Kirchengeschichte des Daniel Bar Maryam – eine Quelle der Chronik von Seʿert?', *ZDMG* Supplementa I (1969), 2, 511–16
Dehkhoda, A. A., *Loghat-nāma* (Tehran: Tehran University Publications, 1994)
Dennett, D. C., *Conversion and the Poll Tax in Early Islam* (Cambridge, MA: Harvard University Press, 1950)
Dentzer, J.-M. and W. Orthmann, eds., *Archéologie et histoire de la Syrie II: La Syrie de l'époque achéménide à l'avènement de l'Islam* (Saarbücken: Saarbrücker Druckerai und Verlag, 1989)
Diacon, T. A., *Millenarian Vision, Capitalist Reality* (Durham, NC and London: Duke University Press, 1991)
Dillemann, L. *Haute mésopotamie orientale et pays adjacents: contribution à la géographie historique de la région, du Ve s. avant l'ère chrétienne au VIe s. de cette ère* (Paris: P. Geuthner, 1962)
Dixon, A. A., *The Umayyad Caliphate 65–86/684–705* (London: Luzac, 1971)
Djaït, H., *al-Kūfa, naissance de la ville islamique* (Paris: Maisonneuve et Larose, 1986)
Donner, F. M., 'The Bakr b. Wā'il tribes and politics in northeastern Arabia on the eve of Islam', *SI* 51 (1980), 5–38
The Early Islamic Conquests (Princeton: Princeton University Press, 1981)
Downey, G. 'Ephraemius, Patriarch of Antioch', *Church History* 7 (1938), 364–70
Dozy, R., *Supplément aux dictionnaires arabes* (Leiden and Paris: Maisonneuve, 1927; second edn)
Dragas, G. D., ed., *Aksum-Thyateira: A Festschrift for Archbishop Methodios* (London: Thyateira House, 1985), 125–42
Drijvers, H. J. W., 'Christians, Jews and Muslims in northern Mesopotamia in early Islamic times: the Gospel of the Twelve Apostles and related texts', in Canivet and Rey-Coquais, eds., *La Syrie de Byzance à l'Islam*, 67–74
'The Gospel of the Twelve Apostles: a Syriac apocalypse from the early Islamic

period', in Cameron and Conrad, eds., *The Byzantine and Early Islamic Near East I*, 189–213

'The testament of our Lord: Jacob of Edessa's response to Islam', *Aram* 6 (1994), 104–14

Drijvers, H., *et al.*, eds., *IV Symposium Syriacum 1984* (Rome: Pont. Institutum Studiorum Orientalium, 1987; Orientalia Christiana Analecta 229)

Duri, A. A., *The Rise of Historical Writing among the Arabs*, ed. and trans. L. I. Conrad (Princeton: Princeton University Press, 1983)

Taʾrīkh al-ʿIrāq al-iqtiṣādī fī al-qarn al-rābiʿ al-hijrī (Baghdad: Maṭbaʿat al-Maʿārif, 1948)

Duval, R., *Histoire d'Edesse, politique, religieuse et littéraire* (Amsterdam, 1975; reprint of *JA* 18–19 (1891–2))

Duval, R., ed., *Lexicon syriacum auctore Hassano Bar-Bahlule* (Amsterdam, 1970); reprint of Paris: Reipublicae typographaeo, 1888–1901)

Elad, A., 'Aspects of the transition from the Umayyad to the ʿAbbāsid caliphate', *JSAI* 19 (1995), 89–132

'The siege of al-Wāsiṭ (132/749): some aspects of ʿAbbāsid and ʿAlīd relations at the beginning of ʿAbbāsid rule', in Sharon, ed., *Studies in Islamic History and Civilization*, 59–90

'Two identical inscriptions from Jund Filasṭīn from the reign of the ʿAbbāsid caliph, al-Muqtadir', *JESHO* 35 (1992), 301–60

El-ʿAli, S. A., 'A new version of Ibn al-Muṭarrif's list of revenues in the early times of Hārūn al-Rashīd', *JESHO* 14 (1971), 303–10

Encyclopaedia Iranica (London and Boston: Routledge & Kegan Paul, 1982–)

The Encyclopaedia of Islam (Leiden: E. J. Brill, first edn, 1913–36; second. edn, 1954–)

Enger, M., 'Notizen, Correspondenzen, and Vermischtes ueber das Vezirat', *ZDMG* 13 (1859), 239–48

Eslami, K., ed., *Iran and Iranian Studies: Essays in Honor of Iraj Afshar* (Princeton: Zagros, 1998)

van Ess, J., *Theologie und Gesellschaft im 2. und 3. Jahrhundert Hidschra* (Berlin and New York: de Gruyter, 1997)

Evans, P.B., D. Ruescheyer and T. Skocpol, eds., *Bringing the State Back in* (Cambridge: Cambridge University Press, 1985)

Fahd, T., ed., *La vie du Prophète Mahomet: Colloque de Strasbourg, Octobre 1980* (Paris: Presses universitaires de France, 1983)

Fattal, A., *Le Statut légal des non-musulmans en pays d'Islam* (Beirut: Imprimerie Catholique, 1958)

Fentress, J. and C. Wickham, *Social Memory* (Oxford and Cambridge, MA.: Blackwell, 1992)

Fierro, M., 'al-Aṣfar', *SI* 77 (1993), 169–81

Fiey, J. M., *Assyrie chrétienne* (Beirut: Imprimerie Catholique, 1965–8)

Chrétiens syriaques sous les Abbassides surtout à Bagdad (749–1258) (Louvain, 1980; *CSCO* 420)

Communautés syriaques en Iran et Irak des origines à 1552 (London: Variorum, 1979)

'Îšôʿdnaḥ, métropolite de Basra, et son oeuvre', *L'Orient Syrien* 11 (1966), 431–50

'Īšōʿyaw le Grand: Vie du catholicos nestorien Īšōʿyaw III d'Adiabène (580–659)', *Orientalia Christiana Periodica* 35 (1969), 305–33 and 36 (1970), 5–46

'Les Marcionites dans les textes historiques de l'Eglise de Perse', *Le Muséon* 83 (1970), 183–8
'Mossoul d'avant 1915', *Sumer* 2 (1946), 31–41
Mossoul chrétienne: Essai sur l'histoire, l'archéologie et l'état actuel des monuments chrétiens de la ville de Mossoul (Beirut: Imprimerie Catholique, 1959)
Pour un Oriens Christianus Novus: Répertoire des diocèses syriaques orientaux et occidentaux (Beirut: Franz Steiner, 1993)
'Tagrît. Esquisse d'histoire chrétienne', *L'Orient Syrien* 8 (1963), 289–341; reprinted in his *Communautés syriaques en Iran et Irak des origines à 1552* (London: Variorum, 1979)
Fleischammer, M., 'Die Banu al-Munajjim', *Wissenschaftliche Zeitschrift der Martin-Luther Universität* 12 (1963), 215–20
Forand, P. G., 'The governors of Mosul according to al-Azdī's *Ta'rīkh al-Mawṣil*', *JAOS* 89 (1969), 88–105
'The status of the land and inhabitants of the Sawād during the first two centuries of Islām', *JESHO* 14 (1971), 25–37
Foss, C., 'Archaeology and the "Twenty Cities" in Byzantine Asia', *American Journal of Archaeology* 81 (1977), 469–86
'The Persians in Asia Minor and the end of Late Antiquity', *English Historical Review* 90 (1975), pp. 721–47
Freeman, P. and D. Kennedy, eds., *The Defence of the Roman and Byzantine East* (Oxford, 1986; BAR International Series 297)
Friedmann, Y., *Shaykh Aḥmad Sirhindī. An Outline of his Thought and a Study of his Image in the Eyes of Posterity* (Montreal and London: McGill–Queen's University Press, 1971)
Frye, R. N., review of Gyselen, *La Géographie administrative*, in *JAOS* 113 (1993), 287–8
Sasanian Remains from Qasr-i Abu Nasr (Cambridge, MA: Harvard University Press, 1973)
'The Sasanian system of walls for defense', in Rosen-Ayalon, ed., *Studies in Memory of Gaston Wiet*, 7–15
Fuller, M. and N. Fuller, 'Continuity and change in the Syriac population at Tell Tuneinir, Syria', *Aram* 6 (1994), 259–77
Gabrieli, F., *Il califfato di Hishâm* (Alexandria: Mémoires de la Société Royale d'archéologie d'Alexandrie, 1935)
'La poesia Ḫārigita nel secolo degli Omayyadi', *Rivista degli Studi Orientali* 20 (1943), 331–72
Garsoian, N. G., *et al.*, eds., *East of Byzantium: Syria and Armenia in the Formative Period* (Washington, DC: Dumbarton Oaks, 1982)
Geertz, C., 'Centers, Kings, and Charisma: Reflections on the Symbolics of Power', in Ben-David and Clark, eds., *Culture and its Creators*, 150–71
Gerber, C., 'Die Umgebung des Lidar Höyük von hellenistischer bis frühislamischer Zeit: Interpretation der Erbegnisse einer Geländebegehung', in Bartl and Hauser, eds., *Continuity and Change*, 303–32
Gervers, M. and R. J. Bikhazi, eds., *Conversion and Continuity: Indigenous Christian Communities in Islamic Lands Eighth to Eighteenth Centuries* (Toronto: Pontifical Institute of Medieval Studies, 1990)
Gibb, H. A. R., 'The fiscal rescript of 'Umar II', *Arabica* 2 (1955), 1–16

Gignoux, P., 'L'Organisation administrative sasanide: Le cas du *Marzbān*', *JSAI* 4 (1984), 1–29

'Le *spāhbed* des Sassanides à l'Islam', *JSAI* 13 (1990), 1–14

Gignoux, P. and R. Gyselen, *Sceaux sasanides de diverses collections priveés* (Louvain: Peeters, 1982)

Gil, M., *A History of Palestine, 634–1099*, trans. E. Broido (Cambridge: Cambridge University Press, 1992; rev. edn)

Gnoli, G., *The Idea of Iran: An Essay on its Origin* (Rome: Istituto Italiano per il Medio ed Estremo Oriente, 1989)

Göbl, R., *Die Tonbullen vom Tacht-e Suleiman* (Berlin: D. Reimer, 1976)

Goldziher, I., *Mohammedanische Studien* (Halle: Max Niemeyer, 1890); trans. C. R. Barber and S. M. Stern as *Muslim Studies* (Chicago: Aldine, 1966)

Gottheil, R., 'On a Syriac manuscript of the New Testament belonging to the Rev. Mr Neesan', *JAOS* 13 (1889), clxxxi–clxxxiii

Graf, G., *Geschichte der christlichen arabischen Literatur* (The Vatican: Biblioteca Apostolica Vaticana, 1944–53)

Gregory, S., and D. Kennedy, eds,. *Sir Aurel Stein's Limes Report* (Oxford, 1985; BAR International Series 272)

Griffith, S. H., 'Disputes with Muslims in Syriac Christian texts: from Patriarch John (d. 648) to Bar Hebraeus (d. 1286)', in Lewis and Niewöhner, eds., *Religionsgespräche im Mittelalter*, 251–73

'The first Christian *summa theologiae* in Arabic: Christian *kalām* in ninth-century Palestine', in Gervers and Bikhazi, eds., *Conversion and Continuity*, 15–31

'The Prophet Muḥammad, his scripture and his message according to the Christian apologies in Arabic and Syriac from the first Abbasid century', in Fahd, ed., *La vie du Prophète Mahomet*, 99–146

'Reflections on the biography of Theodore Abū Qurrah', in S. K. Samir, ed., *Actes du 4e Congrès International d'Etudes Arabes Chrétiennes* (Cambridge: Cambridge University Press, 1992), *Parole de l'Orient* 18 (1993), 143–70

Grignaschi, M., 'Quelques spécimens de la littérature sassanide conservés dans les bibliothèques d'Istanbul,' *JA* 254 (1966), 1–142

'La riforma tributaria di Hosrō I e il feudalesimo sassanide', *Atti del Convegno Internazionale sul Tema: La Persia nel Medioevo* (Rome: Accademia Nazionale dei Lincei 1971), 87–147

Grintez, G. M. and J. Liver, eds., *Sefer Segal: Studies in the Bible Presented to Professor M. H. Segal by his Colleagues and Friends* (Jerusalem: ha-Hevrah le-heker ha-mikra be-Yisrael, 1964)

Grohmann, A., *Arabic Papyri in the Egyptian Library* (Cairo: Egyptian Library Press, 1934–)

Guest, J. S., *The Yezidis: A Study in Survival* (London: KPI, 1987)

Guide Book to the Mosul Museum (Baghdad, 1966)

Guidi, I., *Tables alphabétiques du Kitâb al-Aġânî* (Leiden: E. J. Brill, 1900)

Günther, S., *Quellenuntersuchungen zu den 'Maqātil aṭ-Ṭālibiyyīn' des Abū'l-Farağ al-Iṣfahānī (gest. 356/967)* (Hildesheim and Zürich: G. Olms, 1991)

Gyselen, R., *La Géographie administrative de l'empire sassanide: Les témoignages sigillographiques* (Paris: Groupe pour l'Etude de la Civilisation du Moyen-Orient, 1989)

Haase, C.-P., 'Is Madinat al-Far, in the Balikh region of northern Syria, an Umayyad foundation?', *Aram* 6 (1994), 245–57

Ḥabība, H., 'A Study of Abū Zakariyā's Work', Ph.D. thesis (University of Cambridge, 1965)
Hage, W., *Die syrisch-jakobitische Kirche in frühislamischer Zeit* (Wiesbaden: Harrassowitz, 1966)
Haldon, J. F., *Byzantium in the Seventh Century* (Cambridge: Cambridge University Press, 1990)
'Seventh-century continuities: the *Ajnād* and the "Thematic Myth"', in A. Cameron, ed., *The Byzantine and Early Islamic Near East III*, 379–423
Ḥamīd Allāh, M., *Majmū'at al-wathā'iq al-siyāsiyya li'l-'ahd al-nabawī wa'l-khilāfa al-rāshida* (Beirut: Dār al-Nafā'is, 1983; fourth edn)
A Handbook of Mesopotamia, I (London: Naval Staff Intelligence Department 1118 A, 1916–17; second edn)
Harris, W., *War and Imperialism* (Oxford: Oxford Univesity Press, 1979)
Harvey, S., *Asceticism and Society in Crisis: John of Ephesus and the Lives of the Eastern Saints* (Berkeley and Los Angeles: University of California Press, 1990)
Hasson, I., 'Le chef judhāmite Rawḥ ibn Zinbā'', *SI* 77 (1993), 95–122
Heidemann, S., 'al-'Aqr, das islamische Assur: Ein Beitrag zur historischen Topographie in Nordmesopotamien', in Bartl and Hauser, eds., *Continuity and Change*, 259–85
'The Merger of two currency zones in early Islam: the Byzantine and Sasanian impact on the circulation in former Byzantine Syria and Northern Mesopotamia', *Iran* 36 (1998), 95–112
Herzfeld, E., *Paikuli: Monument and Inscription of the Early History of the Sasanian Empire* (Berlin: Dietrich Reimer, Ernst Vohsen, 1924)
Hewsen, R. H., trans., *The Geography of Ananias of Širak* (Wiesbaden: Reichert, 1992)
Hill, D. R., *The Termination of Hostilities in the Early Arab Conquests AD 634–656* (London: Luzac, 1971)
Hinds, M., 'The first Arab conquests of Fārs', *Iran* 22 (1984), 39–53; reprinted in Bacharach *et al.*, eds., *Studies in Early Islamic History*, 197–231
'Kufan political alignments and their background in mid-seventh century AD', *IJMES* 2 (1971), 346–67; reprinted in Bacharach *et al.*, eds., *Studies in Early Islamic History*, 1–28
Hinz, W., *Islamische Masse und Gewichte* (Leiden: E. J. Brill, 1955)
Hobsbawm, E. J., *Bandits* (London: Trinity Press, 1969)
Primitive Rebels (Manchester: Manchester University Press, 1971)
Hodges, R. and D. Whitehouse, *Mohammed, Charlemagne and the Origins of Europe* (Ithaca: Cornell University Press, 1989)
Hoenerbach, W., 'Zur Heeresverwaltung der 'Abbāsiden', *DI* 29 (1950), 257–90
Hoffmann, G., *Auszüge aus syrischen Akten persischer Märtyrer* (Leipzig: Brockhaus, 1880)
Syrische–Arabische Glossen (Kiel: Schwers'sche Buchhandlung, 1874)
Hohlweg, A., 'Bischof und Stadtherr im frühen Byzanz', *Jahrbuch der österreichischen Byzantinistik* 20 (1971), 51–62
Hole, F., ed., *The Archaeology of Western Iran: Settlement and Society from Prehistory to the Islamic Conquest*, (Washington, DC: Smithsonian Institution Press, 1987)
Holmberg, B., 'A reconsideration of the *Kitāb al-Mağdal*,' in S. K. Samir, ed., *Actes du 4e Congrès International d'Etudes Arabes Chrétiennes* (Cambridge: Cambridge University Press, 1992), *Parole de l'Orient* 18 (1993), 255–83

Honigmann, E., *Le Couvent de Barṣaumā et le patriarcat jacobite d'Antioche et de Syrie* (Louvain, 1954; *CSCO* 146)
Hopkins, K., 'Taxes and trade in the Roman Empire (200 BC–AD 400)', *Journal of Roman Studies* 70 (1980), 101–25
Hopkins, M. K., 'Elite mobility in the Roman empire', *Past and Present* 32 (1965), 12–26
Howard-Johnston, J., 'The two great powers in late antiquity: a comparison', in Cameron, ed., *The Byzantine and Early Islamic Near East III*, 157–226
Hoyland, R., 'Arabic, Syriac and Greek historiography in the first Abbasid century: an inquiry into inter-cultural traffic', *Aram* 3 (1991), 211–33
'Sebeos, the Jews and the Rise of Islam', in Nettler, ed., *Medieval and Modern Perspectives on Muslim–Jewish Relations*, 89–102
Seeing Islam as Others Saw it: A Survey and Evaluation of Christian, Jewish and Zoroastrian Writings on Early Islam (Princeton: Darwin Press, 1997)
Ibrahim, J. K., *Pre-Islamic Settlement in Jazirah* (Baghdad: Ministry of Culture and Information, 1986)
Isaac, B., *The Limits of Empire: The Roman Army in the East* (Oxford: Oxford University Press, 1990)
Isḥāq, Y. M., 'Maṣādir Abī al-Faraj al-Malaṭī al-ta'rīkhiyya wa-atharuhā fī manāhijihi', *Aram* 1 (1989), 149–72
Johansen, B., '*Amwāl ẓāhira* and *amwāl bāṭina*: town and countryside as reflected in the tax system of the Ḥanafite school', in al-Qāḍī, ed., *Studia Arabica et Islamica*, 247–63
Jones, A. H. M., *The Greek City from Alexander to Justinian* (Oxford: Clarendon Press, 1940)
The Later Roman Empire, 284–602: A Social, Economic and Administrative Survey (Norman: University of Oklahoma Press, 1964)
Jones, J .M. B., 'The chronology of the *maghāzī*', *BSOAS* 19 (1957), 245–80
de Jong, P. and M. J. de Goeje, *Catalogus codicum orientalium Bibliothecae Academiae Lugduno Batavae* (Leiden: E. J. Brill, 1866)
Juda, J., *Die sozialen und wirtschaftlichen Aspekte der Mawālī in frühislamischer Zeit* (Tübingen: H. Vogler, 1983)
Juynboll, G. H. A., *Muslim Tradition: Studies in Chronology, Provenance and Authorship of Early Ḥadīth* (Cambridge: Cambridge University Press, 1983)
Juynboll, G. H. A., ed., *Studies on the First Century of Islamic Society* (Carbondale and Edwardsville: Southern Illinois University Press, 1982)
Kaegi, W., *Byzantium and the Early Islamic Conquests* (Cambridge: Cambridge University Press, 1992)
'Heraklios and the Arabs', *The Greek Orthodox Theological Review* 27 (1982), 109–33
'Reconceptualizing Byzantium's eastern frontiers in the seventh century', in Mathisen and Sivan, eds., *Shifting Frontiers in Late Antiquity*, 83–92
Kawerau, P., *Die jakobitische Kirche im Zeitalter der syrischen Renaissance* (Berlin: Akademie Verlag, 1960)
Kazemi, F. and R. D. McChesney, eds., *A Way Prepared: Essays on Islamic Culture in Honor of Richard Bayly Winder* (New York: New York University Press, 1988)
Kelly, J. N. D., *Early Christian Doctrines* (San Francisco: Harper & Row, 1978; rev. edn)
Kennedy, H., 'Central government and provincial élites in the early ʿAbbāsid caliphate', *BSOAS* 44 (1981), 26–38
The Early Abbasid Caliphate (London: Croom Helm, 1981)

Kennedy, H., ed., *al-Ṭabarī: A Muslim Historian and his Work* (Princeton: Darwin Press, forthcoming)
Khalidi, T., *Arabic Historical Thought in the Classical Period* (Cambridge: Cambridge University Press, 1994)
Islamic Historiography: The Histories of al-Mas'ūdī (Albany: State University of New York Press, 1975)
Khan, G., 'The pre-Islamic background of Muslim legal formularies', *Aram* 6 (1994), 193–224
King, G. R. D and A. Cameron, eds., *The Byzantine and Early Islamic Near East II: Land Use and Settlement Patterns* (Princeton: Darwin Press, 1994)
Kiraz, G. A., *A Computer-generated Concordance to the Syriac New Testament* (Leiden: E. J. Brill, 1993)
Kister, M. J., 'The Battle of Ḥarra: some socio-economic aspects', in Rosen-Ayalon, ed., *Studies in Memory of Gaston Wiet*, 33–49
'Land, property and *jihād*', *JESHO* 34 (1991), 270–311
'The social and political implications of three traditions in the *Kitāb al-Kharādj* of Yahya b. Adam', *JESHO* 3 (1960), 326–34
'Social and religious concepts of authority in Islam', *JSAI* 18 (1994), 84–127
Kohlberg, E., *A Medieval Muslim Scholar at Work: Ibn Ṭāwūs and his Library* (Leiden: E. J. Brill, 1992)
Kouymjian, D., ed., *Armenian Studies/Etudes arméniennes in memoriam Haïg Berbérian* (Lisbon: Calouste Gulbenkian Foundation, 1986)
Kraster, R., *Guardians of Language: The Grammarian and Society in Late Antiquity* (Berkeley and Los Angeles: University of California Press, 1988)
von Kremer, A., 'Ueber das Budget der Einnahmen unter der Regierung des Hârûn alrasîd nach einer neu aufgefundenen Urkunde', *Verhandlungen des VII. internationalen Orientalisten-Congresses* (Vienna: Alfred Holder, 1888), 1–18
Krikorian, M., 'Sebēos, historian of the seventh century', in Samuelian, ed., *Classical Armenian Culture*, 52–67
Lammens, H., 'Le Califat de Yazîd Ier (suite et fin) xxv', *Mélanges de la Faculté Orientale* (Université Saint-Joseph), 6 (1913); reprinted in his *Le Califat de Yazid Ier* (Beirut: Imprimerie Catholique, 1921)
'Le Chantre des Omiades', *JA* 9/4 (1894), 94–176, 193–241, 381–459
Landau-Tasseron, E., review article of Donner, *Conquests*, *JSAI* 6 (1985), 493–512
'Sayf Ibn 'Umar in medieval and modern scholarship', *DI* 67 (1990), 1–26
'The sinful wars: religious, social and historical aspects of *ḥurūb al-fijār*', *JSAI* 8 (1986), 37–59
Landron, M. B., 'Les Relations originelles entre Chrétiens de l'est (Nestoriens) et Musulmans', *Parole de l'Orient* 10 (1981–2), 191–222
Lapidus, I., 'The conversion of Egypt to Islam', *Israel Oriental Studies* 2 (1972), 248–62
Lassner, J., 'Did the caliph Abu Ja'far al-Manṣur murder his uncle 'Abdallah b. 'Ali, and other problems within the ruling house of the 'Abbasids', in Rosen-Ayalon, ed., *Studies in Memory of Gaston Wiet*, 69–99
Islamic Revolution and Historical Memory: An Inquiry into the Art of 'Abbāsid Apologetics (New Haven: American Oriental Society, 1986)
The Shaping of 'Abbāsid Rule (Princeton: Princeton University Press, 1980)
The Topography of Baghdad in the Early Middle Ages (Detroit: Wayne State University Press, 1970)

Latham, J. D. and W. F. Paterson, *Saracen Archery: An English Version and Exposition of a Mameluke Work on Archery (c. AD 1368)* (London: Holland, 1970)
Lavenant, R., ed., *V Symposium Syriacum 1988* (Rome: Pont. Institutum Studiorum Orientalium, 1990)
Lavoix, H., *Catalogue des monnaies musulmanes de la Bibliothèque Nationale* (Paris: Imprimerie Nationale, 1887)
Lecker, M., *The Banū Sulaym: A Contribution to the Study of Early Islam* (Jerusalem: Hebrew University of Jerusalem, 1989)
'Biographical notes on Ibn Shihāb al-Zuhrī', *Journal of Semitic Studies* 41 (1996), 21–63
'The death of the Prophet Muḥammad's father: did Wāqidī invent some of the evidence?', *ZDMG* 145 (1995), 9–27
Muslims, Jews and Pagans: Studies on Early Islamic Medina (Leiden: E. J. Brill, 1995)
'Zayd b. Thābit, "A Jew with two sidelocks": Judaism and literacy in pre-Islamic Medina (Yathrib)', *JNES* 56 (1997), 259–73
Leder, S., 'Features of the novel in early historiography – the downfall of Xālid al-Qasrī', *Oriens* 32 (1990), 72–96
Das Korpus al-Haiṯam ibn ʿAdī (Frankfurt a.M.: Vittorio Klostermann, 1991)
Lee, A. D., *Information and Frontiers: Roman Foreign Relations in Late Antiquity* (Cambridge: Cambridge University Press, 1993)
Le Strange, G., *The Lands of the Eastern Caliphate* (Cambridge: Cambridge University Press, 1905)
Lewinstein, K., 'The Azāriqa in Islamic heresiography' *BSOAS* 54 (1991), 251–68
'Making and unmaking a sect: the heresiographers and the Ṣufriyya', *SI* 76 (1992), 75–96
Lewis, B. and R. Niewöhner, eds., *Religionsgespräche im Mittelalter* (Wiesbaden: Harrassowitz, 1992)
Liebeschuetz, J. H. W. G., *Barbarians and Bishops: Army, Church and State in the Age of Arcadius and Chrysostom* (Oxford: Clarendon Press, 1990)
Liebeschuetz, J. H. W. G. and H. Kennedy, 'Antioch and the villages of northern Syria in the fifth and sixth centuries AD: trends and problems', *Nottingham Medieval Studies* 32 (1988), 65–90
Lilie, R.-J., 'Araber und Themen. Zum Einfluß der arabischen Expansion auf die byzantinische Militärorganisation', in Cameron, ed., *The Byzantine and Early Islamic Near East III*, 425–60
Livne-Kafri, O., 'Early Muslim ascetics and the world of Christian monasticism', *JSAI* 20 (1996), 105–29
Løkkegaard, F., *Islamic Taxation in the Classic Period* (Copenhagen: Branner & Korch, 1950)
Lowick, N., *Early ʿAbbāsid Coinage: A Type Corpus*, ed. E. Savage (London: British Museum, 1996)
Lumsden, S., 'Urban Nineveh', *Mār Šipri* 4 (1991), 1–3
Lyonnet, B., 'Settlement pattern in the Upper Khabur (N.E. Syria) from the Achaemenids to the Abbasid period: methods and preliminary results from a survey', in Bartl and Hauser, eds., *Continuity and Change*, 49–361
Madelung, W., 'Apocalyptic prophecies in Ḥimṣ in the Umayyad age', *Journal of Semitic Studies* 31 (1986), 141–85

The Succession to Muḥammad: A Study of the Early Caliphate (Cambridge: Cambridge University Press, 1997)

Magdalino, P., ed., *The Perception of the Past in Twelfth-century Europe* (London and Rio Grande, OH: Hambledon Press, 1992)

Makdisi, G., ed., *Arabic and Islamic Studies in Honor of Hamilton A. R. Gibb* (Leiden: E. J. Brill, 1965)

'The topography of eleventh-century Baghdad: materials and notes, I', *Arabica* 6 (1959), 178–97

Mango, C., *Byzantium: The Empire of New Rome* (New York: Charles Scribner's Sons, 1980)

Mango, M. M., 'The continuity of the classical tradition in the art and architecture of northern Mesopotamia', in Garsoian, *et al.*, eds., *East of Byzantium*, 115–34

'The uses of liturgical silver, 4th–7th centuries', in Morris, ed., *Church and People in Byzantium*, 245–61

Mann, J. C., 'Power, force and the frontiers of the Empire', *Journal of Roman Studies* 69 (1979), 175–83

Mann, M., *The Sources of Social Power, Volume I: A History of Power from the Beginning to AD 1760* (Cambridge: Cambridge University Press, 1986)

Markwart (Marquart), J., *A Catalogue of the Provincial Capitals of Ērānshahr* (Rome: Pontificio Istituto Biblico, 1931)

Ērānšahr nach der Geographie des ps. Moses Xorenaci (Berlin: Weidmann, 1901)

Marlow, L., *Hierarchy and Egalitarianism in Islamic Thought* (Cambridge: Cambridge University Press, 1997)

Mathisen, R. W. and H. S. Sivan, eds., *Shifting Frontiers in Late Antiquity* (Aldershot: Variorum, 1996)

McAuliffe, J. D., *Qur'ānic Christians: An Analysis of Classical and Modern Exegesis* (Cambridge: Cambridge University Press, 1991)

McCormick, M., *Eternal Victory: Triumphal Rulership in Late Antiquity, Byzantium, and the Early Medieval West* (Cambridge: Cambridge University Press, 1986)

Meisami, J. S., review article of S. P. Stetkevych, *Abū Tammām and the Poetics of the 'Abbāsid Age* in *Journal of Arabic Literature* 25 (1994), 66–76

Metcalf, W. E., 'Three seventh-century Byzantine gold hoards', *Museum Notes* (American Numismatic Society) 25 (1980), 87–108

Mews, S., ed., *Religion and National Identity: Papers Read at the Nineteenth Summer Meeting and the Twentieth Winter Meeting of the Ecclesiastical History Society* (Oxford: Blackwell, 1982; Studies in Church History 18)

Mez, A., *The Renaissance of Islam*, trans. S. K. Bakhsh and D. S. Margoliouth (Patna: Jubilee Printing and Publishing House, 1937)

Miglus, P. A., *Das Wohngebiet von Assur: Stratigraphie und Architektur* (Berlin: Gebr. Mann Verlag, 1996)

Millar, F., *The Roman Near East, 31 BC–AD 337* (Cambridge, MA: Harvard University Press, 1993)

Mingana, A., 'An ancient Syriac translation of the Ḳur'ān exhibiting new verses and variants', *Bulletin of the John Rylands Library* 9 (1925), 188–235

Morimoto, K., *The Fiscal Administration of Egypt in the Early Islamic Period* (Kyoto: Dohosha, 1981)

Moritz, L. A., *Grain-mills and Flour in Classical Antiquity* (Oxford: Clarendon Press, 1958)

Morony, M., 'The effects of the Muslim conquest on the Persian population of Iraq', *Iran* 14 (1976), 41–59

Iraq after the Muslim Conquest (Princeton: Princeton University Press, 1984)

'Syria under the Persians 610–629', in Bakhit and ʿAbbās, eds., *Proceedings of the Second Symposium on the History of Bilād al-Shām*, 87–95

Morris, R., ed., *Church and People in Byzantium* (Birmingham: Centre for Byzantine, Ottoman and Modern Greek Studies, University of Birmingham, 1990)

Morrison, C., 'La monnaie en Syrie byzantine', in Dentzer and Orthmann, eds., *Archéologie et histoire de la Syrie II*, 191–204

'Le trésor byzantin de Nikertai', *Revue Belge de Numismatique* 118 (1972), 29–91

Moscati, S., 'Le massacre des Umayyades dans l'histoire et dans les fragments poétiques', *Archiv Orientální* 18 (1950), 88–115

'Nuovi studi storici sul califfato di al-Mahdī', *Orientalia* n.s. 15 (1946), 155–79

Mottahedeh, R. 'Administration in Būyid Qazwīn', in Richards, ed., *Islamic Civilisation*, 33–45

Loyalty and Leadership in an Early Islamic Society (Princeton: Princeton University Press, 1980)

Motzki, H., 'The prophet and the cat: on dating Mālik's *Muwaṭṭaʾ* and legal traditions', *JSAI* 22 (1998), 18–83

Mouterde, P., 'Inscriptions en syriaque dialectal à Kāmed (Beqʿa)', *Mélanges de la Université Saint-Joseph* 22 (1939), 73–106

Muranyi, M., 'Die Auslieferungsklausel des Vertrages von al-Ḥudaibiya und ihre Folgen', *Arabica* 23 (1976), 275–95

Nadler, R., *Die Umayyadenkalifen im Spiegel ihrer zeitgenössischen Dichter*, inaugural dissertation (Erlangen-Nuremberg: Friedrich-Alexander Universität, 1990)

Nagel, T. *et al.*, eds., *Studien zum Minderheitenproblem im Islam I* (Bonn: Universität Bonn, 1973)

Nau, F., 'Un colloque du patriarch Jean avec l'émir des Agaréens et faits divers des années 712 à 716', *JA* 11.5 (1915), 225–79

Nelson, J. L., *Politics and Ritual in Early Medieval Europe* (London and Ronceverte: Hambledon Press, 1986)

Nettler, R. L., ed., *Medieval and Modern Perspectives on Muslim–Jewish Relations* (Luxembourg: Harwood Academic Publishers, 1995)

Newman, J., *The Agricultural Life of the Jews in Babylonia between the Years 200 CE and 500 CE* (London: Oxford University Press, 1932)

Nicol, N. D., 'Early Abbasid Administration in the Central and Eastern Provinces, 132–218 AH/750–833 AD', Ph.D. thesis (University of Washington, 1979)

Nöldeke, T., *Delectus veterum carminum arabicorum* (Berlin: H. Reuther, 1890)

Review of Houtsma's edition of al-Yaʿqūbī's *Taʾrīkh*, *ZDMG* 38 (1884), 153–60

'Die Tradition über das Leben Muhammeds', *DI* 5 (1914), 160–70

'Zwei Völker Vorderasiens', *ZDMG* 33 (1879), 157–65

Nöldeke, T. and F. Schwally, *Geschichte des Qorans* (Leipzig: Dieterich'sche Verlagsbuchhandlung, 1909–38)

Norris, F. W., 'Paul of Samosata: *Procurator Ducenarius*', *Journal of Theological Studies* n.s. 35 (1984), 50–70

Northedge, A., 'Archaeology and new urban settlement in early Islamic Syria and Iraq', in King and Cameron, eds., *The Byzantine and Early Islamic Near East II*, 231–65

Northedege, A., A. Bamber and M. Roaf, *Excavations at ʿAna* (Warminster: Aris and Phillips, 1988)

Noth, A., 'Abgrenzungsprobleme zwischen Muslimen und nicht-Muslimen: Die "Bedingungen ʿUmars (*aš-šurat al-ʿumariyya*)" unter einem anderen Aspekt gelesen', *JSAI* 9 (1987), 290–315

The Early Arabic Historical Tradition: A Source-critical Study (Princeton: Darwin Press, 1994; second edn, in colloboration with Lawrence I. Conrad; originally published 1973)

'Die literarisch überlieferten Verträge der Eroberungszeit als historische Quellen für die Behandlung der unterworfenen Nicht-Muslime durch ihre neuen muslimischen Oberherren', in Nagel *et al*, eds., *Studien zum Minderheitenproblem im Islam I*, 282–314

'Minderheiten als Vertragspartner im Disput mit dem islamischen Gesetz: Die "Nachkommen der Juden von Ḫaibar" und die Ǧizya', in Roemer and Noth, eds., *Studien zur Geschichte und Kultur*, 289–309

Novick, P., *That Noble Dream: The 'Objectivity Question' and the American Historical Profession* (Cambridge: Cambridge University Press, 1988)

Nützel, H., *Katalog der orientalischen Münzen* (Berlin: W. Spemann, 1898–1902)

Oates, D., *Studies in the Ancient History of Northern Iraq* (London: Oxford University Press, 1968)

Olster, D. M., *Roman Defeat, Christian Response, and the Literary Construction of the Jew* (Philadelphia: University of Pennsylvania Press, 1994)

Olyan, S. M., 'What do shaving rites accomplish and what do they signal in Biblical ritual contexts?', *Journal of Biblical Literature* 117 (1998), 611–22

Oppenheimer, A., *Babylonia Judaica in the Talmudic Period* (Wiesbaden: L. Reichert, 1983)

Ortiz de Urbina, I., *Patrologia syriaca* (Rome: Pont. Institutum Orientalium Studiorum, 1965)

Palmer, A., *Monk and Mason on the Tigris Frontier* (Cambridge: Cambridge University Press, 1990)

'Saints' lives with a difference: Elijah on John of Tella (d. 538) and Joseph on Theodotus of Amida (d. 698)', in Drijvers *et al.*, eds., *IV Symposium Syriacum 1984*, 203–16

The Seventh Century in the West-Syrian Chronicles (Liverpool: Liverpool University Press, 1993)

Parry, V. J. and M. E. Yapp, eds., *War, Technology and Society in the Middle East* (London: Oxford University Press, 1975)

Pauly, A. (and G. Wissova), *Real-Encyclopädie der classischen Altertumswissenchaft*, Neue Bearbeitung (Stuttgart: J. B. Metzler, 1894–1972)

Payne Smith, J., *A Compendious Syriac Dictionary* (Oxford: Clarendon Press, 1903)

Payne Smith, R., *Thesaurus Syriacus* (Oxford: Clarendon Press, 1879–1901)

Pedersen, J., *The Arabic Book*, trans. G. French (Princeton: Princeton University Press, 1984)

Peeters, P., review of I. Ortiz de Urbina, *Die Gottheit Christi bei Afrahat*, *Analecta Bollandiana* 53 (1935), 145–6

Pertusi, A., 'Tra storia e leggenda: akritai e ghâzi sulla frontiera orientale di Bisanzio', *Actes du XIVe Congrès International d'Etudes Byzantines* (Bucharest: Editura Aacdemiei Republicii Socialiste România, 1974), 237–83

Peters, F. E., 'Byzantium and the Arabs of Syria', *Les Annales Archéologiques Arabes Syriennes* 27–8 (1977–8), 97–113

Piacentini, V. F., '*Madīnalshahr, qaryaldeh, nāḥiyalrustāq* – the city as political-administrative institution: the continuity of a Sasanian model', *JSAI* 17 (1994), 85–107

Pigulevskaya, N., *Les Villes de l'état iranien aux époques parthe et sassanide* (Paris: Mouton, 1963)

Poliak, A. N., 'Classification of lands in the Islamic law and its technical terms', *American Journal of Semitic Languages and Literatures* 57 (1940), 50–62

Posner, N., 'The Muslim Conquest of Northern Mesopotamia: An Introductory Essay into its Historical Background and Historiography', Ph.D. thesis (New York University, 1985)

'Whence the Muslim conquest of northern Mesopotamia?', in Kazemi and McChesney, eds., *A Way Prepared*, 27–52

Price, S. R. F., *Rituals and Power: The Roman Imperial Cult in Asia Minor* (Cambridge: Cambridge University Press, 1984)

al-Qāḍī, W., 'Early Islamic state letters: the question of authenticity', in Cameron and Conrad, eds., *The Byzantine and Early Islamic Near East I*, 215–75

'Madkhal ilā dirāsat ʿuhūd al-ṣulḥ al-islāmiyya zaman al-futūḥ', in Bakhit and Abbās, eds., *Proceedings of the Second Symposium on the History of Bilād al-Shām*, 193–269

al-Qāḍī, ed., *Studia Arabica et Islamica* (Festschrift for Ihsan Abbas) (Beirut: American University of Beirut, 1981)

Qedar, S., 'Copper coinage of Syria in the seventh and eighth century AD', *Israel Numismatic Journal* 10 (1988–9), 27–39

Rahman, M. J., 'The oath of allegiance', *Islamic Culture* 8 (1934), 258–62

Reinink, G. J., 'Fragmente der Evangelienexegese des Katholikos Ḥenanišoʿ I', in Lavenant, ed., *V Symposium Syriacum 1988*, 71–91

'Ps.-Methodius: a concept of history in response to the rise of Islam', in Cameron and Conrad, eds., *The Byzantine and early Islamic Near East I*, 149–87

'The Romance of Julian the Apostate as a source for seventh century Syriac apocalypses', in Canivet and Rey-Coquais, eds., *La Syrie de Byzance à l'Islam*, 75–86

Reitemeyer, E., *Die Städtegründungen der Araber im Islām nach den arabischen Historikern und Geographen* (Munich: F. Straub, 1912)

Rice, D. S., 'Medieval Ḥarrān: studies on its topography and monuments, I', *Anatolian Studies* 2 (1952), 36–84

Richards, D. S., ed., *Islamic Civilisation, 950–1150* (Oxford: Bruno Cassirer, 1973)

Rieu, C., *Supplement to the Catalogue of the Arabic Manuscripts in the British Museum* (London: Longmans & Co., 1894)

Robinson, C. F., 'The Conquest of Khūzistān: a historiographical reassessment,' in L. I. Conrad, ed., *History and Historiography in Early Islamic Times: Studies and Perspectives* (Princeton: Darwin Press, forthcoming)

'Ibn al-Azraq, his *Taʾrīkh Mayyāfāriqīn*, and early Islam', *JRAS* 3, 6, 1 (1996), 7–27

'A local historian's debt to al-Ṭabarī: the case of al-Azdī's *Taʾrīkh al-Mawṣil*', in Kennedy, ed., *Al-Ṭabarī*

'Al-Muʿāfā b. ʿImrān and the beginnings of the *ṭabaqāt* literature', *JAOS* 116 (1996), 114–20

Review of Palmer, *Seventh Century*, *JRAS* 3, 5 (1995), 97–101

'Tribes and nomads in early Islamic northern Mesopotamia', in Bartl and Hauser, eds., *Continuity and Change*, 429–52
Roemer, H. R. and A. Noth, eds., *Studien zur Geschichte und Kultur des Vorderen Orients* (Festschrift for B. Spuler) (Leiden: E. J. Brill, 1981)
Röllig, W. and H. Kühne, 'The lower Habur: second preliminary report on a survey in 1977', *Les Annales Archéologiques Arabes Syriennes* 33 (1983), 187–99
Rosen-Ayalon, M., ed., *Studies in Memory of Gaston Wiet* (Jerusalem: Hebrew University of Jerusalem, 1977)
Rosenthal, F., *A History of Muslim Historiography* (Leiden: E. J. Brill, 1968; second edn)
Rotter, G., *Die Stellung des Negers in der islamisch-arabischen Gesellschaft bis zum XVI. Jahrhundert*, inaugural dissertation (Bonn, 1967)
Die Umayyaden und der zweite Bürgerkrieg (680–692) (Wiesbaden: F. Steiner, 1982)
'The Umayyad Fulūs of Mosul', *Museum Notes* 19 (1974), 165–98
Rowton, M., 'Enclosed nomadism', *JESHO* 17 (1975), 1–30
'Urban autonomy in a nomadic environment', *JNES* 32 (1973), 201–15
Rubin, U., 'Apocalypse and authority in Islamic tradition: the emergence of the twelve leaders', *al-Qanṭara* 18 (1997), 11–42
The Eye of the Beholder: The Life of Muḥammad as Viewed by the Early Muslims (Princeton: Darwin Press, 1995)
'Quran and *Tafsīr*: the case of "ʿ*an yadin*"', *DI* 70 (1993), 133–44
Rücker, A., 'Das "Obere Kloster" bei Mossul und seine Bedeutung für die Geschichte der ostsyrischen Liturgie', *Oriens Christianus* third series, 7 (1932), 180–7
Russell, J. M., *Sennacherib's Palace without Rival at Nineveh* (Chicago: University of Chicago Press, 1991)
Sachau, E., *Syrische Rechtsbücher* (Berlin: G. Reimer, 1907–14)
Sahas, D. J., 'What an infidel saw that a faithful did not: Gregory Dekapolites (d. 842) and Islam', *Greek Orthodox Theological Review* 31 (1986), 47–67
Said, S., ed., *Hellenismos: Quelques jalons pour une histoire de l'identité Grecque* (Leiden: E. J. Brill, 1991)
Ṣā'igh, S., *Ta'rīkh al-Mawṣil* (Cairo: al-Maṭbaʿa al-Salafiyya, 1923)
Sako, L., *Lettre christologique du patriarche syro-Oriental Īshōʿyabh II de Gdālā* (Rome: Giovanni Carnestri, 1983)
'Les Sources de la chronique de Séert', *Parole de l'Orient* 14 (1987), 155–66
al-Salmān, A. M. A., *al-Mawṣil fī al-ʿahdayn al-rāshidī wa'l-umawī* (Mosul: Maktabat Bassām, 1985)
al-Sāmarrā'ī, Q., *al-Mu'assasāt al-idāriyya fī al-dawla al-ʿAbbāsiyya khilāl al-fatra 247–334/861–945* (Damascus: Maktabat Dār al-Fatḥ, 1971)
Samuelian, T. J., ed., *Classical Armenian Culture: Influences and Creativity* (Chico, CA: Scholars Press, 1982)
Sarkīs, Y., 'Nubdhatān min *Ta'rīkh al-Mawṣil*,' *Lughat al-ʿArab* 6 (1928), 112–16
Sarre, F. and E. Herzfeld, *Archäologische Reise im Euphrat- und Tigris-gebiet* (Berlin: D. Reimer, 1920)
Sayed, R., *Die Revolte des Ibn al-Ašʿaṯ und die Koranleser* (Freiburg: Klaus Schwarz, 1977)
Schacht, J. *The Origins of Muhammadan Jurisprudence* (Oxford: Oxford University Press, 1950)
Schick, R., *The Christian Communities of Palestine from Byzantine to Islamic Rule* (Princeton: Darwin Press, 1995)

Schippmann, K., *Grundzüge der Geschichte des sasanidischen Reiches* (Darmstadt: Wissenschaftliche Buchgesellschaft, 1990)

Schoeler, G., 'Die Frage der schriftlichen oder mündlichen Überlieferung der Wissenschaften im frühen Islam', *DI* 62 (1985), 201–30

'Schreiben und Veröffentlichen. Zu Verwendung und Funktion der Schrift in den ersten islamischen Jahrhunderten', *DI* 69 (1992), 1–43

Schöller, M., *Exegetisches Denken und Prophetenbiographie* (Wiesbaden: Harrassowitz, 1998)

Schmucker, W., *Untersuchungen zu einigen wichtigen bodenrechtlichen Konsequenzen der islamisichen Eroberungsbewegung* (Bonn: Universität Bonn, 1972)

Schützinger, H., 'Abū Yaʿlā al-Mauṣilī. Leben und Lehrerverzeichnis (*Kitāb al-Muʿǧam*)', *ZDMG* 131 (1981), 281–96

Scott, M. L. and J. MacGinnis, 'Notes on Nineveh', *Iraq* 52 (1990), 63–73

Segal, J. B., *Edessa, 'The Blessed City'* (Oxford: Clarendon Press, 1970)

'The Jews of North Mesopotamia before the rise of Islam', in Grintez and Liver, eds., *Sefer Segal*, 32–63

'Mesopotamian communities from Julian to the rise of Islam', *Proceedings of the British Academy* (1955), 109–39

Serjeant, R. G., *Islamic Textiles: Material for a History up to the Mongol Conquest* (Beirut: Librairie du Liban, 1972)

Sezgin, F., *Geschichte des arabischen Schrifttums* (Leiden: E. J. Brill, 1967–)

Shaban, M. A., *Islamic History: A New Interpretation I* (Cambridge: Cambridge University Press, 1971)

Shahid (Kawar), I., 'The Arabs in the peace treaty of AD 561', *Arabica* 3 (1956), 181–213

Byzantium and the Arabs in the Fourth Century (Washington, DC: Dumbarton Oaks, 1984)

Byzantium and the Arabs in the Sixth Century, vol. I, part 1 (Washington, DC: Dumbarton Oaks, 1995)

Shaked, S., 'Jewish and Christian seals of the Sasanian period', in Rosen-Ayalon, ed., *Studies in Memory of Gaston Wiet*, 17–31

Sharon, M., ed., *Studies in Islamic History and Civilization in Honour of Professor David Ayalon* (Leiden: E. J. Brill, 1986)

Shboul, A., *al-Masʿūdī and his World* (London: Ithaca Press, 1979)

Shimizu, M., 'Les finances publiques de l'état ʿabbāside', *DI* 42 (1966), 1–24

Shoshan, B., 'The "Politics of Notables" in Medieval Islam', *Asian and African Studies* 20 (1986), 179–215

Simpson, St J., 'Aspects of the Archaeology of the Sasanian Period in Mesopotamia', D.Phil. thesis (Oxford University, 1992)

'From Tekrit to the Jaghjagh: Sasanian, sites, settlement patterns and material culture in northern Mesopotamia', in Bartl and Hauser, eds., *Continuity and Change*, 87–126

Sklare, D. E., *Samuel Ben Ḥofni Gaon and his Cultural World* (Leiden and New York: E. J. Brill, 1986)

Sodini, J.-P. and G. Tate, 'Déhès (Syrie du Nord) campagnes I–III (1976–8), recherches sur l'habitat rural,' *Syria* 57 (1980), 1–304

Sourdel, D., *Le vizirat ʿabbaside* (Damascus: Institut Français de Damas, 1959–60)

Springberg-Hinsen, M., *Die Zeit vor dem Islam in arabischen Universalgeschichten des 9. bis 12. Jahrhunderts* (Würzberg: Echter, 1989)

Spuler, B., *Iran in früh-islamischer Zeit* (Wiesbaden: F. Steiner, 1952)

Starr, J., 'Le mouvement messianique au début du viii siècle', *Revue des Etudes Juives*, n.s. 52 (1937), 81–92

Stern, S. M., '‘Abd al-Jabbār's account of how Christ's religion was falsified by the adoption of Roman customs', *Journal of Theological Studies* n.s. 19 (1968), 128–85

'Abū ʿĪsā Ibn al-Munajjim's Chronography', in Stern *et al.*, eds., *Islamic Philosophy and the Classical Tradition*, 437–66

'Quotations from apocryphal gospels in ʿAbd al-Jabbār', *Journal of Theological Studies* n.s. 18 (1967), 34–57

Stern, S. M. *et al.*, eds., *Islamic Philosophy and the Classical Tradition* (Festschrift for R. Walzer) (Oxford: Bruno Cassirer, 1972)

Stone, L., *The Causes of the English Revolution 1529–1642* (New York: Harper & Row, 1972)

Streck, M., *Assurbanipal und die letzten assyrischen Könige bis zum Untergange Nineveh's* (Leipzig: J. C. Hinrichs, 1916)

Stronach, D. and S. Lumsden, 'UC Berkeley's Excavations at Nineveh', *Biblical Archaeologist* 55 (1992), 227–33

Suermann, H., *Die geschichtstheologische Reaktion auf die einfallenden muslime in der edessenischen Apokalyptik des 7. Jarhrhunderts* (Frankfurt, Bern and New York: P. Lang, 1985)

'Notes concernant l'apocalypse copte de Daniel et la chute des Omayyades', *Parole de l'Orient* 11 (1983), 329–48

Taylor, J. E., 'The phenomenon of early Jewish-Christianity: reality or scholarly invention?', *Vigiliae Christinae* 44 (1990), 313–34

Ter-Ghévondian, A., *The Arab Emirates in Bagratid Armenia*, trans. N. Garsoïan (Lisbon: Livraria Bertrand, 1976)

'L'Arménie et la conquête arabe', in Kouymjian, ed., *Armenian Studies*, 773–92

Thomas, R. S., *Oral Tradition and Written Record in Classical Athens* (Cambridge: Cambridge University Press, 1992)

Tilly, C., *Coercion, Capital, and European States, AD 990–1992* (Cambridge, MA and Oxford: Blackwell, 1990)

'War making and state making as organised crime', in P. B. Evans *et al.*, eds., *Bringing the State Back in*, 169–91

Tritton, A. S., *The Caliphs and their Non-Muslim Subjects* (London: Oxford University Press, 1930)

Trombley, F. R., 'Monastic foundations in sixth-century Anatolia and their role in the social and economic life of the countryside', *Greek Orthodox Theological Review* 30 (1985), 45–59

Tyan, E., *Institutions du droit public musulman* (Paris: Sirey, 1954–7)

al-ʿUbaydī, M., *Banū Shaybān wa-dawruhum fī al-ta'rīkh al-ʿarabī wa'l-islāmī ḥattā maṭlaʿ al-ʿaṣr al-rāshidī* (Baghdad: al-Dār al-Waṭaniyya li'l-tawzīʿ wa'l-iʿlān, 1984)

Ullmann, M., *Wörterbuch der klassischen arabischen Sprache* (Wiesbaden: Harrassowitz, 1970–)

ʿUmar, F., *al-ʿAbbāsiyyūn al-awā'il* (Baghdad: Maṭbaʿat Jāmiʿat Baghdād, 1973)

Vaglieri, L. V., 'Le vicende del Ḫārigismo in epoca abbaside', *Rivista degli Studi Orientali* 24 (1949), 31–44

Van de Mieroop, M., *The Ancient Mesopotamian City* (Oxford: Clarendon Press, 1997)

Vööbus, A., *History of Asceticism in the Syrian Orient* (Louvain, 1958–88; *CSCO* 184, 197 and 500)

Vööbus, A., ed. and trans., *The Synodicon in the West Syrian Tradition I* (Louvain, 1975; *CSCO* 367–8)

Syriac and Arabic Documents Regarding Legislation Relative to Syrian Asceticism (Stockholm: Estonian Theological Society in Exile, 1960)

Wakin, J. A., *The Function of Documents in Islamic Law* (Albany: State University of New York Press, 1972)

Wallace-Hadrill, D. S., *Christian Antioch: A Study of Early Christian Thought in the East* (Cambridge: Cambridge University Press, 1982)

Wansbrough, J., *The Sectarian Milieu: Content and Composition of Islamic Salvation History* (Oxford: Oxford University Press, 1978)

Watt, W. M., *Islam and the Integration of Society* (London: Routledge & Kegan Paul, 1961)

Wellhausen, J., *The Arab Kingdom and its Fall*, trans. M. G. Weir (Beirut reprint: Khayats, 1963)

Die religiös-politischen Oppositionsparteien im alten Islam, trans. R. C. Ostle as *The Religio-political Factions in Early Islam* (Amsterdam: North-Holland Publishing, 1975)

Skizzen und Vorarbeiten (Berlin: G. Reimer, 1884–9)

Wenke, R. J., 'Western Iran in the Partho-Sasanian period: the imperial transformation', in Hole, ed., *The Archaeology of Western Iran*, 251–81

Wensinck, A. J., *A Handbook of Early Muhammadan Tradition* (Leiden: E. J. Brill, 1927)

Whitby, M., *The Emperor Maurice and his Historian: Theophylact Simocatta on Persian and Balkan Warfare* (Oxford: Oxford University Press, 1988)

'Procopius and the development of Roman defences in Upper Mesopotamia', in Freeman and Kennedy, eds., *The Defence of the Roman and Byzantine East*, 717–35

Whitcomb, D., 'Amṣār in Syria? Syrian cities after the conquest', *Aram* 6 (1994), 13–33

White, K. D., *Farm Equipment of the Roman World* (Cambridge: Cambridge University Press, 1975)

Wickham, C., *Early Medieval Italy: Central Power and Local Society, 400–1000* (Totowa: Barnes & Noble, 1981)

Widengren, G., 'Iran, der große Gegner Roms: Königsgewalt, Feudalismus, Militärwesen', *Aufstieg und Niedergang der römischen Welt, Principat* 9:1 (Berlin and New York: de Gruyter, 1974–), 219–306

'Recherches sur le féodalisme iranien', *Orientalia Suecana* 5 (1956), 79–182

Wiet, G., 'L'Empire néo-byzantin des omeyyades et l'empire néo-sassanide des Abbasides', *Cahiers d'Histoire Mondiale* 9 (1953), 63–71

Wilkinson, J., 'The early development of the Ibāḍī movement in Baṣra', in Juynboll, ed., *Studies on the First Century of Islamic Society*, 125–44

Wilkinson, T. J., *Town and Country in Southeastern Anatolia* (Chicago: Oriental Institute of the University of Chicago, 1990)

Wilkinson, T. J. and D. J. Tucker, *Settlement Development in the North Jazira, Iraq* (Warminster: Aris & Phillips, 1995)

Winkelmann, F., *Die östlichen Kirchen in der Epoche der christologischen Auseinandersetzungen* (Berlin: Evangelische Verlagsanstalt, 1980)
Witakowksi, W., *The Syriac Chronicle of Pseudo-Dionysius of Tel-Maḥrē: A Study in the History of Historiography* (Uppsala: Uppsala University, 1987)
Wolfson, H. A., 'Saadia on the Trinity and Incarnation', in M. Ben-Horin, *et al.*, eds., *Studies and Essays in Honor of Abraham A. Neuman* (Leiden: E. J. Brill, 1962), 547–68
'An unknown splinter group of Nestorians', in his *The Philosophy of the Kalam* (Cambridge, MA: Harvard University Press, 1976), 337–49
Woolf, G., 'World-systems analysis and the Roman empire', *Journal of Roman Archaeology* 3 (1990), 44–58
Worsley, P., *The Trumpet Shall Sound: A Study of 'Cargo' Cults in Melanesia* (New York: Schocken, 1968; second edn)
Wurtzel, C., 'The coinage of the revolutionaries in the late Umayyad period', *Museum Notes* 23 (1978), 161–99
Wüstenfeld, F., *Die Geschichtschreiber der Araber und ihre Werke* (Göttingen: Dieterische Verlags-Buchhandlung, 1882)
Register zu den genealogischen Tabellen der arabischen Stämme und Familien (Göttingen: Dieterichsche Buchhandlung, 1853)
Zakeri, M., *Sāsānid Soldiers and Early Muslim Society: The Origins of 'Ayyārān and Futuwwa* (Wiesbaden: Harrassowitz, 1995)
Zaman, M. Q., *Religion and Politics under the Early 'Abbāsids: The Emergence of the Proto-Sunnī Elite* (Leiden: E. J. Brill, 1997)
von Zambaur, E., *Manuel de généalogie et de chronologie pour l'histoire de l'Islam* (Hanover: Libraire Orientaliste Heinz Lafaire, 1927)

Index

Other titles in the series

Popular Culture in Medieval Cairo
BOAZ SHOSHAN 0 521 43209 X

Early Philosophical Shiism *The Ismaili Neoplatonism of Abū Ya'qūb al-Sijistāni*
PAUL E. WALKER 0 521 44129 3

Indian Merchants and Eurasian Trade, 1600–1750
STEPHEN FREDERIC DALE 0 521 45460 3

Palestinian Peasants and Ottoman Officials *Rural Administration around Sixteenth-century Jerusalem*
AMY SINGER 0 521 45238 4 hardback 0 521 47679 8 paperback

Arabic Historical Thought in the Classical Period
TARIF KHALIDI 0 521 46554 0 hardback 0 521 58938 X paperback

Mongols and Mamluks *The Mamluk-Īlkhānid War, 1260–1281*
REUVEN AMITAI-PREISS 0 521 46226 6

Hierarchy and Egalitarianism in Islamic Thought
LOUISE MARLOW 0 521 56430 1

The Politics of Households in Ottoman Egypt *The Rise of the Qazdağlis*
JANE HATHAWAY 0 521 57110 3

Commodity and Exchange in the Mongol Empire *A Cultural History of Islamic Textiles*
THOMAS T. ALLSEN 0 521 58301 2

State and Provincial Society in the Ottoman Empire *Mosul, 1540–1834*
DINA RIZK KHOURY 0 521 59060 4

The Mamluks in Egyptian Politics and Society
THOMAS PHILIPP AND ULRICH HAARMANN (eds.) 0 521 59115 5

The Delhi Sultanate *A Political and Military History*
PETER JACKSON 0 521 40477 0

European and Islamic Trade in the Early Ottoman State *The Merchants of Genoa and Turkey*
KATE FLEET 0 521 64221 3

Reinterpreting Islamic Historiography *Hārūn al-Rashīd and the Narrative of the 'Abbasid Caliphate*
TAYEB EL-HIBRI 0 521 65023 2

The Ottoman City between East and West *Aleppo, Izmir, and Istanbul*
EDHEM ELDEM, DANIEL GOFFMAN AND BRUCE MASTERS 0 521 64304 X

A Monetary History of the Ottoman Empire
ŞEVKET PAMUK 0 521 44197 8

The Politics of Trade in Safavid Iran: *Silk for Silver, 1600–1730*
RUDOLPH P. MATTHEE 0 521 64131 4

The Idea of Idolatry and the Emergence of Islam: *From Polemic to History*
G. R. HAWTING 0 521 65165 4

Classical Arabic Biography: *The Heirs of the Prophets in the Age of al-Ma'mūn*
MICHAEL COOPERSON 0 521 66199 4

Lightning Source UK Ltd.
Milton Keynes UK
17 November 2010

163042UK00001B/81/A

9 780521 028738